SCANDINAVIAN INSTITUTE OF ASIAN STUDIES
STUDIES ON ASIAN TOPICS
GENERAL EDITOR: KARL REINHOLD HAELLQUIST

ASIAN TRADE ROUTES

SCANDINAVIAN INSTITUTE OF ASIAN STUDIES

STUDIES ON ASIAN TOPICS

STUDIES ON ASIAN TOPICS NO. 13

ASIAN TRADE ROUTES

Edited by
KARL REINHOLD HAELLQUIST

Routledge
Taylor & Francis Group

LONDON AND NEW YORK

SCANDINAVIAN INSTITUTE OF ASIAN STUDIES
84 Njalsgade, DK-2300 Copenhagen S, Denmark

First published 1991
by Routledge
2 Park Square, Milton Park, Abingdon, Oxon, OX14 4RN
270 Madison Ave, New York NY 10016

Transferred to Digital Printing 2006

British Library Cataloguing in Publication Data
Asian trade routes: continental and maritime –
(Studies on Asian Topics. ISSN 0142-6028)
1. Asia. Foreign Trade. History
I. Haellquist, Karl R. (Karl Reinhold)
II. Series
382.095
ISBN 0 7007 0212 1

Publisher's Note
The publisher has gone to great lengths to ensure
the quality of this reprint but points out that some
imperfections in the original may be apparent

CONTENTS

SOUTH ASIA

SOUTHEAST ASIA

EAST ASIA

CONTRIBUTORS

FARUK ABU-CHAKRA
Department of Asian and African Studies, University of Helsinki

ARTUR ATTMAN
Professor of Economic History, University of Gothenburg (since deceased)

LEONARD BLUSSÉ
Centre for the History of European Expansion, University of Leiden

HARALD BØCKMAN
East Asian Institute, University of Oslo

WENG EANG CHEONG
Professor of History, University of Hong Kong

HANS-DIETER EVERS
Professor, Sociology of Development Centre, University of Bielefeld

ANTHONY FARRINGTON
India Office Library and Records, The British Library, London

OLE FELDBAEK
Professor of Economic History, University of Copenhagen

McGUIRE GIBSON
The Oriental Institute, University of Chicago

IAN C. GLOVER
Institute of Archaeology, University of London

ERIK GØBEL
National Archives, Copenhagen

EIICHI KATO
Professor, University of Tokyo

JAN KIENIEWICZ
Professor, University of Warsaw

IRENE NØRLUND
Nordic Institute of Asian Studies, Copenhagen

MINORU ŌMORI
Professor, Hosei University, Tokyo

JAN OOSTERHOFF
Erasmus University, Rotterdam

WALTER RAUNIG
Director, Staatliches Museum für Völkerkunde, Munich

THOMAS RIIS
National Archives, Copenhagen

H. W. VAN SANTEN
Instituut Kern, Leiden

ARCADIO SCHWABE
Department of East Asian Studies, Ruhr-Bochum University

NIELS STEENSGAARD
Professor of History, University of Copenhagen

MAGDALENA TATÁR
Ural-altaic Institute, University of Oslo

TON VERMEULEN
Centre for the History of European Expansion, University of Leiden

JOHN WANSBROUGH
Professor, School of Oriental and African Studies, University of London

BODO WIETHOFF
Professor, Department of East Asian Studies, Ruhr-Bochum University

PREFACE

Research on trade between Asia and Europe is a familiar and prominent field of research in Copenhagen. The Scandinavian — now renamed Nordic — Institute of Asian Studies has benefited from its University of Copenhagen neighbours and colleagues. When the institute was inaugurated in 1968, Professor Kristof Glamann was the Director. He is a well-known pioneer in this field of research. Among scholars invited to give inauguration lectures were Professor Holden Furber, Philadelphia, and Professor C. R. Boxer, Bloomington. Even before the official inauguration, other specialists on Asian trade routes had given guest-lectures at the institute, for instance Professor Owen Lattimore, Leeds, and Professor Cheong Weng Eang, Hong Kong.

The inauguration lectures were published as No. 1 in the *Monograph Series*. Two Copenhagen doctoral dissertations, on Danish and Portuguese trade with Asia, by Ole Feldbæk and Niels Steensgaard respectively, were published in the *Monograph Series* as Nos. 2 and 17. They are now professors at the University of Copenhagen, and both of them contribute to this volume. A former Research Fellow of the institute, now professor at Munich, Dr phil. Carl Steenstrup, has added to our knowledge about European trade with Asia, for instance through an article, 'Scandinavians in Asian Waters in the 17th Century', on Scandinavian participation in early Dutch navigation in Asia. The article was published in *Acta Orientalia*, a journal published at the institute as long as Professor Søren Egerod was both the editor and the director of the institute. In addition to the research pursued at the University of Copenhagen, archivists and scholars at the Danish National Archives, i.e. Erik Gøbel and Thomas Riis, did research on Asian trade routes. Considering these traditions of research, it seemed logical to arrange an international conference on that topic.

The conference 'Asian Trade Routes' was arranged at Krogerup, north of Copenhagen, in August 1984. The conference was arranged by Per Sørensen, Research Fellow of the institute, and Professor Niels Steensgaard of the institute's Board in collaboration with colleagues and other specialists on specific Asian regions, who also chaired the sessions, Dr phil. Mogens Trolle Larsen, Carsten Niebuhr Institute, University of Copenhagen, for the Middle East, Dr Karl R. Hællquist, Research Fellow of the institute, for South Asia, Dr Kristina Lindell, University of Lund, for South East Asia, and Dr phil. Carl Steenstrup for the Far East. Professor Søren Egerod, Director of the institute, opened the conference with a welcoming address and Professor Kristof Glamann presided over the final session of the conference, which was summed up by Professor Niels Steensgaard.

Although dominated by historians, the conference was inter-disciplinary, with active participation of prehistoric archaeologists, economic historians, geographers, anthropologists and linguists, altogether about sixty scholars from fourteen countries in Asia, Europe and the USA.

Two keynote lectures were given, one by Professor Akira Fujieda, Japan, and the other by Professor Artur Attman, Sweden. Professor Fujieda spoke on 'Networks of the Silk Routes and their Cross Roads', illustrating his lecture with colour slides of paintings on silk and wall-paintings in caves. He followed three directions from which the esoteric Buddhism arrived in Dunhuang/Shazhou. He restricted himself to the eighth to the eleventh centuries. Professor Attman spoke on the flow of precious metals from Europe to Asia during the twelfth to the nineteenth centuries. The time-span covered during the conference was from 3000 B.C. to the 1930s, while the sweep of the geographical range was from the Near East to East Asia and across the ocean to the Americas. The conference served as an important stimulus to the participants in that much new material evidence was discussed while placing emphasis on the need for more research. Much needs to be done, not only in the period covering pre-history to about A.D. 1000, but even more so in the period 1000 to 1500 when the European archives became important sources of Asian evidence.

Karl Reinhold Hællquist

1

ASIAN TRADE ROUTES: EVIDENCE AND PATTERNS

Niels Steensgaard

The papers in this volume are bound together by a simple theme: Asian trade routes, but the simplicity of the theme is deceptive. If that large part of the old world, which we habitually call Asia, has its own kind of trade routes, it does not emerge from the papers. There is reason to doubt if trade routes can be differentiated from other kinds of routes and we have equal reason to believe that the trade routes can only be studied in the total cultural and political context. Finally, even the word 'trade' itself escapes our attempts at definition. Trade is not an historical constant, but a complicated social act. So, my task in summing up the papers presented in this volume cannot be accomplished by stating a set of easy generalizations or lines of development. On a much more modest level I shall attempt to direct attention to some problems of evidence and some patterns that may be discerned, if only provisionally, in the papers presented here.

The variety of evidence and the very different problems of evidence, confronting scholars working with various periods and in various regions, have been emphasized by several contributors and were emphasized in the discussions during the conference. The problems of evidence are common to all historians, but they are most obvious when we deal with early periods of history where written information is scant or non-existent and must be supplemented by archaeological evidence. The sophisticated beads and bronzes, presented by Ian Glover, indubitably show a link, a route of cultural interchange between Thailand and its neighbours in a period where other evidence of such links is non-existent, but are they evidence of a cultural interchange only, or do they establish a trade route? The beads or the bronzes will not tell us. Even where archaeological evidence can be supplemented by written evidence, the methodological problems are huge. John Wansbrough gives an example: revised philological readings and systematic source analysis may rearrange the pattern of orthodox interpretations, and enrich our arsenal of potential models. Another example of the problems confronting the historian working in early periods is presented by Harald Bøckman. The evidence he has uncovered concerning Yunnan trade in Han times permits the establishment of a trade link, but is still insufficient to inform us in full of the function and scope of this trade. When new evidence is brought to light — and this may still happen as may be seen in the paper by Bodo Wiethoff, which introduces us to the unexpected survival of a number of Chinese reports on navigation from the eighteenth century — we may catch a glimpse of obscure trade routes and trade relations, but the isolation of scattered documents raises immediately the most difficult problems of interpretation. How shall we use an historical source, if we have no knowledge of the context in which it originated?

As written evidence becomes more ample the position of the researcher changes. He has no need of beads and bronzes in order only to establish the existence of a link. Letters, reports, travellers' tales, even customs registers and merchants' accounts leave no doubt that a link existed, and the philological interpretation of the sources are as a rule uncomplicated. We are able on the basis of the existing material not only to see that the link existed, but also to describe its function as a trade route. The tasks of the historian for these later periods are not limited, however, to describing and analysing and interpreting the evidence, they must also fit the bits of the jigsaw puzzle together in a composite picture.

The papers dealing with the period after 1500, and they form the bulk of this volume, have in spite of all differences two things in common. With few exceptions the sources are produced by foreigners, i.e. usually Europeans, and the trade routes described somehow relate to an expanding world economy, centred in Europe. These two peculiarities should not be confused. The fact that the evidence concerning an Asian trade route is known primarily through sources of European origin, though it undeniably creates special problems of interpretation, does not diminish the inherent interest of the trade route as an Asian trade route proper. The existence of European evidence somehow relates the trade routes under consideration to an expanding Europe-centred world economy, but it does not in itself prove that Asia from the beginning of the sixteenth century was incorporated into a European world economy. It is many years ago when this kind of Europe-centred thinking was unanimously condemned by historians. Our problem now is to determine with more precision the extent to which Asian trade and Asian society remained undisturbed by the European activities and the impact of the quantitatively minute commodity exchange carried on with and through European merchants.

The dimensions of the problem are well illustrated by the paper by Artur Attman and by his tables. Through Europe in the sixteenth to the eighteenth centuries vast quantities of precious metals, primarily from America and Africa, were channelled into Asia. Even the important exports of silver from Acapulco and Japan, which reached the Asian continent from the East, were handled by Europeans. This does not make Asia the bottomless pit swallowing up the precious metals of the world as the mercantilists believed; one might rather think of Europe as a bottomless pit for precious metals as by far the largest part of the American silver production remained there. But the Asian silver import, once we think of it as an economic phenomenon, remains an important fact and a fact which perhaps has not been given due consideration. Economists have told us for more than two hundred years that the mercantilists were silly to be so preoccupied with precious metals. But after all, consumer goods are consumed. Pepper, spices and textiles disappeared, while precious metals remained. The mere fact that precious metals were the one commodity universally in demand should make us wonder. What happened to the precious metals? Obviously the image of the primitive orientals hoarding their gold and silver is unscientific. Precious metals were hoarded everywhere, in Asia as in Europe, but even when hoarded the precious metals had their effect on social values, on power and prestige, and of course this was even more the case when spent or invested, be it in office or in armies or in buildings. Import of pepper or sugar influenced consumers' habits. Import of precious metals influenced the distribution of power and prestige.

Dr. van Santen's study shows us that at least the leaders of the Mughal empire were conscious, not only of their need for bullion, but also knew how to take advantage of trade and navigation in order to strengthen their balance of payments very much in the same manner as we know from European states of the same period. This observation indicates a need for further research into the economic interests as expressed in the trade policy of the Asian powers. In my opinion, but at the present stage I think this can only be pronounced as a hypothesis, the disequilibria caused by the influx of silver into specific regions or specific social strata contributed to the political disruption of the Mughal empire and perhaps of the other gunpowder empires as well, while a few recent studies have hinted at corresponding effects of the increased inflow of silver into China already from the late sixteenth century. Much remains to be done in this complicated field, but first of all I think we should begin thinking of money in this context, not only as a means of payment and a stage on the way to consumer goods only, but also we should remember that money was a key to status and power.

What meets the eye, when we observe the concrete examples of Asian trade routes in the early modern period presented here, is not a uniform picture. Neither 'Asian' nor 'trade' nor 'route' are unambiguous terms, they are historical concepts to be compared with the evidence and to be compared with our more or less conscious model of what trade and markets should be. We have all been brought up to believe that the market through the formation of a price will establish a rational link between the producer and the consumer, and we have also been brought up to believe that price differentials between distant markets will be exploited by ingenious merchants if these differentials are larger than the costs of transport and handling. We find nothing to invalidate such a simple model of trade routes, but we certainly find that a nexus can be established in many complicated ways and that the historical market rarely, if ever, corresponds to the market of economic theory. Jan Kieniewicz did not find in his study of Malabar pepper trade routes any direct connection between the producer and the outward-looking market at all. In twentieth century Indochina Irene Nørlund in her paper found stability in exports and fluctuations in imports and advances the hypothesis that the supply of export commodities depended less on world prices than on fairly predictable local factors in the hierarchical precapitalist agrarian economy. But with or without the incentive of the market price, indubitably the commodities reached the market, and somebody made a profit. It does not invalidate the simple market model, but it indicates that historians should be aware that other social factors than price formation might determine supply.

Not less complex is the picture when we turn to the men of the trade routes proper, the merchants that linked one market with another. The capability and range of the merchants of Asia is illustrated in the paper of Magdalene Tatár. In her paper and in the paper presented by Weng Eang Cheong we see the subtle interconnections between local and long-distance trade. But one problem which in my opinion remains unresolved is the question of the pedlars or the peddling trade in Asian trade. Hans-Dieter Evers in his contribution has given us a marvellous description of the merchant entrepreneurs of Blacksmith Island, true pedlars conforming beautifully to the vision of van Leur. They, according to Hans-Dieter Evers, should be thought of as 'the peasants' of long-distance trade, flexible and impervious to the blows of price fluctuations which would have brought ruin to more capital-heavy entrepreneurs. The activities of pedlars are documented for as long as we have written sources to the history of Asian trade. But what was their significance? Were they archaic survivals in peripheral areas or were they the vehicles which related one market to another and one network to another from one end of the continent to the other until the early nineteenth century? The existence of larger merchants is equally well documented. I think van Santen rightly has pointed to the fact of the presence of such merchants in seventeenth century Gujarat. But we still lack evidence for earlier periods. Perhaps the clue is provided by Weng Eang Cheong and in the joint paper presented by Leonard Blussé, Jan Oosterhoff and Ton Vermeulen. Under the pressure from concerted western efforts the Asian merchant community at least in some cases seems to have reacted with countervailing force, i.e. with concentration of capital and of capabilities in the hand of a few strong merchants. On the other hand, companies might revert to peddling. In the interesting detailed information on sales of English cloth in the uninterested markets of Asia presented by Anthony Farrington we see the apparently contradictory picture of a large company operating in the market as a pedlar selling the cloth literally by the yard.

So the main issue remains the market structure, i.e. the mechanisms of price formation, not the existence of one kind of operators or another. Future research into this problem should be directed towards a closer study of price formation in Asian markets, not in uncovering further evidence for behaviour contradictory to the classification of the entrepreneurs.

If my assumption of a generic difference between a 'peddling' market and a 'Company-type' market is correct, it is fundamental for understanding and describing the new kind of trade routes which were established by the Europeans from the seventeenth century onwards. While even the Portuguese 'Great Ship from Amacao' carried scores of individual merchants to Nagasaki, the Dutch ships, even in the early period presented to us by Eiichi Kato, acted under an united management which could withhold stocks, redirect the flow of commodities and rig the market, looking not only towards Japan but also towards Western Asia and Europe, and which reverted to a purely mercantile role as soon as the unprofitability of piracy was established.

These European-managed routes, even those run by the rather modest Danish East India Company during the seventeenth and eighteenth centuries, gained in importance and range as shown by Erik Gøbel and Ole Feldbæk. They were important to the Danish company as other country trade routes were important to other companies, but one may in reason ask if they were significant from the point of view of Asian economy or not. I have no doubt it was, though it is not possible here to enter into a statistical analysis of the shipping under company management or under a European flag compared to the volume of Asian-owned shipping. But as more evidence is uncovered, particularly from the Dutch company records, concerning the movements of shipping in Asian ports, the early interdependence between trade managed under a European flag and trade managed by Asian entrepreneurs is confirmed. We have a striking example of this in the early and mid-eighteenth century shipping to Canton compared with the very well-documented contemporary Chinese shipping to Batavia.

To an increasing extent the Europeans were able to provoke a concentration of supply, not only for economic reasons, but also to provide protection or alternatively to produce violence which channelled trade into routes and vehicles under European domination. On the other hand we have also increasing evidence of the viability of Asian merchant entrepreneurs and the practical partnership established by European powers and Asian merchants; partnerships explained by the fact that both sides still found more profit in co-operating than in fighting each other. But of course this reasoning is sometimes on a rather high level of abstraction, the same level of abstraction as when we talk of partnership between an armed man and an unarmed man.

And this brings us to one of the most embarrassing complications of the economic market model: the fact that somebody always could control the nexus between consumer and producer and between market and market. It seems to have started early in history according to McGuire Gibson and it seems to have lasted for a very long time according to Thomas Riis, I do not think it has come to an end yet. Seen by the merchant entrepreneur the costs of control and protection might sometimes be predictable; as a rule they were not. Rulers might restrict themselves to being customers in both senses of the word, they might enter the market as producers or as consumers, they might be merchants themselves, they might be robbers, they might provide protection and peace or they might provide the opposite. We have reason to believe that political control, political domination and political collapse lay behind many sudden shifts in trade routes, and that much of the energy and enterprise of merchants has been spent on finding the cheapest and safest route to circumvent the political powers.

If the economic market model survives it is only as a model. The historical reality as presented in this volume is different from the model, but then, of course, it would not be much fun to be an historian if we did not always encounter new examples of the unexpected and the unpredictable.

What is more important: the differences are not easily systematized. We can discern some general developments over time, technical developments, organizational developments, we may talk of the time of the companies, the time of imperial rule, the age of silver, the age of tea, but we cannot describe one general line of development or one common response to challenges of a general nature. We are beginning to have so many bits and pieces of the history of Asian trade routes that we can hope one day to be able to see the whole map, but so far we are still in the stages of discovery and exploration.

2

THE FLOW OF PRECIOUS METALS ALONG THE TRADE ROUTES BETWEEN EUROPE AND ASIA UP TO 1800

Arthur Attman

The trade routes

Throughout the centuries products from the East have been greatly sought after in Europe. This applied to perfumes, drugs, spices, precious stones, silk, cotton, dye-stuffs, coffee and tea. They are light in weight and high in price and are therefore suitable goods for long-distance transportation over land and sea.

The trade routes between Asia and Europe have followed various paths. The oldest route went via the Levant. One route went over the Indian Ocean via Hormuz and across Mesopotamia to Aleppo, where it branched out in various directions to Beirut, to Trebizond and to Tana on the Sea of Azov. Another route across the Indian Ocean went past Aden and up over the Red Sea to Alexandria. The caravan trails came from China via the Silk Road to Kashgar and also from India via Kandahar and Balkh, and they then followed various routes across the Middle East to Aleppo and from there branched out to Beirut, Trebizond or Tana. Thus lines of communication via the Levant terminated in Alexandria, Beirut or the ports on the Black Sea. The European merchants then journeyed to these places in order to collect products of the Orient. Alexandria and Aleppo and its links above all with the ports of the Mediterranean acquired special importance as connecting points.

The route round the Cape became the alternative to the Levantine routes, for the Portuguese from about 1500, for the Dutch and English from around 1600 and thereafter for other European nations as well.

A third line of communication with the Asian markets went from Russia via the Volga and the Caspian Sea to Persia, and from there the caravan trails led to China and India and from Hormuz out across the Indian Ocean. There is a documentary evidence of this line of communication which dates back to the middle of the sixteenth century.

The inter-Asian trade routes were obviously of great importance and constitute a chapter in themselves, and there will be no detailed discussion of them in the present context.

The balance in the trade between Asia and Europe

As a rule there was a distinctive feature of the exchange of goods between Asia and Europe. The products from Asia were of much greater value than the goods from Europe which were given in exchange. As a result there emerged a balance problem which was solved by the Europeans making payment in precious metals for a large proportion of the imports from Asia. This balance problem arose at all the exchange points of Asian-European trade and this condition prevailed — with one exception — throughout the centuries on all the trade routes.

The trade via the Levant

The extant sources from the time of the Roman Emperors onwards all indicate that Europe had large deficits in the traffic with the Orient which went in transit via the Levant. The finds of coins in India show that there was an outward flow of precious metals from Europe, and they confirm the general view expressed by Pliny the Elder shortly after the start of the Christian era. During the later years of classical antiquity and the early years of the Byzantine Empire, precious metals, especially silver, appear to have flowed eastwards, compensated for to a certain extent by supplies of gold which went from Africa to Byzantium via the Sudan and Egypt.

The great change in the Middle East occurred with the Arabian expansion and the founding of the Caliphate. As a result, the conditions of the balance between Europe and the Middle East were also radically affected and this applied throughout the next three centuries from 700 to 1000. In fact the Arabs opened the richly productive silver mines in Pendjir and Shash, and from the eighth century onwards one can detect an increasing flow of silver from the Caliphate both westwards and eastwards. As before, the new Arab-world empire acted as intermediary for the products of Asia on their way to Europe, but the remarkable change consisted in the fact that the Arabs themselves demanded European products on a large scale. These comprised above all slaves, furs and the products of technology such as 'Frankish' swords. The Arabs paid for these European goods partly with transit products but in the main with precious metals, dinars and dirhams. The finds of large quantities of Arab coins in Eastern Europe are evidence of this state of affairs, whereas in Western Europe, especially in the Carolingian kingdom, the premium levied on the coins and the feudalization of the coinage system are reflected in the very rare finds of coins (there was a tax embodied in the coin), and as a result the documentary evidence of balance conditions is tenuous. However, there must inevitably have been a large-scale flow of precious metals from the Caliphate to the areas in Russia which were controlled by the Vikings, and of course to the Scandinavian countries. It is possible to detect this flow from the beginning of the ninth century until the closing decades of the tenth century. This constitutes a clear exception to the 'normal' balance conditions between Europe and Asia and these exceptional circumstances persisted for more than two centuries. 'Normal' balance conditions returned around the year 1000 when the silver from Pendjir, Shash and other Arabian mines dried up.

During the period around 1000 a marked change also took place within the Mediterranean trade. Italian merchants began to travel on business to Egypt and Syria. They came from Amalfi, Venice, Genoa and Pisa, and they established trade links with Alexandria, the Syrian cities and Constantinople. Soon Venice and Genoa became the foremost cities and they extended their contacts as far as the ports on the Black Sea. The Asian products which the Italian merchants collected in the Levantine ports were paid for in part with European goods, but to a greater extent with precious metals, usually silver. This now came from the newly-opened mines of central Europe and at the start of the eleventh century from the Harz mountains. As a result of their export surpluses on the markets of Flanders, the Italian merchants acquired precious metals which they in turn could use for the settlement of balances in the Levant. One of the prerequisites of the prosperity of European trade during the eleventh century was access to the newly-discovered silver of Central Europe. This reached the Russian market from the North Sea region, and especially from Lübeck after the middle of the twelfth century, and it flowed to the Levant via Flanders and onwards via Venice and Genoa. Thus Russian products (furs and wax to begin with) and luxury goods from the Orient reached Europe's consumer areas, and the balances were paid in the east (Russia) and in the Levant with precious metals. Accordingly, the silver of Central Europe from the mines in the Harz mountains and elsewhere passed through the hands of Italian merchants in the Levant and German merchants in Russia, and replaced the Arabian silver from Pendjir, Shash and other mines in the settlement of world trade balances.

For several centuries the prosperous Mediterranean trade played a significant role for the Italian cities and for the rest of Europe. Whereas

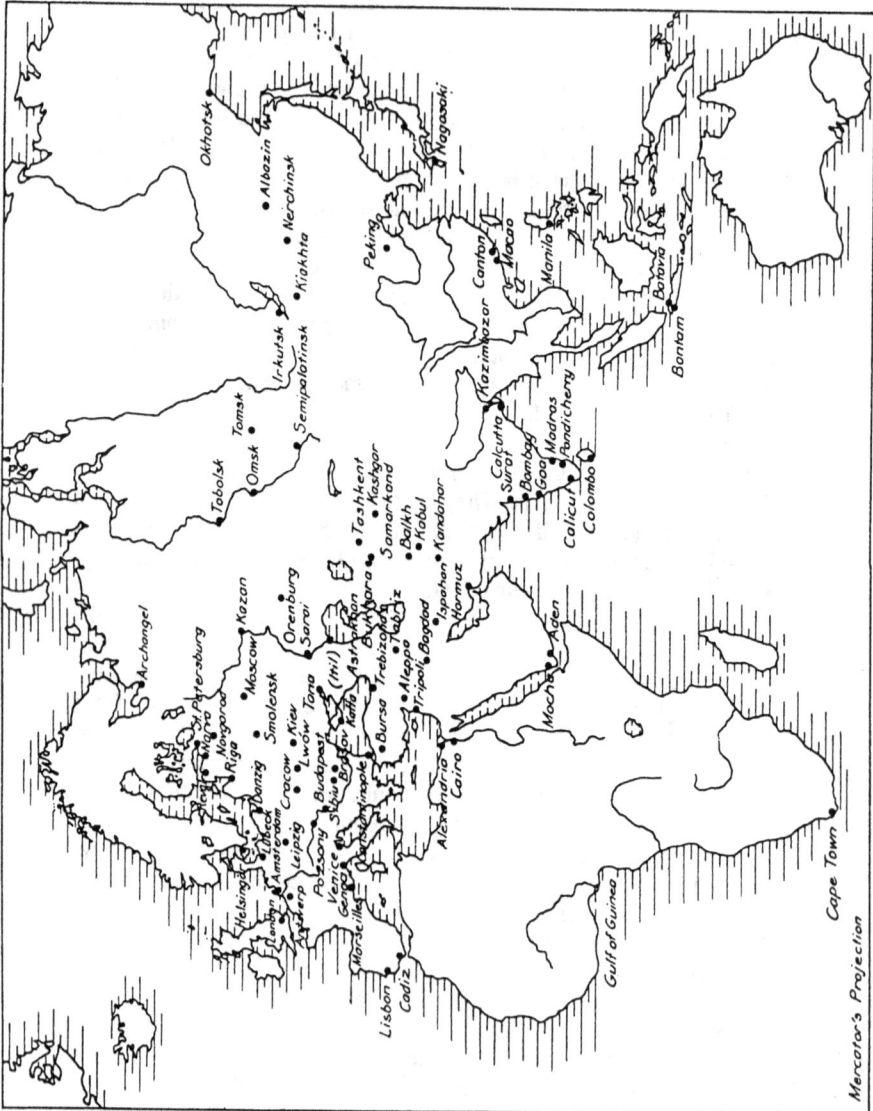

Mercator's Projection

Venice and Genoa had been the dominant trading states in the Levant during the period of the Crusades, a change took place in the course of the fifteenth century: Genoa withdrew to a great extent from this trading area and concentrated instead on the trade with Spain and Portugal. This meant that Venice then gained the supremacy in the trade with the Levant and, as a result, in the fixing of prices in Europe for the products of the Orient. By virtue of the growth in the trade the size of the balance with the trading places in the Levant also increased, and according to E. Ashtor's estimates, towards the end of the Middle Ages they amounted to the equivalent of over half a million rix-dollars (of 25.98 grammes Ag) per year.

The discovery by the Portuguese of the sea route to India certainly heralded a radical change in trading conditions but it did not have a catastrophic effect on the fortunes of Venice. In fact products from the Orient continued to come to the Levant via the traditional routes and to go from there to Venice, but they were now also brought by the Portuguese to Lisbon and Antwerp. This resulted in competitive pricing between Venice and Antwerp as regards the products of the Orient. But Venice was not to be outdone and the city successfully maintained her position, especially during the latter part of the sixteenth century. The catastrophe did not occur until the beginning of the seventeenth century, and was brought about by the appearance of the Dutch and English companies in Asia and by French, English and Dutch competition in the now limited Mediterranean trade in the Levant's own products.

Thus throughout the whole of the sixteenth century trade with the Orient played an important part for Venice, and consequently so did the demand for precious metals with which to pay the balance. At the beginning of the seventeenth century the annual exports of bullion from Venice to the Levant were still equal in value to half a million rix-dollars. When the Western European countries began to trade with the Levant herself, they encountered the same balance problems as had previously confronted Venice with regard to the transit trade from the Orient via the Levant. During the seventeenth and eighteenth centuries the total balances of all Western Europeans in the Levant amounted to some 1 – 1½ million rix-dollars a year .

During the latter part of the Middle Ages and the sixteenth century precious metals also came to the Levant from South-eastern Europe: they came in transit via Poland in payment for Poland's imports of Oriental products and they also came via Hungary as payment for Hungary's imports of goods from the Orient along this route.

The route round the Cape

The Portuguese trade round the Cape soon increased in volume and from the middle of the sixteenth century it achieved significant proportions. Soon it also became apparent that the ships from Lisbon had to carry, in addition to European products, precious metals for the purchase of spices and drugs on the Asian markets. To a large extent this consisted of silver in the form of coins from the Spanish mints, but it also included gold from the Gold Coast on the Gulf of Guinea and later gold from Mozambique on the east coast of Africa as well. However, the major precious metal was the silver coins from the Spanish mints which were able to produce 'reales de a ocho' in vast quantities, thanks to the availability of silver which was imported from America into Cadiz/Seville. These coins were of fundamental importance for the Portuguese in their purchases of goods from Asia and from the latter part of the sixteenth century onwards one may assume that two-thirds of the purchases in Asia were paid for with precious metals. The Portuguese demand for precious metals during the latter part of the sixteenth century totalled approximately 1 – 1½ million rix-dollars a year.

At the beginning of the seventeenth century the Portuguese were faced with serious competition in the European-Asian trade as a result of the establishment of the Dutch and English East India companies (V.O.C., De Verenigde Oost-Indische Compagnie, and E.I.C., the English East India Company, respectively). By the middle of the seventeenth century each of these companies on its own had outflanked the Portuguese. Once the operations of the Dutch and English companies were under way in Asia, their modern methods largely annihilated the traditional transit traffic from the Orient to the Levant and thus largely destroyed the basis of Venice's international trade.

Since the accounts of the companies have been preserved, it has been possible for researchers to establish the scale of their trade with Asia. This has in turn enabled the size of their balances on the Asian markets to be calculated. It has also been possible to establish what precious metals the companies exported from Europe to their offices in Asia to pay for purchases made there. It has become apparent that these exports were substantial.

Later on, at the end of the seventeenth century and the beginning of the eighteenth century, when companies from other countries (including France, Denmark and Sweden) began to send ships on a significant scale to Asia, they too were faced with the problem posed by the Asian trade, viz. the need for precious metals to pay for the purchases there.

In the case of the French company substantial sums were involved during the eighteenth century.

Table 1. *The V.O.C.'s imports of goods from Asia and exports of precious metals 1602 – 1795* (in millions of rix-dollars per year)

Period	Total imports of Asian products into Europe (f.o.b.)	Exports of precious metals from Europe (f.o.b.)
1602 – 10	..	0.26
1610 – 20	..	0.39
1620 – 30	0.61	0.50
1630 – 40	0.87	0.36
1640 – 50	1.02	0.35
1650 – 60	1.07	0.34
1660 – 70	1.26	0.48
1670 – 80	1.35	0 44
1680 – 90	1.78	0.79
1690 – 1700	1.73	1.16
1700 – 10	2.17	1.56
1710 – 20	2.53	1.55
1720 – 30	3.47	2.64
1730 – 40	2.78	1.70
1740 – 50	2.93	1.60
1750 – 60	3.31	2.20
1760 – 70	3.20	2.18
1770 – 80	2.84	1.91
1780 – 90	1.49	1.92
1790 – 95	0.70	1.30

Russia — Persia — India

The Persian market received from India and China products which were sent in transit to Europe. In addition, Persia was producing silk, which was very popular in Europe. During the first half of the sixteenth century these products were distributed to Europe via the Levant, and in return precious metals went from the Levant to Persia on a large

ATTMAN

Table 2. *The E.I.C.'s imports from Asia and exports to Asia 1601 – 1806* (in millions of rix-dollars per year)

Year(s)	Imports from Asia (f.o.b.)	Exports to Asia (f.o.b.)	
		Total	Including precious metals
1601/23		0.20	0.14
1601		0.12	0.09
1610		0.12	0.08
1620		0.39	0.27
1633		0.69	0.49
1660		0.29	0.22
1660/69	0.35*a*	0.48	0.32
1670/79	1.14	1.37	0.99
1680/89	1.72	1.90	1.60
1690/99	0.57	1.14	0.78
1700/09	1.20	1.76	1.56
1710/19	1.94	2.10	1.68
1720/29	2.68	2.74	2.28
1730/39	2.80	2.83	2.18
1740/49	3.12	3.17	2.32
1750/59	3.44	4.53	3.13
1760	3.02	2.19	0.61
1763 – 69		(2.83)	(0.68)
1770 – 77		(2.41)	(0.37)
1778 – 84		(2.06)	(0.02)
1785 – 91		(6.02)	(2.71)
1792 – 98		(6.34)	(1.29)
1799-1806		(11.69)	(3.52

a Relates to 1664 – 69.
Note: The figures for 1763 – 1806 according to *Parliamentary Papers* 1812 – 1813, vol. 8.

scale. From the middle of the sixteenth century this trade was supplemented by one trade route from Russia via the Caspian Sea to Persia, and several sources shed light on the nature of this trade. The value of the Oriental products was considerably higher than that of the European goods which went to Persia, and the difference was made up with precious metals from Europe in the form of rix-dollars and Spanish reals.

From the 1630s it is apparent that Persia had a negative balance with the East, and this was settled with precious metals in the form of Persian coins and European coins which were sent in transit via the Levant and Russia.

Other trade routes

For a long period the supply of precious metals to the Levant involved a considerable transit traffic eastwards through the Arab world. In addition one should take into account the fact that in the direct trade between the various countries in the Middle East on one hand and India on the other, European coins could be sent in transit on a not insignificant scale (e.g. Mocha — Surat). Equally, it is likely that African gold from the Sudan went eastwards along this route and across the Indian Ocean.

The bullion-demanding markets

The sources which are available from the beginning of the seventeenth century onwards are sufficiently numerous and reliable to enable an estimate to be made of the precious metal requirements of world trade. It then becomes apparent that there were three markets in world trade which made great demands for bullion, viz. Asia, the Levant and the Baltic area. The size of the balances on these markets can be calculated fairly accurately, since it is possible in respect of each market to establish the value of exports and imports in the same ports. The resulting figures show that export values are considerably higher than import values and that the difference was made up with precious metals. Further confirmation of this situation is provided by a large number of sources of various kinds.

Thus the starting-point is the invoice figures in Asia and the Baltic area (see Table 3). The figures given for the payments made in precious metals (Ag — Au) are minimum figures: for the Baltic area the proportion is between one-half and one-third and in Asia it is at least two-thirds. It is not possible to give any precise invoice values for the Levant, but in this case estimates must be made on another basis, viz. the actual transporting of precious metals from European ports to the Levant.

Table 3. *Invoice value in millions of rix-dollars per year*

	1600	1650	1700	1750
A. *In Asia*				
Portugal	1.5	0.5	0.5	0.5
The Netherlands	–	1	2	3
England	–	1	2	3
Other countries	–	–	0.5	2
Total	1.5	2.5	5	8.5
Payments ⅔ in Ag-Au	1	1.7	3.3	5.7
B. *In The Baltic and Archangel*				
Total	5	7	7	8
Payment ½ in Ag-Au	2.5	3.5	3.5	4
Payment ⅓ in Ag-Au	1.7	2.3	2.3	2.6
C. *In The Levant*				
Venice	. .*d*	. .	. .	. .
France	. .	. .	(2)*c*	(3)*c*
England	. .	. .	(1.3)*b*	. .
The Netherlands	. .*a*	. .	. .	. .
Total	. .	. .	. .	

a 0.6 in reals, as payment.
b Import value in England.
c Import value in Marseilles.
d 0.5 in specie, mostly reals, as payment.

A closer analysis of the bullion flow from Europe to the East shows that substantial sums are involved and that these increase as time goes by.

A conservative estimate of the yearly exports of precious metals from Europe to the East yields the following figures. In this context it should be noted that during the years 1635 – 1668 the V.O.C. met part of the demand for silver from Japan and this is included in the figure given for 1650 in Table 4.

In the present context the figures for the Levant and those for the route round the Cape are of special interest. In the year 1600 a total of 2 million rix-dollars is involved, in 1650 three and a half million, in 1700

Table 4. *Estimated annual exports of precious metals from Europe to the East*

Year	1660	1650	1700	1750
The Levant	(1)	(2)	(2)	(2)
The Baltic region	1.7 – 2	2.3 – 3	2.3 – 3	2.3 – 3
The route round the Cape	1	1.7*	3.3	5.7
Total	3.7 – 4	6 – 6.7	7.6 – 8.3	10 – 10.7

*Partly silver from Japan

at least 5 million and in 1750 no less than 7 million rix-dollars a year. If the figures for the Baltic market are included, the value of the precious metals which were transported for payment of the balances on the three world markets totalled 4 million rix-dollars in 1600, about 6 million in 1650, about 8 million in 1700 and about 10 million rix-dollars a year in 1750.

Holland's role

Two questions arise: where did these quantities of precious metals come from, and who were the intermediaries in this significant world trade in bullion?

Table 5. *Holland's bullion exports 1600 – 1780*
(in millions of rix-dollars per year)

Trade area	Around 1600	Around 1650	Around 1700	Around 1750	Around 1780
The Baltic	2	2.5	2	2	3
The Levant	0.6	0.8	1	(1.5)	(1.5)
The Eastern Asia	0.3	0.4	2	3	3.5
Total	2.9	3.7	5.0	6.5	8.0

The latter question can be answered as follows. A very large proportion of the transactions in precious metals in world trade took place via Holland. Separate extensive research into this topic has shown that a conservative assessment of Holland's role is to be found in Table 5, which gives minimum figures.

Where did the precious metals come from?

Various kinds of research have enabled an answer to be given to this question.

In fact it becomes apparent that a large proportion of the precious metals imported from America into Spain in the course of various transactions ended up on the Dutch bullion market. Thus it was the Spanish imports into Cadiz/Seville, supplemented from the start of the eighteenth century by Brazilian gold entering Lisbon, which supplied the Dutch bullion market with the large quantities of precious metals which the expanding world trade demanded.

With regard to the sixteenth and seventeenth centuries it is possible to give more detailed figures for the supplies of precious metals from America to Spain.

Table 6. *Imports of precious metals into Europe from America 1531 – 1700* (in millions of rix-dollars per year)

1531 – 35	0.5	1616 – 20	9.8
1536 – 40	1.3	1621 – 25	8.8
1541 – 45	1.6	1626 – 30	8.1
1546 – 50	1.8	1631 – 35	5.6
1551 – 55	3.2	1636 – 40	5.3
1556 – 60	2.6	1641 – 45	4.5
1561 – 65	3.6	1646 – 50	3.8
1566 – 70	4.6	1651 – 55	2.4
1571 – 75	3.9	1656 – 60	1.1
1576 – 80	5.6	1661 – 65	(9.4)
1581 – 85	9.6	1666 – 70	(10.5)
1586 – 90	7.8	1671 – 75	(13.7)
1591 – 95	11.5	1676 – 80	(13.0)
1596 – 1600	11.2	1681 – 85	(7.2)
1601 – 05	7.9	1686 – 90	(12.8)
1606 – 10	10.2	1691 – 95	(11.1)
1611 – 15	8.0	1696 – 1700	(15.0)

The proportion sent to Europe is known primarily through the work of E. J. Hamilton. The imports of precious metals from America into Spain which he recorded have been converted into rix-dollars in the table. Since Hamilton's statistics end in 1660, Table 6 has been supplemented by M. Morineau's estimates for 1661 – 1700, although these appear to be on the high side. They have therefore been placed in brackets.

The discussion that has taken place in recent decades has tended to show that the extent of the decline in imports into Seville, as recorded by Hamilton in relation to the 1620s, has probably been exaggerated. Furthermore, there is a lot of evidence to show that supplies to Europe after the decline in the 1650s were substantial up to the 1680s, when a temporary decrease occurred. But the supply then increased again, and throughout the whole of the eighteenth century significant sums were involved.

At the beginning of the eighteenth century an important new source of precious metal appeared, viz. gold from Brazil, which was transported in increasing quantities to Lisbon. Thus according to estimates which have been compiled, the yearly supply from Brazil to Lisbon during the period 1712 – 1755 had a value of 6.5 million rix-dollars. Therefore these imports of gold into Lisbon which supplemented the silver imports from Spanish America into Cadiz/Seville supplied Europe with large quantities of precious metals. As it had done throughout since the middle of the sixteenth century, the European market obtained in this way the necessary quantities of precious metals for the large bullion trade which commerce with the Baltic area, the Levant and Asia entailed.

As previously stated, much of the flow of precious metals into Cadiz/Seville and Lisbon went onwards into Holland. This is illustrated *inter alia* by the estimate which the Dutch Mint Masters made of the bullion imports from Spain to Holland in 1683: in that year they amounted to 6 to 7 million rix-dollars in value. Thus these imports were sufficient for Holland's bullion exports which amounted to at least 5 million rix-dollars in the year 1700. These imports from Spain into Holland were in turn well covered by the imports from America into Cadiz which, it is estimated, amounted to 10 million rix-dollars a year in value in the 1680s.

The exports of precious metals from Holland to the various markets which made demands for bullion were not made up solely of Dutch coins but also comprised to a large extent coins from Spain (minted in America and Spain) and the Spanish Netherlands, as well as unminted precious metals.

The supply of precious metals to the Asian markets

Summarizing the position, it is possible to establish that a significant proportion of the precious metals exported from Europe went to the

Asian markets. But these also received precious metals from other markets. In all, the following routes were involved.
(a) From and via the Levant;
(b) From Russia via Persia;
(c) Round the Cape;
(d) From Acapulco in Mexico and Callao in Peru across the Pacific Ocean to Manila, whence the precious metals were then dispersed in the trade with the various Asian markets;
(e) From Japan in the form of silver and gold at various periods during the seventeenth century;
(f) From Africa, in the form of gold from the Sudan and Mozambique.

In an appraisal of the different routes, those which ran between Europe and Asia stand out as being by far the most important.

Coin values

Throughout the present text the value figures have been converted into the internationally stable rix-dollar, which contained 25.98 grammes of silver. Conversion rates:

1 rix-dollar = 1½ Dutch guilders (around 1560)
1 rix-dollar = 2½ Dutch guilders (after 1606)
1 rix-dollar = 1 Albertustaler (in the Baltic; 24.65 grammes of silver)
1 rix-dollar = *c.* 1 piece of eight (real)
£1 = 4¼ rix-dollars
£1 = 11 Dutch guilders (after 1606)
1 ducat (3.5 g Au) = *c.* 2.1 rix-dollars (after 1650)
Bimetallic ratios (Au:Ag) in Western Europe: in 1550 10.5 – 11, in 1600 12, in 1660 15, in 1700 15, in 1750 14.5, in 1800 15.5.

3

UGARIT: A BRONZE AGE HANSA?

John Wansbrough

The comparatively abundant, but certainly heterogeneous and discrete documents so far excavated at Ras Shamra have attracted considerable attention and a number of scarcely varying interpretations. There appears to be a kind of consensus that the administrative data from Ugarit attest a dynastic monarchy actively involved in the regulation of what is commonly called a 'palace economy'.[1] While acknowledging that such a view is far from arbitrary, I should like in the following pages to propose an alternative exegesis. The question in my title is thus not rhetorical but quite genuine. It contains, moreover, allusion to the model I have thought appropriate to reinterpretation of the material available, and at least not inappropriate to the venue of this particular conference. But archaeology, it may be recalled, is a notoriously unpredictable pursuit, and it seems methodologically sound that no single hypothesis should remain for long unchallenged.

That Ugarit for some centuries of the second millennium figured significantly in the network of diplomatic and commercial relations through and beyond the Levant is established by the discovery of artefacts, correspondence, records of economic and legal transactions, and explicit mention in the archives of foreign capitals. Even without these, its location on the north Syrian coast and the extent of its already revealed remains would have suggested some such role. As it is, extensive study has produced lists of commodities traded and locally generated, some indication of prices tabulated in terms of precious metals apparently functioning as currency, fragmentary references to shipfitting and other marine enterprises such as haulage and warfare, and allusion to the sojourn of foreigners in Ugaritic territory, evidently in their capacity as merchants. The fact of international commerce is thus indisputable. It is its mode(s) of organization that merit particular scrutiny.

Polanyi's several paradigms for analysis of commercial activity are well known. Their ingeniously hypothetical character makes it difficult to envisage an historical situation to which any one of them might be exclusively applied, but at least the concept of a socio-political matrix consistent with the evidence of such activity is not a required component of every description. On the other hand, the notional opposition 'embedded': 'disembedded' has undoubtedly been over-worked, since the very commitment to 'external' trade is inconsistent with absolute freedom in the choice of partners.[2] In other words, if commerce is meant to include anything more than exchange of symbolic commodities and enhancement of prestige, it becomes susceptible to pressures beyond the control of one or even several agents. I could also add the condition: if it is to prosper, and thereby invoke the factors of profit and continuity. Wherever the initiative might lie, prosecution of trade so defined requires not only the discovery but to some extent also the creation of conditions to ensure its prosperity. These will indeed include a socio-political environment conducive to long-term, and probably long-distance, transactions, but equally one responsive to economic and technological change. Such change might be thought both unpredictable and contingent, in any case well outside the perimeter of a single regulatory mechanism. Nor, of course, is there a single set of conditions, at least historically documented, that could ensure the continued prosperity of trade: it is as much a matter of matching as of making.

Now, to match the commerce of Ugarit to that of a Hanseatic port requires some imagination and moderate adjustment of the data pertinent to expression of authority in that community. These would include both the bodies responsible for taking decisions and the several emblems by which they are designated in the archival material. In this connexion the possibility of an archival (archaeological) bias would have at least to be mooted. From such data it ought to be possible to extrapolate a model of communal organization applicable to, *inter alia*, possession and use of property, production, transport, exchange, brokerage, taxation, and litigation. Limits of space will preclude examination of all these activities. Instead, and by way of introduction of these weightier problems, I intend to consider evidence for the operations of (1) monarchy, (2) assembly, (3) tribunal, and (4) contract.

(1) The presence in Ugarit of a monarchy is documented by the terms MLK and ŠARRU, titles which appear regularly, often but not always accompanied by a PN, in letters, land transfers and legal actions. The collocations MAR ŠARRI, BNŠ MLK, and BT MLK, which occur in commodity allocations and contracts, would seem to invest the titles with some functional significance. Even approximate determination of this function is, however, difficult, since in one series of documents (property transfer) mention of the 'king' plus proper name alternates with that of named 'witnesses' (ŠIBUTU). A juridical equivalence of function between ŠARRU and ŠIBUTU is thus a reasonable, if not

ineluctable, interpretation. Moreover, the epithets MAR ŠARRI and BNŠ MLK appear to be designations of office rather than of descent, i.e. not the 'king's sons' but the 'king's men'. Though the notion of a royal dynasty may not be altogether impressionistic, it is nourished primarily by the recurrent use of a chancery seal bearing the putative eponym YAQARU and a quite unique role of proper names thought to represent a 'king-list'. That YAQARU could be an honorific title and the king-list contain nothing more than a catalogue of random officeholders has not, to my knowledge, been proposed. It may be suggested that Ugaritic MLK is not a translation of Akkadian ŠARRU, but rather, that ŠARRU as employed at Ugarit exhibits a rendering of MLK, possibly influenced by a west Semitic cognate SAR. There is, in any case, no compelling evidence to read MLK at Ugarit as autocratic, dynastic, or 'royal' authority.[3]

(2) In chancery documents there are but few instances of the roots PḤR and QBṢ, which refer to divine assemblies in Ugaritic mythology, and these occur in broken contexts. More important is the recurrent formula ANA PANI amelMŠIBUTI: 'in the presence of witnesses', where (as indicated above) ŠIBUTI occupies the slot sometimes allocated to the 'king'. The etymology of ŠIBU would suggest not merely 'witness' but 'elder', possibly identical with the locution amelABBIM alUGARIT referring, in another document, to those with authority to levy a transit tax. The only Ugaritic equivalent to ŠIBU so far contextually attested is YPḤ which does not, of course, support the rendering 'elder'. It is none the less worth remarking that a (municipal/territorial?) assembly could function in place of the 'king'.[4]

(3) In matters of litigation, and especially those concerned with merchant law, the primary arbiter appears not to have been the MLK but the ŠAKINU. It is he who was addressed by foreign plaintiffs, occasionally even to the explicit exclusion of the 'king', who might also be party to the dispute. That the regulation of such affairs lay within the competence of a special office is hardly surprising, and ŠAKINU is often translated 'vizier'. The extent to which this office was structurally autonomous or in fact merely delegated cannot be determined, though it may we worth recalling that in the Tell Fekheriyeh bilingual ŠAKINMATI is rendered MLK.[5]

(4) A variety of contractual status is expressed in Ugaritic by the root 'RB with the preposition B. Derivatives, in the sense of 'pledge' or 'guarantee', are attested in most Semitic and in several Indo-European languages. In Ugaritic documents the term signifies an act of (reciprocal) obligation, and in Akkadian the parties are designated amelMURUBANU. Two further links are possible but far from clear: first with formation of a 'partnership' (ḪBR/TAPPUTU), second, with 'shares' in a commercial venture ('RB BT PN), in which the PN

slot may even be filled by MLK (see above for the locution BT MLK; and cf. Old Akkadian ANA EKALLIM ERABUM). Such extension of the usage (i.e. 'RB without preposition B) would require rather more documentation than at present available, but there is some evidence for the organization of merchants in 'decumates' ('ŠRM) under a designated head (RB 'ŠRT) and with an established place of business (BT 'ŠRM), that is, 'house' or 'firm' (cf. Akkadian BIT TAMKARIM). It may at least be said that initiative for such contractual arrangements does not appear to lie with the palace.[6]

Analysis of Ugaritic commerce has been, and is still, impeded by a paucity of prosopographical data. Save for several chancery scribes and the celebrated MUDU dossiers, the names of very few persons are attested more than once or twice. It is thus impossible to trace the fortunes of a single merchant or of a trading house. The existence of guilds or of professional sodalities has been mooted but not conclusively demonstrated. One is thus compelled to make do with such epithets as occasionally appear in combination with proper names and/ or occupational types. For example, the term for 'merchant' (TAMKARU) may be qualified by ŠA MANDATTI or ŠA ŠEPI or ŠA QATI, or rendered by Ugaritic MKR and further qualified by BDL. Whether these phrases represent professional status or merely *ad hoc* circumstance is not clear; extrapolation can at best produce a typology, not a history.[7] A further frustration is the absence of a dependable chronology: evidence from Mari, Hatti and Amarna confirm the existence of Ugarit, but shed only faint light on the processes of international commerce. Without some indication of continuity it is impossible, or at least very difficult, to establish causality. These disabling factors ought really to preclude an economic history, but have not quite done so. Desperation has generated the 'palace' model, and it is in this respect that I mentioned the possibility of an archaeological bias. That the vestigial architecture at Ugarit should reveal a 'palais royal' and not, say, an 'hotel de ville' is surely a matter that deserves further examination. Traces, it is true, of temple and funerary architecture have been noted, with some preliminary provisional attempts to identify domestic and even military edifices. The urban configuration of Ugarit has yet to be ascertained, but there is meanwhile no compelling evidence to justify filling the lacunae with symbols of monarchy.[8]

If, for instance, MANDATTU does refer to 'funding' and NTBT/ MIḤD to 'trading ventures', there is not in the relevant texts proof of a concession granted, and certainly not from a 'royal' exchequer. That certain fiscal operations may have been farmed by municipal and other authorities need have no bearing on commercial undertakings. If, moreover, MḪD = KARU and is a reference to 'quai', the equation need imply neither tax-farming nor a single toponym, but more probably a commercial transaction, the named parties to which were free agents.[9] This point may be corroborated by the documentation of commodity prices, admittedly meagre but none the less unequivocal in attesting to considerable fluctuation. Now, whether such can be ascribed to variation in the price of materials, the cost of labour, or of profit margins is impossible to discern. The fact that these texts are undated provokes a further variable, but there is in any case no evidence of monolithic price control. Indeed, the only constant factor in this trade appears to have been the ratio of the basic metals of exchange (gold, silver, copper, tin). Since these, with the possible exception of silver, were not native to northern Syria, the exchange ratio may reflect an international convention. But even a fixed rate would not inhibit the operation of agio, which may have been an additional factor in the fluctuation of prices. Movement of and reckoning in precious metals suggest, at the very least, a technological mode in which profit was a calculable and tangible component. Its ultimate, even immediate, destination would be a fiscal rather than strictly commercial matter.[10]

A further expression of organizational technique is found in reference to shipping. These include not merely routes and cargoes, but also supply and fitting, and name destinations from Ura and Caphtor to Alašiya and Egypt, including several Canaanite ports. To what extent such data may betoken a monopoly of the carrying trade is a question not easily answered, but rough computation based on quantified shipments and anchor weights indicate substantial capacity. Lexical differentiation of ship types as well as terms for shipwright, owner, captain, and crew might be thought to exhibit a sophisticated profession, if not indeed, a developed industry.[11] In the light of my remarks above on the semantic content of MLK, I am of course not inclined to interpret this material as evidence of unilateral regalian enterprise. The often adduced but unique documentary reference to Caphtor occurs in a context perhaps pertinent to the organization of commerce at Ugarit: namely, in a tax exemption to Sinaranu, one of several merchants elevated to the status of 'companion' (MUDU).[12] If that procedure could be read as signalling the emergence of a patriciate, one might find there a clue to membership of the municipal assembly (ŠIBUTU). It is here that the lack of prosopographical data is most sorely felt. A kind of compensation may be sought in the names of the ports, from which an impressive range of gentilics (including Kena'ni) is attested. In what must have been a remarkably cosmopolitan community, regulation of the foreigner's (UBRU) sojourn and status was fairly explicit, comprehending extradition and indemnity of person and property.[13]

If it is not by now absolutely clear, let me acknowledge that the preceding observations are nothing more than random essays at source analysis. That they might generate a narrative history is most unlikely. And yet, my rejection of one and selection of another model must entail some consciousness of the historian's perennial duty. 'Hansa' is itself a problematic term, but was chosen to evoke such notions as government by oligarchy, control of maritime communication, dominant mercantile investment, and of course, a market economy. Corollaries like political independence and establishment of merchant colonies (KARU/MḪD : Kontor/Stalhof/Fondaco) provoke a related but distinct register of questions, that can only be approached by recourse to a further analogy. In some ways Phoenician commerce is better attested than that of Ugarit, and it had certainly been more exhaustively studied. There, the plantation of Mediterranean and Atlantic outposts ('factories') has involved not merely analysis of the variable relations between these and the metropolitan ports, but also of the immediate political configuration in which the latter operated. The structure, or at least posture, of the Neo-Assyrian empire may well have been crucial to Phoenician expansion westward, and it is more than likely that commerce by colonization exhibits an order of priorities rather different from that which had obtained in the second millennium. In recent years a good deal has been written about the 'thalassophobia' of Bronze Age empires, a feature that may have originated in an *argumentum e silentio* for the prosperity of Ugarit. While the danger of a specious circularity must be obvious, it must also be evident that Phoenician commerce required a mode of organization more rigorous than that attested by Ugaritic sources.[14] Several analogies from the late medieval Mediterranean world might be adduced to illustrate supersession of the Hanseatic style. Not long before the entry of Elizabethan England into that world and the metamorphosis by which she became a colonial power, a verdict of the Privy Council defined the Hansa, having neither communal property nor common law nor a common seal or syndic, as a 'confederatio' for the mutual protection of business. That description might just, without serious dislocation, be applied to the role of Ugarit during the documented period of its history.[15]

4

DUPLICATE SYSTEMS OF TRADE: A KEY ELEMENT IN MESOPOTAMIAN HISTORY

McGuire Gibson

Ancient Mesopotamia was a conspicuous consumer of resources, but was also a major producer of some raw materials and finished goods, and took a very active role in long-range trade. It will be argued here that there existed two parallel northwest-to-southeast chains of communication in Mesopotamia, the Tigris and Euphrates system, both of which could tap the same resources and markets. This duplication resulted in long-term trading rivalry and political enmity. It will be proposed that significant shifts in the relations between states after 1000 B.C. can be understood in great part as a result of the opening of alternate routes with the introduction of the camel as a means of transport.

In the following pages, I will be discussing not so much trade and commodities as military and political moves that I suggest were motivated by the need to gain resources, sell finished goods, and prevent rival states from doing the same. The emphasis on states and their relations is dictated by the nature of the written sources. Cuneiform documents are skewed towards those large institutions, such as palaces and temples, that had a need for long-term record-keeping. Thus, we have a view of the ancient world as seen through the eye of scribes who usually recorded only what was of concern to their institutions.[1] Private trade is much less well-represented in the records, although it probably formed the bulk of economic activity in most periods.

Even with the thousands of economic records, there is a large area of doubt on specific items exchanged. Whole categories of human consumption and market activity may go unmentioned in the texts.[2] Important commodities for everyday life, like spices, cannot yet be identified even if they are listed. From the great number of artefacts found in archaeological excavations but rarely if ever mentioned in texts, it must be concluded that most imports were not recorded in documents and the mechanism of their arrival must be inferred from the few archives of private venture trade that we do have.

The main parts of the duplicate systems, Assyria and Babylonia (Fig. 1), although markedly different in environmental features and related resources, were enough alike in their overall potential and needed raw materials that they were in most periods essentially rivals rather than trading partners.

Assyria with the Tigris as its main route for heavy transportation, had mountains and foothills which received enough rainfall to make agriculture possible without irrigation. In very ancient times, the mountain slopes were wooded, affording abundant material for construction and fuel.[3] There were some kinds of fruit trees that would grow more readily in Assyria than in Babylonia, and the area was a natural habitat for sheep, goats, cows, and other animals. Bees thrived in Assyria and the honey was a prized luxury item. The mountains furnished stone for tool-making, for building, and for sculpture.

Babylonia, fed by the Euphrates,[4] could produce a much greater abundance of agricultural goods, but only with irrigation. A few trees with economic value such as the poplar, some fruit trees and the date palm could grow naturally alongside the watercourses. The only significant natural resources of Babylonia were agricultural products such as grains and dates, reeds, fish, pigs, birds, and other wildlife in the marshes and rivers, gazelles and other animals in the deserts, and the domesticates (sheep, goats, cows, donkeys) that had been introduced into the area. Certain processed foods, such as salted or dried fish, smoked meat, dried yoghurt, and ghee may have been items for external trade, but were more probably limited to internal trade. Reeds and reed products were an important resource for construction and for everyday use (mats, baskets) and were most probably traded to Assyria and elsewhere. Dates, grains, and other commodities which could be stored for a time without deterioration or could be processed into forms that would allow storage (beer, wine, sesame oil, linseed oil), would also have been important products for external trade. Manufactured goods made from imported raw materials were probably also exported.

But the main items of export for both Babylonia and Assyria were raw wool and textiles. There is evidence that Babylonian textiles were brought by Assyrians for shipment to their trading colonies in Anatolia (c. 1900 B.C.) and trade is assumed to have gone on between the two rivals in most periods. Such exchange, however, did not negate the basic competition between the two areas.

To a great degree, Assyria and Babylonia were duplicates not only in terms of the most essential exportable products but in their need for many of the same raw materials. For instance, specialty stones for the manufacture of millstones, statuary, jewellery and seals were imported into both Babylonia and Assyria, as were ores, metals, large timbers

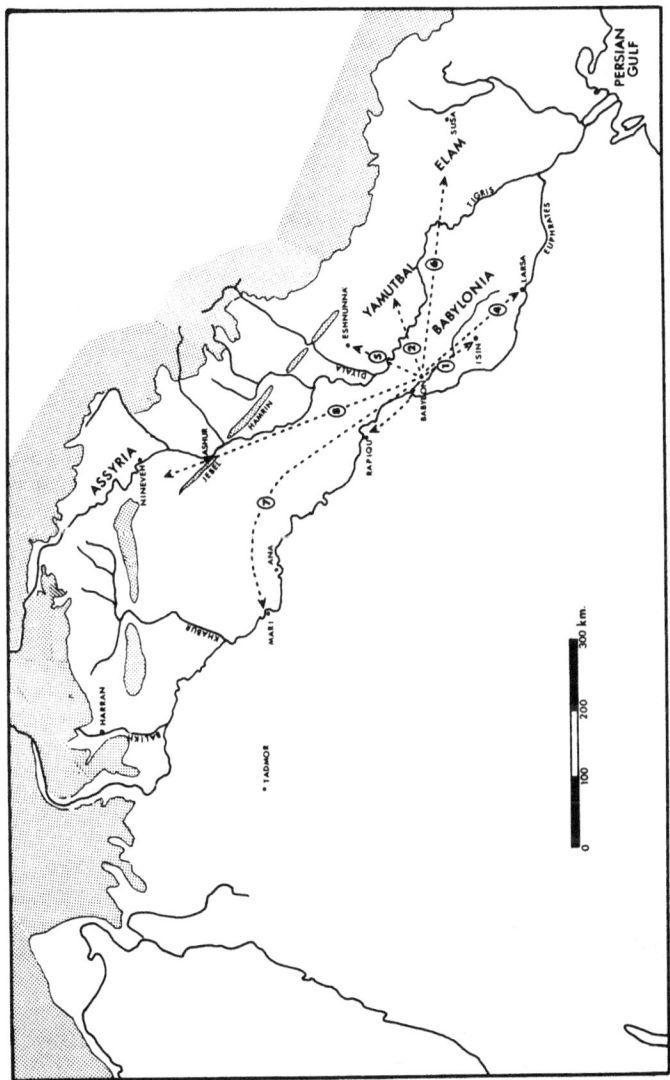

Fig. 1. Mesopotamia in the 18th Century B.C. with conquests of Hammurabi. Adapted from M. A. Beek, *Atlas of Mesopotamia* (London: Nelson, 1962), Map 10.

(e.g. cedars of Lebanon), and numerous other commodities such as shells, ivory, and essences. Large bulk items (stones, timber, grain) were floated down the rivers, while smaller items were carried on the backs of donkeys.

Both Assyria and Babylonia, by linking up with the areas along their respective rivers, the Tigris and Euphrates, could more economically solve their supply problems than they could by co-operating with one another. Each, with its chain of trading partners, had access both to the markets and resources of Turkey and the Levant in the north-west and to the Gulf and Iran to the south-east. Each of the rivals had advantages over the other. Assyria had more direct access through mountain passes to Iran and Eastern Turkey and could make use of well-watered, easy overland routes to the northern Levant and western Turkey. If it could keep as allies its southern neighbours, especially Elam, it also had access to the great Asian trunk roads through Iran and an outlet to the Gulf. Babylonia, on the other hand, was able, through its line of communication along the Euphrates, to tap the markets of southern and central Turkey, Syria, Palestine, and the Levant coast. Its distinct advantage, however, lay in its direct access to the Gulf and the sea-borne trade of Dilmun, Magan, and Meluhha (Bahrain and the Arabian coast, Oman, and Baluchistan/India).[5]

Babylonia's position at the head of the Gulf put it in direct competition with Elam. Babylonia and Elam, even more than Babylonia and Assyria, duplicated resources and needs. It is no surprise that for most of ancient history, these two southern neighbours were bitter enemies, while Elam and Assyria found co-operation to their advantage.

The main communication route across the Zagros, today's Baghdad-Kermanshah road, was of major strategic importance for both Babylonia and Assyria. Whoever held it could deprive the other of its use or force the payment of tolls. Because Eshnunna lay astride that route as well as the Tigris, this kingdom had the potential to play a major role in Assyro-Babylonian relations and did so in one period (19th – 18th century B.C.). Most of the time, however, Babylonia held the pass or attempted to control it.

The chains of communication and co-operation along the rivers were vulnerable. By striking at Elam or any other link on the Tigris side, Babylonia could threaten the interests of Assyria. In like fashion, Assyria, by striking at or suborning Babylonia's trading partners along the middle and upper Euphrates (Ana, Mari, Carchemish) could seriously endanger the economy of that entire line.

The hindering of the lines of commerce and communication can be discerned repeatedly in military movements and diplomatic manoeuvres. The records of the time of Hammurabi of Babylon (c.

1792 – 1750 B.C.) are especially useful for reconstructing the pattern. For almost two centuries prior to this time, Mesopotamia had been split into a number of relatively small states based upon such cities as Isin, Larsa, Eshnunna, Babylon, Mari, and Assur (Fig. 1). Around 1850 B.C., a king of Eshnunna struck west to take the city of Rapiqu on the Euphrates, thus dominating that river's traffic. He then attacked Assyria apparently in an attempt to become the dominant Tigris power. A further raid by Eshnunna into the Khabur river basin of Syria must be seen as a move to threaten Mari, and increase pressure on the Euphrates kingdoms. Mari was so strong in this period that one of its kings was able to campaign to the Mediterranean coast, but its history underwent a great change very shortly thereafter. A new Assyrian king marched to the Mediterranean, presumably to bring the Syrian kingdoms into Assur's sphere. He then captured Mari and set his own son on that throne.

We have there, then, two strong Tigris kingdoms (Eshnunna and Assyria) on a collision course. Eshnunna, with its hold on Rapiqu, could choke off communication between the upper Euphrates and Babylonia. Assyria, with Mari, could do the same. Either was in a position to expand beyond its boundaries to form an empire. The king of Eshnunna, allied with his southern neighbour Elam, attacked Assyria and also made a march up the Euphrates from Rapiqu to put pressure on Mari. Assyria apparently withstood the assaults.

Hammurabi of Babylon, during this time, had consolidated his position by taking Isin in his sixth regnal year (Fig. 1, arrow 1). In the following year he raided Yamutbal and Malgum (Fig. 1, arrow 2), areas east of the Tigris and presumably trading partners of Eshnunna and Elam. In his tenth year, he took Rapiqu from Eshnunna and thereby reopened his main line of communication (Fig. 1, arrow 3). Later, Assyria lost Mari to a local dynast who was allied to Syrian kingdoms and to Hammurabi. With the establishment of this Euphrates axis, the Tigris powers (Assur, Eshnunna, and Elam) now became allies once more.

The Tigris alliance attacked Babylon in Hammurabi's 29th year. The reaction was carefully orchestrated. In the following year, Hammurabi first conquered Larsa (Fig. 1, arrow 4), thus consolidating his hold on all of Babylonia. He then took the kingdom of Eshnunna (Fig. 1, arrow 5). In his 32nd year, Hammurabi conquered Malgum (Fig. 1, arrow 6) to gain a foothold east of the Tigris facing Elam. His next move, in the same year, was to turn on Mari, which he made a vassal; two years later, he returned to destroy Mari after a revolt (Fig. 1, arrow 7). Finally, in his 36th and 38th years, he campaigned against and conquered Assyria (Fig. 1, arrow 8). He did not live to take Elam and much of his conquests were lost by his successor.

The intricate manoeuvres of Hammurabi and his enemies were probably matched by kings in later periods, but we do not have the extraordinary richness of written detail that obtains in the Old Babylonian era. We do know that in the fourteenth to the twelfth centuries (during the Kassite period) international trade and diplomatic relations linked Babylonia with Egypt, the Hittite kingdom (Turkey), Mitanni (eastern Syria and northern Iraq), and Assyria. Trade was brisk up the Euphrates and through the desert oasis of Palmyra as well as along the river to Aleppo. Downriver, Babylonia had a flourishing trade through the Gulf in such goods as exotic woods and spices.

The old pattern of Tigris-versus-Euphrates is reflected in wars between the Assyrians and Babylonians during the Kassite period. Once again the Elamites were allies of the Assyrians in a conquest of Babylonia. Shortly afterwards, Babylonia attacked Assyria successfully, but was itself devastated by an Elamite army.

In Kassite period records there are the first indications of Aramean tribesmen, who were raiding date orchards in Dilmun and menacing caravans in Canaan.[6] Their appearance on the desert fringes of the Fertile Crescent was part of a much larger process in which mass movements of peoples during the late 2nd Millennium toppled, or took advantage of weakness in, the old centres of power. Arameans took over several small kingdoms in north Syria along the Euphrates and even held parts of the upper Tigris at this time. In the following centuries, Arameans were to infiltrate both Babylonia and Assyria to such an extent that Aramaic became the language of everyday speech.

The shreds of evidence available for the period of disorder show that the Tigris-versus-Euphrates pattern still held. Babylonia was harassed by the Elamites until Nebuchadnezzar I (1125 – 1104 B.C.) invaded Elam and sent that country into a decline. Conflict continued between Babylonia and Assyria with one major success for Babylonia and a conquest and burning of Babylon by the Assyrians.

It has been suggested[7] that the inroads of Arameans caused Assyria and Babylonia to make peace in the eleventh century B.C. The following century has been described as a time when '. . . the chief western trade route along the Euphrates lay in the hands of aggressive Arameans and contact with Assyria had been broken off . . .'[8] By the end of the tenth century, Assyrian kings were able to defeat the Arameans and '. . . removed the threat of Aramean invasion from the Assyrian and Babylonian heartlands, and thereby opened the way for renewed Babylonian-Assyrian contacts and for a cultural renaissance in both lands.'[9] The renewal of contacts resulted in the Assyrians' invading Babylonia and the Babylonians' conquering much of Assyria in 892 B.C. Following this war, there was a peace that lasted 75 years.

Thereafter the reassertion of the Tigris-versus-Euphrates pattern can be seen in the placing of Assyrian forts along the middle Euphrates (the land of Suhu) and subsequent revolts by local people there aided by Babylonians.

A late-ninth century revival of Babylonia, especially in its western areas, was accompanied by the first mentions of a group called the Chaldeans. These people, differentiated in ancient sources from the Arameans who were already inhabiting Babylonia in great numbers,[10] established a dominance in the southern part of Babylonia, claimed the Babylonian crown, and led revolts against Assyria when it occupied the country.

At this point in time, a major shift of alliances is evidenced. Whereas heretofore, the Elamites had been the enemies of Babylonia, they were from now on 'Babylonia's traditional ally'[11] against Assyria. What brought about this drastic shift and how did it relate to the model of duplicate trade routes that I am proposing?

The critical element in understanding the change in alliances is the introduction of the camel as a pack animal resulting in the opening or the expansion of trade routes through Arabia (Fig. 2).

There is no question that the desert routes from the Euphrates through Syria were open and used for commerce at least as early as the nineteenth century B.C. Palmyra, ancient Tadmor, was the main stop for donkey caravans to Mari at this time.[12] How much of Arabia was traversed and at what time the routes were used is open to question. In the Eastern Province of Saudi Arabia, I have collected pottery that was made in or copied from Mesopotamian ceramics of the 5th, 4th, 3rd, and early 2nd Millennia. This early pottery was found in oases, in settlements and camp sites along ancient lakes, some of which were a hundred kilometres from the Persian Gulf. Ceramic material found in the Wadi Sirhan, in northwest Arabia, has been dated to the 4th Millennium, but there is considered to be a gap in occupation of that area from then to the 'Hellenistic' period.[13] Until evidence of camels is presented, we must assume that the early sites in Eastern Arabia and the Wadi Sirhan were reached by donkey caravan.

Even though people with donkeys and horses, and knowing the location of wells, could travel the desert routes in early times, it was only with the camel that desert trade became economically viable.[14] It was not just the camel's greater adaptability to the desert that made the difference, but the far greater load the animal could carry.

The date for the domestication of the camel is debated, but a good case has been made for its occurrence sometime around 2000 B.C.[15] Even if domestication did take place then, there is no clear evidence that the camel's use for transport can be dated earlier than about 1200

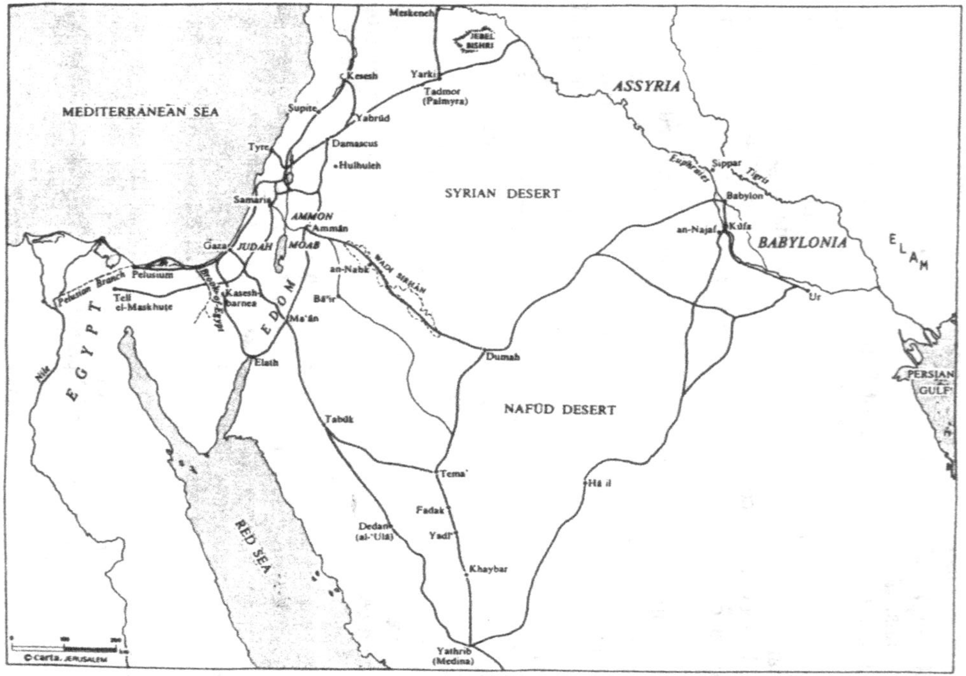

Fig. 2. Main Routes in the Syro-Arabian Desert early 1st Millennium B.C. Adapted from I. Eph'al, *The Arabs of the Desert* (Leiden: Magnes/Brill, 1982), p. 142.

B.C. The caravan trade of the Kassites, linking Babylonia with the Levant and Egypt at about this time,[16] might have utilized some camels, but more probably depended on donkeys and horses (the latter introduced in a major way to Mesopotamia by the Kassites). The great majority of cuneiform references to camels come after this date and the archaeological evidence presents much the same pattern.

With the exception of a few isolated finds of camel bones (which need not necessarily be of pack animals or even domesticates),[17] figurines of camels in excavated sites comprise the best indication of their introduction to Mesopotamia. A few camel figurines have been found in Kassite context, e.g. in thirteenth century Nippur,[18] but they are far more common in later levels, such as houses we can date to the seventh century B.C.

The introduction of the camel into Mesopotamia at about the same time as the Arameans made an appearance might argue for this group as the domesticators. But the fact that the one-humped camel is called in Akkadian by a term that is derived from Arabic would link the animal to the Arabs. On the other hand, the Sumerian term 'horse of the Sealands (i.e., southern Mesopotamia and the east Arabian coast)' would seem to show that the camel made its first impact in the southern fringes of Babylonia, where the Arameans are first mentioned and were eventually concentrated. Since Arabs are not attested in Mesopotamian sources until the ninth century, we must assume either that the Arameans brought in the camel, calling it by terms learned from its probable Arab domesticators in the southern part of the peninsula, or that the Arabs were already on the fringes of the settled areas in the thirteenth century, some four hundred years before their first recorded mention in cuneiform. Future analysis of texts may indicate a different conclusion, but it would seem logical to assume that Arabs in the southern part of the peninsula domesticated the camel and introduced it to Syria and Mesopotamia where Aramean/Chaldean people adopted it. I assume that the Arameans and Chaldeans developed the long-range desert trade in co-operation with the Arabs, using profits from ventures to buy agricultural and orchard land, and city property, and putting the profit from those holdings into further ventures.

When the Arabs were first mentioned (836 B.C.) they were a camel-owning force in opposition to the Assyrians in Syria.[19] A century later, they were most usually allied with the Babylonians as enemies of the Assyrians, but could sometimes be integrated into the Assyrian provincial administrative system.[20]

The importance of the Arabs in international trade can be seen in the taxes and booty taken from them (gold, spices, camels, precious stones) by Assyrian kings.[21] In the reign of Sennacherib (c. 700 B.C.) the Assyrians received tribute from Taima (Tema'), an important oasis deep in Arabia. In the year 689 B.C. the same king carried out a campaign against Adummatu (modern Dumah), an oasis almost equidistant from Babylon, Medina, and the Mediterranean coast. In the Assyrian annals, there is also mention of gifts from the king of Sheba. The entire peninsula was obviously in contact and major trade was being carried out in gold, precious stones, spices and incense.[22]

I would suggest that the trade across the desert changed the relationship between Elam and Assyria on the one hand and Elam and Babylonia on the other. In previous times Elam had little to gain by co-operating with Babylonia. Even though its merchants probably had to pay a large number of tolls on the well-watered overland routes through Assyria, that was its logical partner. In the first Millenium, however, with Babylonia linked to the incense sources of south Arabia and to the Mediterranean by camel caravan, it would have been more profitable for Elam to co-operate with the Babylonians and their Arab allies (partners?). Camel caravans, even when they travelled somewhat close to the Euphrates, could not be forced to pay the tolls exacted on the river routes.

The Chaldeans in Babylonia, by using the desert, made ineffective the traditional Assyrian stratagem of taking a portion of the middle Euphrates and fortifying it. Though militarily stronger, Assyria could do little to restrict the trade and consequent accumulation of wealth in Babylonia. Assyrian kings might invade and set up client kings, put Assyrian princes on the Babylonian throne, or take the Babylonian crown personally, but they could not stop Chaldean and/or Arab caravans from delivering goods to the southern heartland of the Chaldeans. The campaigns into Arabia, to interdict the trade there, must be seen as the next logical step by the Assyrians, but such forays must have been of little value.

Attempts by the Assyrians to control the marshy area of southern Babylonia, the Chaldean heartland, were equally futile. Just as the Arabs would retreat farther into the desert, the Chaldeans would retreat deeper into the marshes or over the border to Elam, and wait for the Assyrians to leave.

Military aid to the Chaldean kings of Babylonia was given by the Elamites, usually in exchange for large gifts of gold and silver. But it was not just for these payments that the Elamites would have fought, but also to keep open the trade routes.

The Assyrians finally attacked and completely destroyed Elam, but were themselves then conquered by a combination of a new Iranian element, the Medes, and the Babylonians. The Babylonians took over much of the Assyrian empire and inherited its attitudes and enemies. Thus, initially, they tried to hold Syria but eventually withdrew from the west.

The Babylonian king Nabonidus (556 – 39 B.C.), made a great effort to integrate his Arabian interests with the rest of the Babylonian empire. Late in his reign, he moved his court from Babylon to Taima, from which he consolidated his hold on the oases as far south as Medina.[23] Caravans linked Taima with Babylonia, the Gulf, South Arabia, the Red Sea, the Jordan Valley, Damascus, and Harran. His move, although perhaps motivated in part by religious considerations (a shift to the Moon God as the main deity), was a logical attempt to operate from his main economic base, the desert trade, while being in a position to deprive his enemies, the Medes and Egyptians, of some of their necessities.

It should be mentioned that by opening the desert routes, a group of highly-prized commodities (incense, myrrh) could now be brought from south Arabia to Mesopotamian and Levantine markets more directly and probably more cheaply than the same products could be brought by Egyptians from the alternate sources on the Upper Nile. The establishment of this Arabian route in the early 1st Millennium B.C. created an Egyptian/Arabian duplicating system of trade analogous to that in Mesopotamia. The Arabian route may have cut into Egypt's trade significantly and it may have been partly this factor that brought Egypt to take military action at this time in Asia.

After the fall of the Babylonians to the Achaemenid Persians, Mesopotamia became part of increasingly larger empires with an east/west orientation. The opening up of the desert routes and their attachment by long-range camel caravan to the Silk Route, made the northwest-southeast chains of contact along the Tigris and Euphrates of secondary importance. The duplicate systems still retained a vital place in Asian trade, but as feeder lines in a much larger network.

5

TRADE AND TRADE ROUTES OF THE QURAYSH

Faruk Abu-Chacra

Essential geographical features

Although surrounded by five seas, the Arabian Peninsula has hardly any islands to diminish its isolation nor any hospitable harbours except Aden, and there is not a single river to facilitate transport and communication through the vast sunburned deserts.

The peninsula is a land of great contrasts. The soil in the south is fertile and the climate favourable, a Garden of Eden, or Arabia Felix, whereas the adjacent region to the north-east is a veritable hell on earth, known as the Empty Quarter, the most savage part of the area and the most extensive area of continuous sand in the whole world. The camel is indeed the 'ship of the desert'.

An important feature of the pre-Islamic period was that Mecca had won control of the caravan trade (a position held previously by Petra and Palmyra) which extended up the west coast of Arabia from Yemen in the south, to Damascus and Gaza in the north. Southwards, the trade routes continued into Ethiopia and, utilizing seasonal winds (monsoons), the merchants went to India by ship when the south-west wind was prevalent. In the north there was the Eastern Roman or Byzantine Empire, a receptive market for Oriental products from India and East Asia. By 610 the trade through Mecca had become very profitable, and the main entrepreneurs had become wealthy merchants, and most of the town shared the prosperity.

Mecca had, however, attained this dominant position by ruthlessly preventing Yemeni merchants from coming to Mecca and subjugating the rivals in the neighbouring town of Ta'if after defeat in battle. Mecca became especially important because of the Abyssinians' occupation of Yemen, and the merchants of Mecca were mediators between Yemen and Abyssinia.

By 610 the people of Mecca were earning their living almost exclusively through commerce. One can say that the Meccan people established the commerce and the rules of trade (*ganun al-tigara*) by the practice they acquired during their journeys and through their knowledge of the world. They regulated the terms of trade concerning companies, investments, contracts, ownership, taxation (*al mukuus*) and punishments (fines).

Mecca depended principally on trade, unlike Medina, which was more dependent on agriculture.

The social tensions in Mecca about 610 were mainly due to the conflict between the new mercantile economy and the old nomadic economy. Commerce encouraged the acceptance of material values and of an individualistic spirit. From the Qur'an it appears that the great merchants, often heads of clans, were no longer willing to use their wealth to help the poor and unfortunate clansmen. This shows a disintegration of the tribal solidarity which was a prominent feature of nomadic society.

To this state of affairs the Qur'anic call to generosity and care for the unfortunate was very relevant.

The tribe Quraysh

The Quraysh constituted the noblest of all tribes in the area. The Prophet Muhammad himself belonged to this tribe; moreover, the Quraysh had the custody of the Ka'ba. In the Qur'an, Muhammad's tribe and their journeys are praised by winter and summer:

Sura 106: Quraysh or The Quraish (Custodians of the Ka'ba)
In the name of God, Most Gracious, Most Merciful.
1. For the covenants (of security and safeguard enjoyed) by the Quraish,
2. Their covenants (covering) journeys
   By winter and summer
3. Let them adore the Lord
   Of this House
4. Who provides them
   With food against hunger,
   And with security
   Against fear (of danger).

Nearly all the inhabitants of Mecca belonged to the tribe of the Quraysh, and acknowledged a common ancestry. The tribe was divided into clans which varied in importance, partly according to numbers, partly according to the degree of success or failure in commercial ventures. The leading men of the more powerful clans were great merchants who had gained a monopolistic hold over some sectors of the trade of Mecca. Muhammad's clan, that of the Hashim, had failed to maintain a place among the leaders, but had become head of a league of less powerful clans which opposed the monopolists. Since Qur'anic teaching was directed against the monopolists or great merchants, the clan of Hashim, though mostly disavowing Muhammad's religion, agreed for several years to give their full support against the great merchants.

The Caravan

The caravan trade was dominated by the tribe of the Quraysh. The budget was shared among all members and anyone, man or woman, could participate in the journey. There were two caravan journeys a year, one to Damascus in Syria, in the summertime, and one to Yemen during the winter because of the climate. Besides these, many minor journeys were made every year. The Quraysh stored their merchandise in Mecca and sold it not only in the local markets but elsewhere, as well.

Once when a caravan which was lead by Abu Sufyan (leader of the Umayyad house) was returning from Damascus, Muhammad, who was then in exile in Medina, sent 300 of his supporters and followers to attack the caravan of Abu Sufyan, who had three times as many men as Muhammad, a thousand camels and capital amounting to 50,000 dinars. Now Muhammad won his first important battle (the battle of Badr) in the year 622. The Quraysh used to leave for their journeys from the administrative centre of Mecca (dar al-nudwah). When the caravans, which might comprise one thousand camels, departed or returned, there was always a great celebration. The Quraysh used Badr as their halting-place. On their arrival there, they slaughtered cattle and drank wine.

We are told that when Muhammad was praying with his believers and they heard the bells of the arriving caravans, they started to run one by one to the caravans. Later on Muhammad scolded them in the words of the Friday sura, verse 9: 'O true believers, when ye are called to prayer on the day of assembly [Friday], hasten to the commemoration of God and leave merchandising.'

In Gaza and Syria the Quraysh bought Mediterranean products such as raisins, glue, metals for war equipment, olive oil and white slaves. They sold Indian and East Asian products such as spices (some names of spices come from the Arabic language: safran, balsam, camphor, pepper, cumin), incense for religious ceremonies, pearls, perfumes, medicines and leather. From Africa they imported mainly cotton, silk, ivory, wood and black slaves.

The trade routes by land were often very insecure because of the Bedouin raids, and that is why the caravans often travelled by night, frequenting the coastal routes which were less susceptible to attack. They had three main routes to avoid the sand desert areas, especially the area of red sand in Al-Rub' Al-Khali. It was these caravans which went across Arabia in all directions to Syria and the Persian border and brought back news of the outside world, and which also made the Arabs aware of the civilizations around them.

The first of the three routes went from Mecca to Yemen by the Red Sea and continued to the Indian Ocean and the Persian Gulf; the second from Mecca by the Red Sea to Petra, Gaza and Syria; the third connected Hijaz with the Persian Gulf through the Najd area. All these routes were later used also by the Muslim pilgrims to Mecca.

The roads

On the roads there were road markers and markers for frontiers and sometimes mileage signs. The merchants used the mile as a measure; one mile was as long a distance as you could see. Some of the roads were paved with asphalt (*Qir* in Arabic), a material also used for painting boats in order to prevent leakage and sea damages.

The harbours

The most important harbours were Aden in Yemen with its connections to India and Mocha with connections to Africa, lending its name to Mocha coffee.

Money

In the pre-Islamic period there was no form of Arabian currency; in those days the money in use was Byzantine, Persian and Egyptian. Purely Arabic money appeared first during the reign of Caliph El-Malik (685 – 705).

Suq (market)

The *suq* (market) system was the same as it is today in some Arabic countries; the market moved every day from one area to another. The most important market was Suq Akkazah which took place seasonally, situated in the Meccan area and dominated by merchants from Mecca.

The purpose of the market was not only the selling and purchasing of products; it was also the scene of poetic debates where special judges evaluated the poems. Later, when Islam became predominant, Akkazah was destroyed by the Muslims because of opposition to their religion. At the *suq* in Akkazah animals, white and black slaves, both male and female were traded. Even Khadigah, the first wife of Muhammad, bought a slave at Akkazah.

The white slaves came from the Mediterranean area and the black slaves from Africa. The latter were cheaper and less qualified. The slaves in Arab countries sometimes had the right to inherit their owners. It is related that a woman called Barira came to Khadigah and asked her (Khadigah) to buy her; but Khadigah said she did not need Barira. On hearing this, Muhammad compelled Khadigah to buy her. When Muhammad opened Mecca in 630, he released all the slaves.

In those days the women in Mecca had more liberty than after the introduction of Islam, they were very independent, and divorces were common. Many women became wealthy entrepreneurs. Khadigah was one of the most prominent female merchants at that time. She had been married twice before she met Muhammad. She used to hire men to carry her merchandise outside Mecca on a profit-sharing basis. When Khadigah heard about Muhammad's truthfulness and trustworthiness, she arranged for him to go to Bostra in Syria as leader, overseeing her merchandise. He executed the commission very well. After his return, Khadigah offered him marriage which Muhammad accepted. At that time Muhammad was 25 years old and Khadigha was 15 years his senior. She was a woman with a strong personality and a noble character, and as long as she lived, Muhammad took no other wife.

This marriage to Khadigah was an important turning point in Muhammad's career, for subsequently it afforded him the opportunity to meet Christians and Jews in the course of his wider travels abroad.

6

TRADE ROUTES IN EARLY NINETEENTH CENTURY SYRIA AND LEBANON

Thomas Riis

In contrast with today, early nineteenth century Syria was thought to comprise the region between the Mediterranean and the desert and between Egypt and Anatolia. Due to her position her international trade was transacted overland as well as by sea. For some reasons, such as the lack of suitable ports, there was no significant international seaborne trade in the southern part of the region, only the pilgrimages to Jerusalem, cf. Table 1. We are thus justified in concentrating upon the region's northern part that corresponded to the later French mandate area or to present-day Syria plus Lebanon.

Table 1. *Navigation in the Levant 1839 – 41[a]*

| | 1839 | | 1840[b] | | 1841 | |
	Ships	Tonnage	Ships	Tonnage	Ships	Tonnage
Smyrna (Izmir)	928	96,995	956	96,822	861	95,228
Larnaca	50	8,828	109	14,989	83	12,620
Limassol	183	28,834	147	9,479	47	7,462
Alexandretta	34	5,266	–	–	46	6,338
Latakia	22	2,975	–	–	–	–
Tripolis (Syria)	17	2,113	–	–	–	–
Beirut	150	15,518	27	6,366	155	16,432
Sidon	15	–	–	–	–	–
Jaffa	–	–	–	–	–	–
Alexandria	321	62,360	655	135,936	1,034	214,952

Source: AST. I.R. Governo per il Litorale (Küstenländisches Gubernium): Atti Presidiali Busta 46 (1843) fase 8/5 3 Gub. 999/P ex 1843.

(a) Austrian military years, i.e. 1 November 1838 to 31 October 1841. The table is not comprehensive, as it comprises only Austrian, British, French, Greek, Hanseatic, Ionian, Neapolitan, Sardinian and Swedish ships, but excludes e.g. Turkish and Tuscan vessels. (b) 1840 was a year of war in Syria.

International land trade with Syria had for centuries been undertaken by caravans to and from Baghdad, and to and from Mecca. The latter coincided with the annual pilgrimage and consequently its return to Syria could be predicted; the numbers were considerable due to the religious nature of the pilgrimage. In 1876 it was estimated that 6,000 people took part in the caravan. In Syria, these pilgrimages set out from and returned to Damascus.[1]

The Baghdad caravan was only part of a much larger transport system that formed one of the transit routes between Europe, Persia and India; goods went by ship to Basra and from there to Baghdad. In the early nineteenth century caravans connected Baghdad with two cities in Syria, Damascus to the south and Aleppo to the north. River transport was possible only between Basra and Baghdad, but was no longer in use north of Baghdad. It had been so, however, until the early seventeenth century, when barges were used on the Euphrates for most of the distance between the point where the desert route from Aleppo met the river and the point at Baghdad's latitude where the route again left the river.[2] We notice that barges were employed, but in the 1830s animal hides filled with air were used; very conveniently they could be emptied and folded after the navigation or they could be filled with water for the desert journey.[3] As late as on the eve of World War I, rafts were used for transport on the Euphrates; the entire journey between Aleppo and Basra would take about a month.[4]

It seems that a large caravan left Aleppo for Baghdad every year in July or August. The departure would be known several months in advance.[5] The size of the caravans varied considerably: in December 1824 a caravan of 1,500 camels arrived in Aleppo from Baghdad, a week before its arrival it had been estimated at 1,400 camels.[6] At the beginning of July 1825 a small caravan from Baghdad that had joined the one from Mosul, arrived in Aleppo. Together they numbered 1,000 camels;[7] at the other end of the scale we find a caravan of 7,000 camels that came to Aleppo from Baghdad in November 1863.[8]

The desert route from Damascus was also of ancient origin. During the first centuries A.D., it took the direction of Palmyra and continued from there toward the Euphrates where it met at present-day Abu Kamal or Hit.[9] About 1840 the British camel post between Damascus and Baghdad went by Hit,[10] but probably taking a course not very far from the present road through Rutba. The precondition of the post route was that the camels and their riders were to be independent of the water sources, thus they carried their own water supply in animal hides. At the same time the risk for assaults by robbers on horseback was diminished because the watering places were avoided and the range of action for horses was small in the desert.[11] It is not quite clear whether or not the caravans took the same route as did the camel post, but the possibility is not to be excluded, as some of them were organized by the British agents in Damascus and Baghdad. They gave marked competition to the slower and less regular native caravans. Consequently the British caravans were increasingly gaining ground.[12] Apparently they were of recent date at that time.

For the camel post, we can calculate the average speed at the end of the 1830s, because the Damascus agent often informed his Baghdad colleague of his letters' date of arrival. The number of days employed between Baghdad and Damascus oscillated between eight and fifteen with an average of eleven.[13] As the day of departure I have considered the date of the letter which, however, may have been written one or two days before the actual departure of the post. Obviously, the caravans were slower, but the speed of the post means that merchants at either end of the route would know in advance that a caravan might be expected at a certain time with a certain number of camels and with certain kinds of goods — information that was hardly available in the Syrian merchant's maritime trade before the construction of the telegraph in the 1860s.

Although the post was less regular on the Baghdad – Aleppo route than the British camel post (that often carried the India mail) merchants would inform each other of the departure of caravans in order that their correspondents might take the necessary measures.[14] Even on the smaller routes with mainly regional traffic, correspondents informed each other of the departure of caravans or even helped in their preparation. Thus at the beginning of this century the Aleppo trading house Vincenzo Marcopoli & Cie organized caravans for Mosul, apparently regularly, as an envoy would turn up in the Ḥān Marcopoli sent by the Blackfriars of Mosul about two weeks before departure. He would help with the preparations and return with the caravan.[15]

Of the goods that had arrived in Aleppo or Damascus from Mesopotamia, some of them were bound for Europe. Which route would a merchant choose in the first half of the nineteenth century?

In 1835, the Stock Exchange of Trieste had mentioned St Jean d'Acre, Sidon, Beirut and Tripolis as Damascus' ports.[16] Tripolis had been important in the sixteenth century but had now mainly regional trade (apart from the silk trade), also St Jean d'Acre was mainly regional despite the fact that it could export corn.[17] It had flourished in the late eighteenth century due to the policies of its pashas, but apparently their successors had not continued their work.

Thus the Damascus merchants' choice was between Sidon and Beirut. The latter's road was dangerous to ships (as was that of Tripolis),[18] and Sidon was too small and did not give sufficient shelter, although it seems to have been less exposed to winds than the port of Beirut.[19] When Volney travelled in Syria in the 1780s, the pashalik was governed from St Jean d'Acre to which town the pasha had recently moved from Sidon.[20] To the Frenchman Beirut seemed to have too many disadvantages to promise a brilliant future,[21] and when in 1819 or 1820 the French consul-general of Aleppo, Guys, advised his government to concentrate upon Damascus, he suggested the transfer of the consulate-general from Aleppo to one of the ports closest to Damascus, preferably Sidon where France had a hān.[22]

Two facts may have influenced Guys in favour of Sidon: access from Damascus was easier than from Beirut, and the existence of a French building which could be used would save the Treasury money. Beirut, however, had its supporters, also among the French. In 1777, Baron de Tott visited the ports on the Syrian coast in order to reform the administration of the French nations. According to him Sidon's trade could expand in the direction of Damascus, and in opposition to Volney, he found Beirut's road one of the best in Syria and appropriate for big vessels. Furthermore, he stressed the Maronites' preference for France which would eventually give her commercial advantages over other nations.[23]

It is clear that Tott was the more far-sighted of the two Frenchmen; despite Guys's opinion c. 1820, Beirut was considered the port of Damascus by 1822,[24] which must be explained by the fact that the French had been evicted from Sidon and St Jean d'Acre in 1790.[25] European trade had thus to pass through the ports between Beirut and Alexandretta.

Tripolis and Beirut were, as we have seen, reckoned among Damascus' ports, but the former could be viewed as the southernmost of Aleppo's ports as well; the other two were Latakia and Alexandretta. As becomes clear from the trading statistics of these ports, Tripolis' role was insignificant in the international transit trade through Syria though it had some regional trade. The town was too far from Aleppo and Damascus to become their natural outlet — despite the relatively easy land communications — and the port was not very good; thus Beirut became Damascus' port while Alexandretta and Latakia disputed between themselves which should be Aleppo's outlet.

Latakia and Alexandretta were situated almost equally far from Aleppo[26] and in either case travellers had to pass through mountains where they might fall into highwaymen's hands, especially between Alexandretta and Aleppo. Alexandretta's road was recognized as the best in all Syria, but the place was unhealthy because the swamps were not sufficiently drained, and a source of much disease — perhaps especially malaria. Latakia's harbour was much too narrow to serve large numbers of ships, and larger vessels had to stay in the road 30 to 45 minutes off shore. Some captains preferred this port to Alexandretta, probably in part because of the better climate.[27] The British consul of

Damascus who visited Latakia in 1837 found one more advantage, as he told his colleague Werry in Aleppo: 'I saw such fine girls here yesterday, delightful creatures — I really thought of you and how you would have enjoyed to ruffle about the petticoats . . .'[28]

Despite the local beauties Latakia's role as Aleppo's port was drawing to an end by 1845. According to the head of the house Cubbe in Aleppo all the city's merchants preferred their goods to be unloaded in Alexandretta rather than in Latakia,[29] and in August 1845 he admonished his captain not to unload in Latakia but in Alexandretta. The Aleppo merchants had promised the pasha of Aleppo to instruct their captains to use Alexandretta, not Latakia, and thus take advantage of the Customs that belonged to the pasha of Aleppo.[30] Apparently the Aleppo pasha had granted some reduction of Customs or other advantage to the merchants who promised, in return to instruct the captains to unload at Alexandretta. The agreement did not apply to loading in Latakia which becomes clear from the Cubbe papers.

By the mid-nineteenth century the pattern of trade had thus stabilized itself round two axes, Aleppo — Alexandretta and Damascus — Beirut. Each of them carried the regional trade, both import and export, and they were in this respect mainly independent of each other because of the different economic structures of the hinterland. Only in the transit trade between Europe, Mesopotamia and Persia did the two routes compete, and then only for certain goods.

During our period of study steamship lines were established between the Syrian coast and Europe. In 1837, a line run by the French government began to transport passengers and mail between Marseilles and the Levant, but as it did not take goods, its profitability was unsatisfactory.[31] On 1 June 1839 the Austrian Erste Donau Dampf-schiffahrts-Gesellschaft (DDSG) opened its line from Smyrna to Syria. In Cyprus, Larnaca was the port of call, from there the steamer proceeded to Jaffa whence she sailed along the coast towards the north calling at Beirut, Tripolis, Latakia and Alexandretta; from the latter port she returned to Smyrna;[32] the line was later extended to Alexandria. DDSG's Aleppo agent, Vincenzo Marcopoli, at once organized a main service between Aleppo and Alexandretta corresponding with the arrival of the steamship.[33] Later in the summer, the DDSG's Baghdad agent planned a fortnightly mail service Baghdad—Aleppo—Alexandretta corresponding with the calls of the steamer.[34] Despite this promising beginning, it was decided before the end of the summer to call only at Beirut, mainly for political reasons.[35] At the end of 1840 the line had to be stopped entirely because of the war in the region and because the *Seri Pervas* that sailed on the line had an accident that took her out of service for a considerable span of time.[36] The line had not been reopened when in 1845 the Austrian Lloyd shipping line of Trieste took over all the DDSG's lines in the Mediterranean.[37]

In 1852 the French Messageries Nationales (Impériales) opened a regular service with steamships to the Syrian coast where Alexandretta, Latakia, Tripolis and Beirut were the ports of call as well as Jaffa.[38] Probably it was this French initiative that obliged the Austrian Lloyd to open a regular service with Syrian ports other than Beirut. Unlike the Messageries it did not call at Tripolis, but at Haifa and at Cyprus (Larnaca, between Latakia and Beirut).[39] Both lines had connections with Constantinople and Alexandria. From the distances given in the French sources and the sailing times in the Austrian timetable of 1853 we learn that the scheduled speed was — as could be expected — considerably higher on the longer parts of the voyage,[40] e.g. 8.5 knots between Smyrna and Rhodes, but only 5.7 knots between Mersin and Alexandretta.

By 1858 a Russian line had been opened that connected Odessa with the Syrian ports and Jaffa via Constantinople, Rhodes and Mersin. Furthermore there were less regular services. The French company Bazin's ships would not leave Marseilles until they had a full cargo, their ports of call were Cyprus, Beirut, Alexandretta and Mersin. The arrival of the Turkish boats was 'uncertain from defects in the administration and navigation'. About four British steamers arrived monthly at Alexandretta from Liverpool with manufactures and colonial products, but apparently without passengers.[41]

Before 1837 when the first regular line with Syria was opened the arrival of ships was less predictable than the arrival of caravans. This is amply clear from the correspondence of the Aleppo branch of the house Cubbe. When the captains arrived at one of the Syrian ports, generally from Leghorn where the house had another branch, they would send a message to the firm in Aleppo that then would give them further instructions. In March 1834 Cubbe thus wrote from Aleppo to Captain Antonio Pioggio who was apparently waiting in Latakia. Cubbe had learnt by letters from Baghdad that a caravan would be leaving for Damascus within a given time. It would probably bring merchandise for Europe and Cubbe told the captain to sail for Beirut to fetch as much as he could before returning to Latakia where he would get a further cargo. After that, the season for new wool, would have come in Cyprus where Pioggio should complete his cargo.[42] In May Cubbe informed the captain that the Baghdad caravan might not arrive before the end of May, but that he should wait in Beirut and then later sail to Latakia.[43] A month later Cubbe wrote to Pioggio (now in Latakia) that the Baghdad caravan had arrived in Damascus at the end of May, and had been in Aleppo two or three days before. He expressed the hope that Pioggio had found freight in Beirut, and in Cyprus.[44]

This example — which is but one of many — shows us that although the arrival of caravans was known in advance, ships might nevertheless be held up for several months on the Syrian coast, and that the captains had to act on instructions from their Syrian partners as well as rely on their own sense of business.[45]

The opening of regular services transporting passengers, mail and goods introduced an element of regularity at least on the Mediterranean leg of the trade route. The calls after 1852 at the smaller Syrian ports rendered it more probable that the vessels could complete their cargoes bound for the final destinations Europe, Constantinople or Egypt. At the same time they outrivalled the coastal trade that had been undertaken, especially by local Syrian, Turkish or Greek ships.[46]

On the other hand, the lack of regularity in the volume of goods for exportation from Syria was incongruent with the steamers' regularity. In his report for 1862 the Aleppo agent for the Messageries Impériales, Nicola Marcopoli, stressed that the vessels often had too little room on board which meant that merchandise had to be left at Alexandretta. Consequently the exporters preferred to ship their goods, especially cotton that was very much in demand because of the American Civil War, on board sailing ships that could be chartered at lesser cost. Other steamship companies exploited the situation and the Messageries lost lucrative opportunities. Marcopoli found that the Messageries could have prevented this development by sending bigger steamships or even supplementary vessels to Alexandretta.[47]

In his report for 1863 Marcopoli recognized the company's efforts in sending supplementary vessels to Alexandretta, but they were not large enough and the rival companies had all found cargoes. The agent asked the company not to neglect Alexandretta, whose staple goods of wool and gall nuts were little influenced by the price fluctuations caused by the American Civil War. Syrian cotton fetched high prices because of the war, and could thus support the Messageries' high freight rates. This was momentary, Marcopoli stressed, because after the war, cotton prices would fall and exporters would be obliged to use the sailing ships' cheaper freight.[48]

Steam did not supplant sail during our period except perhaps in the coastal trade and navagation; this was caused, above all, by the number, regularity and size of the steamers that were often considerably bigger than the small vessels employed on the coast. Steam was clearly competitive in the transport of passengers, mail and money; similarly the luxury goods carried by the Venetian galleys four centuries earlier. In the transport of heavy goods, sail might still be profitable under certain conditions. Several essays had been made at creating faster communications overland from the Mediterranean to the Persian Gulf, but none had been realized apart from the improved

British caravan service Damascus — Baghdad and the toll road between Damascus and Beirut[49] when the Suez Canal was constructed. Britain had been the driving force in these undertakings (except the Damascus—Beirut road) a fact that should be seen in a wider perspective. The main routes to India from the Mediterranean passed either through Egypt and the Red Sea or through Syria, Mesopotamia and the Persian Gulf. France under Bonaparte had shown her interest in Egypt and had been stopped by Britain. In the 1830s France supported Egyptian pretensions at domination in Syria, where Britain counteracted her and at the same time worked hard at improving communications with India. Rivalry between the two European powers continued in Syria: when the French supported the Lebanese Maronites, Britain was recognized as protector of the Druses. After World War I the region was divided between Britain and France as mandatory powers, and their rivalry ceased only when they both withdrew from the region after World War II. Behind their antagonism was not only the concern for British exports to Syria and French imports, but also the much more important question of the way to India.

7

THROUGH THE SAYAN MOUNTAINS: TRADE ROUTES BETWEEN MONGOLIA AND SIBERIA

Magdalena Tatár

Asian trade routes have always interested historians, but most of our knowledge is limited to the long-distance routes and those with major traffic. We know much less about local routes leading to the periphery of the world as known by Europeans in olden times. Mongolia, however, was not so peripheral as many seen to have believed. *The Secret History of the Mongols* (§ 182) mentions a Muslim merchant called Asan (= Hasan) coming from the south to the Argun River, where he wanted to trade sheep for sable and weasel furs. This happened before Jenghiz Khan unified the Mongols into a mighty state. In this paper I would like to speak about a little-known direction — namely that from the south, the Chinese-influenced Mongolia, to the north, Siberia; and about a very little-known peripheral area, namely the Sayan mountains and the area of the Xövsgöl Lake, in Mongolia. Today the Sayan area is divided politically: Tuva, South Xakassia and part of Buryatia belong to the Soviet Union, whereas the Darxat region belongs to Mongolia. In olden times this area was one political entity with a mixed population, speaking the Turkic, Samoyed and Mongolian languages.

The existence of Chinese connections with Siberia is clear enough from the Chinese sources and from the Chinese-inspired influence expressed in the culture of the Siberian peoples. The best-known contact zone is the region of the River Amur, in Mongolia and Central Asia. These connections extended to the Yukaghirs by the Lena, who informed the first Russians in this place about the route from the Lena through the region of the Lamut people to the Amur.[1] It was easy enough to follow the River Selengge from Mongolia to the north. This is the most important route to Siberia; at the present time the railway between the Baykal and Ulan Bator follows this track still.

But were there any possible routes through the Sayan mountains? One often reads[2] that this area was very isolated, but the reindeer-breeding people in Eastern Tuva did not even know about money as late as in this century. At the same time archaeologists found a lot of remains of different ancient cultures, among others Uygur and Chinese buildings, agriculture, e.g. near Ulan uul,[3] which is traditionally held to be the most isolated place in Mongolia. The first written documents about a road in this area are from the eighth century. The Turkic Empire had many connections — mostly of a military kind, of course — with the Khirgiz and As and other peoples in the Sayan, as well as with peoples on the northern side of the mountains. Tonyuquq's inscription by the Orkhon informs us about the road the Turkic army followed when conquering these peoples. They could not follow the only route through the Kögmen, (= the Sayan mountains), because of deep snow; so an As man led them from a place called Ak termel through the Ibar mountains, passing the northern Sayans beside the Ani River. The dramatic journey from Ibar to the Ani took ten days. The way beside the Ani was so narrow, that there was place for just one horse beside the river. After the victory, they came back on the northern side of the mountains. From this description it is clear that there were three routes through the Sayan mountains, of which one was the most commonly used. It was possibly the same route that Bilge gayan took in his campaign against the Cik and As people crossing the Kem, i.e. the Yenisey River. War, robberies, taxes and gifts between foreign peoples all have a mercantile character. These martial trading methods between the barbarians and China or among the barbarians themselves, were very important in times when normal trading connections were disturbed by politics. This was the relevant situation between Mongolia and China up to the twentieth century. Such martial methods were used also by the Mongols when they looted furs from the country of darkness, i.e. Siberia, as Marco Polo (Chap. 61) reported it. But he also reported about the difficulties the Mongols had in finding the way there. At the time of Jenghiz Khan conquering the Sayans, the Mongols took the route east of the Darkhat region to the west, to the Altay, with the help of local people (*The Secret History*, § 239). This is an interesting fact because such a route was not mentioned in our sources for many centuries after this occasion. In Western Tuva the Mongolian army went on the ice of the River Kem-Kemjiüt (i.e. Kem = Yenisey; Kemčik> plur. Kemjiüt was the people staying by the river).[4] The Mongolian army sent by Jenghiz Khan spread false news about the campaign along the usual roads and ways, and followed a track called the way of the red ox. The soldiers cleared the way, passed the mountains unexpectedly and pacified the Tümet tribe (*The Secret History*, § 239 – 240). It is quite evident that the routes followed the rivers in this mountainous country. It looks as though travel occurred mostly in winter, on the ice. It is interesting that there are some routes called 'usual ways'. Basing my conclusion on these facts I judge that there was relatively heavy traffic in this area. We do not know what happened to these connections after the Yuan dynasty. The Mongolian khans, especially the West Mongolian khans of Dzungaria used their diplomacy, and sometimes their weapons, too, to enforce the trade with China which was being carried on at different places along the Mongolian border since 1571 at four market-places. By a Chinese law of 1488, silk textiles and some products of iron were bartered for animals, furs, manes of horses, etc. After the sixteenth century the trade in tea, a state monopoly, was used to pay for Mongolian horses.[5] The Sayans were a part of the Dzungarian interest area, so some of this merchandise possibly came also from this territory, first of all from Western Tuva. The Oyrat khans of Dzungaria tried to build up close trading connections with the Russians, too, who came now to Siberia and Central Asia. Trade was the easiest way to wealth for the first generation of these Russian Cossacks. I would like to mention here Yerifey Khabarov, the founder of the town Khabarovsk. He was a warrior who ate aborigines in wintertime, if necessary, possessed farms and mines, and traded a lot in fur and horses along the Lena River. The latter he could buy only from the Mongols.[6] It is known that the first Russian colonists bought livestock from the Mongols. At the beginning of the seventeenth century the Oyrats went to the market-places in the Russian forts such as the one by the Yamiščcvo Lake, and to towns as far off as Tobolsk, Tjumen', Tomsk and Tara. In 1640 they invited Russian and Bukharian merchants to Dzungaria. Trading at Tunkin Fort in Buryatia is documented from 1685.[7] To reach this place they had to cross the Sayan mountains. The Russians, rivals with Dzungaria for dominance in Tuva, built a fort on the Kemčik River in 1629.[8] Russian merchants reached China, crossing Dzungaria and the Gobi.[9] The Mongols sold mostly livestock, fur and saddles, but Chinese products given as gifts and sold as merchandise are reported from the first meeting between the Mongols and the Russians.[10] Russians drank the first tea by Altan gan Ombo Erdeni in 1638. This drink rapidly became popular, and the Russians included it, along with gold, silver and precious stones, on their list of items exchanged in their trade with Mongolia. Another important article of exchange was slaves. Russians bought slaves from Dzungaria, and sold, in turn, such items as textiles, silver and gold products, and paper. In 1646 the Russian government gave licence of free trade to Dzungarians in the Siberian towns. Russian traders transmitted these goods to Moscow and Archangel, and from there to Europe.[11] Because of political difficulties and the fall of Dzungaria, Western Mongolia lost its importance in Russian trade. The most important trade route between Siberia and Mongolia followed the Selengge valley with a market-place first in Selenginsk (1673), since 1727 in Kyaxta. We know only the official part of the Mongolian trade. Both the Chinese and the Russian governments tried to cut down both the transit trade and the local trade by the border. So, China forbade merchants to enter into the Tagna and Uryangxay Province, i.e. the Sayan area.[12] After 1706 trade with China was a Russian state monopoly, while that with Mongolia was a private business, permitted only for professional traders, of course.[13] But all the strict regulations resulted in a flourishing smuggling activity. Many lamas, country lords, even the governor in Urga himself, carried on this kind of business. In this way a lot of smuggled Russian goods came to Kalgan, Peking and Tibet. The forbidden trade was very important on the Russian side, too. As S.L. Raguzinskij wrote to the Czar's government, it was the main way of life for the local people, and therefore he proposed that the trade be made free in this province.[14]

One example of the difficulties comes from the Sayans. In 1717 the Russians built a harbour on the northern side of the Xövsgöl Lake to stop the local Xaasuud tribesmen entering with their merchandise into Russia. It was of course a very sensitive area, and they were pressed by the Peking government to give up the harbour. They judged the Russian activity as aggressive in this time of the border commissions. In 1727 according to Russian-Chinese border agreement, the Chinese government ordered the Darxat tribe to stay at all times on their former summer pasture by the Beltes and Agar Rivers.[15] They wanted to cut off the connections between Darxats and border-soldiers.

New trade routes were opened by the Russians in the eighteenth century. In 1765 they organized a ferry crossing the Baykal, and at the end of the century a way round the Baykal was built.[16] Their intentions were not mercantile; at the same time they tried to cut down the whole Mongolian trade. But the trade was growing; in 1756 Russians sold merchandise in Mongolia for 450,768 roubles and Chinese traders sold to Russians for 241,252 roubles; in 1784 it was almost 2.5 million roubles for each country, all together 5 million roubles. This is the official number. In practice, we must assume a much larger sum. From the 1730s, forts were built for Manchu/Chinese soldiers in Mongolia. The nearest to the Sayan was by the Orxon River, built in 1735. Already in 1746 there existed a mercantile town as well. Trade was made unlimited, first in 1757 by the forts, and in 1796 by the administrative centres in the country. In 1780, the trade in the countryside (in the *xošuu*-s and by the *šabi*-s) was fixed at 200 *lang* silver a year.[17] The Russians made the local trade free first in 1800. Crimes against the traders were somewhat reduced after this (cf. Uryangxay tribesmen from the Russian territory robbed and killed a Chinese merchant in 1781). Now the Buryat tribesmen could sell animals and wool, and the Buryat soldiers (so-called Kazakhs) could sell bread to Mongolia in years when there was a good crop.[18] After the agreement in 1862, Russian merchants could work in the places where a Chinese official resided, and custom-free trade was licensed up to a

Fig. 1. The old Russian-built ship, the *Suxbaatar*, on the Xovsgol lake.

Fig. 2. The Ulyastay-Morom-Xatgal road near Xatgal.

Fig. 3. *Obos* (offering places) on the main pass between Moron and Cagaan Nurr.

Fig. 4. Fishing factory in Cagaan Nuur.

Figs. 5 and 6. Ferry between Zoolon and Cagaan Nuur.

distance of 100 *li* on both sides of the border.[19] At the same time 2000
Polish captives built the new route round the Baykal. The Trans-
Siberian railway was built to Cita in 1899, with a ferry crossing the
Baykal up until 1915.[20] Russian-Mongolian trade continued to grow; in
1863 it reached 260 thousand roubles, by 1900 it reached almost 17
million roubles. At that time one sheep cost 12 – 15 pressed tea-blocks.
Both Chinese and Russian money were accepted, but people liked the
Chinese money more than the Russian.[21]

   This evolution opened the Sayan area for a trade which was no longer
occasional, but constant. In the 1860s A.P. Šubin, a Russian merchant
from Irkutsk, called Andrey the Russian by the local people, settled
down beside the central Buddhist monastery at Zòòlon. He bought fish,
furs and animals from the Darxat people and paid for them with
everyday household objects. The price was very arbitrary. At the
beginning of the twentieth century the Darxat Province exported 4000
sables and 10,000 squirrels to Russia. One sable cost 25 – 35 roubles,
one squirrel cost 12 – 17 kopeks, 1 *pùù* (= 16 kg) 'white fish'
(*taymen'*) cost 20 – 30 kopeks. Šubin built fishing industries in two
places: by the Sisged River at a place called Golyn am, i.e. Cagaan
Nuuryn Zagasny Uyldver, 'Fishing Factory at Cagaan Nuur' today,
and at Xogorgyn am. These factories produced and exported 800 – 960
kg fish to Russia yearly. He employed 30 – 40 workers in these
industries.[22] At the same time, five Chinese merchants were staying in
the same place.[23] We do not have any statistics about their trade, but we
can take a closer look at some other traders' statistics. In the 1890s, a
Chinese merchant, called Dašinxùù by the Mongols, who also had
business with the Uriangxay provinces, sent yearly 80,000 sheep from
Xovd to Köke gota. In 1892, another man called Aršaan in Mongolia,
who was also trading with the Soyots (a tribe in the Sayans), sent
45,000 sheep and 500 camels from Xovd to Köke gota. In comparison
with this, in 1900, Mongolia exported 500 horses, 15,320 sheep and
12,000 other livestock to Tunkin, one of the busiest Russian-Mongolian
trade points.

   The Russians modernized all the time. They began to trade in
companies, and to sell through Russia to Europe, and through the
Chinese harbours to Japan and America. In 1893 a Russian state official
of high rank, P. Badmaev, a Buryat by birth, founded a company in St.
Petersburg and in Cita to trade with Russia, Tuva, Mongolia, China and
the Buryat minority in Russia. Mongolian exports to Russia grew from
3.5 million roubles in 1903 to 8 million roubles in 1909. One quarter of
it crossed the border at Kyaxta and in the following three towns in the
Sayan area: Koš-Agač, Zaysan and Usinsk. In the same period, Russian
exports to Mongolia fell off from 4 million to 2.5 million roubles.

Russia bought and then re-exported a great deal of fur as before; only in February 1911 American merchants bought 70,000 pieces of fur at the markets in Kyaxta, Biysk and Irbit. The Russian textile industry in Simbirsk and Yekaterinburg used more and more Mongolian wool, so Russian merchants founded wool-washing factories in Mongolia, one of them by the Delger mörön River in the Sayan mountains.[24] The Darxat Province exported livestock, fish, wool, butter and fur (sable and squirrels) for 157,000 roubles in 1904 – 1905.[25] Russia, using the Trans-Siberian railway, had better chances in western and northern Mongolia than in China. China planned a railway from Kalgan through Urga (today Ulan Bator) — Ulyastay-Xovd, i.e. south of the Trans-Siberian railway, more or less parallel with it, in 1909 – 1910, but as both Russia and Japan were against this, the railway was never built.[26] So China slowly lost the northern provinces. In 1910 Russian merchants came to Tuva, and the hated Chinese had to leave. All Russian colonists in Eastern Tuva were merchants. They sold tobacco, tea and textiles for squirrel skins which were to be paid in the next hunting season, and if people could not pay, which was very common, the trader took the reindeer skin they slept on for 20 squirrel skins in spring. In autumn people begged for it back, but by then it cost 40 squirrel skins. All the goods were sent by the Yenisey River to Minussinsk.[27]

The most detailed description of roads in this area was given by Carruthers at the beginning of this century. All roads mentioned by him followed old routes beside the rivers. We know little about other roads. The excellent Danish traveller and scholar, Haslund-Christensen used a route from Buryatia to Urga, following the Uur and Egiyn gol River. He heard about it from Russian merchants dealing in fur in this area.[28]

After the revolution a great deal changed. West-Sayans, i.e. Tuva, became a part of the Soviet Union, as it is now. There is no more local traffic of any importance between the region around the Uvs Lake in Mongolia and Tuva, or between Tuva and the Xövsgöl area. But the route from Central Mongolia to Xatgal and from there over the Xövsgöl Lake to Xanx is now very important, both for export and for import. An old Russian ship of 1260 tons, now called Süxbaatar, started on the Xövsgöl in 1925, going with cargo 120 km from Xatgal to Xanx, from June till October. From Xanx, which is called Türt now, the traffic today follows an old route through the pass Mongon Davaa to Slyudyanka, the railway station by the Baykal. In 1938 the government converted the old monastery in Zöölön into a factory, which produced textiles and furniture. In 1959 this factory moved to Xatgal, the new industrial centre in the area, with a wool washing factory, etc. The old fishing factory in Cagaan Nuur — the only one of its kind in Mongolia

— was reorganized in 1942.[29] Its products are sold only to the Soviet Union, the so-called Siberian white fish, i.e. *taymen'*, as human food; the other kind, dried fish, as animal food.[30]

We can conclude that this province was not isolated at all, and that cultural and linguistic connections were realized by these martial and mercantile routes.

8

SOME ASPECTS OF TRADE IN BADAKHSHAN (AFGHANISTAN) BETWEEN 1880 AND 1980

Walter Raunig

Introduction

Badakhshan, the north-east province of Afghanistan, is the moun-tainous land (covering an area of 10,886 square kilometres) drained by the Kokcha River and its tributaries. In the year 1975 some 300,000 people lived there; today it would be difficult to estimate the number since many were forced to flee or were killed in the war. Confined among the high mountains of the Hindukush to the south, the Pamirs in the east, and the mountains of Darwaz and Shoghnan in the north, this province lay for a long time isolated and cut off from the centres of East and West Turkestan with which a lively trade and exchange of culture was once carried on. The position of this area is best designated by the term 'remote'.

The main rural settlements lie in the extensive valleys and basins. The population is composed above all of Tajeks and Mountain-Tajeks. The Ozbaks and Pashtuns also live here though in much smaller numbers. The few Hazaras, Qarlugs, Moghols, Vigurs and Nuristani as well as the Kirghiz of the Pamirs, all of whom were still living here years ago, must also be mentioned though it is difficult to say whether any at all are living there now. (I refer here to the flight of the Kirghiz from the Pamirs to Pakistan. Today most of them are in Turkey.)

Since ancient times an irrigation system, and to a lesser extent also a natural cultivation of the soil, have formed the basis of a livelihood for the inhabitants of Badakhshan along with the cultivation of fruit, stock-farming and the production of walnuts. The inhabitants of Badakhshan form an essentially permanent, rural traditional society though in summer they often migrate to the upper pastures with their animals (seasonal nomadism). Only the Kirghiz in the easternmost parts, living on the plateaux of the Pamirs are, or were, genuine i.e. full nomads. Moreover, in summer other full nomads move into the province with their herds from Qataghan in the west to seek grazing areas to the north and east of Fayzabad. Singly, small groups of nomads (Gojors) from the south come over the main chain of the Hindukush into the Monjan Valley and carry on trade during their wanderings.

The province of Badakhshan has an ancient tradition of handicraft and trade, well-known far beyond its borders. Along with a pronounced home industry there have always been actual centres for the production of certain goods. Further, these were favoured by the position of trading centres, markets, routes or, for example, in the case of iron-casting and the production of wrought-iron work by the iron-ore sources northeast of the capital city. The earlier salt mining which today lies outside the boundaries of the province or on the other side of the state border in the Soviet Union was once of great importance for the economy and trade. To a modest extent it is also of importance today because the salt, imported from the neighbouring province to the west, must be brought into the farthest corner of the land, to the plateaux of the Small Pamirs in the east. Importation of salt from the Russian Pamirs, where earlier (i.e. before 1920) the Kirghiz mined salt to the north of both basins of the Rang-Quol, is no longer possible. The Kirghiz exported their salt to the west in exchange for wheat. Salt also served as currency for various wares and products.

Still of importance to Badakhshan today, as export articles often going far beyond the borders of the land, are livestock and the beautiful horses of the province which are greatly in demand.

Not only in trade but for the whole of the cultural-historical development of Badakhshan of eminent significance throughout thousands of years were the lapis lazuli sources lying in the upper Kokcha valley. Since lapis lazuli in the Old World was, practically speaking, only to be found here the working and wearing of this popular stone, from ancient Egypt to China, was an indication of the very old tradition of Badakhshan's trade over numerous intermediate stations in areas lying thousands of kilometres apart. The mining of lapis lazuli doubtless took place throughout the entire history of this province.

In the Middle Ages the Badakhshan area was famous for another stone as well. This was the ruby of which Marco Polo spoke (along with silver, copper and lead). Rubies were being mined up to and into this century though no longer in land of the Badakhshan of today but in Garanj, north of Eskhashem near the Panj River on the other side of the state border. Other mineral wealth, for example gold, which was sought (gold washing) throughout the entire course of history and which even to the present day is being sought, has never at any time played a significant role for Badakhshan.

As 'remote' as the area mentioned has been for at least 70 years, it had a significance as a land of passage for the long-distance traffic between Near East and East Asia and between Central and South Asia.

The mountain lands on the Amu-Darya, the Oxus of antiquity, had been known to the Greeks for some 2,500 years.

Various parts of Badakhshan, above all the broader valley landscapes where the laiger villages are situated, have been — though at different periods — of great importance since ancient times as areas of passage for north-to-south and east-to-west trade relations extending over a vast distance. These ancient trading routes were, of course, also the old military roads over which the foreign powers and peoples had entered the land since the days of Alexander.

Through the province of Badakhshan a branch of the famous Silk Road runs from Balkh over Khanabad, Taloquan, Keshm, Fayzabad, Baharak, Zebak, Eshkashem and the Wakhan upwards over the Pamir to Tashqorghan and further into the Tarim Basin. From Zebak one of the branches of this famous Silk Road crosses southwards over the Anjoman Pass to Bagram by Kabul and further to India.

In the eighth century the Arabs reached the area. This set off a great Chinese military expedition over the Pamirs to the west. The Tibetan Empire extended to the easternmost regions of Badakhshan; this area was then, to the greater part, conquered by the Mongols. Marco Polo sojourned in Badakhshan. Al-Yaqubi calls the area 'important for the trade with Tibet' etc. Therefore, the role of this north-east province of Afghanistan as an area of passage for the long-distance trade in practically every epoch is undisputed.

Long-distance trade

Up to the beginning of this century, i.e. to about 1920, trade relations existed over an extensive area, reaching far beyond the borders of the province — nevertheless the extent and significance of this trade had already been radically reduced in contrast to earlier times. This is evident, for example, in the observations of Olufsen who, around the turn of the century, confirmed the remote position of the area mentioned from the great trade routes of Asia.[1]

Nevertheless at that time, for example, the following European wares were being imported through Russia to North and North-east Afghanistan: textiles, vessels, hardware, tea, sugar, matches, paper, tobacco etc.[2] In the opposite direction the region of the Russian Pamirs was a market outlet for metal wares from Badakhshan[3] and it drew people from Shoghnan and the Wakhan over Pamirski-Post, where there was a constantly inhabited Kirghiz settlement, a caravanserai and a bazaar, to East Turkestan.[4] The bazaars of Badakhshan also offered wares from Bokhara and India. For Fayzabad, for example, is mentioned: 'Sugar, tea, indigo and all sorts of articles of European manufacture are brought from Peshawar by Bajaur merchants via Chitral and Zebak; Khokand and Bokhara merchants bring Russian sugar, cloth, cutlery and other articles of commerce, and pack horses and sheep.'[5] Wood speaks of a trade route through the province which was once so important but also refers to the fact that this route had lost its significance. In its day Jorm was perhaps the most important bazaar of the province to which people travelled from afar. Of particular importance in Jorm was the salt and hardware trade.[6] From time immemorial tea had been brought into the land by native and by Chinese traders so that earlier Chinese money was also in circulation.[7] Up to the final seizure of power by the Communists in China traders from Badakhshan came as far as East Turkestan where they picked up silk and cotton goods or other textiles.[8]

This long-distance trade existed into the twenties and remained up to the first years after World War II. Afterwards, it became impossible due to political events in this part of the world. A long-distance trade to the south, i.e. over the passes of the Hindukush to Nuristan and Chitral still continued but its significance could no longer be compared with that of the old trade relations of the west to east. Wood speaks of these trade relations with Chitral[9] while Olufsen mentions the Nuristani traders in the Badakhshan of the previous century.[10] Over the Hindukush passed the most important export products of the province. These were, along with horses, woollen goods and livestock, in particular salt and lapis lazuli.[11] Woollen goods and livestock also went over the Anjoman Pass to Kabul from where, in the opposite direction, industrial goods, tea, sugar and cotton products came.[12]

This trans-Hindukush trade still exists today though to a much reduced extent. The two routes which still possess some measure of significance for long-distance trade and which do not follow the modern road network are: (1) that from Keshm in a north-east direction to Fayzabad, the capital of the province, and (2) the other from the upper Kokcha Valley through the Anjoman Valley and over the pass of the same name into the Panjsher Valley and thus to Kabul. This latter route is even today important for the transport of livestock and of lapis lazuli by horse in Badakhshan to Kabul.[13] Of the remaining — and thereby, in part extremely difficult — routes over the Hindukush Passes only that leading from the Anjoman Valley to Nuristan (Weran Pass) will be mentioned because of the special role it plays, even now, in the traffic of goods and persons. Today, it is no longer salt which is being traded over the Hindukush from Badakhshan to Nuristan in exchange for honey, wax and wooden products but, practically speaking, only heavy-laden material, some cotton textiles and coats serve as articles of export. From Nuristan honey, wood carvings, earthenware, metalware, skins, furs, textiles, fat, livestock and, allegedly, horses as well as wickerwork[14] are brought into Badakhshan.

For the last three decades a long-distance trade significant for the economy of Badakhshan was only possible to the west, that is from and over the provinces Takhar, Baghlan and Qondoz lying to the west and important to the whole of Afghanistan (intensive cultivation of the soil and cotton). In other words, during the last three decades almost the entire long-distance trade of the province has taken place over these three northern provinces of Afghanistan. Thereby the following is of importance.

Within the last few decades — as also in most other areas of Afghanistan — a completely new traffic and trade situation has arisen due to the construction of roads and the use of automobiles. Since the 1950s the truck has almost completely driven the pack-animals from most of the main traffic and trade routes.

By far the most important and most used route (in the summer of 1975 between 5 to 10 cars in each direction per day) for the automobile traffic (powerful trucks and smaller cross-country vehicles) leads from the important city of Quondoz in North Afghanistan through Khanabad and Keshm to Fayzabad. This road was completed in 1937.[15] Since the second half of the 40s[16] the road has led from the province capital further up the Kokcha to Baharak and then over Zebak to Eshkashem.[17] This road, though, is of no great significance. For many years a route has led (though only for cross-country vehicles, from Eshkashem on the Afghanistan side of the Wakhan Valley on to Qala-e Panja.

From Baharak a branch road leads off to the south through Jorm and partly up the Kokcha, almost to the lapis lazuli mines of Sar-e Sang while a second such road stretches from Keshm down to the west border of the province and on southwards for a distance.

Along this road today is brought the greatest part by far of all wares and products which do not come from the land itself but from outwards, for example all modern industrial wares, textiles (materials and clothes), cotton, beautiful glazed pottery, gasoline, petroleum, conserves, rice, tea and sugar. Along this route as well the greater part of Badakhshan's export products such as wool, skins, nuts, livestock and some textiles (for example the cape coats which are so popular in Kabul) and other particular handicrafts are transported. Only the lapis lazuli export, so important for Afghanistan, is still extensively carried out by pack-horses over the Anjoman Pass (see above).

Domestic trade

The domestic trade of the province of Badakhshan is sustained by wandering traders who travel regularly, in smaller groups or often alone with pack animals, from the capital Fayzabad or from other larger bazaars over the land to the isolated valleys or to the heights of the Pamirs, Hindukush or Darwaz. They bring articles of use in daily life for household, farm and livestock into the smallest settlements and to the nomad camps. These articles include both handmade wares from the handicraft centres of the province of Badakhshan as well as goods imported in long-distance trade as, for example, vessels of metal (iron, copper and aluminium pots, bowls, dishes, kettles), pottery, simple and cheap materials, light trousers of cotton, rubber shoes, secondhand European-American clothing, lathe-turned bowls, spades, pitchforks, tools for craftsmen (shoemakers, smiths and saddle-makers), cape-coats made in Fayzabad, saddlery, needles, knives, aluminium spoons, tin trays, small boxes, felt mats and blankets, felt bags, cheap jewellery (today even of plastic), tea, salt, sugar, rice, cigarettes and opium.

When travelling through Badakhshan one meets these wandering traders again and again. From the different parts of the land they naturally bring back those products and wares which they are able to sell — with almost no exception at a high profit in the various towns.

In the summer of 1975 I repeatedly met traders from the larger villages — as well as native traders — who were transporting giant balls of wool through the eastern Wakhan to Khandud or Eshkashem, that is, to the auto route by means of donkeys or yaks. At the same time Mr. Singer also met such traders who were trading in the Little Pamirs with the Kirghiz,[18] exchanging textiles, tea, wheat, sugar and opium for sheep and the pelts of wild animals.

Opium represents not only a reason for the impoverishment of health and of social structure of some parts of Badakhshan's population but also one reason for its economic decline. The role played by the wandering traders coming from the larger villages is an extremely negative one. The sale of opium and other reprehensible trading practices have proved the main evils for the rural population of the province.

The domestic trade of the province is sustained not only by the professional wandering traders, but also by the indigenous farmers and nomads (see above). Not only do they sell their goods to the trader but also they offer them for sale in their native villages in a more or less extensive area. What the farmer in Badakhshan can offer the traders from the bazaar villages or towns is quickly enumerated: cattle, sheep, goats, horses, walnuts, almonds, pistachios, rendered butter, yak tails, and products of native handicrafts. While the transport and sale of wheat and walnuts is possible over great distances, even in export beyond the boundaries of the province, the transport of fruit (apples, pears, cherries, morello cherries, quince, apricots) is fraught with difficulties. Almonds, pistachios and dried apricots, on the other hand, can easily be transported with no loss of quality. The mining of lapis lazuli is now under state control as is also the salt-mining in the province of Takhar, from where the so important salt is introduced into Badakhshan. The yield of the iron sources north-east of Fayzabad is today of no more than local significance.

Apart from the skins of wild animals, livestock (sheep, goats, camels, horses and, by the Kirghiz, the yak too) is practically the only source of income for the nomads if they are not active as traders as well. Above all, the wool of animals and also the animals themselves are traded over great distances throughout the land.

Alongside the professional traders and farmers and the industrial centres in the bazaars of the larger villages and towns, products of the handicrafts of rural areas are sold by the craftsmen themselves (in part as wandering craftsmen) in other valleys, regions and markets. The most important of these products are objects of daily use made of wood, metal and clay, along with textiles. Pottery, heavy, coarse woollen materials of sheep's wool or light materials of cotton, blankets, shawls and runners, also items of felt, bags, leather and carvings are traded in independent undertakings.

Many villages have specialized in the production of certain goods. For example, good quality pottery wares are made in Anjoman, Jorm, Shognan and in West Wakhan, Yaftal, Ragh, Kolala near Zebak and Fayzabad. Their production results sometimes with a commission, sometimes without, and the products are mostly sold in certain defined market outlets. The pottery wares are well packed and loaded on to donkeys by men to be traded from village to village. According to the amount of wares (one to three pack-animals), the sales quota and the length of the way these journeys last from one to two weeks. Several such trips are usually undertaken during the course of a summer. In winter only commissioned utensils are delivered. These smaller trips last but a few days and the goods are mostly carried by the man himself.

Badakhshan's manual skills are also evidenced by the beautiful textile handwork. The Tajek women have become known for their products of cotton, sheep and ibex wool. From these the following articles are made and traded within the land: stockings, socks, caps, pullovers, gloves, scarves, blankets, shawls, bags, coats and raw textiles such as undyed coarse wool material and felt. Various districts and villages have specialized in the production of particular textile handicrafts (see above).

The most widespread productions are those of wood, leather and wicker products because the raw materials are found easily and everywhere. The best work, though, is to be found in the larger bazaar centres. Carpenters are few; carvers are more readily to be found. These make bowls, spoons, chests, boxes, forks, ploughs, yokes, etc. and musical instruments. Good quality carvings come from the Monjan Valley while the few turners work above all in Wakhan and in Shoghnan. Shoghnan, moreover, is known for the production of good string instruments (*rabâb*) which are traded from there.

In the working of metal both the wrought-iron as well as the casting technique have been known since ancient times. But while iron-casting (cooking cauldrons, ploughshares and oil-lamps) can only be carried out in three centres (Fayzabad and Zardeu Valley, near the iron sources, as well as Qoran), there are blacksmiths in practically every valley (but not in all of the villages) who have their fixed market areas. Coppersmiths and filigree workers or silver- and goldsmiths now work, practically speaking, only in bazaars though once goldsmiths and silversmiths travelled through the land as wandering craftsmen.

Conclusion

The itinerant trade, carried on within the borders of the province, extends — as we have heard — to all parts of the land, even to the most isolated valleys and heights. Far from the automobile highway, trade is carried out by porters or by the use of pack-animals. In conclusion, a few words on this topic still remain to be said.

The forms of travel and transport in the style of the ancient Orient, which appeal to the European sense of the romantic, are still extensively in use due to the lack of roads, bridges and safe passages over the mountains. Along with the donkey, which is the chief animal for transporting goods and people, the horse — above all the riding horse — and the dromedary, used both as beasts of burden as well as for riding, and to be found right into the Wakhan, play the most important roles in the traffic of the land. Recently the yak, in increasing numbers, has taken over the role of the ideal pack and riding animal of the Central Asian highlands in Badakhshan, also beyond the Pamirs though at the end of the last century it was scarcely to be found even in Wakhan. The most westerly appearance of the Bactrian camel is in Badakhshan, east of Qala-e Panja. While this famous caravan animal of Central Asia is used for work by the Kirghiz, the Wakhi seem to look upon these beasts as objects of prestige. In any case no one has heard of them being used for any sort of work nor did I ever see a single animal being used in this capacity.

9

PROBLEMS OF SETTLEMENT OF THE EASTERN WAKHAN VALLEY AND THE DISCOVERIES MADE THERE IN 1975

Walter Raunig

The Wakhi people, according to the present point of view, cannot simply be subordinated under the great Afghan people of the Tajik either linguistically or solely in manifestations of culture. Some 10,000 inhabitants of the Afghanistan part of the Wakhan, with respect to language, form a group in themselves in Badakhshan and this group, in contrast to the West Iranian Tajik, can be traced back to northeast Iranian forebears in Afghanistan. Its language is limited to the large east-west valley of the Wakhan. Besides their mother tongue most Wakhi today understand and speak Dari (a form of the Persian dialect usual in Afghanistan) — the most important lingua franca of the country. But few — and these mostly clergy (Mollahs) or teachers — can read and write Dari.

The economy of the Wakhi is based on irrigative agriculture and stock-farming as can be consistently observed in the areas of settlement from the western village of Futur (2600 m. above sea level) in Wakhan, on over Qal'a-e Panja (2800 m.) as far as Sarhad (3320 m.). Langar (3590 m.) about 30 kilometres from Sarhad is the easternmost hamlet. Here the area of the sedentary Wakhi joins the area inhabited by the roaming, nomadic Kirghiz who lived there under Haji Rahman Qul Khan in the Pamir-e Khurd up to 1978.[1] Consequently, the Wakhi area of settlement extends over a distance of 200 kilometres. Along this stretch — mostly in the valley but also, in part on the heights above — ruins of various ages are to be found. Some of these old ruins, discovered on the valley terraces of the eastern Wakhan in the year 1975 by the 'Austrian Exploration Pamir 75'[2] are of interest for an understanding of the settlement of this area.[3]

On the northern moraine terrace, lying about 200 metres above the floor of the eastern Wakhan Valley, four ruin-complexes with their former fields and irrigation ditches were found. One of the old main irrigation ditches once led from a Pamir valley above the terrace along the mountainside (Fig. 1).

From: Spuren alter Besiedlung auf den
      Talterrassen des östlichen Wakhān
      (Nordost-Afghanistan) - W. Raunig.

In: P. Snoy (Ed.)
    Ethnologie und Geschichte:
    Festschrift für Karl Jettmar,
    Beiträge zur Südasienforschung, Vol.86.
    Wiesbaden, Franz Steiner Verlag 1983

■ ruins of houses
● ruins of a fortification

These fields, irrigation systems and ruin-complexes were, very probably, once permanent settlements which, because of their isolated position, offered people more security than the settlements in the valley. The once-cultivated areas around these courts, relatively flat and lying at right angles to one another, were extensive enough to sustain several large families under normal climatic weather conditions (Figs. 2 and 3). A few meadows and the alpine pastures, lying at the rear of the Ptukh Valley and, according to the testimony of the natives, still used up to a few decades ago by the present-day villagers of Ptukh, offered meagre but sufficient sustenance to a modest herd of livestock.

The dilapidated buildings of both valley terraces would seem to differ in no way from those of the valley below.[4] The walls are of gathered stones; chaff mixed with clay served as mortar and the inner rooms (main living quarters) were plastered with fine clay mortar. However, on closer scrutiny, the old buildings on the north just as on the south terrace, do indeed show some differences from the buildings usual today in the Wakhan Valley. These divergences are to be noted in the straight walls and manner of construction of the exact rectangular corners. Moreover, these straight walls have openings for windows — and this, again, is in contrast to practically all of the present constructions in Wakhan.

The best preserved buildings of the northern terrace at the present time consists of nine rooms, including a tower. Its entire length runs to some 20 metres, the width is 12 metres. The tower, set off from the building but lying directly on the house wall along the mountainside and even today some 2.5 – 2.7 metres high, has a ground area of about 4.5 square metres. The thickness of the wall ranges from 40 to 60 centimetres. The entrance would seem to have been to the east; in front of the building is a sunken space surrounded by a wall of earth about 4.5 metres wide and 20 metres long — a type of catchment which may have served as a water reservoir. Here, as well as beside the other three smaller ruin-complexes, a number of rock engravings and also food storage spaces are to be found, partly set into the ground.

On the moraine terraces on the south side, i.e. the Hindukush slope, also lying some 200 metres above the floor of the valley and sharply divided into individual sections, are several (in all about 15) ruins of varying size along with their former fields, irrigation ditches and even some rock engravings. A few of these ruins are, even today, used as temporary lodgings, for example, during the time of harvesting, because here on the southern terrace of the valley some of the fields are cultivated. However, the very extensive old irrigation system is today almost wholly useless.

All the ruins found on this southern valley terrace — corresponding to those of the northern terrace — stand singly, surrounded by fields;

Fig. 1. The northern valley terrace of the easternmost Wakhan Valley, *c.* 200 metres above the floor of the valley (running horizontally through the middle of the Figure). Above it on the right-hand side is the old irrigation ditch as a hairline running parallel to the terrace.

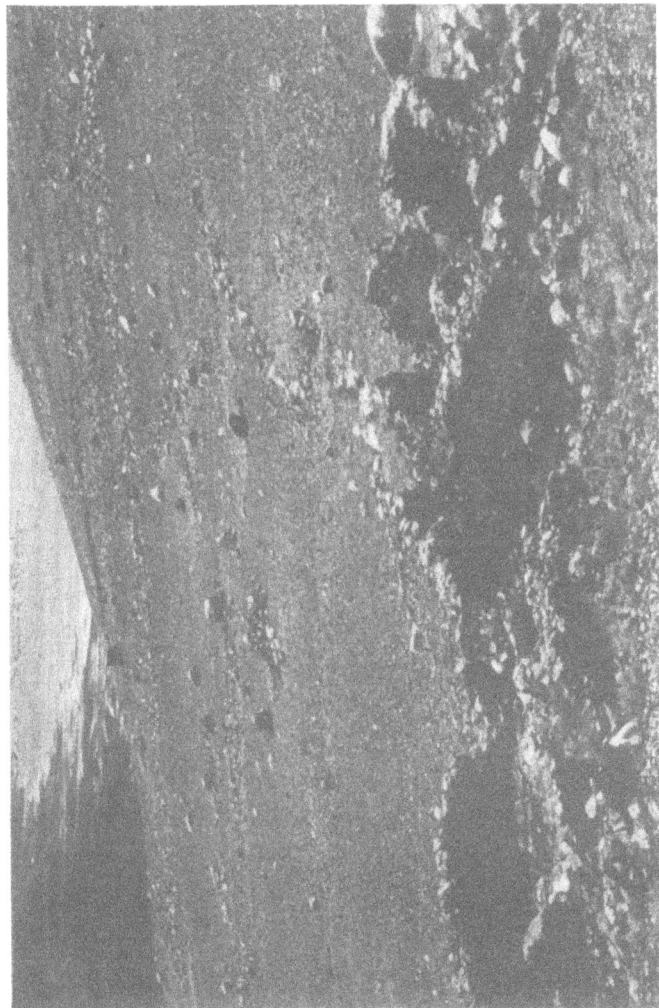

Fig. 2. One of the four ruins on the northern terrace with old fields and irrigation ditches in between.

Fig. 3. The same ruin as in Fig. 2 with a view to the east looking downward to the end of the Wakhan Valley at Tshehel-Kand and Sarhad.

Fig. 4. Ruin of a fortified building on an isolated hill, lying before the southern terrace of the easternmost part of the Wakhan Valley.

i.e. they form no village or hamlet. One of these former buildings, found on an isolated hill, lying before the actual terrace, with an excellent view over the entire eastern part of the Wakhan Valley, undoubtedly served as a type of fortress or fortified structure (Fig. 4).

South of Sarhad, the last i.e. the easternmost village of the Wakhan Valley, high on the slopes on both sides of the entrance to the valley in the direction of the Broghil Pass, there are also some ruin-complexes. A visit to these, unfortunately, was forbidden by the former Police Commandant in Sarhad. Judging from the location of these ruins, in contrast to those mentioned above on both terraces of the valley, they would, in all probability, be the former fortifications — perhaps dating from the time of the Tibetan occupation. Here, by Sarhad, in the year A.D. 747 violent conflicts occurred between the Chinese troops which came over the Pamir (Po-mi-lo) and the Tibetan Troops entrenched in the fortifications (the first documentary mention of Sarhad).[5] Regretfully, we were unable to determine the size, type of construction, and other architectural details, nor could we investigate possibilities of water supply, etc. of the ruins south of Sarhad.

While the age of these as yet unexamined ruins has not been established with certainty, the radiocarbon, lichen growth and weathering examinations of the stones of the ruins on both moraine terracces conducted at the Universities of Vienna, Bonn, Graz and Innsbruck, resulted in the following data:

The main water conduit on the northern terrace was built in the second half of the fourteenth century. The beginning of agriculture on the terrace is also assumed to date from this time. Repair of the water system was carried on between A.D. 1490 and 1650. Judging from the variations in lichen growth on the blocks of the loose stone wall, more than 200 years must have passed between the building and the restoration of the water system so that the date of repair can be assumed to be at the beginning of or within the first half of the seventeenth century. The dates determined for the buildings go back only as far as the seventeenth century. It has, therefore, been established than an enlargement of the agricultural acreage took place in the second half of the fourteenth century and a construction of single farms occurred at the beginning or in the first half of the seventeenth century at heights no longer attained in Wakhan today. The settlement was probably abandoned at the beginning of the nineteenth century, perhaps because of the destruction of the water drainage system which could not have been repaired with the technical means available.

As far as the dating of the buildings of the southern valley terrace is concerned, there is less documentary evidence than for the ruins of the northern terrace. They presumably date back, at least in part to the same time. This has also been suggested by the lichen growth

(*Xanthoria elegans*) along the wall surface of one of the old irrigation ditches now in disuse.

The dates mentioned for the buildings on the terrace 200 metres above the eastern valley floor tell us nothing of the actual age of settlement of the Wakhan Valley or of the beginning of agriculture. Our colleague, Prof. Patzelt from the University of Innsbruck, found, near the village of Rawtshun on the south bank of the Wakhan Darja (3200 metres above sea level) in a wind-protected cave in the rock of the slope, remains of a fire with charcoal remnants which according to radiocarbon examination date back to the period between 2190 and 2120 B.C. These remnants from the Neolithic are the oldest indications of human presence in the valley, up to now. This, however, offers no proof of a permanent settlement. Rather, such a camp-fire puts one in mind of transient hunters or shepherds, and the earliest datings (radiocarbon and pollen analysis) for cultivation of the soil in the eastern Wakhan Valley go back to the first and seventh centuries A.D., respectively.

A decline in agriculture (and, therefore, a decline in the population as well) in the following centuries, as proved by the pollen-analysis examination, could probably be attributed to a change in climate (drought) rather than to an historical event. In the fourteenth century an increase in population necessitated an expansion to the valley terraces, and a permanent settlement was made on the terraces at the beginning of the seventeenth century at the latest. Just how much the need for security played a role in the settlement of the terraces is unknown. At any rate, the construction of the main water conduit occurred on the northern terrace in the time of Timur (1360/70 – 1405). Doubtless, for well on 2000 years, the Wakhan retained a significance as a thorough-fare (e,g, southern branch of the Silk Road). The route to China, over Badakhshan and thereby through the Wakhan Valley and over the Pamirs would have been used by that famous Venetian traveller, Marco Polo.

In the last century a decline of population in the eastern Wakhan clearly seems to have taken place. This may have been responsible for the migration from the southern terrace. However, the abandonment of the northern terrace as an area of settlement was most likely due to the failure of the water supply in the first half of the nineteenth century.

10

ASIAN MERCHANTS AND EUROPEAN EXPANSION: MALABAR PEPPER TRADE ROUTES IN THE INDIAN OCEAN WORLD-SYSTEM IN THE SIXTEENTH CENTURY

Jan Kieniewicz

The purpose of this paper is to present some hypotheses concerning the connections that existed between the routes of the Malabar pepper trade and the World-System of the Indian Ocean in the sixteenth century. On this occasion I would also like to determine in what way European expansion affected those connections and how much it was itself affected by them.

The following are my presuppositions:

1. When speaking of Malabar, I refer to the economic entity connected with the western coastal region of India from Mt. Dely down to Cape Comorin in which pepper growing and pepper trade probably played the key role. It is of course an open question whether we can consider Malabar as a socio-economic system. For, in spite of very strong economic ties and cultural unity, it resembled rather a loose conglomerate of villages. In addition, caste divisions strengthened political divisions which in their turn made the creation of one country or one state out of Malabar difficult.

2. By the designation 'trade routes', I mean permanent communication links connecting production centres with sales depots. They are determined by the social attitude towards those goods which are the object of exchange, and also by the interests of dominant individuals or whole groups of people.

   At the same time these trade routes are connections between people created by transportation, trade, and exchange of information, and form a network around the chosen or imposed communication links. In the sixteenth century, the Malabar routes of the pepper trade constituted the only stable and extra-political network.

3. I consider the Indian Ocean to be a 'World-System', not solely an aquatic system. It represents an economic system that still has not been well defined. It seems not to correspond to such concepts as 'World-Economy' or 'World-Empire'. The structure called the 'Proto-World-Economy', suggested by Wallerstein, impresses me

78

as artificial.[1] I feel intuitively that a supra-regional organization linking the various societies and connected by the sea must have existed. How extensive was this system in the sixteenth century? We may conclude from European accounts that there existed between Malacca and Aden something more than a network of trading contacts. Were these trade connections indispensable to the existence of totally different local systems? Was it such networks that moulded the Indian Ocean into a World-System?[2]

4. The European expansion lifted Europe above its socio-cultural origins to become a part of a world-economy. The nature of the influence of the expansion in the Indian Ocean World-System has not been exhaustively explained. Did the activities of the Portuguese, or the functioning of the Estado da India reflect in Asia the expansion of the sixteenth century European World-Economy? Did that European economy in the sixteenth century possess the possibility of subordinating its external areas?

5. Asian merchants did not create a community — I use this term 'Asian merchants' to describe that group which quite apart from the origin of its component members, had ties with the World-System of the Indian Ocean. The role played by these Asian merchants in the Indian Ocean World-System, is an important distinguishing factor.

The routes of the pepper trade in Malabar were shaped by the distribution of pepper cultivation, the territorial topography, the structure of property, the political system and by the permanent sixteenth century prevalence of demand over supply.[3] The area suitable for intensive pepper cultivation was determined by the quality of the soil, its degree of salinity, the altitude above sea level, and the relative costs of transport. Temperature and humidity were obviously a *sine qua non*, but did not represent a differentiating factor, since they did not influence localization within Malabar. We can distinguish several areas specializing in the cultivation of pepper, but to demarcate them precisely is not so easy. Contemporary sources seem not to attach importance to the precise determination of the region of cultivation. They describe more or less precisely the dimensions of supply at the coast. It was only very gradually that it began to be noticed that this was not synonymous with the whole of production. The sixteenth century information provides, at the most, a basis for no more than an estimate of the order of the size of production, and does not go beyond generalizations on the question of localization. For some reason, observers did not find closer details worthy of their notice. Perhaps they did not have access to them.

In the sixteenth century the cultivation of pepper intended for export was concentrated in the area to the south of Paliakar and

Kotamangalam, above all on the estates of the Rajah of Vadakkumkur, 'Reyno da Pimienta', and the Rajah of Tekkumkur, that is, from the Periyar River to the Anchekoil River. The axis of concentration of the gardens can be established at the 150 m. contour level. The gardens lying further south, to the Kallada River, were of less significance. Nor do we know whether pepper cultivation had even developed in Attingal and Peritali in the sixteenth century. There were however definitely no major areas of pepper cultivation in the northern regions — and indeed not until the nineteenth century. The earliest to be developed, from the sixteenth century, was the cultivation in the Chirakkal and Kottayam regions, just as in south Kanara.[4]

The question of the quality of the pepper was a disputed matter for the European authors, but they were not interested in the grade but above all in the yield. We know very little of the conditions operating in cultivation. It is therefore difficult to formulate questions about the motivations for economic activities. In particular the matter of the relation of demand for pepper to the behaviour of the cultivators is problematic. It is only with great caution that one can make use of reference to our period of observations recorded at the end of the eighteenth century.[5] Therefore the majority of concepts considered below should be treated as provisional.

The concentration of cultivation, the slow process of expansion of the area under cultivation, the garden form, the small units of production and use — these were all elements which exercised an extremely strong influence upon the formation of the routes of the Malabar pepper trade. The distance from the regions of cultivation to the coast was not great, transport conditions were excellent. But despite this, large-scale cultivation, concentration of property, merchant domination and capacity for swift reaction to external stimuli did not develop. These matters are not part of our concern here, but they indicate the importance of the trade routes. These were not simply transport tracks.

The scale of cultivation was of less significance. Given the plenitude of water routes and the availability of timber, it was apparently not a problem to construct the required number of boats or ships. We know that sometimes the ships came to the weekly markets in such great number that they could not be moved.[6] The pepper transport in the sixteenth century must have made use of boats of various shapes and sizes. But we may conclude that it was mainly the larger ships known as *tones* that reached the ports. Their cargo was between 2 and 8 tons, and they probably carried the pepper loose rather than in sacks. In any case, this was the form in which it was delivered at times to the Portuguese factory at Cochin.[7] However, I do not think that this was the only or even the most common form of transport used for supplies to the Arab ships. In any event, about a thousand *tones* of this kind would have been required for the Malabar pepper trade. This cannot have been difficult to achieve.

However, the relationship between supply and demand was the factor of decisive importance in the pepper trade. During the sixteenth and seventeenth centuries, the area under cultivation in Malabar grew considerably, while conditions on the coast did not change. The demand from distant markets, evidenced by the merchants in Malabar, rose steadily, and systematically exceeded the supply available. Social, demographic and cultural conditions which prevented those cultivating the pepper gardens from reacting swiftly must have played a role here. Cultivation on a larger scale must have been highly profitable, but there is no sign that this had any effect on production.[8] The extensive network of river routes greatly reduced transport costs, and there was nothing to prevent the producers themselves from reaching the coast with transports.[9] They were indeed present on the coast but this clearly did not lead to change in the sphere of production. Competition among the merchants on the coast led them to attempt to ensure certain supplies, and therefore to make advance payments on crops. But this did not produce dependence of the cultivators on the merchants.[10] The rajahs and Kartavas controlling the routes inland organized the collection of customs and dues. The Portuguese tried to persuade the local rulers to participate in the organization of deliveries to their factories, but without great success. Thus the Portuguese were for the whole of the sixteenth century dependent upon the local merchants. In any event, they did not manage to carry out their plans to effect control of the routes or to subordinate the cultivators.[11]

The routes linking the coast with the interior of the country obviously served in the transport of exports and imports of other products. Among these were such varied items as timber, coconuts and rice. The permanent rice deficit, combined with the ready possibility of obtaining rice supplies from neighbouring countries, exercised an enormous influence on the functioning of the Malabar economy.[12] This was almost certainly one of the conditions leading to continual expansion of the pepper gardens. The motives of economic decision-making in Malabar, especially among producers, need to be further investigated.

The trade routes started in the interior of the country, where in the zone of garden cultivation there must have been very numerous local bazaars. Pepper could have been sold there by *janmkarans, kāṇamkarans* and/or *kuḷikāṇamkarans*, groups representing different titles to land and its fruits. One could find in these groups people from different *jatis* and caste-like groups, such as *nayars* and Syrian Christians. Their social status and mutual ties did not influence the trade routes. On the other hand, the traders were not only active at the local bazaars but they also reached the gardens directly. Anyway, in the sixteenth century traders did not manage to subjugate cultivators. Similarly the rulers who profited from customs and other levies, and who intervened in the organization of supplies to the harbours, would never try to tax the producers directly. Political fragmentation, and the multiplicity of frontiers and conflicts could not contribute towards the improvement of transport, but these were probably factors that prevented the traders and rulers from dominating production.

Can we speak about pepper trade routes in Malabar? We can do it in so far as it was precisely the pepper trade that determined the formation of the internal market. Keeping in view the character of those routes we can demarcate two spheres of commercial activity in Malabar.

The first I would call a local sphere for it appeared in connection with the process of commercialization of pepper. The trade routes ran to and from the local exchange centres. The waterways and the land-routes — the latter often rather footpaths than routes — in the regions of intensive pepper cultivation converged at the local bazaar and/or at the weekly market. Such centres, as a rule with good communication with some other larger trade centre, were quite numerous. It seems that they always could have been reached within one day-long march.[13] In the eighteenth century, in the southern part of the garden region, Krishnapura, Puttenkavai, Tumbanur, Karibanda, and Tavalikara were centres of this kind. From here, the routes ran outwards at roughly the same parallel of latitude, but in two different directions: towards the coast, and towards the mountain passes. There were very many rivers leading to the sea, mainly the Kallada, Anchekoil, Pambai, Kakkad, Kajama, Vadakka and Periyar. To some extent the tributaries of the Ponnani were probably also used. On the other hand, the routes running towards the passes in the Western Ghats were very few and heavily frequented. These routes ran from several larger trade centres like Kotamangalam, Kanjirapalli or Kottarakara, which functioned very much like harbours. The markets of Erattupetta and Erimaly, from which however the road east led through Kanjirapalli, played a similar role.[14] A few other centres for the organization of exports through the Western Ghats may have been located actually in the zone of cultivation, and have also made use of water export routes. This could have been the case with Corgeira, Paleacate Cheri, Zaruquly, Ramapurata, Ciuncam and Mohatushe, mentioned in the later reports.[15]

Only a few passes were suitable for caravan transport: the road from Padmanabhapuram to Tinneveli, which led through Aramboli,[16] and the road from Kottarakara to Aryankavu, which ran in the same direction, through the Shencottah Pass.[17] The Anchekoil Pass may also have been used. The road from Kanjirapalli through the Gudalur Pass led to Periakulam, Tanjore, and Negapatam.[18] The route from Kotamangalam through the Bodinaikur Pass ran in the same direction. From

Kotamangalam and other centres, e.g. via Angamali-Trichur, the caravans may have headed in the direction of Mysore, Trichinopoli and Pulicat.[19] The pepper transported by the land routes reached deep inland in India, to the Koromandel coast, to Bengal or even to China.[20] The existence of these land routes was of great significance in all matters connected with the pepper trade and the Portuguese expansion in Malabar.

For the local sphere, changes of ownership, and not the nature of the tracks nor the kind of transport, was of decisive importance. There can be no doubt that pepper reached the ports also directly from the cultivators, and was even transported there by them. More frequently, however, some passed through the hands of merchants in centres like Mavalikara, Tiruvala, Changanachery, Kottayam, Viakam, Vadetha, Chembe, Triniputra, Diamper, Edapalli, Alwaye, Alangadi and others. It was there that the *tones* may have been loaded, although we do not know whether they took a cargo belonging to one or more persons. It is probably not accidental that these places were also centres of local authorities, and that the rajahs were involved in organizing the transports. The process of concentration of cargoes which took place before the pepper reached the ports was of fundamental significance.

We may speak of a second sphere, the intermediary sphere, characterized by the creation of longitudinal links, utilizing both the sea and the fresh water bays as well as the coastal lakes and canals. This was also characterized by a different trade activity. The network of longitudinal links provided optimal conditions for linking the interior of the country with the coast.[21] These routes above all were connected with the main centres of export, such as Cannanore, Calicut, Cochin and Kollam. From time to time, and to a certain degree, a similar role was played by centres of lesser rank such as Kayankollam, Porakkad, Kodungallur, Ponnani, Chettuwai, Putuppattanam, Chaliyam, Parappanangadi, Beipur, Pandarani, Kapokate or Kottakal. This coastal transit region in which the goods moved along a north-south axis and were concentrated on a few markets or store-houses, was a sphere of intensive penetration by traders from outside Malabar.[22] But even here local traders dominated, although these traders differed from those dominant in the local sphere. This created an exceptionally broad plane of economic links. Despite the existence of distinct centres for export, smaller ports retained their independence and functioned for the benefit of their hinterlands. This was certainly the result of favourable communication links. None the less, the trade routes in Malabar corresponded above all to the requirements of an economy vitally interested in relationships with its surroundings.

This intermediary sphere in the most natural way was connected with the sea-routes system which linked Malabar with the Indian coast from

Gujarat round to Coromandel. Here two processes took place which were of paramount importance for the economy of Malabar. Goods from the whole of Asia and from outside it were exchanged for the money indispensable for buying pepper profitably. The considerable amounts of rice necessary to make up for the permanent deficit of food were also bought in the same circulation system. These two processes made the society of Malabar stable. [23]

These two spheres were separated neither territorially nor economically, but they undoubtedly did exist. In the local sphere pepper became the item of trade, and the trade routes, especially the short ones, were dominated by the local people. Concentration of cargoes here was weak. The intermediary sphere determined the basis of 'export'. The traders from the coast dominated it and the concentration of cargoes was increasing. Indirectly this sphere meant that the trade routes fully belonging to Malabar participated in the Indian Ocean World-System. Such intermediary spheres like that of the Malabar coast, were most important for world trade. [24] Without them the sea navigation would remain marginal. This point of view is confirmed by the history of European expansion.

Thus hypotheses concerning the routes of the Malabar pepper trade can be formulated in the following way:
— the trade routes in Malabar were determined by the pepper trade.
— the narrowly localized zone of cultivation had a sufficiently dense network of local bazaars to make efficient commercialisation possible.
— the routes between the local market and the ports served not only for transport; the transactions resulted in displacements in time and space and in the concentration of cargoes.
— the system of routes was connected with the intermediary sphere.
— as to size, density and significance of cargoes, the routes leading to the coast were definitely predominant, as compared to the routes leading inland. It would appear that the pepper trade in the inland direction took a different form from that in the intermediary sphere. None the less, the overland routes represented an essential complement to the stabilizing mechanism for Malabar as a social system.

It is also possible to put forward a few hypotheses on the subject of the European expansion and the Asian merchants:
— the military and trading presence of the Portuguese created a system for making use of the Asian trade, or to be more precise, the ocean-going trade. This did not affect the routes of the Malabar pepper trade. However, in the intermediary sphere, it had an overwhelming

effect in that it did allow the Portuguese to make contact and to carry out their expansion.[25]

— the intermediary sphere remained dominated by Asian merchants, and this is not in contradiction to the presence in the trade of cultivators, rulers and the Portuguese. From the perspective of the Malabar communication routes and the pepper trade, it can be seen that the Asian merchants were not able to create stronger links as a community with supralocal interests, and they remained dispersed. Their activities embraced distant seas and distant markets, but their roots were to be found in exactly these structures intermediate between local markets and continental trade.

— the activities of the merchants were of decisive importance in the continued existence of local social systems. This did not affect social mobility or the system of values. In the intermediary sphere, trading activities transmitted destabilizing stimuli, while at the same time contributing to the creation of mechanisms that protected functional balance.[26]

— participation in the pepper trade became a process of adaptation for the Portuguese.

The Malabar with which the Portuguese came into contact on the pepper trade routes never ceased to be an alien reality for them. But these contacts resulted in the Portuguese becoming Asian merchants.

Consideration of the pepper trade routes finally enables us to formulate a few conjectures on the subject of the Indian Ocean. It seems probable that the phenomenon termed the intermediary sphere was the most permanent link amongst the various societies situated on the Indian Ocean. The small cargoes, the small-scale but numerous contacts, and the intensity of meetings limited to a relatively narrow group of people, all determined the specific nature of the trade amongst the societies of the coast. It was indeed essential to the existence of these societies. Despite this, there is no sign that these societies integrated around the ocean or that the merchants became a predominant factor in them. It would be more correct to emphasise the links of these societies with the coast rather than with the sea.[27] It was these societies, with their mutual linkages through the intermediary zone, and the relation of the coast with the surroundings, that created the real Indian Ocean World-System.

In the light of the above comments, it would seem that the question of the Malabar pepper trade routes deserves greater attention. That is, of course, in fact trade routes *tout court*, and we are discussing pepper because of its local importance and also because of the greater quantity of source materials. We should also consider whether the specific conditions of the Malabar coast did not exert a decisive influence upon the form of trade relations.

Can the conclusions suggested here be applied to other areas? With this in mind, I will treat my final remarks as hypotheses to be challenged in the light of further research into the trade routes in Asia:

1. The Indian Ocean as a World-System was moulded by the ratios of exchange established in the intermediary spheres. The existence of the intermediary spheres was subordinated neither to any core of any world-economy, nor to the distant markets, not even to the traders dominating within them. The Portuguese did not change anything in this regard during the sixteenth century. The routes of the Malabar pepper trade did not change either.
2. The trade-routes system in Malabar contributed to the creation of the Indian Ocean World-System but was not dependent upon it.
3. The sixteenth century Portuguese expansion did not modify the existing relations; it was precisely the Portuguese who had to adapt to conditions in the intermediary sphere.
4. The continuation of the Malabar pepper trade and stability of its routes, as well as the adaptation of the Portuguese among the Asian merchants, give ample proof of the strength of the World-System of the Indian Ocean. A more precise definition of this system, also taking into consideration the relations with other World-Systems, is becoming an urgent research task.

11

TRADE BETWEEN MUGHAL INDIA AND THE MIDDLE EAST, AND MUGHAL MONETARY POLICY, c.1600 – 1660[1]

H. W. van Santen

As is well known, the Dutch East India Company (VOC) traded in a bewildering variety of goods. With Batavia as its Asian entrepôt an extensive trading system was set up, in which hundreds of ships were engaged in shipping an enormous variety of Asian and European products to the most profitable markets. My aim here is not to give an endless list of all the different trade goods, their places of origin and their destinations. The object of this paper is much more limited: I will concentrate mostly on one type of merchandise, i.e. cotton goods, and on one trading area — the north-western part of the Indian Ocean. Both the VOC and a large group of Gujarati traders were active in this trade, making comparison between these two types of traders possible.

A significant feature of this particular trade was that the Dutch and Gujarati merchants operated in a highly competitive market, not only in Gujarat or the North Indian plains where these cottons were produced but the selling markets of Mocha and Persia as well. Here, the VOC market position differed greatly from that in other Asian products. Another important Asian product, cloves, became subject to a Dutch monopoly as the result of the enforced control of the production areas in the Indonesian Archipelago on the one hand, and Dutch dumping policy in the selling markets on the other. Market control over this product was virtually complete in Europe and Asia during the period 1680 – 1730, but the foundations had already been laid by the middle of the seventeenth century. Even in the 1630s very few cloves arrived in Europe by way of the old land route through the Middle East, the VOC having successfully deflected the spice trade to its new route around the Cape of Good Hope. As a consequence, the structure of indigenous trade in western Asia changed, and many Indian merchants, who for centuries had specialized in the spice trade, were forced to shift their attention to trade between India and the Middle East.

I will not digress any further upon this well-known 'success story' in the history of the Dutch Company. The only point worth emphasizing here is that such a comfortable monopoly was the exception rather than the rule. The bulk of Asian products or markets were never subject to monopoly, or controlled in any other way.

In the first part of this paper I shall describe Dutch and Gujarati trade in the western part of the Indian Ocean, and in doing so, shall make some observations on the competitiveness of Asian traders in general *vis-à-vis* a western company. Secondly I shall draw attention to the amazing role of the Mughal government in this trade. Because the Middle East was important in providing precious metals, Gujarati merchants were sometimes encouraged — if not pressed — to maintain the cotton export trade.

After having compared Dutch and Gujarati performance in the same trade in the same trading region, my second aim in this short essay is to explore the hypothesis that trade cannot be studied in isolation as a purely economic phenomenon, but that the whole socio-political and military context should be taken into account.

In the trading system of the VOC in Asia, its factory at Surat fulfilled several important functions. It was here that the cargoes destined for Mughal India were unloaded, including Asian products such as spices, copper, pepper, tin, and European merchandise such as vermillion, quicksilver and woollen cloth. From Surat Indian products such as indigo, saltpetre and cotton goods were exported together with a host of other goods destined for the Asian and European markets. Further, Surat acted as a trans-shipment port for the Western Asian region. With Surat as its centre, the Company traded in Indian goods between India, Persia and the Arabian peninsula. The money earned in this regional trade was used partly to finance the purchase of Indian export goods for the European and Asian markets.

Dutch trade in Indian goods to Persia began in the 1630s, and mostly cotton piece-goods worth between *f* 50,000 and *f* 150,000, were shipped in the ensuing years. Although not much is known about the *total* import of cotton goods into Persia (see below) we may safely assume that the Dutch market share was only marginal — definitely lower than ten per cent. Dutch profits were low, gross profit being 40 per cent in 1640 but only 4 per cent in 1651 and 7 to 8 per cent in 1659. In fact, each year profits turned out to be lower than expected so that, as the Governor-General remarked, 'all our exertions amount to virtually nothing, taking interest costs and other expenses into account.'[2] An average gross profit of 40 per cent was considered the minimum needed to break even in this intra-Asian trade.

The Dutch, being dissatisfied with their own performance, were astounded by their Gujarati rivals' capacity for competition. It was indeed amazing: how could these Indian merchants compete with the VOC — which did not pass on any transport costs to the retailer (because the VOC ships had to go from Surat to Bandar Abbas anyway, to pick up the cargo destined for Batavia and Amsterdam), and which paid lower tolls in Persia? A few VOC sources seem to confirm this picture of the generally low profitability of this trade. Indian merchants, freighting their goods in Dutch ships, were said to make a mere 11 per cent profit, whereas gross profits of about 16 per cent seem to have been normal on goods shipped by Indian vessels (to which a lower freight rate was applied). Dutch merchants were undoubtedly right in saying that average *net* profits must have been very low indeed. How was a humble Gujarati merchant able to compete with the mighty VOC? The answer given by the company servants themselves sounds quite convincing. The Indian trader simply operated at far lower costs and could afford to accept much smaller profits. Besides, as the Dutch servants admitted, he often had a much more thorough knowledge of how the market worked when he bought and sold his *baftas, tapechindes* or *chelas*. After several decades of disappointing financial results the VOC admitted defeat, and in the 1660s it ended this trade in piece goods between Surat and Bandar Abbas.

In 1642 the Dutch Company began shipping cotton goods to Mocha, where the situation had finally improved, peace having been restored there after the successful revolt of the Zaidi imams of Sana against their Ottoman overlords. As in the case of Dutch trade to Persia, profits turned out to be extremely low. On the average, gross profits amounted to about 15 per cent, resulting in unacceptably low net profits after the deduction of interest losses, the loss of silver due to reminting in Surat, presents to the Mocha officials, etc. Despite numerous objections from local company servants, the Governor-General at Batavia ordered them to carry on with this trade, hoping to 'finally reap the profits from this trade, and hence, receive enormous quantities of cash.'[3] Several measures were considered for improving the situation. However, the same methods the Company had used elsewhere in Asia (sometimes with great success) were useless here. There were several reasons why a dumping policy or the use of force, or both, simply would not work. As some company servants pointed out, a dumping policy, glutting the Middle Eastern markets with cotton goods to deter other merchants would not discourage the many thousands of pilgrims who went to reduce travel expenses. Besides, would the Company be able — financially and logistically — to flood the Mocha market for years on end? Finally, they thought it highly unlikely that the Mughal government would not retaliate on seeing this vitally important trade threatened. Of course, this last argument could also be applied to the proposal to obstruct Indian trade to Mocha by force.

Clearly, a direct and aggressive trade policy was not feasible, and the Company was forced to operate as one trader among many others. This proved to be too difficult: in 1655 this trade was ended. As in the

VOC's Persian trade, it had only a small share in the market, exporting about 76,000, 60,000 and 77,000 pieces of cotton cloth in the years 1645, 1646 and 1647. This was a mere trifle when compared with the export of 702,000, 555,000 (and 116 bundles) and 990,000 pieces by Gujarati traders.

Much to his regret in 1677 the Governor-General was forced to admit 'that the Indians ship large amounts of precious metals from Mocha, Basra and Bandar Abbas. They are able to purchase their goods in Northern India and Gujarat much cheaper than the VOC, having small expenses and less costs.'⁴ We may conclude, therefore, that the Dutch position in this western Asian trade was structurally weak, as very high gross profits were necessary, since the VOC had to take its enormous overhead costs into account. Gujarati merchants on the other hand, operated at far lower costs, and could thus afford to accept lower profits. Another possible factor which may help to explain the Dutch inability to compete successfully, was that — at least in some years — the Mughal authorities pressed their subjects to maintain the cotton export. I will return to this point later.

Much about the commercial activities of Indian traders remains in the dark. There are some shipping lists in the Dutch archives, giving details of the cargoes of ships arriving at and departing from Surat. However, the problem with these lists — which were probably copied from the official toll registers — is that we do not know how reliable they are, nor how much was smuggled in or out. Another major problem is that we do not know how many vessels sailed from other Gujarati ports. Besides, how much was transported to Persia over land by caravan? Because of this lack of statistical information I will only point to two general features of Indian trade to the Middle East.

A most remarkable characteristic of Indian trade to Persia was the persistence of the old land route. In the seventeenth century a large proportion of Indian transport goods, especially those grown or manufactured in the North Indian plains, seem to have reached their destined Persian markets by land rather than by sea. Dutch company servants admitted that it cost more to transport goods from Agra to Surat, shipping them to Bandar Abbas and bringing them to Isfahan, the central market of Persia, than to take the land route from Agra to Isfahan via Lahore and Kandahar. Each year a total of between 20,000 and 25,000 camels loaded with Indian export goods are reported to have arrived in Isfahan from Lahore. In 1663 a company servant estimated transport costs on the land route from Agra to Constantinople to be even lower than those on the route Agra-Surat-Mocha-Constantinople or Agra-Surat-Basra-Constantinople. These references — few as they are — should make us aware of the fact that during the seventeenth century the old land route had not yet become negligible. For many merchants purchasing cotton cloth or indigo in the North Indian production areas, it was often more economical to have their goods transported by land rather than by sea.

'Unpredictable' was the epithet most often used by Dutch company servants for describing market conditions in Mocha. In Mocha one did not know what to expect; one year high profits were being made, but the next year supply was so enormous and/or demand so low that each merchant had to sell at a loss. The situation in Mocha was considered worse than anywhere else in Asia. The market situation at Surat or Bandar Abbas, for instance, was considered much more transparent. Several reasons were given to explain the huge price fluctuations and the structural imbalance between supply and demand. Firstly, Mocha was mainly a port of trans-shipment, acting as a complex and delicate nodal point between two trade worlds — the Asian and the Mediterranean. Most of the products shipped to this port were not used or consumed locally, but were transported to the great Muslim fairs at Mecca and Medina, or to Suez, Cairo or Constantinople. In this long-distance trade, supply and demand were rarely in balance, hence the enormous price fluctuations. Secondly, price-stabilizing factors were absent due to the structure of the market. Gujarati, as well as Bengali and Coromandel merchants, tried to sell their cotton goods here, making any market control by one or a few important merchants almost impossible. And more important still, thousands of pilgrims arrived in Mocha each year, all carrying a few cotton goods which they tried to sell as quickly as possible. The diversified supply by these 'pedlar' pilgrims thwarted any attempt at market control or stockpiling.

In his famous study Niels Steensgaard has explored the hypothesis that *all* Asian traders had to operate in a non-transparent market and that — unlike the companies — they were not able to influence price developments through stockpiling or some form of monologistic market behaviour.[5] This contrasted with the situation in the Netherlands, where in the seventeenth century we can discern a trend towards greater transparency of the market, and where several merchants were able to influence price developments by stockpiling and monopolistic market behaviour. Working in a more 'modern' way, these merchants were able to maximize their immediate income and to reduce price fluctuations. Steensgaard considered the Dutch Company to be a good example of this more modern attitude, whereas the Asian 'pedlar traders' are said to represent a more traditional kind of market behaviour.

Where the subject of this paper is concerned, perhaps something can be added to this interesting theory, my hypothesis being that differences in market behaviour between an Asian and a western trader were quite small, and that we have to look for other factors to explain Dutch superiority in some Asian markets. Of course, the situation at Mocha seems to be almost in accordance with the 'ideal-type' Asian market described by Steensgaard. But then, this market can hardly be called 'normal', being a port of trans-shipment, characterized by a very diversified supply. And when we try to apply this idea of the 'Asian pedlar' (operating in a highly non-transparent market) to other regions, we encounter even more serious difficulties. Let me give some examples of monopolizing and stockpiling Gujarati merchants. In 1661 Haji Zahid Beg, one of the greatest merchants of Surat, had bought all the tin the Company had shipped to Surat (about 200,000 pounds). Afterwards, an English and a Gujarati ship arrived from Atjeh carrying 265,000 pounds of tin. Haji Zahid Beg made an offer to the owners to buy the entire shipment 'because he wants to be master of this product.' Or else, so a Dutch writer added, 'he would spoil the market and would take reprisals against the President of the English East India Company whom he had lent quite a sum of money.'[6] In this way Haji Zahid Beg was able to monopolize the tin market in northern India for one year, at least. Another example of a monopolizing merchant is Virji Vohra, a Gujarati entrepreneur, who headed a huge trading network stretching from the Archipelago to the Middle East. For several decades he and his partners bought up virtually all the cargos of VOC ships arriving at Surat, and this enabled him to monopolize many selling markets of northern India. The Dutch could not teach him anything about how to effect a policy of dumping, use stocks to stabilize prices, or maintain a monopoly. Once, Virji Vohra even threatened to dump his stocks of cloves if the Company persisted in its plan to sell its goods to another merchant! Several similar examples could be given, showing that Gujarati merchants sought after market control — and sometimes attained it.

But not all market conditions proved favourable to some form of control by one or a few merchants. As I have tried to show, in Mocha the structure of the market did not allow for any stockpiling by a small group. Merchants from many different regions tried to sell their goods there, and the situation was complicated by the presence of this large group of pedlar pilgrims. Moreover, the fact that Mocha acted as a port of trans-shipment in a complex structure of long-distance trade made demand very unpredictable. Mocha was simply not a 'typical' Asian market. In fact, in my opinion many objections could be raised against the attempt to describe *the* Asian market or the behaviour of *the* Asian trader. The situation turns out to be so diverse that it is almost impossible to generalize. Market behaviour varied according to the conditions encountered in a particular market, the merchant sometimes trying, as the French company servant Georges Rogues remarked, to spread his risks by selling in many different markets, 'so that if in one place no profits are made, fortune favours him in another. This compensation permits him a subsistence.'[7] In many other markets however, the Indian merchant tried as hard as his Dutch colleague to diminish his risks by monopolization and to influence price developments by stockpiling.

But one may object that, if differences in entrepreneurial behaviour between the Asian and the western trader are considered to have been so small, how could the Company have appropriated a large proportion of intra-Asian trade, and monopolized trade in some very important products? What advantages did a Company have in Asia? F. S. Gaastra has rightly emphasized the difference in scale between the Asian and the Dutch trader, the world-wide trade connections of the VOC enabling it to compare market conditions in say, Amsterdam, Taiwan and Persia. The ability to gather information and to survey the situation in the whole of Asia (and in Europe as well) could have greatly influenced its position — at least in some markets.[8] Another major point is made by Steensgaard when he states that the companies successfully 'internalized their protection costs'. Looked at from a slightly different angle, one might say that the companies seem to have had at their disposal far greater technological and maritime means for enforcing their policies than were available to their Asian competitors (or to the Portuguese, for that matter). In most cases market control over a certain product was established only after the use of violence against Asian traders and their rulers. In short, force was a necessary and integrated part of the market strategy of the VOC.

One might add here that this use of force was not always possible or successful. At least two conditions had to be fulfilled. In the first place it was necessary that the production area of the crop, mineral, or manufactured article in which the VOC was interested should not be too large or too widely dispersed. Pepper, for instance, was grown in many different regions, and any attempt at monopolization would necessarily encounter many more difficulties than was the case with cloves or cinnamon. The second essential condition for any successful attempt at market control was that its effects on the other commercial interests in that area should not be too detrimental. The conflict necessary to deter the other merchants, or to force the local ruler to grant a monopoly position, should remain under control. The Company had realized very well that the attempt to monopolize the trade in cotton goods to the Middle East would have had serious consequences for its profitable trade in copper and spices with Mughal India, and for the export of cotton goods and indigo to Europe. In other words, the diversity of its trading interests in Mughal India acted as a guarantee against a total, all-pervading conflict between the Company and the Indian merchants and their rulers. As a consequence, Gujarati competition had to be tolerated. The risks of a more aggressive policy were simply too high.

We may conclude that in a situation where the Dutch could not make use of their world-wide 'information system', or where the risks of enforcing a more aggressive trade policy were considered too high, their position was rather weak. And, one might speculate, it possibly weakened still further during the eighteenth century as Dutch naval and military costs — necessary to maintain their monopolies — continued to rise, thus enabling other traders (such as the European country-traders with their low overhead costs) to take over.

In the preceding pages only one side of the trade between India and the Middle East has been described. But the Middle East was of importance to the Mughal economy not only as a selling market for piece goods and other Indian products. The precious metals with which the Gujarati merchants returned to Surat were equally important. The Middle East has, with some justification, been called 'the treasure chest of the Mughals'. Concluding this paper, I would like to give an interesting example of official Mughal interference in this trade — an example perhaps of a pre-modern policy aiming at export promotion. In my opinion there is a definite link between two phenomena: on the one hand a growing import of silver and gold by Gujarati merchants after 1650 (from an estimated Rs. 2 to 4 million a year before 1650 to approximately Rs. 3 to 6 million and more afterwards) and on the other hand a clearly increasing official involvement in this trade in the period 1651 – 1662.

It had always been quite normal for the Mughal and his family to own a few ships and to transport goods and pilgrims to the Middle East. But in the year 1651 Mughal involvement grew dramatically. Shah Jahan ordered the governor of Surat to have ten or twelve big ships built which were to be used in the carrying trade to Mocha and Persia. At the same time merchants were forbidden to ship any goods on non-Mughal vessels, at least as long as the 'King's ships' were not yet fully loaded. Until 1662 when Shah Jahan's successor Aurangzeb sold them, these huge Mughal ships virtually monopolized the carrying trade from Surat to Bandar Abbas and Mocha. But why did a Mughal king with his warrior ethos begin to act like a *bania* entrepreneur? Of course, one might suppose that he was simply lured by the profits to be made in the carrying trade. The VOC director at Surat gave, however, a much more fundamental and interesting reason for the entrepreneurial behaviour of Shah Jahan and Aurangzeb. According to him it was part of a more comprehensive policy. He wrote: 'Unless the king forced his subjects to continue this trade [to Persia and Mocha] few merchants would risk their money. All merchants of Surat are being taxed, however, in that each has to send several bales of goods to Mocha. But even while the king is aware that they will make very little profit, he forces them to do it. His aim is to sell the cotton goods produced in Hindustan and Gujarat (in which profession most of his subjects have to make a living) and thus attract an enormous sum of Spanish pieces of eight and ducats to his realm (the Mughal empire having no gold or silver mines of its own). And that is why the merchants have to continue in that trade, or else the craftsmen would be reduced to poverty.'⁹

In other words, by imposing an export quota upon the Gujarati traders and by providing the necessary ships to transport these goods, the Mughal hoped to stimulate foreign trade and to increase the amount of precious metals flowing into India. The ideas behind this policy do not seem to differ much from the arguments used by the so-called 'monetarists' or 'bullionists' of sixteenth and seventeenth century Europe. But why was this policy put into effect in the 1650s? And why was this experiment in a government-controlled carrying trade brought to an end after a few years, when Aurangzeb sold most of his ships? Was this temporary involvement perhaps connected with the declining Dutch import of gold and silver (which declined from between ƒ 500,000 and ƒ 1,100,000 a year to between ƒ 200,000 and ƒ 400,000), thus perhaps necessitating a more active policy to increase the total inflow of precious metals into India? And had Mughal involvement become superfluous after the big 'push' in the 1650s? We do not know exactly why but it is clear that, for some reason, official involvement was ended. In the first half of the eighteenth century there was absolutely no direct Mughal involvement in foreign trade, according to Das Gupta.¹⁰ A much more detailed knowledge of Mughal policy and the Indian economy will be needed before we are able to answer this question. The general point I would like to stress in this paper is, that we simply cannot treat trade as an isolated — and purely economic — phenomenon, and that the whole political and military context should be taken into account. We cannot describe a trading company like the VOC without analysing the use it made of its maritime and technological superiority, nor should the commercial activities of the Gujarati traders be studied without paying attention to outside influences. Trade and power, or trade and official policy, were never unrelated categories.

12

COUNTRY TRADE UNDER DANISH COLOURS: A STUDY OF ECONOMICS AND POLITICS AROUND 1800

Ole Feldbæk

Trade in Asia

'Country trade' may be defined as maritime trade between Asian ports. That is a fairly precise definition. But one should keep in mind, that country trade also includes the islands of Isle de France and Isle de Bourbon — present day Mauritius and Réunion — a fact which is important in this context. It also includes ports on the coast of east Africa, including the Cape of Good Hope — a fact which is of less importance here.[1]

One should also keep in mind, that country trade was not just a matter of Asian ships, Asian shipowners and merchants, and Asian goods. Admittedly, a very large portion of the country trade can be defined in this way. But country traders were also the East Indiamen, who called at ports on the coast of India on their way to Canton, or who 'lost' their voyage, and used the more or less enforced waiting period to sail between Asian ports, before they could return to Europe. And country traders were also Asian-built ships destined for Europe, which around 1800 quite often sailed between Asian ports picking up cargo and accumulating capital, before they finally set sail for Europe.

Furthermore, one should keep in mind the chronology. Country trade meant different things in 1500, 1600, 1700 and 1800. Around 1500 the Portuguese had encountered an old and wide network of maritime trade routes in Asia: routes between ports in East and Southeast Asia; routes between Malacca and ports on the coasts of India; and routes between India and ports in the Red Sea and the Persian Gulf, just to mention the main routes. These trade routes the Europeans entered mainly for two reasons. One was to procure cargoes for the European market. The other was to accumulate profit from the country trade, for their King, for their company — and for themselves as private individuals.

The main characteristics of the traditional country trade survived the arrival of the Europeans, but the European presence did, on the other

96

hand, bring changes. The most characteristic feature of the Portuguese
— and after them of the Dutch and the British — was their effort to
force this country trade — by military means, and by political and
economic means — to centre on Portuguese Goa and Malacca, Dutch
Batavia and English Madras. But the Europeans also opened up new
routes and introduced new types of goods. The most remarkable
example was the export of opium in large quantities from English
Calcutta to southern China, partly as an ancillary source of finance for
the English East India Company's China trade, partly as a trade in its
own right and for its own profit.

   Another important factor in the country trade was the emergence of
large European settlements in South and Southeast Asia: Spanish
Manila, Dutch Batavia, French Pondicherry and Port Louis, and British
Bombay, Madras and Calcutta: settlements whose existence to a high
degree depended upon country trade and upon economic enterprises in
the hinterland. Furthermore these European settlements were dependent on European goods — mainly consumer goods and naval stores —
and on remittance of goods and capital to Europe, both in peace and in
war. And the commerce of these settlements was no longer just a matter
of a few company servants and some free merchants and free mariners
who needed outlets for their private economic activities — be they
lawful or be they unlawful. Towards the end of the eighteenth century
regular merchant houses or agency houses were operating, with
widespread economic and financial interests, and in close contact with a
host of correspondents in Asian and European ports, regardless of
company monopolies and nationalities.

   Towards the end of the eighteenth century this country trade under
various European flags was a tangled web of competition and co-
operation. To a certain degree it was competition in the basic economic
sense of the word. But it was also a matter of political competition, as
the European governments and companies gradually realized the
dependence of their Asian settlements upon the country trade. But
country trade was also a form of co-operation. The European
shipowners and merchants suffered widely from divided loyalties. They
were torn between their loyalty to their masters in Europe, and their
loyalty to their own private economic interests and those of their
foreign business connections, be they English, Dutch or French, or be
they for that matter Protestants or Catholics. For a long time the
Europeans who were engaged in country trade simply refused to permit
a state of war in Europe to interfere with their trade. They just carried
on an uninterrupted trade with one another, covered for decency's sake
by some neutral flag; and company servants and free merchants and
mariners alike obligingly shut their eyes to the flimsy camouflage under
which their political opponents operated.

But this Arcadia was not to last forever. For one thing, commanders of English and French squadrons in Asian waters had other loyalties — and also a healthy appetite for rich prizes and for prize money. And the governments in Europe — acknowledging the rising political and military importance of the settlements in Asia — began to take over the political and military management of the settlements from the companies. The French did it in 1769; the English did it with the India Act in 1784; and the Dutch did it in 1796. Wars in Europe were no longer just something one read about in letters and newspapers from home. War between the European powers became a harsh reality to the European shipowners, merchants and agency houses, and to the European governors in the settlements in the East. War in Europe interfered with the country trade for the first time during the Revolutionary Wars. From February 1793 France and England were at war. In 1795 Holland joined the war against England. And in 1796 Spain did the same. The four great maritime powers were now at war. That meant business to the neutrals, and among the neutrals were the Danes.

Exploitation of Neutrality

The Danish governor in Tranquebar and the Danish chief in Serampore were authorized to issue passports for ships belonging to Danish subjects, including of course Indian shipowners resident in the two small Danish settlements. As soon as the news of the war reached India, the number of Tranquebar and Serampore ships started to grow. And with the spread of war — and with the intensification of the warfare — this growth accelerated.

Statistics on Serampore ships — their owners, their tonnage, their captains and their destinations — have not survived. We can see the number of Serampore ships growing, but we are not in a position to give serial statistical information, such as we are able to do for Tranquebar during some — though not all — of the war years from 1793 to 1807. We shall therefore concentrate mainly on the Tranquebar ships which — by the way — represented the majority of the country ships under Danish colours around 1800.[2]

Before the war there had only been a handful of country ships from Tranquebar, scarcely totalling a thousand tons. In 1793, however, passports were issued for at least 20 ships of an aggregate tonnage of about 5,000 tons. In 1794 another 20 passports were issued, also totalling about 5,000 tons. In 1795 — when news of Holland's entry into the war reached India — the number of Tranquebar passports rose to 43, totalling more than 16,000 tons. In 1796 the number of passports rose further, to 67, now totalling almost 25,000 tons. And in 1797 the number of passports reached 74, likewise totalling almost 25,000 tons.

Here the statistical series is broken for the following five years, and it will be necessary to rely upon an impression based on other types of material.[3] The impression is, that the number of country ships under Danish colours remained at this level — or perhaps *almost* at this level — till the war between England and Denmark in 1801 and the short-lived peace between England and France 1802 – 1803, where the country trade under Danish colours was reduced to its low pre-war level. But when the war broke out again in 1803, the tonnage under Danish colours once again started to grow. It did not, however, grow above the level of the early war years of 1793 and 1794. In 1804 and 1805 the governor of Tranquebar issued some twenty passports totalling about 5,000 tons per year. But this was not to last. In 1807 war broke out between Denmark and England; Tranquebar and Serampore were occupied by the British; and the Danish flag totally disappeared from Asian waters for a period of seven years.

Without going into the details of, *why* this remarkable rise in country trade under Danish colours happened, or *how* it did, it can be said that the belligerents transferred a large number of their ships ostensibly under Danish ownership — although one should not overlook the fact that a considerable number of Danes did actually participate in the shipping and trade for their own account as well. From 1793 onwards, however, a significant part of the European country trade was carried on under cover of the neutral Danish flag — mostly the French, the Dutch and the Spanish country trade, but also to some extent the English country trade.

A regular traffic in passports from Tranquebar and Serampore now developed. In some cases the owner of the ships in question ordered his Danish agent to take out passports, and furnished the Dane with the relevant information about the ship. In other cases blank passports were taken out by a Dane, that is, where the data about the ship was not filled in until need arose. It is a fact that most of the Danish civil servants — if not all of them — and most of the Danes residing in Tranquebar and Serampore acted as agents in this way, and procured the requested neutral camouflage in return for a handsome bribe or even a fixed percentage of the venture. The second-in-council in Tranquebar, Frantz von Lichtenstein, became quite notorious in this line of business, and was referred to all over the Indian Ocean as '*notre ami le cinq pour cent*' or as '*le marchand des passeports*'.[4] The Danish authorities were not squeamish, but surprise was registered in Tranquebar, when a Danish ship was stopped by a French privateer from Isle de France, which requisitioned some provisions from the Danish ship — and then paid for them with a bill of exchange drawn on von Lichtenstein.[5] And being a God-fearing man, the governor of Tranquebar was regularly embarrassed, when twenty-year-old Danish mates pledged their souls and testified on oath that they were the real and true owners of formerly French ships of 500 tons or more. But it is part of the picture, that they got their passports, all the same.[6]

Areas of operation

We meet with these Tranquebar and Serampore country ships everywhere in the network of maritime trade routes, as far West as Surat and Muscat, and as far East as Canton and Manila. In 1799 a Serampore ship even had the honour to sail as a tender ship for the Acapulco Galleon. But the significant areas of operation were the coastal trade of India, the traffic with Isle de France, and the trade 'to the Eastward', that is the trade with Malayan ports, with Dutch ports in Indonesia, and with Canton and Manila.[7] It should be emphasized, though, that although there was a certain specialization as to routes and goods, the ships moved fairly freely between these three areas of operation.

The most important area of operation — as far as the number of ships was concerned — was the coastal trade of India, including the West Coast and Ceylon, but with the East Coast being where most ships operated.[8] The ships upheld the trade between the various European settlements, and they transported indiscriminately European goods — such as consumer goods, naval stores and metals — and Indian goods like rice, salt, piece goods and pepper.

Quite another type of country trade was the traffic between India and Isle de France.[9] The French islands were thorns in the flesh of the British, primarily because they were bases for privateers; but also because the French government in Europe — by way of the Islands and Tranquebar — was able to keep up contacts with Indian princes hostile to the British. Not until 1810, however, were the British able to occupy these last strongholds of the French in the East. Till then, therefore, privateers and naval vessels from the islands cruised in the Indian Ocean and in the Bay of Bengal, and a considerable number of British ships were taken and brought to the islands for sale. The Tranquebar and Serampore ships were instrumental in furnishing the French islands with provisions, and to a certain degree, also with the naval stores so desperately needed for fitting out the privateers. Furthermore, the country ships under Danish colours were busily engaged in transporting the formerly British owned cargoes to buyers in Asia and Europe. And last, but not least, a number of the British prizes, which were sold cheaply in Port Louis, returned to India under Danish colours, and here they were sold back to the British at prices considerably lower than the costs of buying or building new ships.

Still quite another type of country trade was the traffic to the Eastward: the trade between India and the Malayan Archipelago, Canton and Manila. This was primarily a trade in Indian textiles and opium, and the ships returned to Calcutta and Madras in ballast, with chests of Spanish silver dollars. Calcutta's commerce to the Eastward was in 1793 a fairly new branch of trade, but an extremely lucrative one. After 1793 Serampore ships were used in this traffic, partly to cover the property of the English agency houses in Calcutta and partly to cloak the trade of the wealthy Armenian merchant community in Bengal.[10]

Trade and politics

Taking a look at the country trade under Danish colours in the decades around 1800, it is, therefore, not possible to say that it *only* helped Britain's enemies, and that it *only* operated against British interests. The picture is more complicated than that. On the other hand, all things being considered, there can be no doubt, that it *mainly* helped Britain's enemies, and that it *mainly* frustrated Britain's war efforts, just as most activities under neutral flags tended to do during the Revolutionary wars and the Napoleonic Wars all over the world.

The question is, therefore: why didn't the British do anything about it?

One possible answer is that they did not know what was going on under the neutral Danish flag. But that possibility can be dismissed off hand. They knew all they needed to know — and a good deal more than that.[11] That was why the British envoy in Copenhagen flatly declared that open war with Denmark would be preferable to the Danish version of neutrality.[12] And that was why the governor-general in Calcutta urged the British cabinet 'to render a most important service to our national interests in this part of the world, if you could devise any means of annihilating the whole of these petty European states throughout the continent of India, but above all those of Tranquebar and Serampore'.[13]

Both London and Calcutta knew very well that if there were no neutrals to buy the prizes and their cargoes in Port Louis, French privateering would be deprived of its economic incentive, and would come to a stop of itself.[14] They also knew that without neutral shipping and trade the Dutch in Java would find it very difficult to keep the Indonesian princes dependent, while Britain as a great power had all the material resources necessary to put pressure on a neutral small power such as Denmark with minuscule and totally defenceless settlements in India.

Part of the answer lies in the fact that the British cabinet traditionally gave a much lower priority to Indian affairs than to European affairs. It considered it inexpedient to provoke even one of the smaller European powers such as Denmark to such an extent that it sought closer political contacts with France. English governors-general knew that London would not allow them to intervene against the smaller European powers in Asia to a degree that might create trouble between the courts in Europe — and the representatives of the smaller European powers in India knew that too — and acted accordingly. Even a forceful British governor-general such as Lord Wellesley, therefore, had to accept most of what was going on in Tranquebar and Serampore, however detrimental to British interests in Asia. He did force an official English agent upon the governor of Tranquebar, in order to put a stop to the French contacts with Tipu Sahib of Mysore by way of the Danish settlement, and to put a stop to the collecting of naval and commercial intelligence for the benefit of the French privateers.[15] But when it came to the large-scale Danish sale of neutral camouflage to the shipping and trade of Britain's enemies, he did virtually nothing.

This is even more surprising, considering that he in fact had the legal means to do so. According to English law, a former British ship taken by the enemy and sold to neutrals, could be given back to the original British owner, just by paying the neutral owner one eighth of the value of the ship in salvage.[16] But Lord Wellesley did not even use this legal instrument, which would undoubtedly have removed at least part of the economic incentive behind the French privateering.

Why he did not do it — and why he did not make use of the other means he actually had, to set limits to these activities so harmful to British warfare, we do not know for certain.

It is, however, possible to point to what might have been at least part of the reason. Namely, that although the governor-general since the India Act of 1784 was the representative of the British cabinet in the political sphere, the days of divided loyalties in Asia were not yet over. The British agency houses in Calcutta, Madras and Bombay did also benefit from the easy access to neutral camouflage, not least in their trade to the Eastward. Furthermore, they much preferred to buy back their ships taken by the French, at a reasonably low price by way of agents in Tranquebar and Serampore, rather than paying high prices for new ships. And after Parliament in 1793 had refused to give the trade between England and India free, they still needed neutral settlements like Serampore and Tranquebar for their remittance of goods and capital to Europe in circumvention of the English East India Company's monopoly.[17]

Such were *their* interests. Also, an ambitious governor-general such as Lord Wellesley knew very well that he needed the financial goodwill and the active economic support of the agency houses for his aggressive policy towards establishing a British hegemony over India. He also knew that the agency houses knew that he knew![18]

So even around 1800, the days of divided loyalties and of divided interests between home government and colonial administration were not yet over. That may — at least to some extent — provide an answer to the question why the country trade under Danish colours flourished so remarkably in the years around 1800.

13

DANISH COUNTRY TRADE ROUTES IN ASIAN WATERS IN THE SEVENTEENTH AND EIGHTEENTH CENTURIES

Erik Gøbel

Introduction

From the middle of the seventeenth century to the middle of the nineteenth, Denmark was one of the minor European colonial powers, but even so, the Danish king held sway over a complete Lilliputian overseas empire.

Apart from Norway with the Faroe Islands, Iceland and Greenland, Denmark's most important possessions in the tropics were: a territory on the Gold Coast with the principal forts Christiansborg and Fredensborg (occupied from the middle of the seventeenth century to 1850); the three small Caribbean islands of St. Thomas, St. John and St. Croix (acquired in 1671, 1718 and 1733 respectively, but all sold in 1917); as well as Tranquebar on the Coromandel Coast (from 1620 to 1845) and Serampore in Bengal (from 1750 to 1845) both in India. Furthermore, the Danish crown possessed some lesser factories in Asia at times, e.g. in Masulipatam on the Coromandel Coast, Pipli and Balasore in Bengal, Cochin and Calicut on the coast of Malabar, Bantam in Java and Macassar in Celebes.

Although the adjoining overseas land areas remained small, their importance to Denmark was not inconsiderable. This was true especially from an economic point of view, as the main purpose of the acquisition of colonies was to establish and advance Danish overseas navigation and commerce. This policy was a success in the eighteenth century, particularly during the many world wars between 1756 and 1807. In this period the Danish government succeeded in keeping the country neutral, and consequently Danish vessels and merchants were able to take over a considerable share of international shipping and trade, while the merchant fleets of the warring great powers were greatly restricted.

A number of the basic political and economic conditions relevant to a small power like Denmark were to some extent atypical of the European Asia trade as such. But conditions imposed by nature, that is on the seas, were fully applicable to all nations, as were technical and navigational circumstances. These common conditions were reflected in the common nautical patterns.

Let us then take a preliminary look at the Danish material, to learn what information it contains about proper country trade as well as about European shipping between different trading ports in Asia.

Literature and unpublished material

Danish literature on navigation in Asian waters is scarce, and deals mainly with the eighteenth century — a fact resulting from the very fragmentary archival material, relating in particular to the seventeenth century.

Another bias in the maritime sources is that they contain information predominantly about European ships, especially those of the chartered trading companies. Thus the Danish Asiatic Company's archives contain a lot of information about navigation between Copenhagen and Asia from 1732 on. Among other things ships' logs and ships' ledgers from all Company expeditions to India, Isle de France, Batavia and Canton are preserved. On the other hand, private Danish India trade is only poorly represented in the sources, although it outnumbered that of the Company after 1775.

To throw light on the short-distance country trade along the coast of Coromandel, I have made use of the Tranquebar sea-toll registers, which are presented below.

Long-distance country trade is investigated by means of the Tranquebar sea-pass protocols, supplemented by ships' logs and the like.

A later section of this paper contains a presentation of the most important literature about Danish navigation in Asian waters throughout the seventeenth and eighteenth centuries.

Country trade in the seventeenth century

As suggested, country trade under the Danish flag or in Danish ports in Asia throughout the seventeenth century is rather difficult to define, but its main features were as follows.

As early as in the 1620s, cotton cloths were exported from Tranquebar to Achin in Sumatra, Bantam in Java and Macassar in

the Celebes, from where rice, pepper and spices, respectively, were
imported. In addition, the Danes were at the same time in
commercial contact, although less profitably, with Siam, Bengal and
Cochin.

Towards the end of the 1630s and in the beginning of the 1640s, the
most important Danish country trade route connected Masulipatam,
if convenient via Tranquebar, with Macassar. Furthermore, vessels
were sent to Persia. But gradually Bengal became an important
destination for the Tranquebar vessels. Of course the trade centre of
Madras, situated just 200 kilometres to the north of Tranquebar, was
a most important trade partner throughout, and might even be
reached by rather small craft.

Around 1645, the most significant ports of trade for the Danes in
India were: Porto Novo, Tegnapatam, Pondicherry, Palicat (all on
the Coast of Coromandel); moreover Macassar; and to a lesser extent
Bantam, Achin, Kedah, Banjarmasin, Cherapon, Japara (in the
Sunda Isles); Emeldy (in Bengal); as well as ports in Ceylon, such as
Cotiari.

Often trade was conducted at several places on the way. In 1647 a
vessel sent from Tranquebar to Macassar, called at Bantam,
Cherapon, Batavia and Japara — on its way out, as well as on the way
home.

The years from 1648 to 1669 were slack and a strain on the Danes
on the Coromandel. They lacked capital and personnel, and most
trade connections were interrupted. According to an English letter,
written in Madraspatam in 1651, the Danes 'are quite blown up'.

Nevertheless, around 1670 navigation to Porto Novo, Achin and
Bengal was resumed, while shipping to Malacca, Bantam and Japara
was particularly flourishing. At this time, sporadic sailings from
Tranquebar to China were attempted as well. (Otherwise this remote
country was not reached directly from Denmark until 1731.)
Furthermore, an active trade with Arabia grew up in the 1670s —
which was cancelled in 1681.

For the rest of the seventeenth century, the Danish colours were
most frequently seen along the Coromandel, in Achin and Malacca.
Also the coast of Malabar, and in particular, Bengal, became of
increasing importance as trading partners to Tranquebar.

As mentioned, the source material from the seventeenth century is
exceedingly fragmentary, and often in a bad state of preservation.
Consequently, it is not possible to assess the number of expeditions
or quantities of goods. The country trade of that century is known
only in broad outline.

Country trade in the eighteenth century

During the Northern War 1709 – 1720, both the Dano-Indian society and country trade under the Danish flag languished. However, the establishment of the Danish Asiatic Company in 1732 resulted in Danish activities being resumed on a full scale.

During the eighteenth century, by far the most important long-distance country trade routes were those connecting the Coromandel with Bengal, and Bengal with China. But besides this general trend, the Danes experienced some years of hectic activity between Tranquebar and Isle de France around 1800. Still, however, the short-distance country trade along the coast of Coromandel was the most extensive.

I have investigated the Tranquebar sea-toll registers for the accounting years of 1780/1781, 1785/1786 and 1790/1791. (The accounting year ran from 1 August to 31 July.) These sea-toll registers are preserved in a nearly unbroken series from 1778 to 1823. The only *lacunae* cover the two periods from 13 May 1801 to 16 August 1802 and from 1 August 1807 to 19 September 1815, when the Danish possessions were occupied by the British.

In the accounts, one will find an entry for each vessel arriving at or departing from Tranquebar — but of course only vessels that had a cargo to declare. In the beginning the entries recorded the date, owner of goods, type of vessel, port of departure or destination, cargo, and amount of customs paid. For instance, on 20 April 1790: 'a thony came to Harrop & Stevenson from Pondicherry, in which was [description of cargo]', plus specification of customs dues paid.

But rather soon after 1778, the practice of recording ports of departure or destination was often neglected. So the number of entries for which this sort of information is missing was 5% in 1780/1781, 1% in 1785/1786, and as much as 42% in 1790/1791.

Furthermore, many commodities did not have to be declared, they just passed the bonded warehouse of the town. On the whole, the government was very pragmatic, and endeavoured to charge trade as little as possible. Tariff rates consequently amounted to only 4% on imports and 2% on exports. Finally one has to keep in mind, when evaluating these as well as other customs accounts, the existence of smuggling, as well as the practice of giving false indications of localities.

Probably for these reasons, the Tranquebar sea-toll registers have so far only been made use of by only one or two researchers.

Anyway, let us investigate the registers — and keep in mind the reservations mentioned above. This means that all the following numbers are to be regarded as minima.

The three years, i.e. 1780/1781 and 1785/1786 and 1790/1791, constitute a random sample. In this a total of 744 expeditions are mentioned, of which 504 were arriving and 240 departing vessels. Correspondingly, 290 craft arrived in Tranquebar during the year 1782/1783 while 147 departed.

The geographic distribution of ports of departure of the vessels arriving in Tranquebar did not vary in the years examined. Destinations of departing vessels changed in the following way: while the nearest ports on the Coromandel were visited by 34% of all vessels in the war-year of 1780/1781, their share more than doubled in the years of peace that came after; on the contrary, 1780/1781 experienced a dense traffic to Madras with 15 vessels, which implied that the ports far away on the Coromandel were visited by 34% of the departing vessels, while this proportion was reduced to about 20% in the two years of peace, 1785/1786 and 1790/1791.

Besides, the complete figures for the three years combined are shown in Table 1.

Table 1. *Ports of arrival and departure for vessels at Tranquebar*

1780/1781, 1785/1786, 1790/1791	arriving vessels		departing vessels	
Near Coromandel	343	68%	154	64%
Rest of Coromandel	74	15%	55	23%
Ceylon	32	6%	13	5%
Malabar Coast	5	1%	3	1%
Bengal	11	2%	1	0%
Nicobar Islands	2	0%	–	–
Sunda Islands and Malacca	14	3%	1	0%
China	3	1%	1	0%
Europe	6	1%	8	3%
Unknown position of departure/ destination	14	3%	4	2%
Total	504		240	

Noteworthy is the fact that, in addition to the vessels in the table, the sea-toll registers mention 123 vessels without indication of place of departure and 67 without place of destination. But as 106 and 61, respectively, stem from the year of 1790/1791, this matter of missing information is only of minor importance to the results of the analysis.

Among those without indication of departure or destination quite a lot of European ships to or from Europe or engaged in country trade are hidden. Europe, and especially Bengal, are mentioned too seldom in the sea-toll accounts. Control against supplementary information, containing captains' names and the like, has indeed shown Europe or Bengal as ports of departure or destination for a number of these ships.

In the table, Near Coromandel has been defined as ports within a distance of 100 kilometres from Tranquebar, the most important places to the north thus being Pondicherry (French) and Porto Novo (Dutch, but functioning as a quasi-free port and international mart). To the south the most essential ports were Carical (French), Nagore (British) and Negapatam (Dutch).

Among the ports nearby, the 1780s apparently saw a strong increase in the interchange with Pondicherry and Nagore; whereas the Dutch towns or Porto Novo and Negapatam lost their former importance as suppliers to the Danes in Tranquebar.

The rest of the Coromandel was first and foremost represented by Tondi and Madras (British). These towns were situated on the coast about 200 kilometres to the north and south respectively.

Fluctuations in Tranquebar sea customs receipts between 1779/1780 and 1806/1807 are shown in Fig. 1. Receipts are in Tranquebar current rix-dollars, and include both imports and exports.

It is obvious that the town experienced the peak of its activities between 1779/1780 and 1785/1786. On the other hand, a new boom set in during the Revolutionary and Napoleonic Wars.

With a reasonable degree of certainty, it can be seen from the sea-toll registers how nautical activities were distributed according to the seasons.

During three different five-year periods chosen at random, i.e. 1779/1780 – 1783/1784 and 1789/1790 – 1793/1794 and 1799/1800 – 1800/1801 with 1802/1803 – 1804/1805, a significant seasonal variation is seen. This is clearly demonstrated by computing three-months moving averages from the shares of the months of the sea-toll receipts for each of the five-year periods. The result is shown in Fig 2, in which each five-year curve is shown twice.

From this it is evident that shipping was most infrequent in winter, mainly from October to December, when local navigation was

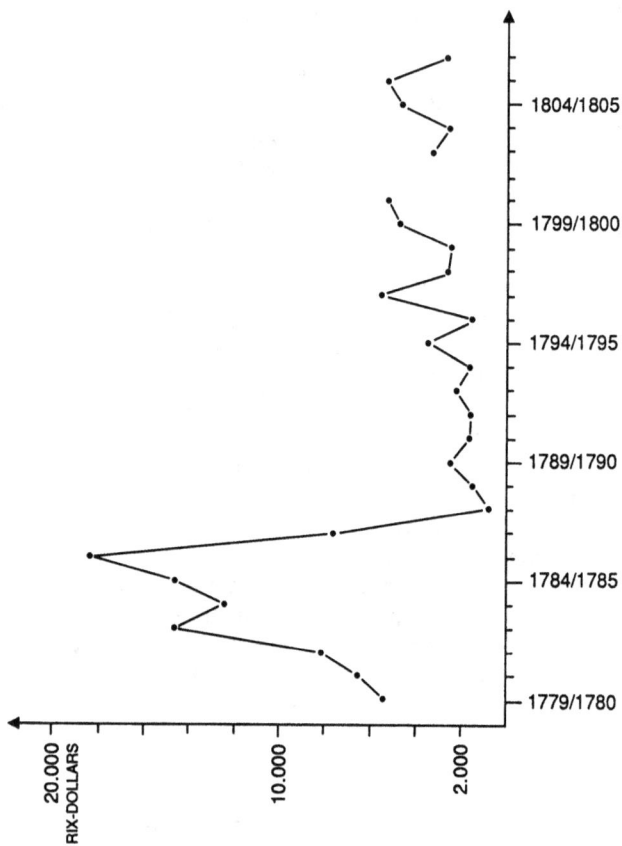

Fig. 1. Sea Customs receipts at Tranquebar.

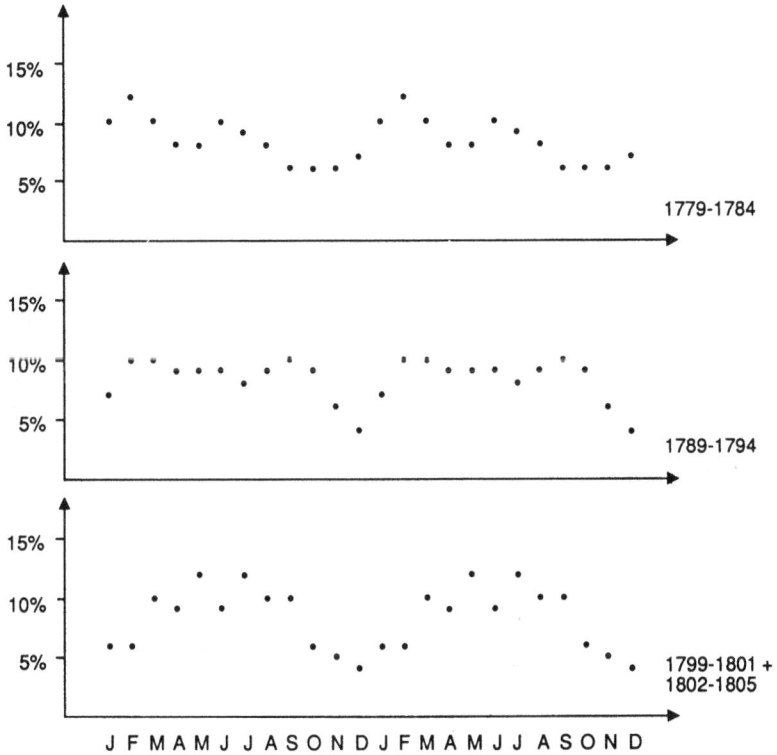

Fig. 2. Seasonal variations of sea-toll receipts averaged for each of the five-year periods.

heavily impeded by the north-east monsoons, and at a time of year when ships from Europe had not yet arrived.

Conversely, shipping activities at Tranquebar reached their peak in spring and summer, especially in March and July. This picture in the sea-toll registers may partly be attributed to the fact that during this season, as a rule, the big ships arrived from Europe with rather extensive cargoes to declare.

Among the small coasting vessels, the types most frequently mentioned were: *selling* and *thony*, of which the latter was named *double selling* also. Even bigger, but still rather common, were *sloop* and *ship*, while *catamaran* and *boat* were smaller than the *selling*.

A common feature of all the above-mentioned — and many other types of what we may call pure country trade vessels mentioned in the Tranquebar customs accounts — was that as a rule they were the property of Indians. Their crews consisted of Indians, too, who were engaged in a kind of tramp trade or *cabotage* up and down the coast.

The bigger ships that went by the routes to distant destinations were owned mostly by Europeans. These freighted products e.g. from Dutch or French colonies to Tranquebar — or directly to Europe. A few of these ships are mentioned in the Danish customs accounts, but most of them did not export goods from or import commodities to Tranquebar. At most the cargoes passed the bonded warehouse of the town, where they were allowed to stay for a year without being declared.

The volume of this navigation with big European ships is suggested by the issue of sea passes in Tranquebar. This is known for the years from 1793 to 1797 only, during which period 242 passes were issued; each was valid for one expedition. But as was the case with the sea-toll registers, the sea-pass accounts record only minimum figures. These are shown in Table 2.

In addition, we know that 84 big ships owned by Europeans arrived in Tranquebar in 1800. In 1795 – 1796 the corresponding number was 104 vessels, of which 69 were under the Danish colours, 25 were British and 10 were of other nations.

In dealing with conditions in Tranquebar, it must be kept in mind that after the American War of Independence, the centre of gravity of Danish Asian trade was no longer on the Coromandel Coast, but in Bengal. The factory in Serampore, which bore the official Danish name of Frederiksnagore, was situated 150 kilometres up the River Hugli, immediately north of Calcutta.

From Serampore no customs accounts whatever are preserved. On the other hand, it is known that in the accounting year of 1793/1794, customs receipts amounted to around 14,000 Tranquebar current rix-

Table 2. *The issue of sea passes at Tranquebar*

	number of sea passes issued	of which for exp. to Isle de Fr.	of which for exp. to Batvia
1793	27	3	–
1794	23	2	1
1795	37	17	1
1796	71	13	15
1797	84	17	15
Total	242	52	32

dollars in Serampore, compared to only a little more than 2,000 rix-dollars in Tranquebar. In the years up to 1807, receipts in Serampore were continually twice as high as in Tranquebar. In 1796, therefore, the Danish Asiatic Company had taken the consequences of the altered situation and ordered the factory at Tranquebar to be closed.

At the same time, however, a new trade came into being under cover of the Danish colours. The phenomenon in question was navigation between Danish possessions and Isle de France — a trade in which the role of Serampore was inferior. As early as during the American War of Independence, a few ships had been sent to Isle de France and Isle de Bourbon from Tranquebar, together with one from Copenhagen. But as the normal lines of supply to the islands were interrupted by the British blockade during the Revolutionary and Napoleonic Wars, navigation under the Danish flag was established instead. Furthermore, the wars meant that French privateers operated from the islands, where British prizes were now sold at rather cheap prices — a possibility Danes learned to profit by.

The volume of Danish navigation to the French islands is reflected in the above-mentioned number of sea passes issued in Tranquebar. Between 1793 and 1797 a total of 53 such documents mentioned Isle de France as destination. But Peter Anker, governor of Tranquebar, 1788 – 1806, made an official report to the Board of Commerce in Copenhagen, calling attention to the fact that the majority of ships at that time went to Isle de France, no matter what was written in their sea passes.

Furthermore, he mentioned that of the rest, a great part went to Batavia — as the Dutch, just like the French, had become involved in a war with Britain, the ruler of the seas.

Besides Danish intra-Asiatic navigation to the foreign colonies blockaded by the British, ships were sent out from Denmark. No less than 55 of these so-called return voyages to Isle de France were carried out in the period from 1794 to 1806 (16 of these from 1794 to 1797), as well as 73 voyages from Copenhagen to Batavia in the years from 1795 to 1807 (14 of these from 1795 to 1797).

European ships in country trade

Danish trade and navigation between Copenhagen and Asian ports has been rather thoroughly investigated already. But a particular aspect of this trade was navigation between different Asian towns carried out by the big Danish ships arriving from Europe. These activities are most reliably studied in relation to the Asiatic Company's ships.

Between 1732 and 1807, the Company equipped 125 'Chinamen'. As a rule they did not call at any Asian ports on their way to or from Canton. Only at the Sunda Strait did they make a short stop to get fresh water and food on board.

But from 1758 on, some of the Company's 'Chinamen' made use of the Middle or, more often, the Outer Passage through the Indian Ocean. By doing so, they were able to call at Tranquebar on their way to Canton. This practice became more and more common in the following years; thus each year from 1771 to 1785 a ship bound for China visited Tranquebar, (except for 1774, but against this two called in 1784).

In 1758, the Danish Company tried to send one of its 'Chinamen' via Surat on its way out, but this experiment was never repeated. During the American War of Independence, three expeditions were attempted, sailing via Malacca to Canton.

During the Revolutionary and Napoleonic Wars, the Danish Asiatic Company sent two 'Chinamen' via Manila — a trade which had been of some importance to the Danish pure country trade since the Spanish crown in 1742 issued a *cedula* opening Manila to Danish ships; this trade was resumed after 1814. Finally, an attempt to send a 'Chinaman' from Copenhagen via Bombay in 1795 was tried, but without success.

The aim of these deviations from the direct route was of course to conduct trade in the different Asian ports. In Tranquebar the

European cargo, if any, was unloaded, and instead Bengal cloth was taken on board, as well as saltpetre and opium for the Chinese market. Part of the opium was often sold in Malacca, which was situated *en route* from India to China; often Malayan tin was taken in at Malacca.

From Canton, all ships returned directly to Denmark with no calls in Asia. Only one of the Asiatic Company's ships fell outside this pattern. The little *Frederiksnagore* of 400 tons burden departed from Copenhagen in February 1775, and after having called at Coromandel and Bengal, it arrived in Canton, from where it returned to Tranquebar to form a part of the country trade fleet of that town.

During the Danish Asiatic Company's second charter period from 1772 to 1792, more than half of 37 proper East Indiamen went both to Tranquebar and Serampore — as well as to foreign trading stations along the Coromandel Coast. In that way operations in Indian waters lasted on an average of 221 days, compared to 89 days among ships that only called at either Serampore or Tranquebar.

Part of the extra time, of course, was spent *en route* between Tranquebar and Serampore. But often the Danish ships took in cargo along the Coromandel; for instance, there is the example of the East Indiaman *Disco*, which in 1790 – 1791 on its way from the Cape of Good Hope called at Port Louis in Isle de France, from where it continued to Tranquebar, and further on with anchorings for a few days at Madras, Masulipatam, Coringo and Vizagapatam, eventually to reach Serampore. On its way home the ship stopped at Vizagapatam, Coringo and Tranquebar to take aboard the cloth ordered. At the same time, the *Prinsen af Augustenborg* touched at Tranquebar, Madras, Pondicherry, Tranquebar, Pondicherry, Madres and Serampore, before returning directly from Bengal to Europe.

During the period from 1792 to1807, the Danish Asiatic Company's Indiamen seldom called at both Tranquebar and Serampore. Out of 25 expeditions, only 6 touched at both Danish towns.

To what degree these European Company vessels constituted part of the country trade between the Coromandel and Bengal is debatable. The same applies to the private return expeditions under the Danish flag between 1775 and 1807. Of these, at least 51 ships of 22,000 tons total burden are known to have called at Bengal as well as ports along the coast.

In particular during the Revolutionary and Napoleonic Wars, Danish private ships participated in long-distance interchange of goods within Asia. The most prominent ports were, besides the Danish ones: Port Louis, Pondicherry, Madras and Batavia. Thus, for example, the *Expedition* in 1804 – 1805 went by the route from

Copenhagen to Isle de France, Tranquebar and Batavia, before
returning to Copenhagen.

Conclusion

What has been presented above is certainly but a preliminary and
cursory draft.

The material indicates, however, that it will be possible to
reconstruct the main features of Danish country trade routes in Asian
waters in the seventeenth century and especially the eighteenth
century.

In the preserved Danish material, to a certain degree supplemented
by foreign sources and literature, two main types of activities stand
out. One has to do with the Danes involved in long-distance country
trade carried out in big European ships. The other concerns the
Indians who were involved in short-distance country trade by means
of small local vessels, predominantly engaged in trade along the
coast of Coromandel.

But as suggested, it is impossible to make a clear-cut distinction
between European trade and pure country trade. After all, it is
evident that the Danes in Asia belonged to a neutral small power.
Consequently, they experienced the culmination of their activities
when the great powers were at war with each other.

14

BEADS AND BRONZES: ARCHAEOLOGICAL INDICATORS OF TRADE BETWEEN THAILAND AND THE EARLY BUDDHIST CIVILIZATIONS OF NORTHERN INDIA

Ian C. Glover

Much is asserted, little is proven. In the absence of a suitable, easily accessible body of evidence, hypothesis replaces fact and the passage of time produces the assumption that what was tentatively suggested in a previous decade is, in the absence of contravention, established proof.[1]

In this paper I am presenting some relatively new evidence from excavations at the cemetery site of Ban Don Ta Phet in Western Thailand which bears directly on the question of the economic, social and religious transactions between India and mainland Southeast Asia at the turn of the Christian era.

Introduction

The influence of Indian Hindu-Buddhist civilization in Southeast Asia from the middle of the first millennium A.D. is undeniable and found almost everywhere other than in the remote and forested mountainous interior of the mainland and larger islands, or in the eastern islands of Indonesia and the Philippines.

From this time onwards, we have numerous religious icons and monuments modelled on Indian prototypes, inscriptions using Indian scripts and languages, and a few ambiguous external historical sources; Chinese and Indian. These data have provided most of the evidence for Indianization, and are fully presented and analysed in numerous books and articles of which I will only mention Coedes' authoritative *The Indianized States of Southeast Asia*, Wolter's *Early Indonesian Commerce*, and Wheatley's *Nagara and Commandery*.

Most historians treating this period accept that this pervasive Indian influence developed along an established commercial network with roots extending back into prehistory; van Leur, for instance, writing on early Indonesian trade[2] states, 'In my opinion there must have been

Indian trade in the archipelago earlier than Chinese trade . . . the trade
was in valuable high quality products. In it spices, drugs, expensive
sorts of wood, exotic birds and other curiosities were shipped out of
Indonesia and similar Indian and Near Eastern wares were brought in'.
To identify such transactions before the period of written history the
only reliable form of data is that produced by field archaeology and
this, for various reasons, has been slow to develop in Southeast Asia,
particularly in the area of later prehistory and early protohistory.

Historical and archaeological sources

A generation ago Wheeler published a comprehensive and still useful
survey of the archaeological evidence for the long-distance trade of the
Roman World. With the aid of Western historical sources such as the
Periplus, Strabo, Ptolemy and Pliny, and Indian epigraphic and
archaeological finds he was able[3] to develop a convincing framework
for Indian commercial links with the west. Since he wrote there have
been new finds (summarized in Raschke 1978 and Christie 1979) but
not so many as to require a complete revision of Wheeler's thesis.
Discussing Southeast Asia, Wheeler was able to point only to a few
imported pieces of sculpture and the famous bronze lamp from P'ong
Tuk on the Meklong River in Western Thailand,[4] and the more or less
systematic excavations by Malleret[5] at Oc-eo in the Mekong Delta of
Vietnam where sculpture, inscribed gemstones and rings, and a coin of
Antoninus Pius of A.D. 152 point to clear, if not very precisely dated
links with India and the Mediterranean world. The Periplus and other
western historical sources provide no intelligible framework for
commerce with 'Chryse the Golden, the very last land towards the east'
and the reports of the Chinese envoys K'ang T'ai and Chou Ying in the
middle of the third century A.D.[6] inform us about political, religious
and social affairs in the land of Funan, but say little about commercial
links to the west, although they do testify to the adoption in Funan
(Cambodia) of an Indian writing system and the presence of Brahmin
priests and rulers with Sanskrit names.

   On the basis of this sparse evidence Wheeler[7] was unwilling to extend
to Southeast Asia the well-structured trading systems he could describe
for India and the Erythraean Sea and attributed these Western-derived
items found in Thailand and Vietnam to 'drift' rather than to 'organized
intercourse with the West'. And Raschke[8] writing on the Roman spice
trade with the Far East, argued that, 'Archaeological evidence of Indian
contact with Southeast Asia can scarcely be put before the present era,

and the main thrust in Western Malaya does not appear until the 3rd – 6th centuries. Even at commercial centres such as Oc-eo the evidence of Indian contact is quite limited'.

In the past few years only a few new finds which bear on this problem have been made, recognized or published from Southeast Asia. These are:

1. A copper coin of the Western Roman Emperor Victorinus (A.D. 268 – 270) minted in Cologne was found a few years ago at U-Thong in Thailand and is preserved in the National Museum there.[9]

2. A few sherds of the Indo-Roman pottery known as Rouletted Ware of the first century A.D. have been recognized by Walker[10] among other pottery belonging to the Buni Complex, grave assemblages of this period, distributed along the north coast of Java.

3. Bronson's excavations at the early town site of Chansen in Central Thailand in 1968 – 69 provided one undoubted Indian object, a fine ivory comb[11] from Period II which the excavator dates to the 1st – 3rd centuries A.D.

4. Excavations at Beikthano in Central Burma[12] have provided substantial evidence for a town with a palace and stupas modelled on Indian lines. Among the finds one etched agate bead was found (see discussion below) and a number of Indianizing 'Pyu' coins. The excavator, with the aid of four C-14 dates and stylistic comparisons with various Indian prototypes, dates the settlement to 1st – 5th centuries A.D. but the coin evidence[13] indicates that Beikthano was occupied well into the 8th century A.D.

It is at this stage that I wish to turn to our excavations at Ban Don Ta Phet in Western Thailand which, though not primarily directed to this goal, have provided abundant evidence for contacts with India.

The cemetery of Ban Don Ta Phet

The archaeological site of Ban Don Ta Thet lies on the southern edge of the village of that name, between Kanchanaburi and U-Thong in West-Central Thailand.

Antiquities were found there by schoolchildren in September, 1975 and excavations were undertaken by the Thai Fine Arts Department between November 1975 and May 1976. A number of burials were identified, richly equipped with iron tools and weapons, bronze vessels and jewellery fashioned from bronze, bone, ivory, glass and semi-precious stones. An exhibition of finds from the site was held at the National Museum in Bangkok in 1976 and for that occasion a booklet describing the excavation and some of the finds was written (in Thai) by Chin You-di (1976) who was in charge of the excavation from February to May 1976.

The cemetery was attributed by Chin You-di to a settled farming community of the late Iron Age, dating to between 50 B.C. and A.D. 250; a period before the appearance of centralized kingdoms organized according to political and religious models introduced from India. Nevertheless, certain items of jewellery, particularly the etched agate and carnelian beads, provided evidence for contacts with India where this technique has a long tradition.[14]

Following the Thai excavations of 1975 – 76 Warangkhana Rajpitak[15], undertook the metallurgical examination of the bronzes in which she identified some unusual characteristics of the Don Ta Phet bronzes; namely the use of very high tin:copper alloys (in the range of 20 – 28%) and a manufacturing process which involved the lost-wax casting of containers with exceptionally thin walls (on some vessels this is as little as 0.3 – 0.5 mm.), followed by limited hot-working, annealing and quenching and rotary polishing. This is the first appearance of a distinctive Southeast Asian tradition of the manufacture of bronze ritual vessels which has been described by Mourer in recent times in Cambodia.

Following the Thai work of 1975 – 76, further excavations were undertaken in 1980 – 81 and 1984 – 85, jointly by the Institute of Archaeology, London and the Fine Arts Department, in which about 55 funerary deposits were revealed with a generally similar range of furnishings. I have already published on the need for these excavations,[16] and two preliminary reports on the first of these two seasons are available[17] and I will not repeat the details here. Five radiocarbon samples have been dated all from different graves, and all give the same age. The weighted mean of these results gives an age of 2265 ± 37 BP, which, when calibrated, gives 2340 – 2310 BP or 360 – 390 BC with a two sigma variation. The samples were calculated from organic material (mainly rice) incorporated in the pottery and thus there is no question about the association of the dated samples with the archaeological remains.

The material evidence from Ban Don Ta Phet

There are two categories of finds which provide evidence for trade, or more properly perhaps, gift-exchange between India and Thailand at this time. These are the beads and the bronze vessels. Other items, for instance, low-fired earthenware and the many wrought-iron socketed and tanged tools and weapons[18], are entirely local, even parochial in character.

Beads

It is convenient to divide these into two categories; glass beads, and those made from semi-precious stones such as agate, crystal and carnelian. Nearly 3,000 beads were found in every burial for which proper documentation is available. Numbers varied from two or three up to several hundred, although some burials which had few beads were rich in bronze and iron.

Glass beads were most commonly moulded into cubes, rectangular forms, six-sided prisms, or small rings. Red, green, yellow, and blue beads are present but bright or intense colours are rare and most common are very pale whitish-green, almost clear beads.

From the point of view of contacts with India, the most interesting of the glass beads are some large, translucent green, six-sided prisms (Figs. 1 and 2). Parallels for these in glass are hard to find in the archaeological literature, but they are remarkably similar to the famous beryl crystals of South India which were so popular at this time and which attracted the attention of Pliny the Elder.[19] Examples are portrayed in Gandaran sculpture and glass imitation of these beryls are referred to by Pliny. I suggest that these are 'glass beryls' made in India and traded to the east. Far-fetched though this may seem on its own, I believe the suggestion makes more sense when the evidence from the etched stone beads and the bronzes is taken into account.

Of the 3,000 or so beads found at Bon Don Ta Phet, more than 500 were made of hard semi-precious stones and of these, by far the most common were spherical carnelians ranging from 5 to 22 mm. in diameter. Rather less frequent were small, facetted lozenge carnelians, cylindrical and barrel-shaped banded agates, very small unmodified crystals, and a few small green stone beads. All these beads are drilled for suspension with cylindrical holes 1.0 – 1.5 mm. in diameter, and are very finely ground and polished so that the spherical beads vary by no more than 0.1 – 0.3 mm. from a perfect sphere. Lamb has already commented on the technical mastery shown by the makers of early Southeast Asian hardstone beads.

Carnelians and agates are found in Southeast Asia and one deposit of carnelian was located north of Lopburi in Central Thailand by our survey team in 1983, but there is no evidence of their exploitation at this time. Nevertheless, sites in Western Thailand of the late prehistoric-early historic period are very rich in carnelian and agate beads, and these are also widely distributed throughout continental and island Southeast Asia, and we must think of a number of yet undiscovered manufacturing sites in the region, or accept, at least for the moment, the notion that they were imported from India where manufacturing sites are well documented and sources of stone abundant. Bibliographic references to this tradition are very numerous and are not cited here, but see for instance, Possehl 1981. Bellwood[20] discusses the distribution of these plain spherical and facetted carnelians within Southeast Asia and the arguments for and against their ultimate source in India.

But however probable it may be that the plain carnelian and agate beads were imported this is difficult to prove given their ubiquity and simple forms. But among these stone beads there is a particular variety known to archaeologists as 'etched beads' about which there must be less doubt. More than 50 such etched beads were found at Ban Don Ta Phet and a small number have come from looted sites in the region around U-Thong town.[21] Most of these (Fig. 3) belong to the well-known Type 1 etched beads characterized by Beck, Mackay, and Dikshit in which a white design is etched (more properly stained) with a strong alkaline paste on to the natural red or black of the polished stone surface.

Etched beads went through periods of popularity and relative decline in India.[22] After the Harappan period there was a revival in the craft in the Buddhist cultures between about 300 B.C. and A.D. 200, and then a further appearance of them in Muslim, Mediaeval sites, particularly in the region from Iran east to Sind, although they have been found as far west as Crimea and the Caucasus.

The etched beads from Ban Don Ta Phet match most closely those of the second Indian period as Chin You-di recognized, and detailed examination by Williams and myself of the Don Ta Phet beads and of those in the British Museum and in the Beck Collection at the University Museum in Cambridge confirm this resemblance, although we found that there is greater variability in the detailed application of the etching medium and its effect on the beads than either Beck or Mackay recognized.

But not all the etched beads from Thailand can be easily referred to Indian types of Beck's second period, and there is one variety in particular, of large asymmetric pendants stained in alternating bands of black and white on the natural red carnelian (Fig. 4) that has only one close parallel so far published from India proper, from Bhita near Allahabad[23] where it is dated to between the third century B.C. to the sixth century A.D.[24] Examples of these beads have come from Don Ta Phet, Kok Samrong, Don Makhak and Ban Tung Ketchet, all within 25 km. of U-Thong town.

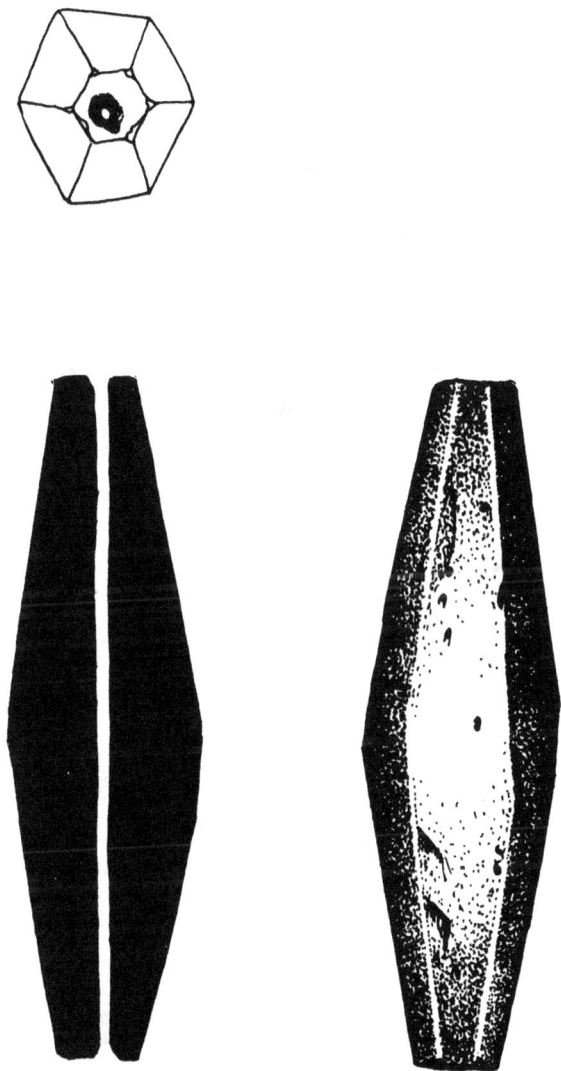

Fig. 1. Large translucent six-sided glass bead found at BDTP by villagers in 1975-6.

BDTP 80
LOC 990 — 485
56 20 12
cm

Fig. 2. Three six-sided green glass beads, during excavation 1980-1.

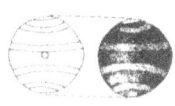

(73)

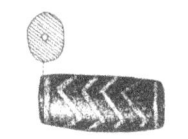

(73)

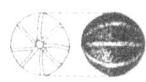

(46)

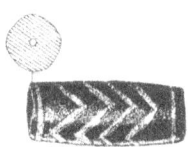

(55)

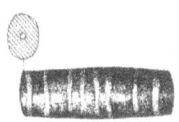

(46)

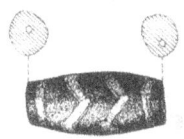

(56)

(73)

Fig. 3. Etched agate and carnelian beads from the 1980-1 season.

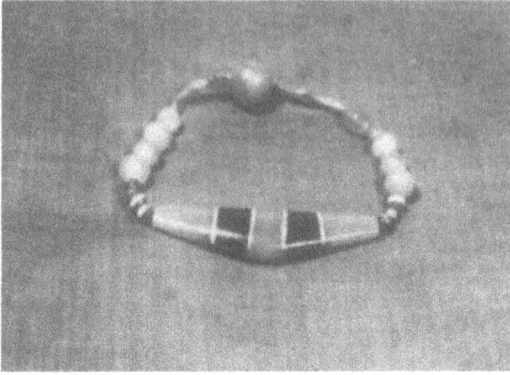

Fig. 4. Large red carnelian bead with bands stained white and black, 1975-6 season.

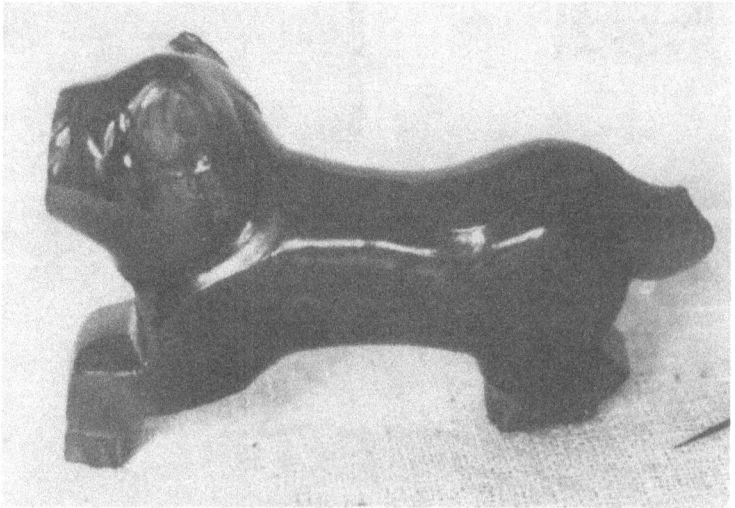

Fig. 5. Carnelian pendant in the form of a leaping lion, 1980-1 season. Length to break in tail, 7 cm.

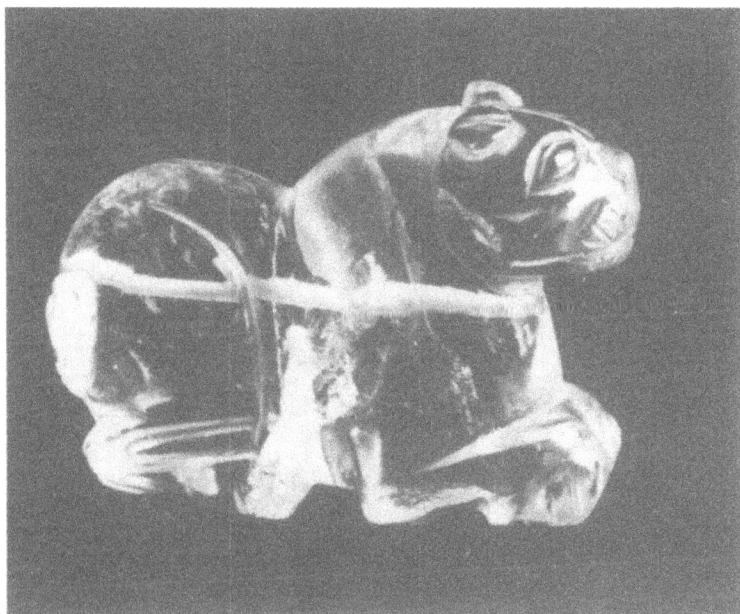

Fig. 6. Crystal lion pendant from Dharmarajika stupa, Taxila, Pakistan (Marshall 1951 III: Pl. 496).

Fig. 7. Bronze vessels, beads and iron tools in burial context 46, 1980-1 season.

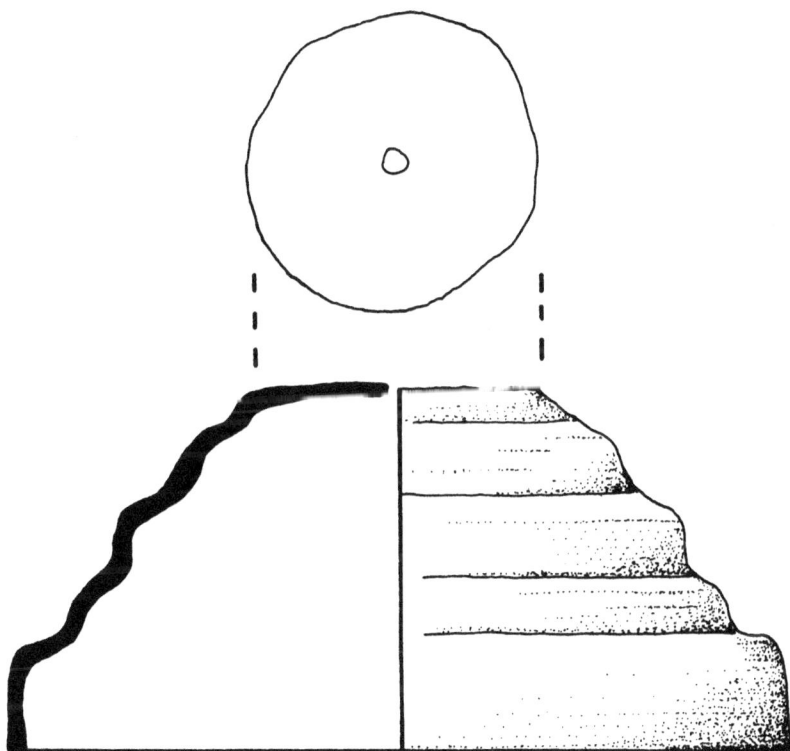

Fig. 8. Bronze object in the form of a stepped truncated cone, possibly representing a stupa, 1980-1. The diameter at the base is 12 cm.

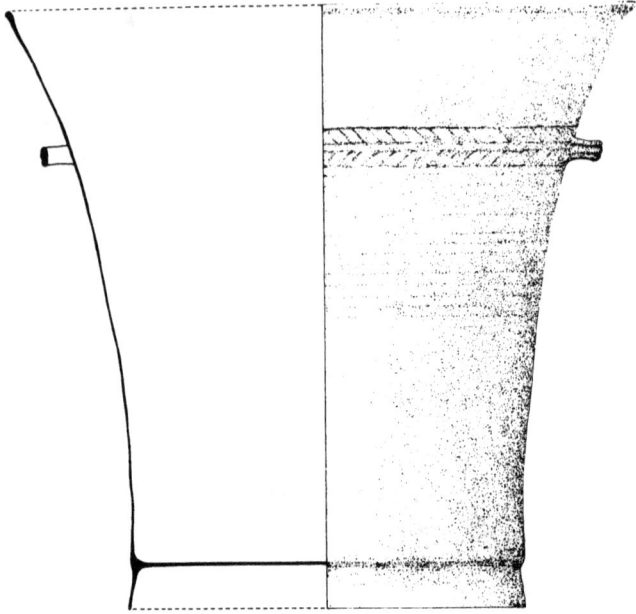

Fig. 9. Large bronze vessel of copper-lead-tin alloy, perhaps an import to BDTP form the Dong-s'on Culture area of Vietnam.

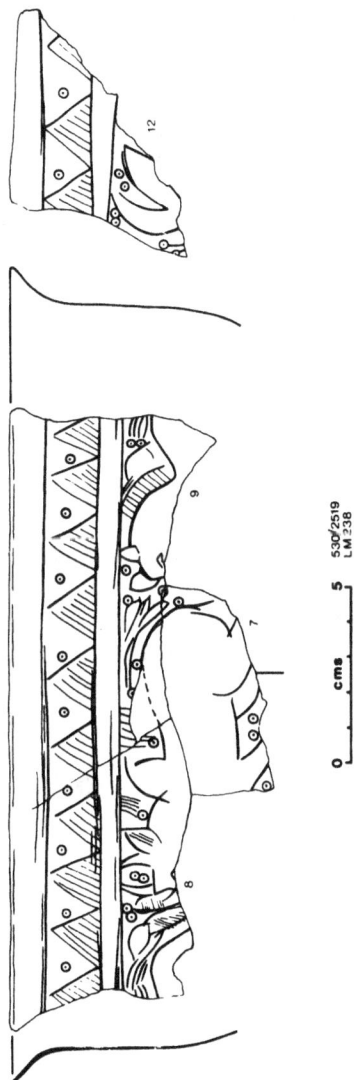

Fig. 10. Fragment of a high-tin bronze vessel showing a procession of animals including humped cattle and a horse. Found by villagers in 1975-6.

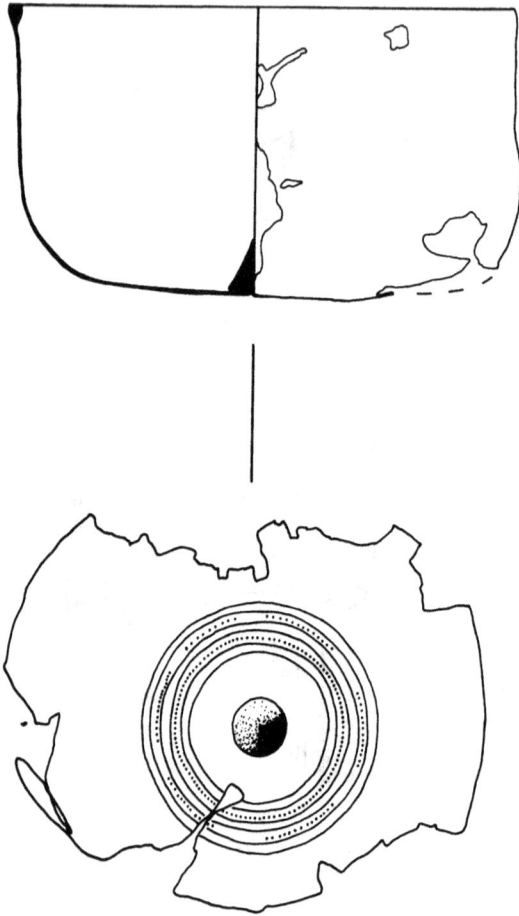

Fig. 11. High-tin bronze vessel with a central conical boss and concentric rings, 1980-1 season.

Fig. 12. Fragmentary high-tin bronze vessel with central conical boss and concentric rings, 1980-1 season.

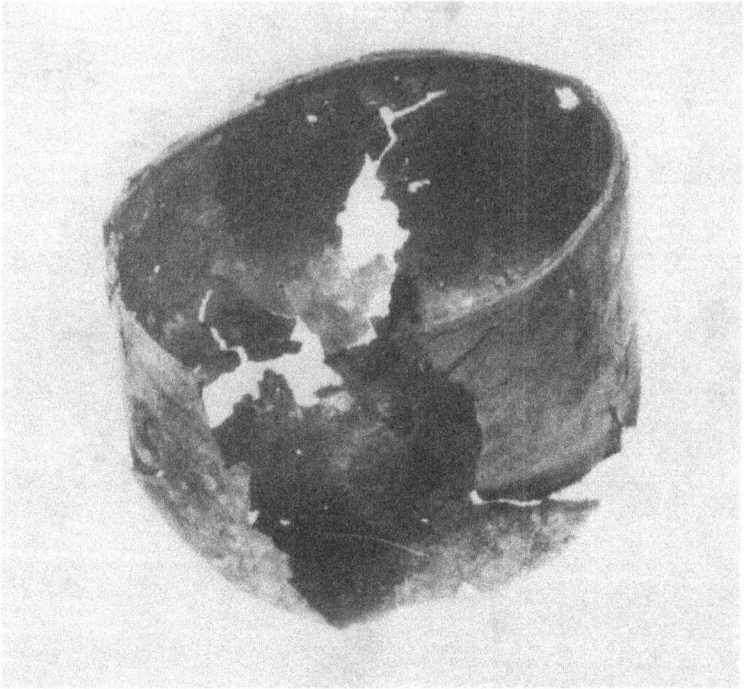

Fig. 13. As Fig. 12.

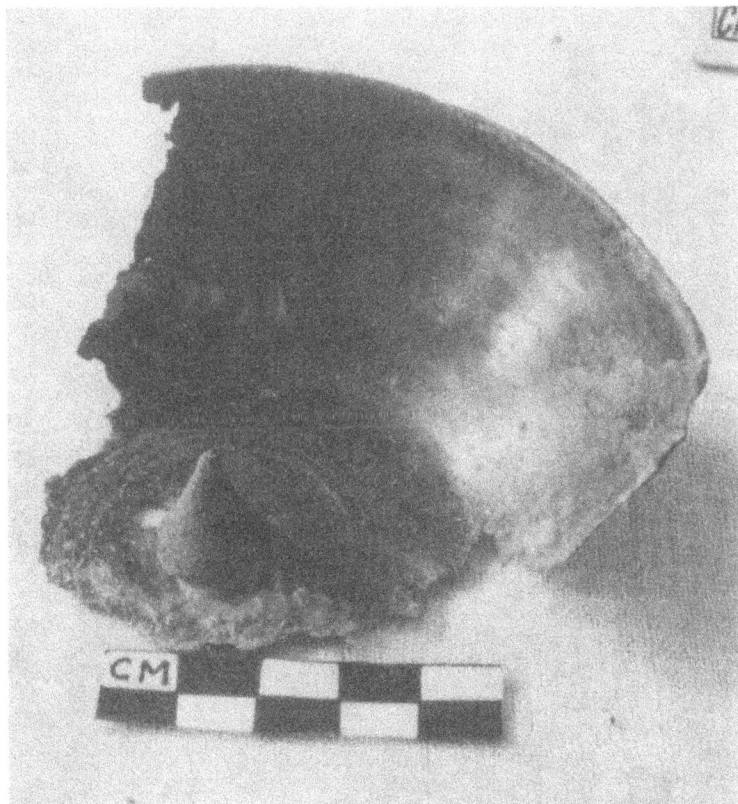

Fig. 14. As Fig. 12.

Fig. 15. Pottery 'knobbled ware' vessels from Sisulpalgarh, Orissa, India (Lal 1949: Pl. XLVIb). Courtesy of the Archaeological Survey of India.

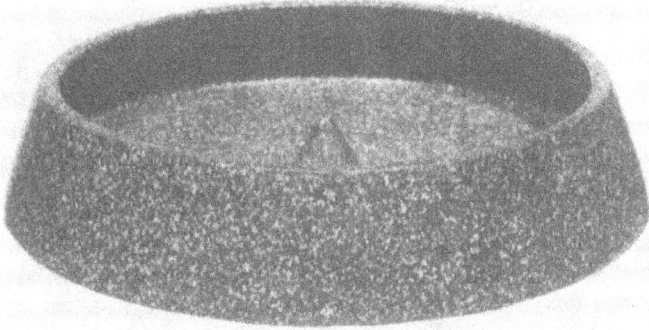

Fig. 16. Black granite bowl from Taxila, Pakistan, with central conical boss surrounded by concentric circles (BM 1867: 4.27.1). Courtesy of the Trustees of the British Museum.

Apart from those from Don Ta Phet and its neighbourhood very few etched beads have so far been described from sites in Southeast Asia, and despite the lack of systematic excavation in most countries it is my feeling that they will always be rather rare east of India. In Thailand I know of other examples only from Ban Chieng;[25] one is in a private collection of antiquities from Saraburi, north of Bangkok; and there are said to be some in collections from the rich bead sites of Peninsular Thailand. A few have also been published from the island of Palawan in the Philippines,[26] and three were excavated at Leang Buidane cave in the Talaud Islands of North-Central Indonesia,[27] one has been published from the excavations at the early city of Beikthano in Central Burma,[28] and one etched carnelian was found in Tomb 13 at Shi Zhai Shan in Yunan Province, South China.[29] This is quite securely dated to the Western Han Period (175 – 118 B.C.), and it is very similar to two of the beads from Burial Context 73 at Don Ta Phet and many in India.[30]

Apart from the etched beads, there is one large carnelian pendant (Fig. 5) carved in the form of a leaping lion[31] which is almost certainly Indian in origin (and there is a small, broken fragment of another or similar animal). No exact parallel for this piece is known, but smaller crouching lion pendants are commonly found in the Buddhist reliquaries of the Gandara civilization such as the one (Fig. 6) from the Dharmarajika stupa at Taxila.[32] Before the Buddha was represented in human form, about the second century A.D., he was often shown in the guise of *Shakyasimha*, the 'Lion of the Shakyas', and there can be little doubt that this lion bead from Ban Don Ta Phet is a Buddhist icon.

Bronze Vessels

Bronze was used for three categories of grave furnishings at Ban Don Ta Phet: 1. containers; 2. bird figurines; and 3. ornaments such as bracelets, anklets, and small bells. The latter are either very simple forms, ubiquitous in Southeast Asia, or so far unique to this site, as are the figurines. The bronze vessels, however, present strong evidence for contacts with India; already raised in the paper reporting Warang-khana's preliminary results.[33]

Nearly 300 bronze containers were found in the 100 or so funerary deposits excavated during the three seasons (Fig. 7). Many of these were incomplete, having been deliberately broken or crushed before burial, and the thin walls and brittle alloy employed in manufacture meant that we have had many problems in recovery and conservation. A full classification of these vessels has not yet been made, but it is clear that there is considerable variation in size, form, and presumably, function.

There are flat-bottomed, cylindrical canisters, small cups or beakers, more-or-less hemispherical bowls in various sizes, and a few unique pieces such as a stepped, truncated cone, or stupa-like form (Fig. 8) and a large bucket or situla (Fig. 9) with thicker walls than usual, made from a high lead, low tin bronze. This last vessel is so far unique to Thailand and most closely resembles some objects in bronze and pottery found in the contemporary Dong-son Culture of North Vietnam from whence I believe it was derived. The stepped cone form is also a unique piece in Thailand, but here the links are rather to the west for comparisons can be made with the terracotta miniature stupas from the Mediaeval Buddhist monastery of Antichak in Bihar.

There are several characteristics of these bronze vessels to which I want to call attention: metallic composition and manufacturing processes, forms and decoration, distribution, and finally, their possible function.

The composition and manufacturing methods have already been mentioned earlier in this paper, and rather fully discussed by Rajpitak and Seeley[34] so I will only summarize the main points here. Most of the vessels were made of a high-tin bronze, cast with thin walls, and were hot-worked, quenched and annealed to varying degrees. Some vessels had bands of fine incised decoration below the rims and a few included scenes of peoples, houses, and horses, cattle, and buffaloes (Fig. 10) which remind one of the processional scenes on the famous Kulli vase in the British Museum, and on some Buddhist sculptural friezes such as those from Amaravati.

Rajpitak and Seeley suggest that this intractable alloy was chosen because of its resemblance, when freshly cast, to yellow gold, and they point to the occasional finds of high-tin bronze bowls in India with similar properties, such as those from Coimbatore, Adichanallur in the Nilgiri Hills, and Taxila where Marshall (1951) found 28 in the Mauryan strata at the Bhir mound. They refer to an interesting observation made by Nearchus when he travelled through this region with the Macedonian army in the fourth century B.C. and preserved in Strabo's *Geography* (15.1.67) that the local people used 'brass that is cast, not the kind that is forged . . .' with the strange result that, 'when they [vessels] fall to the ground they break to pieces like pottery'. Such a description fits equally the bowls from the Bhir mound at Taxila and those from Ban Don Ta Phet. As India is deficient in tin, and copper-tin alloy artifacts are rare in India at this period, it is highly probable that these high-tin vessels were imports from outside India. About this time Indian artisans were developing brass (a copper-zinc alloy) which enabled them to overcome the difficulties of working with pure copper, and to use the abundant zinc ores of Western India.

Within Southeast Asia bronze vessels with identical composition and similar forms have been recovered from the tin gravels of Western Malaya;[35] one was found in Ongbah cave on the Kwae Yai River in Western Thailand,[36] and fragments of high-tin vessels were identified by Rajpitak from the site of Kok Khon in Sakon Nakon Province of Northeast Thailand.[37] The Tham Ongbah bowl is dated by one C-14 date of 2180+180 B.P. (K.300), and the other finds have not yet been, or cannot be, dated because of the lack of context.

Most of the bowls are undecorated and flat, or gently curved inside, but a number (perhaps 20 – 30 including fragments) are finished on the inside base with a series of concentric circles surrounding a conical boss (Figs. 11 – 14) which is sometimes cast integrally with the vessel and sometimes rivetted on. No other examples of this form are known from Southeast Asia but in India it occurs in a modified form on at least one of the Nilgiri bowls now in the British Museum, and also is replicated in pottery in the 'knobbed ware' of Sisulpalgarh, Jaugada and Dhouli, early historic towns in Orissa (Fig. 15).[38] There seem to be no more recent finds or discussion of this unusual ceramic type by Indian archaeologists, but our collaborator during the 1982 – 83 survey season in Thailand, Mr. Kalyan P. Gupta, was strongly of the opinion that the Sisulpalgarh knobbed bowls were primarily ritual vessels, and also that they were a local variant of the Rouletted Ware which I have already discussed and which has a wide distribution in Eastern and Central India from the final centuries B.C. to the first century A.D.

Finally, I must mention in this context, a black granite bowl from Taxila (Fig. 16) which is now in the British Museum (Cat. No. 1867: 4.27.1).[39] Described as a reliquary, this striking object unfortunately lacks any firm context and appears to have been acquired by the museum from the collection of Sir Alexander Cunningham in the nineteenth century. Although made from a very different material, with its angular form, conical boss and concentric circles it provides a remarkable parallel to the Thai bronze knobbed bowls and the Sisulpalgarh knobbed pottery, and reinforces the connections already proposed for fairly close links between the Buddhist civilization of northern India and western Thailand in the early centuries of the Christian era.

Summary

I think that we can demonstrate that many of the beads recovered from the burial site of Don Ta Phet were made in India and they were objects of contemporary use and value among the thriving Buddhist societies there. And further that some of these communities were using for ritual and perhaps domestic purposes cast, high-tin bronze vessels which the balance of evidence available suggests were manufactured in Southeast Asia, perhaps in the modern territory of Thailand (where by far the largest number of pieces have been found) and exported westwards. Some of these bronze vessels were made in a distinctive Indian design and almost certainly for use in temple rituals.

The presence of two categories of material: bronze ritual vessels, and a carved carnelian lion, both having symbolic functions in Indian Buddhism, together with the other evidence for mutual exchange between Northern and Eastern India and Thailand strongly suggests that Buddhist missionaries were already active, indeed established in Southeast Asia by the second century A.D. Wheeler was correct to argue thirty years ago on the basis of evidence then available to him that the few western items found in Southeast Asia came there through 'drift' rather than through organized commercial relationships, but enough evidence is not on hand to refute this interpretation and to show that Southeast Asia was already part of that world trading system developed by Imperial Rome and Han China.

Acknowledgements

The field-work on which this paper is based was done in co-operation with the Fine Arts Department of Thailand and I particularly wish to thank the Director-General of Fine Arts and Mr. Pisit Charoenwongsa for their very great help. The research was supported by the British Academy, The Hayter Fund and the Gordon Childe Fund of the University of London, the British Institute in Southeast Asia, the Evans Fund of Cambridge, the Royal Society of Antiquaries, and the British Museum. I am especially grateful to Kalyan P. Gupta of the Archaeological Survey of India for his valuable commentary on the Indian comparisons for the material from Ban Don Ta Phet. We presented a joint paper to the VIIth International Conference of South Asian Archaeologists in Brussels, in July 1983 which emphasized the Indian comparisons for the etched beads from Southeast Asia.

15

TRADITIONAL TRADING NETWORKS OF SOUTHEAST ASIA

Hans-Dieter Evers

Introduction: The Debate on Asian Trade and Society

On 22 June 1596, after a long and unlucky passage around the Cape of Good Hope and northeast across the Indian Ocean, the four Amsterdam ships of the first Dutch 'Company for Afar' came to anchor before the Javanese town of Bantam, thus ending a voyage that had begun on 21 March 1595 . . . The accounts of the first voyage transport us into the midst of everyday life in the town of Bantam — ceremonial visits are exchanged with the town authorities, the governor, and the *shahbandar*; nobles and merchants come on board: 'There came such a multitude of Javanese and other nations as Turks, Chinese, Bengali, Arabs, Persians, Gujarati, and others that one could hardly move . . . They came so abundantly that each nation took a spot on the ships where they displayed their goods, the same as if it were on a market.'[1]

With this lively description van Leur embarks on his well-known analysis of early Asian trade. The long-distance trade spanning the whole of Asia from the Mediterranean to Japan was, according to van Leur, organized as a peddling trade of many merchants carrying small loads of valuable goods over long distances. The economic mentality of the traders and the organization of their international trade must be thought of in terms of handicraft forms. Reviewing early reports one is constantly struck, says van Leur, by the large numbers of traders, the bustle on shipboard and in the harbours, and the trading voyages with hundreds of single merchants.[2]

Because of the long duration of voyages settlements of merchants were necessary. These settlements with their entrepot markets formed a far-flung market system on which also regional trading networks converged. Access to trading networks and inclusion in the market system became a major stimulus for state formation throughout Southeast Asia, giving rise to powerful states like Aceh, Malacca or Macassar and a multitude of rich coastal principalities like Passai, Lingga, Banten, Buton and Ternate.

The aristocracy and the rulers were passive in trade, 'the active ones were the handicraft traders undertaking journeys with commenda money or commenda merchandise and alongside them the independent handicraft traders, among them peddlers [sic] travelling with packs on their backs, journeying individually or in company with peddler caravans. Shipping too manifested the same forms, the commander and crew carrying on trade on their own account alongside the transport of people and goods'.[3] Nevertheless, it would be wrong to connect peddling with poverty as one might be inclined to do today. The value of goods transported was high and cash was needed to start on the peddling trade. This was often provided by the local ruler or the aristocracy.

In the same way as van Leur tries to point out the similarity of trading patterns in the ancient Mediterranean, in the Middle East, and in South and Southeast Asia, he also stresses historical continuity. He argues 'that pictures sketched above had undergone little change for at least two thousand years up to and into the seventeenth century'.[4] The question, of course, arises how long the basic trading pattern of peddling trade could survive after the seventeenth century. Possibly up to the present? Van Leur seems to think so, as his occasional reference to a description of present-day harbour principalities in the Persian Gulf seems to indicate.[5] Trade, particularly peddling trade, is indeed seen by van Leur as an 'historical constant'.[6] There was no evolution 'from barter to world trade'.[7]

Van Leur's thesis was criticized by Meilink-Roelofsz.[8] According to her 'Asian trade was not predominantly a peddling trade' as van Leur had suggested, nor was it 'a shipping trade carried on mainly by independent citizens.' In any case Southeast Asia trading patterns of the sixteenth and seventeenth centuries were much more diverse than European ones at the same time. Meilink-Roelofsz does not detect any signs of the formation of a local Southeast Asian middle group of traders carrying on trade on its own account. Throughout the Malay-Indonesian Archipelago the local ruler had a prominent share in trade and shipping or at least promoted his interest with the help of foreign traders. Luxury goods but also mass products were traded by rulers and officials, and only cheap goods were left to van Leur's pedlars.

The Portuguese were able to penetrate the Asian trading networks because their trade was organized on a higher level and larger scale. But they in turn had to succumb to the Dutch and British Companies. As Steensgaard[9] has pointed out they remained victorious both over the Portuguese and indigenous Southeast Asian trade 'by virtue of their greater control of the market and the internalization of protection costs, i.e. by subordinating the production of protection to the market mechanism, they utilized the resources more economically than the older institutions.'

European ascendancy was already beginning to manifest itself, but it was only around 1800 that Europe started to outstrip the East, though much earlier Java was already transformed to a producer of bulk goods (sugar, coffee) for the European market. But was Southeast Asian shipping 'degraded' to coastal trade, piracy or small-scale peddling trade as a result?[10] Was van Leur misled by the observation of today's hawkers and petty traders, as described by Geertz, and has he just projected the present into the distant past?

Indeed, an evaluation of Asian trade leads to a number of rather far-reaching questions. How are we to explain the world of Southeast Asia up to the eighteenth century? Was precolonial Southeast Asia caught between two world-systems, China and India? Or was there an independent Southeast Asian world-system at least during certain periods? When did Southeast Asia become the periphery of the emerging European world-system? It appears that Wallersteinian world-system analysis is hard to apply to the diversity of Southeast Asia though it might help to put our analysis of trading networks into a wider perspective.

Another set of questions may be drawn from the work of Karl Polanyi.[11] Was precolonial Southeast Asia a non-market economy according to Polanyi's theory? This would be very hard to argue for the states on the straits of Malacca thriving on entrepot trade (Srivijaya, Malacca, Aceh *et al.*). On the other hand, Malay texts, like the Malacca code or similar works from Makassar prove that serious attempts were made to regulate prices, shipping and trade.

Van Leur's thesis on peddling trade as a typical and enduring model of Asian trade makes sense, even if it was not the only or the predominant way of Asian trading at all times. But this peddling trade, though carried on by individual traders on a small scale, was certainly not anarchic. Van Leur stresses quite rightly the flexibility of this kind of trade but neglects the systematic aspects of the trading networks that made its persistence possible. Peddling trade appears to be a phenomenon on the same level of generality as peasant production. The forms and customs remain stable over long periods of time, but the configurations in which they occur, the articulations with other forms of trade, and the relative significance change over time.

The persistence of the Southeast Asian peddling trade, similar to the persistence of Asian peasant production, can convincingly be demonstrated by the existence and even growth of contemporary trading networks. But before embarking on this endeavour a general discussion on the definition of trading networks is necessary.

Definition of Trading Networks

Trading networks are social processes of exchange. They are social processes in the sense that social interaction takes place between persons with the primary purpose of exchanging goods over more or less greater geographical distances.

Market places (as defined by Polanyi 1957) can be the nodal points of trading networks. The interrelation of these more or less permanent market places can be called a 'market system'. Trading networks can span 'world systems' as defined by Wallerstein,[12] but also 'local systems' that have no place in Wallersteinian analysis. It is important to note that these intermediate trading networks or market systems do not have to be bounded by national boundaries. To the contrary, they seldom are; e.g. an important type of trading network, namely smuggling, is dependent on straddling national boundaries! But this is rather an empirical question to which we are going to return later.

What are the criteria that define a trading network? At least a preliminary checklist can be provided as follows:
— there is usually an ethnic or religious homogeneity of traders, but diversity of partners,
— a regular interaction between trading partners along definite trade routes,
— an evolution of the trading network over time,
— a typical inventory of trading goods,
— the development of distinctive trading practices, customs and types of exchange, including typical ways of travelling and typical means of transport,
— the utilization of a market-place system.

Trading networks can vary in extent without necessarily forming an hierarchy. In Southeast Asia thousands of small traders peddle fish directly from the fishermen to nearby villages or peasants trade agricultural products at weekly village markets.[13] Intermediate trading networks extend over long distances but traders transact business in small lots and individually. Their trade would be classified as part of the so-called informal sector in contrast to the commerce of trading companies.

An Overview of Contemporary Nusantara Trading Networks

The identification of contemporary and past Southeast Asian trading networks is a formidable task. Taking only Island Southeast Asia, the

'Nusantara', into consideration, we should like to identify the following
intermediate trading networks that are still active or have been active
until recently in the Malay world:
  Nusantara intermediate trading networks:
    (1) The northern straits of Malacca (Aceh)
    (2) The Riau-Singapore network
    (3) The Buginese network
    (4) The Butonese network
    (5) Minangkabau petty trade
    (6) The Sulu network
    (7) The Trengganu/Kelantan-Thai network
    (8) Networks of the Java Sea
This list is by no means exhaustive and there are many other
examples of small-scale and intermediate (i.e. intra Southeast Asian)
networks. But peddling trade networks can extend throughout Asia,
like the network of Nepalese pedlars and smugglers, connecting their
Nepalese home valley with Hong Kong, Singapore and many other
Southeast Asian market places. The South Indian Chettiar community,
peddling, as it were, money and loans, had established a no less
extensive network throughout Asia, the Pacific and beyond.[14]
  The following examples of trading networks will provide us with
some clues as to the long-term development and current workings of
intermediary peddling trade in Southeast Asia.

*Analysis of a Trading Network: The Maritime Pedlars of the
Blacksmith Islands*

One of the most important and historically relevant trading networks
connected the spice islands of the Moluccas with eastern Java. The
sailing route from the ports of the Javanese empire of Majapahit passed
around the two southern tips of Sulawesi where local chiefs rose to
power and formed coastal principalities on account of their access to
shipping and trade. The Javanese inland states probably exported rice
— a bulk trade overlooked by van Leur — through its ports on the Java
Sea to the East Indonesian islands, particularly the Moluccas.[15] Here
the valuable spices were grown that eventually attracted Portuguese,
Spanish and Dutch merchants who vied for the monopoly of the spice
trade to Europe.
  One such harbour principality, the kingdom of Wolio, which after
islamization became the Sultanate of Buton, controlled the islands of
south-eastern Sulawesi. It was connected with the powerful trading

Sultanate of Ternate and came eventually in 1908 under Dutch colonial rule. To its realm belonged the strategically located group of the Blacksmith Islands (Kepulauan Tukang Besi) with the three major islands of Wangi-Wangi, Kaledupa and Binongko. Here, on these rather dry and infertile islands, a group of daring seafarers, shipbuilders and maritime traders became settled, who up to now carry on a brisk maritime peddling trade throughout Eastern Indonesia and the Java Sea.

It would be wrong, however, to argue that these maritime traders are relics of the past. Their profound knowledge of the Southeast Asian world and beyond, their quick adjustment to changing trading opportunities, and their adoption of new maritime technologies demonstrate that they are very much of this age, that they are fully integrated into the Indonesian, the Southeast Asian, and eventually the world economy.

The maritime pedlars of the Tukang Besi islands built their own vessels (*perahu lambo*), a relatively modern type of sailing vessel of between 5 to 75 tons loading capacity. Their trade routes are still very much determined by the changing monsoons but they are also happy to launch trading expeditions to wherever their fancy and adventurous spirit might suggest.

Perhaps the best way to give an impression of the trading network is to relate in some detail the recent voyage of Captain Haji Ibrahim and his crew.

Haji Ibrahim, a native of the village of Pongo, Wangi-Wangi, owns a sailing vessel, a *perahu lambo*, of 20 tons, which he and his crew had built themselves some years ago. In January 1983, he assembled a crew of six villagers, borrowed some additional cash from relatives and set sail for the Banda Islands in the Moluccas with a cargo of household goods, cement, textiles and other small items they had bought in Surabaya on a previous voyage. They arrived on the Banda islands after ten days but decided to sail on to the Gorong and Watubela islands about 110 nautical miles to the east between the southern tip of Ceram and Irian (New Guinea). Here they traded their merchandise for nutmeg. By mid-April, when the north-east monsoon (*musim timor*) started, they had assembled 12 tons of nutmeg nuts and 1 ton of nugmeg flowers.

With the brisk eastern monsoon they arrived back in Wangi-Wangi within six days and nights, stayed with their families for ten days and then continued to Ujung Pandang in South Sulawesi, where they arrived after a fast passage of two days. When they contacted Chinese traders in the market they were dismayed to learn that the price of nutmeg had dropped considerably. After haggling and waiting for two weeks they decided, after long deliberations among the crew, to cut their losses and to sell at a lower price.

They had bought 15 tons of nutmeg at Rp. 175.-/kg, which they had to sell for Rp. 150.-/kg. Losses due to price fluctuations occur occasionally, but usually profits are made and distributed as follows: The creditor of the advanced capital receives half and the crew, including the captain, receives an equal share of the remaining half of the net profit. Harbour dues, gifts to officials and the ship's share of one-twelfth of the proceeds from the sale of the cargo have been deducted beforehand. In this case the total proceeds were used to buy new goods, among others rice, cement, household goods (*barang dapur*), and fashionable furniture. With this cargo they returned to their home village on the Blacksmith Islands, without, however, discharging it. In June they set sail again and arrived after four days and five nights at Pulau Dowora at the southern tip of Halmahera. Here they started to trade their goods around the villages on various islands for about four months. Because of the earlier loss they decided not to buy any spices, but to return to their village on the Blacksmith Islands. They arrived safely in the first week of November, hauled the sailing ship up on to the beach for repairs, distributed their profits which amounted to about Rp. 25,000 per crew member, and dispersed.

Similar trading expeditions are regularly undertaken by the 169 sailing vessels (*perahu lambo*) owned by maritime pedlars on the island of Wangi-Wangi of the Blacksmith Islands of Southeastern Sulawesi. The general pattern is clear: merchandise is bought in a major market place like Gresik near Surabaya or Ujung Pandang and then peddled around the islands of eastern Indonesia. Though occasionally adventurous crews sail to new destinations, like captain Ibrahim, who had once sailed to Singapore and once to Kuching, Borneo, with the help of an Indonesian school atlas, trade is usually carried out on among groups of islands between Sulawesi, the Moluccas and Irian. Sea captains and their crew members tend to know village headmen, with whom they trade. As orders are quite often placed for the next voyage, long-lasting relationships are developed. Copra is still the major item of trade, though the efforts of the government bureaucracy to monopolize trade in copra and spices through government-dominated co-operatives lead to frequent clashes with officials and with the police.

In recent years some traders have bought or rented land in the villages of their trading partners and have started to open up plantations for coconuts or cloves. Other villagers have followed and established settlements on many of the eastern islands. Considerable migration is currently taking place, trading vessels now carry passengers, and the motorization of ships allows more regular service irrespective of the monsoon season.

The Deterioration of a Trading Network: Smuggling in Aceh

At the same time the Javanese empire of Majapahit extended its influence to eastern Indonesia by activating the spice trading network to the Moluccas, the Acehnese principalities of North Sumatra gained through the pepper trade with Java. From the fourteenth century onwards Aceh and its trading networks gained in importance until the Dutch-Acehnese war led to a decline at the beginning of the twentieth century.

The Acehnese states were organized to serve long-distance trade. The Acehnese aristocrats (*uleebelang*) were not rulers of an area or state (*nanggrou*), but rather traders in pepper from the Acehnese west coast, or in rice from the coast along the straits of Malacca. 'The relations between subjects and rulers in these states were all within the framework of commerce'.[16] The Acehnese trading network during the nineteenth century became increasingly concentrated on Penang, but also extended to other ports along the straits of Malacca as far as Singapore and to India.

This trading network is now defunct, or rather has shrunk to miniscule proportions. Each week a coastal vessel from Singapore arrives at the free port of Sabang discharging international merchandise, ordered by local Chinese traders. These in turn are picked up by Batak women who smuggle these goods across to the mainland, where they are sold on a specific corner of the *pasar* of Banda Aceh. Some of these articles, like drinking glasses from France, sarongs from India, or plastic containers from Singapore eventually find their way to Medan and other Indonesian towns.

Similar smuggling networks are found all over Southeast Asia, particularly along the Thai-Burmese border, the Riau archipelago around Singapore, in Southern Thailand and the Sulu Sea of the Philippines. Most of these networks have a long history, but are, of course, subject to change through government policies and vacillating market relations.

The Rise and Decline of a Trading Network: Chettiar Money-lenders in Southeast Asia

The term 'Chettiar' refers to a group of castes found throughout South India. In 1891 there were more than half a million members of these castes in Madras state speaking either Tamil or Telegu.[17] The typical caste occupation is commerce and money-lending, but as usual other occupations are also found like weaving or farming. We are here concerned with one of the endogamous groups or castes only, namely the Nattukottai Chettiar, who numbered 7,851 in 1891. They were, and apparently still are, concentrated in an area popularly known as 'Chettinad', comprising the eastern part of Ramnad District (Tirupattur and Devakottai Divisions) and some part of the Pudukottai Division of Tiruchirappali District.

They trace their origin back to the Chola empire (10th – 13th centuries) and appear to have been in the banking or money-lending business before British times.

The Nattukottai Chettiar form a Tamil-speaking South Indian caste whose traditional caste occupation has been banking and money-lending for a considerable period of time. Their activities as money-lenders have slowly expanded throughout British India during the nineteenth century and have experienced a sudden and phenomenal rise overseas in the 1870s and 1880s. While maintaining their head-offices in the Madras Presidency, Chettiar agents have set up branch offices in South Africa, Mauritius, Ceylon, Burma, Malaya, South Vietnam, and Indonesia.

Already at the turn of the century they were known for their wealth, and contemporary commentators have noted that 'they are the most go-ahead of all the trading castes in the South', and that their first and major aim is 'to make as much money as possible'.[18] There appears to have been very little change in their reputation in this respect, because also the 1961 census report comments that 'they are always keen on their trade, and to make money and to become rich is their sole aim at all times'.[19]

The Chettiar are Saivites and most of their temples are dedicated to Lord Subramaniam, son of Siva. The temples are managed by a committee whose chairman is to be the God Subramaniam himself, who is at times 'affectionately called Chetty Murugan'.[20] The 'appointment' of one of the major deities of the Hindu pantheon as chairman of a council of money-lenders certainly testifies to the confidence and claim to righteousness the Chettiar place in their business activities.

The temple serves as the major bank of the Chettiar who may obtain credit from the temple funds. Thus the main Chettiar temple in Rangoon was known as the 'Chettiar Exchange' in the 1930s.[21] Repayment of advances are guaranteed by religious sanctions, as no money-lender will want to disappoint or cheat the owner of the temple fund, Lord Subramaniam himself.

It is difficult to pinpoint when Chettiar migration overseas started. In addition to their banking activities in Southern India they appear to have been engaged in trade with Ceylon in early British times, but most must have migrated to Ceylon only with the coffee boom during the nineteenth century.[22]

The difficulty in evaluating earlier reports lies in the fact that the term 'Chetti' also means trader and refers to many castes in South India. An eyewitness report of the 1830s refers, however, explicitly to the Nattukottai Chettiar in Ceylon who had been dealing in raw cotton. By then the nearly 150 firms in Colombo had changed to importing textiles and rice and exporting coffee.[23]

According to some local Chettiar in Singapore, the first members of their group arrived in Malacca about 1800 and in Penang and Singapore in the 1840s. These dates are backed by the fact that the main Chettiar temple in Singapore was built about 1855 to 1860.[24] Chettiar must also have become active in money-lending soon after the British influence extended to the Malay Peninsula after the Pangkor engagement of 1874.[25] Data from our own urban landownership study show that loans advanced by Chettiar money-lenders were entered into the land registry in the early 1880s, i.e. soon after it was started.

J. R. Andrus[26] mentions that some Chettiar probably migrated to Burma by the middle of the nineteenth century but confined their activities mainly to Rangoon and other urban centres until about 1880.[27] But even in 1910 there were only 350 Chettiar firms in Burma; by 1930 their number had increased to more than 1650.[28] Chettiar activities in South Vietnam must have started later, according to one source, only after 1925. Though South Africa, Mauritius, Thailand and Indonesia are always included in the list of countries to which the Chettiar extended their business, nothing definite can be said about their date of migration or their activities in these countries.

From these data it appears that some connections with Southeast Asian countries must have started in the early 1800s, but the main migration and expansion of Chettiar activities abroad must have occurred after 1870, when British rule was established in Burma and Malaya. Thus the Cyclopaedia of India of 1885 mentions that Nattukottai Chettiar 'have lately entered their commercial transactions to distant countries'.[29]

It is likely that up to the 1930s Chettiar money-lending activities concentrated on the export-crop-producing areas or the few commercialized rice-growing districts. The prevalence of Chettiar in the Straits Settlements (Singapore, Malacca, Penang) or the larger towns in the Federated Malay States also indicate the importance of lending to the commercial sector.

Around 1930, the Chettiar money-lending network extended from its centre in South India throughout Southeast Asia. Big trading centres, like Singapore, Penang, Medan or Saigon had larger Chettiar communities, but also in small provincial towns Chettiar agents were found. Money was transferred freely and members of the big Chettiar families could travel from *kitingi* (Chettiar dormitory and business house) to *kitingi* through colonial Asia.

Meanwhile the Chettiar network has dwindled, but remnants are still intact on a smaller scale.[30]

Conclusions

The very existence of interregional maritime peddling trade today appears to give credence to van Leur's theory. Some of the features we could observe today are remarkably similar to those described by van Leur for early Asian trade up to the seventeenth century. The Tukang Besi islanders buy world-market products as well as local items at a major market place. These goods are then peddled in small quantities over long distances. The maritime pedlars receive their capital from rich villagers, government officials, or from their families. The proceeds are distributed according to fixed proportions, and the maritime pedlars part after a trading expedition. Relations with trading partners, however, are long lasting and an enduring trading network has evolved.

But despite these social relations, regulated by custom and long-term communicative interaction, the impingement of other forces is occasionally felt. When the traders arrive at a major market place they may have to contend with prices determined by the world market or by government exchange regulations. The long-established network of money-lending may be severely curbed by new banking laws. In short, the social organization of the trading network meets the constraint of the market system, which in turn is part of a modern world-system. The persistence of local trading networks over long periods of time, in fact through several 'world-systems', speaks, however, for their relative autonomy.

16

FRENCH—INDO-CHINESE TRADE RELATIONS 1885 – 1930: WITH SPECIAL REFERENCE TO THE TEXTILE TRADE[1]

Irene Nørlund

This short study will examine the trade structure and the policies France applied to her Indo-Chinese colonies, in particular Vietnam, from the earliest years of her colonial implantation in the 1880s up to the outset of its disintegration which, as generally conceded, began in the aftermath of the Great Depression. Since no major or systematic study of Indo-Chinese foreign trade is available in published form for this period, the question of raw data — accessibility, veracity, quantity and quality — poses itself with painful acuity and is by no means of secondary importance.[2] In particular, to what extent do the sources at hand lend themselves to treatment by modern, economic, historical methods? Despite the methodological limitations underlying this study, we nevertheless attempt to answer some of the nagging economic questions concerning the development of trade between France and Indo-China. 1. What were the immediate and long-term consequences of the politically motivated decision by the French government in 1892 to implement severe protective tariff regulations in place of formerly more lax controls? 2. Did the French colonial trade policy, faced with sharp competition from Chinese interest, manage to bring about exclusive relations with Indo-China? 3. Finally, what can we conclude from the trade balance between France and Indo-China during this period with respect to the dominant economic interests inside France herself?

We hope that this study will contribute to the broader debate concerning French – Indo-Chinese relations, in particular to the question whether or not the Indo-Chinese colonies were profitable to French economic interests, and whether the export of goods from France to Indo-China was more important than the exploitation and extraction of raw materials.

The study is divided into four sections. The first section presents an overall picture of the Indo-Chinese foreign trade and considers the methodological difficulty involved in establishing a volume index expressed in fixed prices for measuring trade development.

The main trends of Indo-Chinese trade development with France, its empire, and neighbouring Southeast Asian countries, are dealt with in the second section.

The third section examines one particular commodity group, namely textiles, amongst the principal commodities exchanged between France and Indo-China. Import of textiles was in fact of major importance to Indo-China, both from its Asian neighbours (Hong Kong and China), and from the French Empire. Throughout this period, textiles were the most important import commodity from France, and therefore involved substantial economic interests in France herself. To what extent did textile trade really develop in this period?

The fourth section deals with the development of maritime trade between Indo-China and her various trading partners. In particular we find that an increasing amount of tonnage is being transported by French fleets parallel to changing maritime relationships between Indo-China and her other trading partners, notably China, Japan, Great Britain and the United States. By 1930, the French fleet still carried only about a quarter of the total shipping tonnage, although the actual amount of trade with France was somewhat higher.

For the period prior to 1913 our main statistical source is the French language yearbook *Administration des douanes et regies. Indochine Francaise. Rapport sur les statistiques des douanes* published in Saigon. However we have only had access to the years 1885 – 1898. This data has been supplemented with statistics from the official French economic journal, *Bulletin Économique de l'Indochine* which first appeared in 1897. In addition we have been able to consult other archive documents found in France (Paris and Aix-en-Province) as well as in Vietnam itself (Hanoi). For the period beyond 1913 statistical data has been taken from the official French *Annuaire Statistique de l'Indochine*, which first appeared in 1927 and is our main source of documentation. The statistical bulletin regroups data going back to 1913. Furthermore these data have been supplemented by various other documents to gain a clearer picture of Franco-Indo-Chinese trade relations over the period under consideration.

Foreign trade of Indo-China

Figure 1 shows the Indo-Chinese foreign trade from 1885 to 1930. It is expressed in francs up to 1915 and in gold-francs for the period thereafter. It should be noted that the period after the outbreak of World War I was marked by a heavy inflation of French francs, and therefore monetary values are expressed in gold-francs from 1915 and onwards, the latter being much more stable than the francs, and fluctuating little with respect to the Vietnamese piastre.

Already by the 1890s trade — both exports and imports — is exanding rapidly. A noticeable import boom occurs at the turn of the twentieth century, most certainly due to the increasing needs in materials and equipment felt by a growing colonial administration and an expanding economic infrastructure (construction, transport, factories etc.).

Measuring foreign trade in current prices for each year has its limitations as an indicator of trade development since fluctuations cannot be taken into consideration. Nor can the total volume of trade tonnage be used as an indicator because very disparate commodities are simply lumped together regardless of their different values and weight (i.e. silk and coal). For example the export tonnage from Indo-China during this period was 4 to 10 times higher than the import tonnage, whereas the actual trade value does not differ appreciably. Furthermore, total tonnage does not indicate anything about the composition of the commodities exported or imported.

To deal with the problem of measuring the growth of import-export trade we will consider the exchange of certain major commodities based on their fixed prices in 1914. In this way, we can describe the development trends of trade volume over the total number of goods included in the sample for the period under consideration.[3]

The index for the export trade is based on 19 principal commodities.[4] Given the changing types of rice export over the period 1899 – 1929, this major export commodity has been broken down into white rice, broken rice, cargo rice and paddy. For the period 1885 – 99 we only know the total volume of rice export, but we may assume that its composition does not change significantly before 1899, whereafter we consider the four different rice products separately.

In Figure 2 rice is used as the sole basis for the export index up to 1899. In 1904, rice represents 78% of the total export volume. Afterwards, rice export diminishes somewhat in percentage but is still by far the major export commodity. By 1914 rice represents 65% of the total export volume, and the above mentioned 16 commodities constitute 81% of the total export volume and 79% of the total value.

On the other hand an import index is much more difficult to establish in the same manner because the import volume is based on changing items of heterogeneous character. Obviously it is easier to measure the volume and value of a ton of rice than of a stock of machinery or a batch of hardware. In order to determine an index from any given volume according to a fixed price it is necessary for the different commodities under consideration to be comparable over the same given period. For example, commodities lumped together as 'metal products' or

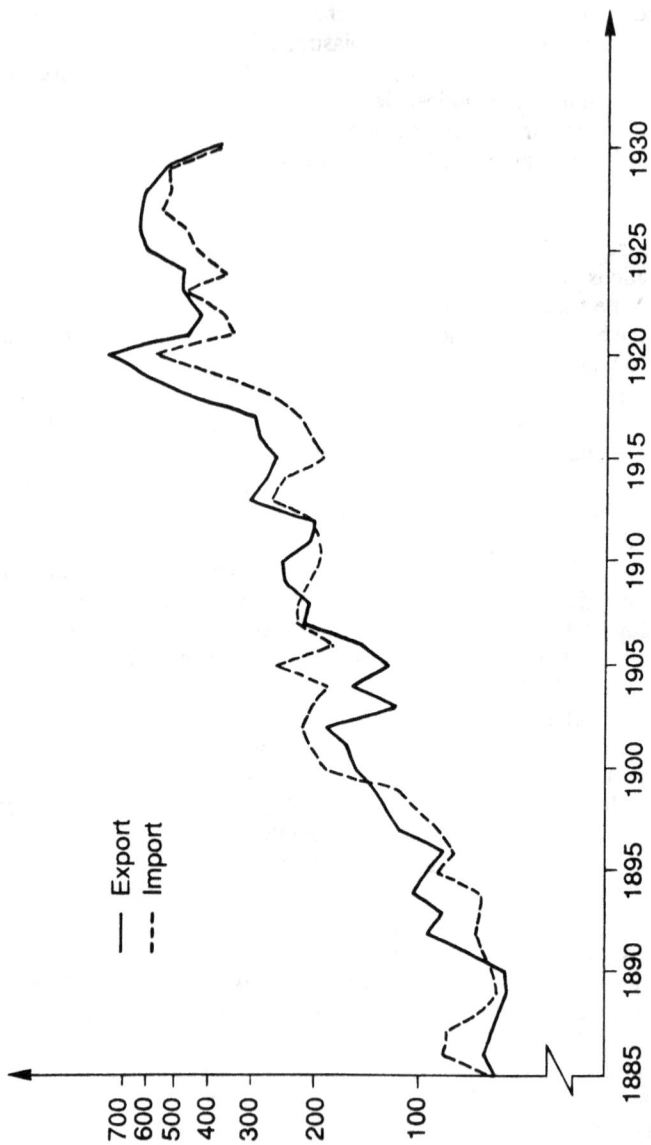

Fig. 1a. Import to Indo-China and export from Indo-China, 1885-1930 (Francs).

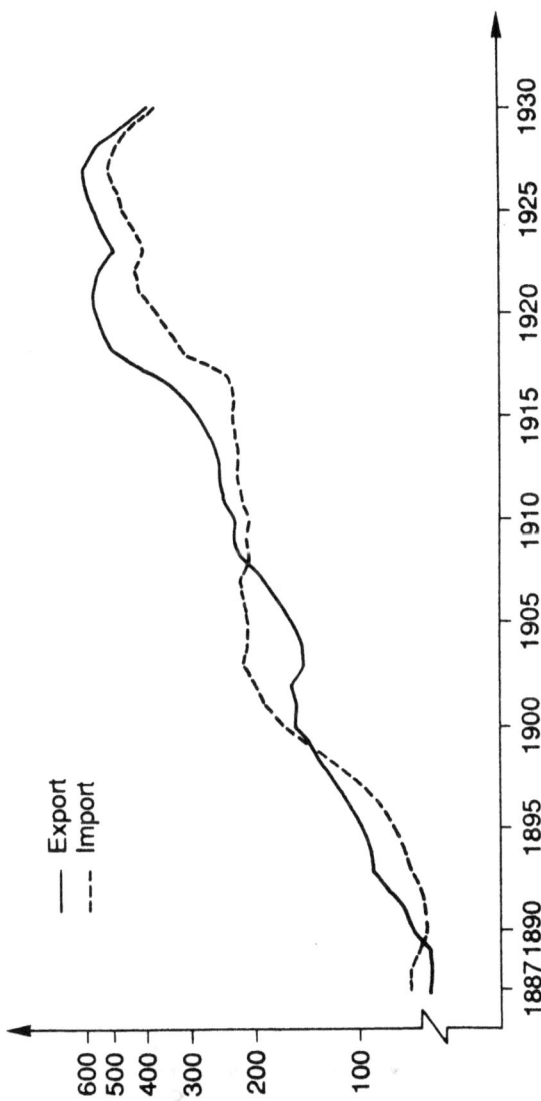

Fig. 1b. Import to Indo-China and export from Indo-China, 1885-1930. Five-year moving averages.

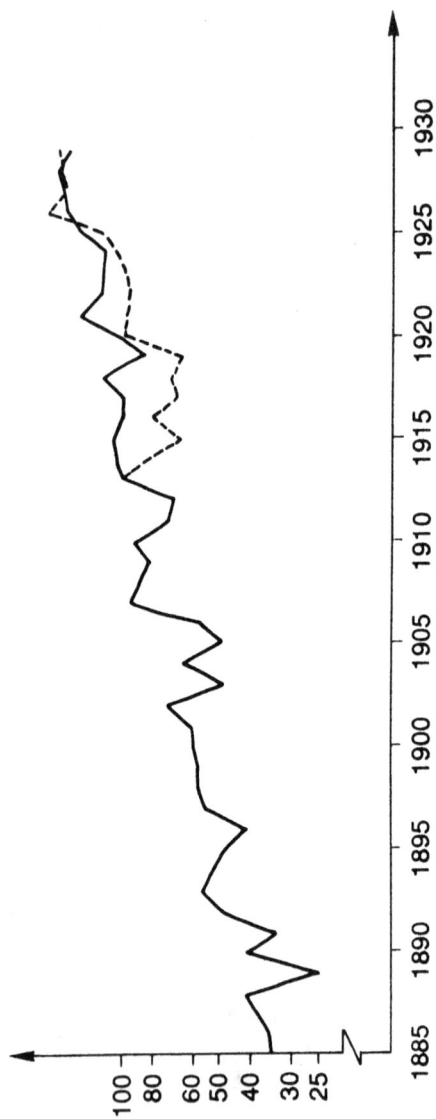

Fig. 2a. Export and import. Indo-China 1885-1930. Volume in 1914 prices. Index 1913 = 100.

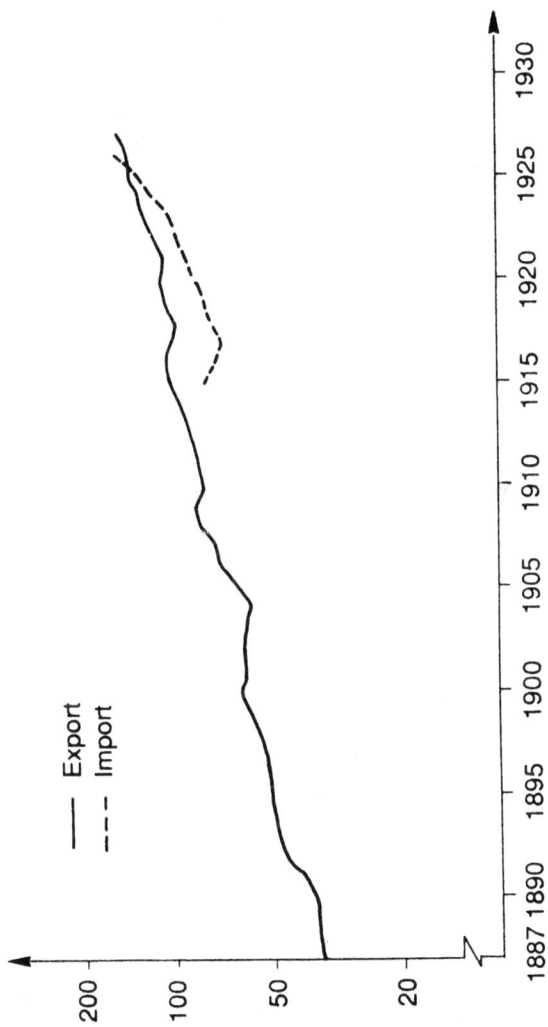

Fig. 2b. Export and import. Indo-China 1885-1930. Volume in 1914 prices. Index 1913 = 100. Five-year moving averages.

'machinery' are often so heterogeneous as to weight and value that they are not comparable. Since the latter two categories represent no more than 6% in 1913 and 10% in 1928 of the total import value, we will only include a few items from these types of goods.

We will base the volume/price import index on more commodities, 31 in fact,[5] than the above used export index. Textile products form the major share followed by foodstuffs, beverages, oils, metals and some simple hardware products. Nevertheless it must be stressed that these 31 commodities make up no more than 39% of the total import value in 1914, albeit 42% in 1913, and 53% of the total import volume. Certain important commodities such as gold, silver and especially opium, have not been included for reasons relating to the changing monetary standard, and in the case of opium, to the obvious lack of official accounting of pertinent statistical data.

As can be seen from Figure 2, import commodities can only be traced back to 1913 since statistical data prior to this date are only available in current prices and not in tonnage. As in Figure 1, the export curve of Figure 2 steadily grows from 1885 onwards, however, exports increase slower albeit more regularly in fixed prices, in fact 3.7% yearly on the average. In Figure 1 the yearly increase of exports was 5.1% on the average. Contrary to Figure 1, the growth rate of Figure 2 does not slack off towards the end of the period under consideration. Nevertheless, World War I did adversely affect importation, as Figure 2 shows, whereas the last 7 years of the 1920s indicate a sharper increase of import commodities than in Figure 1.

Figure 1 plots trade growth expressed in francs between 1885 and 1930, whereas Figure 2 employs our constructed volume price index. Calculating trade growth by means of this index allows us to neglect price fluctuations, and therefore changes in trade volume reflect actual production changes. The trade development shown in the two curves of Figures 1 and 2 represent two different ways of looking at the trade relations. The first relates to prices and the second to the volume of trade. By comparing the two types of trade development, especially towards the end of the 1920s, it is interesting to observe that trade, measured in prices, is falling off whereas the actual volume of trade seems to be increasing. This seemingly contradictory tendency points to a serious foreign trade problem facing Indo-China during the 1920s. However the statistical material available is not detailed enough to permit a deeper analysis, and therefore throughout the rest of this study we still continue to use current prices whenever it is not possible to follow the trade volume of the various commodities.

Development of trade with France and its empire compared to that with other countries

In this section we no longer consider the dynamics of the developing trade with Indo-China in the light of overall import/export figures, but according to the trade relations between Indo-China, France and her empire on the one hand, and between Indo-China and all other countries on the other.[6] Beginning with a small share during the early days of colonialism, in so far as export trade is concerned, France quickly increased her percentage both on the import and export side (Figure 3). Nevertheless, it was only with the enactment of the Kircher tariffs in 1928, which aimed at assimilating the French colonies, that France became Indo-China's major trading partner. However, throughout the whole period, the financial interest of French exporters to Indo-China seems to supersede those of the exporters from Indo-China to France. This can be seen from the fact that rice, the main export commodity, still went to the huge ports of Hong Kong and Singapore to be consumed mainly on the Asian market. But with the promulgation of the Kircher tariffs in 1928, Indo-China had increasing difficulty maintaining her traditional export markets. Amongst other reasons, the export duties levied by the French colonial administration suddenly made Indo-Chinese rice too expensive for regional competition, and therefore France herself soon had to become the new outlet for rice, maize and rubber, despite the seeming irrationality of this long-distance trade.

If we look at the trends in exports and imports, we note substantial variations in the development rate depending on which trading partner is being considered. The graphs, Figures 4 and 5, follow import and export trends, respectively, with France and her empire — and other foreign countries for the period 1885 – 1930. Up to 1913 the basis used is current prices in francs, and afterwards the Vietnamese piaster. The index we employ allows our graphs to follow development trends regardless of the currency changes from francs to piasters.

Figure 4 shows a stable *export* development between Indo-China and her Asian trading partners, namely Hong Kong, Singapore, China and the Dutch Indies. However, Indo-Chinese exports to France, though in general rising very rapidly after 1885, drop around World War I and do not regain their pre-war level before 1925, after which exports again increase markedly. It is interesting to note that throughout the entire period from the middle of the 1890s to the 1930s, exports from Indo-China to her Asian trading partners increase slowly but steadily. There was no drop off between World War I and 1925, contrary to the trend with France.

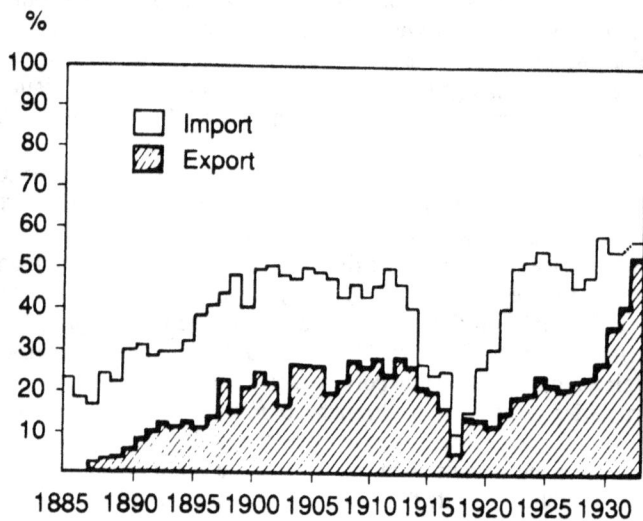

Fig. 3. Trade between Indo-China and France (including the Empire) 1885-1930. Percentage of total import and export respectively (values).

The overall *import* commodity trend, contrary to that of exports for the entire period, is quite unstable. For the period from 1885 to the end of the 1890s, just when imports from France were increasing rapidly, imports from all other countries decreased somewhat, and stagnated until about 1897. After 1897, imports from outside the French empire rose quickly for the next few years only to level off between 1903 and 1917. A new period of quickly rising imports from neighbouring countries took place towards the end of World War I when imports from France were at their lowest level. However, the growth rate of French imports once again surpassed that of imports from other countries during the 1920s.

Imports from France increased a bit more rapidly than exports to France, with the same drop occurring around World War I and lasting until 1925, after which imports rose again as quickly as exports (Figure 5).

The greater fluctuation in the import trade by contrast to the export trade between Indo-China and her various trading partners can be explained by the greater vulnerability of imports to external factors such as the changing world market prices, international conflicts, protective tarrifs, etc. The export of commodities from Indo-China depended mainly on local factors, parameters that were fairly predictable in the hierarchical pre-capitalist agrarian economy which characterized Indo-China at that time. In the predominating rice economy of Indo-China, natural factors such as rainfall and soil fertility would, of course, strongly influence the yearly crop output.

The role of the textile trade with Indo-China

Taken over the whole period from 1885 to 1929, textile imports in the form of ready-made fabrics, averaged about 25% of the total import value, cotton, silk, jute and woollens being the major items.

From 1879 to 1919 the overall import of textile fabrics increased from 18 mill. francs to 50 mill. francs. Table 2 shows the share of imports from France slacking off in the beginning of the 1900s, but increasing steadily thereafter up to 1925, after which time fabric imports dropped off, because textile products on the whole were not keeping up in percentage with the general overall commodity increase which included many new products (Table 1). Nevertheless, measured in current prices, textile imports did increase somewhat, and considered in volume, they actually seem to grow steadily. Of the three major textile items, cotton fabrics were by far the most constant import item for Indo-China throughout this whole period. The import of silk

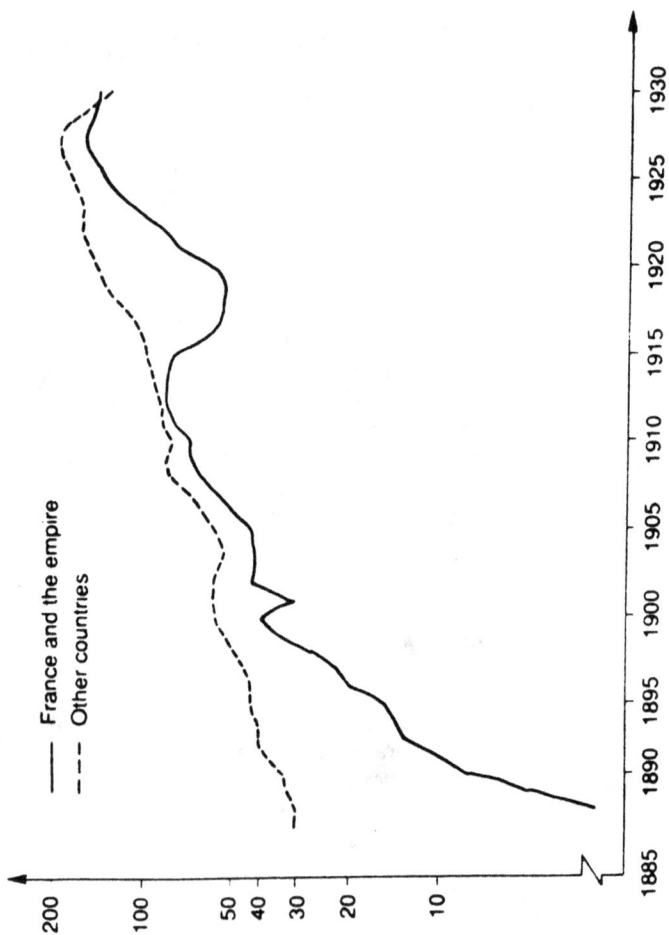

Fig. 4. Export from Indo-China to France (including the Empire) and to other destinations, 1885-1930. Current prices. Index 1930 = 100. Five-year moving averages.

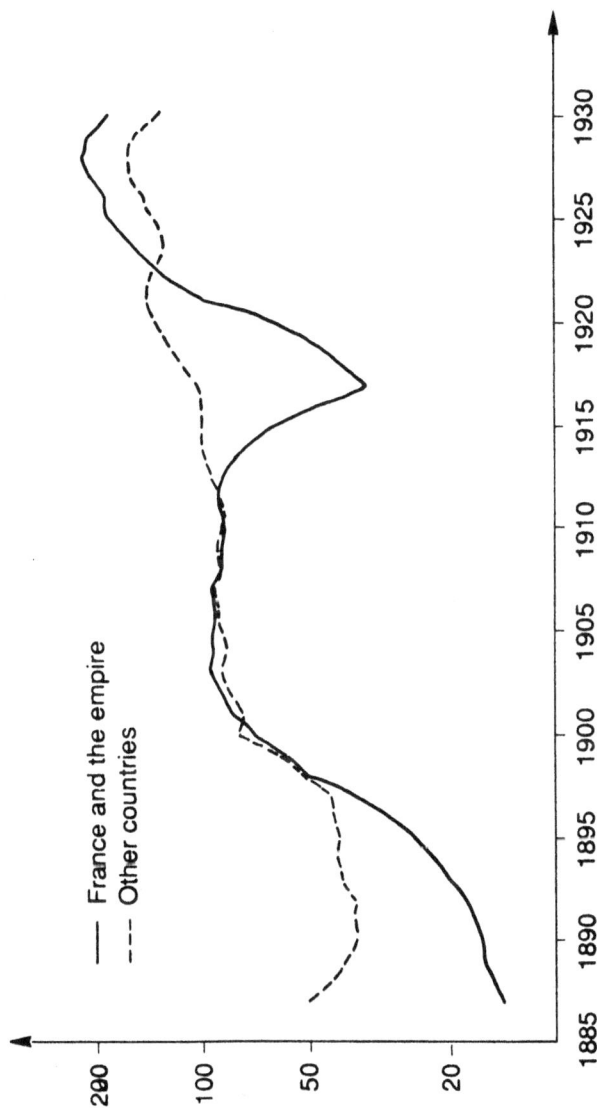

Fig. 5. Import to Indo-China from France (including the Empire) and from other destinations, 1885-1930. Current prices. Index 1913 = 100. Five-year moving averages.

Table 1. *Import of fabrics to Indo-China 1885 – 1929. Percentage of total import value*

1885	24%	1910	23%
1890	27%	1915	25%
1895	25%	1920	26%
1900	23%	1925	25%
1905	16%	1929	17%

Sources: Rapport des douanes, 1896; *Bulletin Economique de l'Indochine*, 1912; *Annuaire Statistique* 1913 – 22, 1923 – 29.

Table 2. *Import of French textile fabrics into Indo-China as a percentage of total imported fabrics (in values)*

1885	3%	1910	45%
1890	22%	1915	48%
1895	39%	. . .	
1900	51%	1929	74%
1905	58%		

Sources: as Table 1, and BEI 1915.

fabrics increased especially in the 1920s, whereas jute imports decreased considerably in the same period.

Now, if we consider the development of textile imports to Indo-China uniquely in terms of trade with France, we find that the French share increases dramatically from 1885 to 1905 (Table 2). By 1900 France had conquered more than 50% of the imported textile fabric market in Indo-China, and even though her share seems to drop considerably after 1905, between 1915 and 1929, the French recover and surpass their former level to the extent that by 1929 France controls 74% of the import value of fabrics to Indo-China.[7] The very high share of imported fabrics from France in 1929 is probably due to the revised tariff policies introduced in 1928 which favoured French textile capital in the face of foreign competition.

The market for cotton fabrics was almost totally dominated by French products as far as imports are concerned before the turn of the century and remained so until the economic crisis brought about by World War

Table 3. *Import of cotton fabrics from France as a percentage of total import of cotton fabrics (in tonnage)*

1897	78%	1913	99%	1922	80%
1904	96%	1914	93%	1923	90%
1906	98%	1915	69%	1924	92%
1907	97%	1916	39%	1925	92%
1908	97%	1917	25%	1926	94%
1909	93%	1918	27%	1927	94%
1910	89%	1919	31%	1928	95%
1911	93%	1920	32%	1929	97%
1912	94%	1921	68%		

Sources: Archive Nationales. AOM. Carton 237 N 02 (7). BEI 1905, 1908, 1914. *Annuaire statistique* 1913 – 22, 1923 – 29.

Table 4. *Export of raw silk and cloth from Indo-China (tons)*

	raw silk	silk cloth	silk embroideries
1899	185	3.4	–
1903	117	3.5	–
1908	80	3.6	–
1913	93	12.6	0.7
1918	9	5.2	0.4
1923	64	22.0	6.7
1928	32	35.6	5.0

Sources: Leurence: Étude statistique sur le développement économique de l'Indochine 1899 a 1923, BEI 1923. *Annuaire statistique* 1913 – 22, 1923 – 29.

I. After 1922 French cotton fabrics again dominated imported textiles and cornered 80% of the market (Table 3).

Silk has traditionally been a special trade item, entirely apart from cotton and jute. In the beginning of the twentieth century, raw silk was still an important export commodity for Indo-China, but as the national production of silk fabrics of higher quality developed, so did its export, with the foreseeable result that raw silk exports decreased steadily (Table 4). The implantation of several silk factories by French enterprises parallel to the growth of cottage industries accounts for this

Table 5. *Import of silk cloth into Indo-China (tons)*

	from France	From China/Hong Kong
1903	–	214
1908	5	229
1913	5	263
1918	20	245
1923	47	199
1928	545	384

Sources: BEI 1905. *Annuaire statistique* 1913 – 22, 1923 – 29.

evolution. At the same time, the import of silk fabrics from both France and China increased in general much more than the export over the same period from 1903 to 1928 (Table 5). This seemingly contradictory development can probably be explained by a growing national consumption of silk products.

As for the cotton textile trade, overall imports of raw materials, thread, and fabrics measured in tonnage, developed rapidly after the 1890s and the French had actually conquered the fabric market by the turn of the century (Table 6). The implantation in the early 1900s of three important French cotton factories with important spinning capacities would lead us to expect a decrease in the importation of threads especially, but the available figures indicate the contrary, and the import of thread from other countries actually increased. Increased national consumption as well as the proliferation of local markets was furthered by improved transport possibilities underly this development.

Just as in the case of silk exports, Indo-China exported mainly raw cotton and a small portion of her manufactured thread, relying mainly on importation for ready-made fabrics. However, the export of finished silk fabrics did become an appreciable source of revenue for Indo-China, or rather, the French enterprises and merchants in Indo-China, even though import of silk fabrics greatly surpassed export. Cotton fabrics never became an export item since they were entirely consumed by the home market. Only in the case of cotton lace — a handicraft product — did export increase considerably in the 1920s (Table 7).

The overall pattern of textile trade from 1892 to 1930 indicates an unfavourable import-export balance for Indo-China for all ready-made cotton and silk fabrics. From the turn of the century onwards France dominated the cotton trade, and the Chinese, the silk trade. Colonial protective policies and tariffs definitely favoured and encouraged the interest of the French textile capital in Indo-China, especially the cotton

Table 6. *Import of raw cotton, cotton thread, and cotton fabrics (tons)*

| | From France and the colonies | | From other countries | | |
	thread	fabrics	raw cotton	thread	fabrics
1892	2.682	–	–	3.608	–
1897	–	2.891	–	–	817
1904	480	4.380	3.182	1.722	202
1908	511	6.139	2.782	3.472	176
1913	434	9.376	5.326	1.255	83
1918	134	1.225	4.056	1.623	3.385
1923	106	6.696	5.707	2.524	720
1928	394	7.239	4.592	2.894	341

(a) The figures only include imports to Tonkin, which, however, was by far the most important consumer of thread. Certain kinds of thread are counted in metres, but converted into weight according to the weight/price relations of the major import item (unbleached thread). (b) Thread counted in metres is not included.

Sources: BEI 1905, 1907. Rapport des douanes, 1893. Archive Nationales. AOM. Carton 237. N 02(7).

Table 7. *Export of raw cotton, cotton thread and fabrics*

	raw cotton (tons)	ginned cotton (tons)	thread (tons)	fabrics (tons)	cotton lace (kg)
1899	510	1,693	–	–	–
1903	2,100	2,300	–	–	–
1908	4,250	3,130	–	–	–
1913	6,400	3,450	1,712	75	–
1918	2,240	1,910	341	8	490
1923	1,410	1,920	702	132	18,455
1928	489	510	246	136	21,863

Sources: as Table 4.

entrepreneurs. Therefore it is not surprising that the textile industries and commercial enterprises of Paris and Lyon should take a substantial interest in colonial trade with Indo-China. However, it is noteworthy that, during the same period, the same textile establishments have invested a considerable amount of capital in Vietnam to set up modern textile factories.

Sea trade with Indo-China

We conclude this paper with some observations concerning the distribution of seaborne trade with Indo-China amongst the major naval powers operating in Southeast Asia during this period. Unfortunately, available statistical data do not allow us to follow the general development of sea trade prior to 1912. However, it is safe to say that by this date France controlled roughly one quarter of the overall shipping tonnage to and from Indo-China.

Table 8 provides figures for incoming tonnage over the period from 1912 to 1929 from ships flying the French, British, Chinese, Japanese and the United States flags. Clearly the data reflect the changing power relations in Southeast Asia. Up to World War I the British Empire's tonnage share outclassed that of the French, which must be explained by the overwhelming importance of the Hong Kong rice outlet for Indo-China.

However, by 1929 Britain's share of tonnage had dropped from 36% to 14% mainly due to the French colonial tariff and monetary policies which led to overpricing raw materials from Indo-China for the traditional Asian markets. Japan, whose trade with Indo-China rapidly increases throughout this period, especially during World War I, takes second place only to France by 1929. With the exception of the war years, China's sea trade with Indo-China remains limited and accounts for less than 10% of the total shipping tonnage, and of course much of this trade is carried out by junks. The United States, a late-comer to the sea trade with Indo-China, showed herself an unstable trading partner throughout this period.

The low percentage of Chinese shipping tonnage to Indo-China seems surprising in view of the importance generally accorded to the position of Chinese merchants in Indo-China and the merchant houses of the Saigon-Cholon area in particular. Apparently most of the rice bought by Chinese middlemen from Vietnamese peasants was shipped to Hong Kong in vessels flying under British or French flags. A considerable quantity of Indo-Chinese exports handled by Chinese intermediaries — especially products from the north of Indo-China —

Table 8. *Number and tonnage (in percentages) of boats entering Indochina divided into flags 1912–29*

	France		Britain		China		Japan		U.S.A.		
	boats	% of tonnage	boats	% of tonnage	boats/junks	% of tonnage	boats	% of tonnage	boats	% of tonnage	total tonnage
1890	55	16	239	31	3/ 877	2	19	3	2	0.3	743,578
1912	263	35	431	36	44/ 890	4	243	19	51	4	1,565,000
1915	304	29	281	17	247/ 965	15	284	25	139	11	2,429,000
1918	343	21	382	23	298/ 960		291	19	238	14	2,242,000
1921	289	24	347	22	83/1183	5	216	16	71	7	3,171,000
1924	331	34	232	15	196/ 919	9	244	21	18	3	3,448,000
1927	354	36	231	14	180/1027	3	270	21	28	4	4,045,000
1929	349	26									4,569,000

Sources: Rapport des douanes, 1891, *Annuaire statistique* 1913–22, 1923–29

entered China via overland routes and rail, but the seaborne trade was
by far the most important. In any case the figures of Table 8 do question
the generally held assumptions concerning the dominant role of Chinese
merchant houses in Indo-China *vis-à-vis* rice exports.

Final remarks

For a number of reasons mainly related to scarcity of data, our
conclusions concerning the foreign trade of Indo-China from 1885 to
1930 remain provisional in character. It is certainly true that trade with
France and the French Empire takes on growing importance throughout
this period, but only after 1930 does France become the exclusive
trading partner of Indo-China. There is no doubt that the French
colonial trade policy had a major effect on the changing trade relations
with France and the empire *vis-à-vis* trade with other foreign countries.
This is especially true for incoming commodities where colonial tariff
policies were partly able to control the entry of goods from countries
outside France and the empire. On the other hand, rice as well as other
local exports had difficulty competing with their Asian neighbours
faced with less restrictive tariff controls; therefore it is not so surprising
that even for such homegrown products, trade relations between Indo-
China and France should expand steadily over the period in question.

The actual development of foreign trade shows remarkable growth,
both of imports and exports, and there seems to be a rather close
connection between the trend of the export trade with that of imports. In
the 30 year period from 1890 to 1929, the export value surpassed that of
the import value except for the short interval from 1900 to 1908, during
which time the implantation of factories as well as the extension of
infrastructure and communication systems absorbed a considerable
amount of French capital. The depression did, of course, influence
Indo-Chinese trade activities, and the value of trade decreased in
absolute terms. In spite of this world crisis, the volume of trade did not
drop considerably, which is a good indicator that productive activities
continued — at any rate during the early years of the depression — even
though the actual revenue from trade decreased. The volume/price
index confirms the general tendency underlying the entire trade
development, i.e. that exports developed steadily, albeit at a slower rate
than prices.

By and large, not enough interest has been accorded to the import
trade with French Indo-China in comparison with the considerable
attention paid by economists and historians to the export interests of
metropolitan France and their colonial proteges. Moreover the
quantitive importance of the Chinese trade needs to be re-evaluated.

Finally the above observations concerning the difference in trends between the Indo-Chinese export and import trade need to be elaborated; especially our contention that the volume of export commodities in contrast to imports seems much less sensitive to external factors such as fluctuating world market prices or international, political conflicts. However the pre-capitalist social relations of production characterizing the Indo-Chinese agrarian society throughout this period, tend to substantiate this contention. Closer inspection of the available documentary sources concerning foreign trade relations between Indo-China and her different trading partners will surely provide further insight into the important economic and social transformations occurring within Indo-China during this ascendant period of French colonialism.

17

YUNNAN TRADE IN HAN TIMES: TRANSIT, TRIBUTE AND TRIVIA

Harald Bøckman

Yunnan has traditionally been regarded as the transit area for a flourishing trade between the Indian region and the Han-Chinese region. This activity is said to have originated long before the Han dynasty (206 B.C. – A.D. 220), but at least for the period under discussion, there is still too scant evidence for proclaiming it a 'Southern Silk Road'.[1]

The trade in the adjacent regions to the east and south-east has been treated in Wan Gungwy's study of the Nanhai trade,[2] but there exists no similar thorough study for the Yunnan region. Pelliot's monumental 'article' covers a later period, and does not attempt to substantiate an early tradition. Chen's study is useful to check the basic facts, but sins grossly against most basic rules for textual criticism. Ji[3] has useful information scattered throughout his work, but concentrates, as the title indicates, more on the purely cultural matters like religion, language and literature. Cammann deals mostly with the northern passage, and even the standard study for the topic by Yü, gives only peripheral treatment of the south-west. This paper will outline some fields of investigation for this topic. It will concentrate on Yunnan as a transit and tribute region, and not go into detail about the regional connections like Yunnan and the Chu region in the north-east, the Yelang region in the east, the Jiaochi region in the south-east and the little-known but probably important link with the Kam region in the north-west. The written historical material is a good starting-point, but a composite and unruly region like Yunnan will profit greatly from future interdisciplinary collaboration.

Sima Qian, the Grand Historian of China, sums up his account of the Southwestern Barbarians (Xinan Yi Liezhuan) saying that the whole affair of Han relations with the south-west came about because someone happened to come across some relish of betel pepper from Shu (Sichuan) in Panyu (Guangzhou), and because the people of Daxia (Bactria) carried canes made of Qiong bamboo from Sichuan in West China.[4] This passage is an almost frivolous commentary from the author and was probably meant to be so. The context he refers to was Tang Meng's visit to the Southern Yue people[5] and Zhang Qian's involuntary prolonged exile in Central Asia.[6] This last affair has direct bearing on our study, so we will discuss this story in some detail.

Transit trade

When the Han emissary Zhang Qian returned to the capital of the Han dynasty from his prolonged stay in Central Asia some time before 122 B.C., the Han had just relinquished their efforts to get permanent control over a part of the south-west, especially the Yelang region (present-day Guizhou). The reason for this was that the Southern Yue had just been subdued and by that, Yelang had lost much of its strategic importance. Furthermore, the upkeep and permanent presence in the regions, which had been 'opened up' by Sima Xiangru and Tang Meng,[7] had proved both costly and difficult because of factors like climate, topography and revolt from the indigenous peoples.[8] And more serious worries were brewing on the northern border.

Zhang Qian, during his visit to Bactria, had discovered what he was told was cloth from Shu and bamboo canes from Qiong, both in the Sichuan region, which had come to Bactria through the land of Shendu, i.e. India. Zhang was told that Shendu was not too far from Shu, and since the roads through the north-west had been blocked by the Xiongnu and the Quangs, he memorialized after his return that the court should initiate efforts to establish a passage through the south-west to Shendu.

Accordingly, expeditions were sent out in four directions to the Mang, Ran, Xi and Qiong and Bo, the peoples of which are representatives of the Sino-Tibetan marches of today, but the emissaries were blocked in the north by the Di and the Zuo, and in the south by the Xi and the Kunming, and none reached their destination. When one of their delegations arrived in the Dian kingdom in Central Yunnan, it was well received and invited to stay. The Kunming tribes to the west of them had a reputation of robbing and killing Han emissaries,[9] so the King of Dian sent out several of his own people through Kunming territory to find a passage to Shendu. After a year of efforts, they returned with the task unfulfilled.[10] Even a subsequent army of 20 – 30 thousand men, which was raised by freeing the criminals in the three districts of the capital and replenished by men from Ba and Shu, was repelled by the Kunming.[11]

The hospitality and co-operation of the King of Dian left, however, such a deep impression on the Han emissaries that they proposed to the

Emperor that the court should initiate friendly dealings with Dian and annex it. This was completed in the year 109 B.C., when the Hans had pacified most of the lesser tribes of the region, which, as the custom was, 'begged to become vassals of the Hans with Chinese officials to govern their land.'[12] The King of Dian mended his ways and ceased his resistance, and was appointed to remain nominal ruler over the newly established prefecture of Yizhou.

There are several noteworthy conclusions to be drawn from this first successful Han domination of the central Yunnan region. In the first place, the arguments for opening up the south-west were not commercial, but military and strategic. If the road between Shu and Shendu could be opened up, it would bring states like Daxia, Dayuan and Anxi closer to the Han in their strategic deliberations in the north-west.[13] In this sense, the Han policy in the south-west did not differ from the policy in the north or from the fundamental Han tradition that political and military strategy takes predominance over trade and that trade should be regulated by military power as a defensive measure.

Zhang Qian's encounter in Central Asia with products allegedly from Shu did indeed have a great impact on the geopolitical manœuverings of the Han. The products in question seem to have been renowned in their days, but the way Sima Qian relates the incident, it seems that Zhang Qian accepted the story without being able to verify that the products really were from Shu. As Cammann[14] has pointed out, it just does not make sense to carry bamboo half-way across South-Central Asia, and we do not really know what kind of material the 'cloth' (bu) from Shu was.[15] P.-t'Serstevens, on the other hand, refers to Laufer and maintains that the bamboo was of such special quality that it could quite likely have been transported far through intermediaries.[16] In the writer's opinion, Zhang may just as well have been subject to a promotional trick from local merchants similar to the magic which the 'right kind' of label invokes on shoppers today.

Furthermore, it seems that there was not only no direct contact and knowledge about India and Burma at the Han court, but that there also had been no direct contact between Chang'an and the kingdom of Dian. This is revealed in a passage in the Shi Ji where the King of Dian says that he had, as had the King of Yelang, been pondering over the extent of the land of the Han ruler.[17]

Thus, we can rule out the existence of *officially initiated* transit trade between China and the regions beyond Yunnan, and this is probably valid for the whole period under discussion. This does not at all mean, however, that there are no signs of transit trade in the region at the time. The fact that there was a notion in the bazaars in Daxia about far-away regions like Shendu and beyond reveals the existence of sophisticated long-distance networks of trade. When the Han emissaries were at the Dian court, they were told that beyond the Kunming tribes to the west of them, there was the land of Dianyue and that the merchants from Shu sometimes went there on trading missions[18]

The Sichuan region is of great interest and obviously of great significance as far as early trade is concerned. There are two reasons for that. One is that it virtually existed as an independent state for several centuries during the Zhou dynasty until it was conquered by the Qin in 316 B.C. The social formation in the region seems to have had a distinct regional flavour, and was an operating-base for a prominent class of merchants.

The other reason was that the region was a major producer of sophisticated handicrafts and was rich in raw materials. Shu was famous for its bronzes, gold and silverware, lacquerware and iron before it was taken over by government control during the former Han dynasty, and in the Shi Ji, we can read that the region also produced large quantities of dye, ginger, cinnabar, bamboo and wooden implements. The southern part of the region seems to have had a certain suzerainty over the Dian and the Bo, the latter noted for its young slaves. Nearby to the west were the regions of the Qiong and the Zuo, the former famous for their horses and the latter for their yaks.[19] It is clear that the merchants from Shu were in control of the regional trade and had established communication with both the south-eastern region around Guangzhou through Dian and even the hostile Kunming. The men of Shu seem to have been the Pantays (Huis) of their day.

Later in the dynasty, the regional and long-distance transit trade was boosted by the establishment of the Han military forward position of Yongchang in the middle of the first century A.D. In the biography of the Ailaos in the *History of the Later Han Dynasty (Hou Han Shu = HHS)*, we can read the following about the Yongchang Commandery: 'From the region comes copper, iron, lead, tin, gold, silver, precious stones, amber, crystal, cowry shells, clam pearls, peacock, jadeite, rhinoceroses, elephants and monkeys.'[20]

The fourth-century regional gazetteer *Record of the Lands South of Mount Hua (Huayangguo Zhi = HYGZ)* describes the region in the same vein and adds products like brocade, embroidery, calico and silk.[21]

It is clear that Yongchang must have been an important transit centre, because several of the products mentioned (amber, pearls, cowry shells) are beyond doubt from the regions further to the south and the west. And it seems that the place also developed beyond an entrepot and into a true trade centre, as the HYGZ mentions the presence of people from Piao (Pyu = Burma) and Shendu (India), who undoubtedly must have been connected with trade.[22] The prospects for finding out to what extent Yongchang also developed into a trade centre with a market structure as well, should be good, because the remains of the Han garrison town have just been located by Chinese archeologists near present-day Baoshan.[23]

But until now, there have been very few archaeological indicators of the volume and the types of commodities that were traded. The rich excavations of the Dian royal tombs in Shizhaishan in Central Yunnan do contain large quantities of cowry shells, but they may just as well have originated in the littoral south-east, and only a few pieces of glass were contained in these tombs. The one cocking lever from a Han crossbow which Cammann identified from the finds in Taxila, must undoubtedly have come through Central Asia, and as yet, there have been no significant archaeological finds in Burmese sites from the period.[24]

The fact that there is so little substance beyond the general listings of commodities in the written sources may be interpreted in two ways.

One is that the sheer volume of trade was fairly limited, both because of the obvious difficulties with the extreme geographical conditions, and the seemingly persistent hostility of the Kunming tribes. The Shi Ji does in fact say that because of the constant harassment by the Kunmings, envoys would rather journey to the foreign states by the northern route, and that the regions in the north-west had become so surfeited with Han goods that they were no longer regarded with special esteem.[25]

Another possible explanation can be that there was a constant flow of commodities; that the trade was more of a low-keyed, long-term nature, more of the Southeast Asian type of 'accumulation rather than replacement'[26] and accordingly different from the more spectacular fast money trading in the northern passages. And since the trade seems to have been in the hands of regional traders all along, it has probably been an unbroken activity throughout the centuries.

Tribute trade

Another form for trade that merits our attention is the tribute trade. The term was first discussed in its Chinese context by Lattimore.[27] By tribute trade we do not mean just the ceremonial tribute offered in connection with tribute missions by the lesser rulers to the more powerful rulers, which could be said to function within a gift-exchange structure. I am primarily thinking of the considerable concentrations of wealth amassed by local and regional prominent persons within the framework of officially sanctioned trade which took place in the shade of the proscribed gift-exchanges between the courts.

The earliest mention of tribute missions from the remote regions in the south-west is found in the HHS, which relates that the Ailaos, the Daners and others offered tribute to the imperial court in the year A.D. 74.[28] This was the beginning of an active period of exchange that lasted well into the second century.

The most detailed listing of tribute-objects is found in the biography of the Ailaos in the HHS. There, it says that towards the end of the first century A.D., the local kings sent rhinoceroses, elephants, water-buffalos, cattle, ivory, golden seals and purple ribbons. Of special interest is the mention of the tribute sent by the Shan King in the year A.D. 120, which included musicians and magicians, who said themselves that they were people from beyond the ocean in the west, which the author of the history associates with Rome (Da Qin).[29]

The most common tribute objects from the Han court seem to have been, not unexpectedly, gold, silver, silk and brocade, as well as seals and cordons. Another prestige object that probably will be unearthed some day in the region adjoining the south-west is the famous lacquerware from the government-controlled workshops in Shu and Guanghan, because such objects have been found in other border regions as far as Pyonyang, Noin Ula and Qingzhen.[28]

As mentioned, tribute trade was not limited to the objects exchanged at the court. The exchange of commodities taking place in the shade of the ceremonies was regulated to fixed market days, and it is likely that these market days were the scene of intense barter primarily from the side of the guests from the outlying and far-away areas. There is little evidence about what were really the most favoured items and what was exchanged. One interesting incident is found in the Biography of the Southern Yue in the *Shi Ji*, which relates the anger of Prince Zhao Tuo of Nan Yue when the Empress Dowager Lü Hou banned the trade of iron implements in connection with the tribute trade because of Zhao Tuo's separatist movements.[31] It seems that tension around strategic commodities is by no means limited to our times.

In the rich archaeological yields in the Dian tombs of Shizhaishan in Yunnan from the second century B.C., there is a very interesting group of figurines in bronze on the lid of one of the cowrie-shell containers. This highly artistic creation has been named 'The Tribute Scene' (*nagong chang*),[32] and represents beyond doubt such an occasion. No less than seven groups of people are depicted, and they are seven distinct ethnic groups all presenting different produce. There is no indication as to what kind of prestige goods the tribute bearers might have been given in return, but the evidence from the Shizhaishan tombs shows that products of bronze, iron, gold, silver, jade and lacquer were produced locally.[33]

The tribute from Shizhaishan shows that there were several layers of tribute structures, and that it may be a regional indigenous tradition just as well as a copy from the Chinese. Even if the long-standing Chinese tribute system is a sophisticated system for political and social interaction with foreign and remote regions, it is definitely incorrect to regard it as a purely Chinese invention.

Trade with trivia

Finally, I would like to mention briefly to what extent it is possible to spot local produce, or trivia, in the material I have gone through. Such a trade would probably include a whole line of products, starting from the near-ritual prestige objects to basic necessities like cloth, pottery and foodstuff. That such trade existed is indicated in the *Shi Ji*, which relates that in the Shu and adjacent regions, there was a network of plank roadways in the remote areas which made it possible for the areas which had a surplus to exchange their goods for things which they lacked.[34]

But so far, there is little archaeological evidence — and the little there is must again be sought in the Shizhaishan tombs. On one of the lids of the cowry-shell containers, there is an elaborate scene which depicts a ritual of human sacrifice.[35] But there are also other actors on the scene besides those taking part in the ritual. There are figurines sitting beside baskets, figurines discussing over a basket, figurines with baskets on their heads, a man who carries a big fish, and others who seem to be just hanging around. The contents in the baskets are difficult to discern, but the scene no doubt depicts a barter transaction of agricultural by-products. It is striking that, judging from the scene, the trade activity seemed to have been the almost exclusive domain of women. The scene demonstrates clearly that trade activity took place in the shade of ritual activity, and indicates that formal markets in a separate setting, typical for a peasant economy, had not yet come into existence.

The Dian culture in the Former Han dynasty shows a culture which on the one hand must have been a civilization with a sizeable social surplus, because of the tremendous amassment of ritual objects and prestige goods of a high technological quality, which at the same time had not yet developed an urbanized level of market-town activity or a distinct class of merchants. This fact, in the context of Chinese history, poses a challenge to our understanding of the local culture in the south-western fringes of China.

18

FROM PIRATES TO MERCHANTS: THE VOC'S TRADING POLICY TOWARDS JAPAN DURING THE 1620s.

Eiichi Kato

Introduction

The Dutch began to trade with Japan in 1609. On 1 July two ships detached from the fleet under the command of Admiral Pieter Willemsz. Verhoeff called the *Roode Leeuw met Pijlen* and *Griffioen* entered the port of the island of Hirado (Firando). Two months later the Dutch delegates, having been granted an audience by the Shogun Tokugawa, received from his government a guarantee of unimpeded trade and the right of abode in Japan: they decided to open a depot for the Dutch Company at Hirado. From then on and until 1641 in which year, on the Shogun's orders, the depot was transferred to Nagasaki, Hirado was to play an important part in the history of Far Eastern international relations both as the strategic and commercial base of the Dutch East India Company (VOC) and as the most important staging post at the extreme north of the Dutch sphere of interest.

The activities of the VOC in Japan were characterized by an aggressive attitude towards its competitors, particularly at the outset, and its behaviour verged on the piratical. However, following upon the achievement of Japanese national unity symbolized by the strict control of the Shogun's power, the VOC had to moderate its policy.

As for the activities of the VOC in Japan prior to 1620, from which date even the details are generally known to us, it must be admitted that we know all too little about them. We do certainly have access to a number of documents preserved in the Dutch general state archives (*Het Algemeen Rijksarchief,* i.e. ARA) at The Hague, but these provide too little information about the activities of the VOC in Japan during the first two decades of the seventeenth century. That is why I want to elucidate this problem despite the absence of primary sources: my method being to study the merchandise handled by the VOC using those documents still in existence despite the ravages of time.

Raw Silk from China and Silver from Japan

During the sixteenth and seventeenth centuries Japanese foreign trade was more or less limited to the import of raw silk from China and the export of silver. This form of barter was to all intents and purposes continuous and reciprocal.

Following the interruption of official traffic between China and Japan in the mid-sixteenth century these goods were almost exclusively transported by the Portuguese, who had recently arrived within sight of the Chinese and Japanese coasts. The acquisition and founding of the town of Macao gave the Portuguese access to the market of Canton where they purchased finest quality raw silk. Taking advantage of this ideal situation, the Macao Indiaman on its annual journey to Nagasaki was able to realise profits of between 200 and 400 per cent.

The Market for Raw Silk

It is estimated that the amount of raw silk exported annually to Japan between 1620 and 1630 rose from 200,000 to 400,000 catties (100 catties are equivalent to one picul).[1] But at the beginning of the seventeenth century the amount had been decreasing and had sunk below the level of 200,000: in fact the Macao Town Council proclaimed at the end of the sixteenth century that the quantity of raw silk sold to Japan must not exceed 160,000 catties per annum.[2] A Spanish document dated about 1600 mentions that a Portuguese ship *en route* to Japan loaded 50,000 to 60,000 catties of the best quality raw silk and 40,000 to 50,000 catties of other kinds, which would mean an estimated profit of twice the purchase price.[3] It is estimated that the VOC's imports of raw silk into Japan exceeded 100,000 catties per annum after 1635.

The Proportion of Merchandise Imported and Exported

We have no data on the first years of the seventeenth century, but the figures appearing in the accounts ledgers of the VOC trading depot at Hirado known as the Comptoir Firando give us an idea of the frequency and importance of commerce in Japanese waters during the first half of that century, both European and Asian.

The day-books (i.e. *Negotie Journaal* and *Grood Boek*) of the Firando Bank still exist and we have their records since 1620; also we have other more fragmentary documents relative to the earlier period such as invoices, bills of lading etc: they are still in the archives of the

VOC mainly filed under the heading *Overgecomen brieven en papieren uit Indie.*

According to the Firando records of 1636 during that year the Dutch unloaded goods to the value of f. 1,593,011: – :3; at the same time their exports were worth f. 3,192,809: – :3. In the figures given, including imported items f. 921,298:7:6 worth of Chinese raw silk and f. 327,619:10 worth of other kinds of silken materials and of items exported one finds f. 2,811,950 worth of Japanese ingots (*Japans gemunt silver* or *Japans schuit geld*). And the percentage of chauns to the total value whether imported or exported is as follows: 59.43 per cent for raw silk, 21.13 per cent for silk goods i.e. 80.56 per cent; and that of money in ingots is 88.49 per cent of the total value of exports. This means that f. 1,248,917:17:6 worth of silk and silk materials imported into Japan produced sales worth f. 2,811,950.

By this time Spanish travel to Japan had already been banned, the English had beaten a retreat and the Shogun's edict shutting off the country forbade the Japanese all commercial journeys. After 1635 Portuguese business transactions declined and Chinese activity stagnated. As shown by the figures cited above (see Table 1) one could simplify the details of Japanese commerce by stating that it was limited to the import of raw silk from China and the export of silver during the first part of the seventeenth century.

The Development of Japanese Foreign Trade

In view of the amount of space available I shall endeavour to illustrate my observations by referring to the tables below.

Imports of raw silk

Table 2 shows the increase in the quantity of raw silk imported by Japan between 1600 and 1639 via both European and Asian ships. The figures for Dutch imports are taken from the accounts of the Firando trading depot and they are relatively accurate particularly if one compares them with those produced in previous years. For the years prior to 1620 it is impossible to determine the total quantity of imports.

The figures for the years 1622, 1623, 1624 and 1630 show the total sales; from 1628 to 1632 the Bakufu (the Shogun's government) placed an embargo on Dutch merchandise as a result of the 'Nuijts affair' on Taiwan which brought Dutch and Japanese merchants into conflict. Statistics for other nations are more approximate and depend on the character of the various sources cited.

Dutch imports of raw silk rose to the level of those of the Portuguese after 1635: this was the year when the decree shutting off the country was promulgated, forbidding overseas travel to the Japanese; in 1639 the Bakufu, inaugurating its official policy of persecuting the Christian faith, banned the Portuguese from the whole of its territory.

General view of VOC Transactions after 1620

Table 3 shows the development of VOC trade with Japan from 1624 to 1640 with the exception of the embargo period 1628 – 1632; it gives the statistics of the value of imports and exports, of silver exported and of the amount of raw silk imported annually. One can thus establish that the amounts of the transactions varied in direct proportion to fluctuations in the quantities of silk and silver handled by the VOC.

In 1624 the VOC made Formosa its strategic and commercial centre for the area and built Fort Zeelandia there. Mastery of Formosa enabled it to trade prosperously and to be the link between China and Japan: its imports doubled and its exports quadrupled compared with the previous year. Although trade with Japan was interrupted by the 'Nuijts affair' which erupted in 1628, the tendency to growth took off again as soon as the Shogun, having extracted tokens of obedience to his authority from the VOC, authorized the resumption of trade with Japan.

The Firando Trading Depot, the VOC's Strategic Base: VOC Trade Before the 1620s

When comparing the period before 1620 with that after 1630 one must agree that the character of VOC trade with Japan is marked by the difference between this period and the two others. During the 1630s, as mentioned above, the import of raw silk and export of silver were the main elements of Japanese foreign trade. Inversely, during the second decade of the seventeenth century and at the beginning of the 1620s, the Dutch failed to show a very great interest in the demand for raw silk on the Japanese market; sometimes they even sent quantities of it back from Firando.

The Firando Trading Centre without External Support

During the early years Dutch trade with Japan was intermittent, even arbitrary. In 1610 and 1613 not one Dutch vessel visited Hirado; in

Table 1. *List of cargoes imported and exported by the VOC to Japan in 1636*

	IMPORTS			EXPORTS	
Commodities	value in guilders	(%)	Commodities	value in guilders	(%)
raw silk	f. 921,298: 7: 6:	(59.43%)	silver ingots	f. 2,811,950: – : – :	(88.49%)
silkenware	f. 327,619:10: – :	(21.13%)	copper	f. 198,437: 1:13:	(6.24%)
woollen goods	f. 83,410: 5: 8:	(5.38%)	copper money	f. 45,075:12: – :	(1.42%)
cotton goods	f. 18,279:16:12:	(1.18%)	iron materials	f. 12,765: 4: 9:	(0.40%)
linen ware	f. 8,029: 9: – :	(0.52%)	building timber	f. 13,365:14:11:	(0.42%)
leather goods	f. 86,785: 8: – :	(5.60%)	camphor	f. 2,955:17: 9:	(0.10%)
sapan wood	f. 20,324: 1:10:	(1.31%)	foodstuffs	f. 65,516:11:10:	(2.06%)
spices and drugs	f. 24,628: 7:13:	(1.59%)	lacquers	f. 14,248: 8:11:	(0.45%)
sugar	f. 33,795:12: 8:	(2.18%)	assorted goods	f. 3,582:14:13:	(0.11%)
ivory	f. 10,364: 2: 8:	(0.67%)	re-exports	f. 9,834: 9: – :	(0.11%)
metal ware	f. 11,334:14:12:	(0.73%)	Total	f. 3,177,734:14:12:	(100.00%)
assorted goods	f. 2,963: 8:10:	(0.19%)			
domestic items	f. 10: 8: – :	(0.00%)			
special articles	f. 1,398: 6: – :	(0.09%)			
Total	f. 1,550,241:18: 7:	(100.00%)			

Source: Negotie journaal Firando, Anno 1636. MS. ARA. Japans Archief No. 836

Table 2. *Raw Silk Imports to Japan, 1660 – 1636*

Year	Portuguese ships	[a]Dutch ships	Japanese ships	Chinese ships	Spanish ships
1600	[b]25,000 catties				
1601	No voyage				
1603	[c]140,000 catties				
1604	[d]Such a good cargo of Chinese silk				
1605					Wrecked 50,000 crusados
1606	[e]Profitable				
1607	No voyage				
1608	No voyage				
1609	[f]260,000 catties				
1610	No voyage				
1611	[g]20,000 catties				
1612	[h]130,000 catties		_____[h]500,000 catties_____		
			_____[i]200,000 catties_____		
1613	No voyage				
1614	[j]30,000 catties				
1615	[k]90,000 catties				
1621		5,688^1/16 catties			
1622	No voyage	9,056 catties			
1623	[i]Rich cargo	3,231 catties	[m]12,000 catties	[l]Rich cargo	
1624		2,847.5 catties			
1625		29,017 catties			
1626		33,227 catties			
1627		91,362¼ catties	[n]_____200,000 catties_____		
1628		28,980.5 catties			
1629		—			
1630		[o]25,189 catties			
1631		—			
1632		—			
1633	[p]12,000 catties	1,409 catties	[q]100,000 catties	[r]150,000 catties	
1634	[s]20,000 catties	64,530 catties	[s]150,000 catties	[s]170,000 catties	
1635		132,039 catties			
1636		142,251 catties			
1637	[t]157,589 catties	110,306 catties		[w]150,000 catties	
1638		142,194 catties			
1639		111,387 catties			

* Quantities of silk are shown in *catty*: 100 catties equal 1 picul.
After: E. Kato. The Japanese Dutch Trade in the Formative Period of the Seclusion Policy. (ACTA ASIATICA 30. 1976)

Notes to Table 2

(a) The figures in this column are cited from the *Negotie Journaels Firando* 1620 – 1639 and also the *Groot Boecken Firando* 1624 – 1639.

(b) Fernão Guereiro, *Relaçào Annal*, II, p. 204.

(c) C. R. Boxer, *Fidalgos in the Far East*, p. 50. The cargo for this year, however, was confiscated by the Dutch.

(d) Francisco Pires, *Pontos do que me alembrar* (C. R. Boxer, *The Great Ship from Amacon*, p. 68, note 133).

(e) ibid.

(f) *Copie brief van Jacques Specx de Nangasacque, 3 Nov. 1610* (Kol. Arch. Oude Brieven uit Indië, Japan). The Portuguese ship which arrived in 1609 was *Nossa Senhora da Graça* or *Madre de Geos*. She sank outside the port of Nagasaki in January 1610.

(g) *Journael ende Verhael van de reyse gedaen door P. W. Verhoeven.* 1607 et seq.

(h) Report of Father Valentim Carvalho, S.J. translated into French by Léon Pagés (*Histoire de la religion Chrétienne au Japon, depuis 1598 jusqu'à 1651*, t II, Annex pp. 164 – 5).

(i) *Sunpu-ki.* (Shiseki zassan II. p. 236). The two figures given for the silk imports in 1612 are rough estimates.

(j) The letter of R. Cockes to A. Denton at Patani, Firando, 25 Nov. 1614 (Foster, *Letters Received by the East India Company*, Vol. II, p. 203).

(k) The same to John Gourney at Siam, Firando, 20 Dec. 1615 (Ibid. Vol. III. p. 265).

(l) *Originele missive van Cornelis van Neijenroode uijt Firando, 20 Dec. 1623* (Kol. Arch. 995, ff. 257 – 260).

(m) IWAO Seiichi, *Shuinsen bōeki-shi no kenkyū*. Tokyo. 1958, pp. 252, 253.

(n) *Copie Missive van Pieter Nuiyts uijt Firando, 17 Feb. 1628* (Kol. Arch. 1006, ff. 155, 156).

(o) Trade at the Dutch Hirado factory was suspended from 1628 to early 1633 by orders of the bakufu, but the Hollanders were allowed to sell part of their stock. The figure here, therefore, represents the amount of sales.

(p) *Copie brief van Carel Lauwrens aen N. Couckebacker, Nangasacqui, 13 Sept. 1633* (Kol. Arch. 11722).

(q) *Originele Generale Missive door H. Brouwer ende Raden aen de XVII, 5 Aug. 1634* (Kol. Arch. 1028).

(r) *Copie brief van Carel Lauwrens aen N. Couckebacker, Nangasacqui, 12 Sept. 1633* (Kol. Arch. 11722).

(s) *Originele Missive van N. Couckebacker uijt Firando aen Batavia, 24 Nov. 1634* (Kol. Arch. 1026) and also *Originele Generale Missive door H. Brouwer ende Raden aen de XVII, 8 Jan. 1635* (Kol. Arch. 1023).

(t) *Translaet van gesegelde memorie der goederen door de ses Portugesche galiotten 1637 in Japan gebracht* (Kol. Arch. 1035).

(u) IWAO Seiichi, "Kinsei Nisshi bōeki ni kansuru sūryōteki kōsatsu" (*Shigaku zasshi* LXII – 11, 1952).

Table 3. *The commerce of the VOC with Japan, 1624 – 1640: analysis of the principal elements*

Year	Value of imports (*Guilders*)	Value of exports (*Guilders*)	Value of silver (*Guilders*)	Raw silk by weight (*Catties*)
1624	f. 72.311	f. 74.672	–	2.847,5
1625	f. 364.590	f. 554.409	f. 338.513	29.017
1626	f. 230.048	f. 342.745	f. 236.207	33.227
1627	f. 630.494	f. 1.022.563	f. 851.045	91.362,3/4
1632	–	f. 800.419	f. 643.273	–
1633	f. 134.664	f. 375.980	f. 194.803	1.409
1634	f. 740.051	f. 1.201.030	f. 849.579	64.530
1635	f. 1.009.262	f. 1.636.833	f. 1.403.119	132.039
1636	f. 1.593.011	f. 3.192.809	f. 3.012.450	142.251
1637	f. 2.351.907	f. 6.829.891	f. 4.024.200	110.306
1638	f. 2.625.265	f. 4.892.880	f. 4.753.800	142.194
1639	f. 3.470.910	f. 7.564.034	f. 7.495.500	111.387
1640	f. 6.295.366	f. 2.691.147	f. 1.795.500	229.032
			f. 410.893*	

*The figures indicate the total of gold money exported in 1640
Sources: Negotie journaal Comptoir Firando, 1624 – 1640. Ms. ARA. Japans Archief 830 – 840.

Table 4. 'Retour Vloot' for the year 1617

Ships' names	Departure from Bantam	Cargo value	Destination
Orangieboom	1 sep. 1617	f. 56.566: 2:10:	Hoorn
Postpaert	12 nov. 1617	f. 48.766: 4: — :	Enkhuizen
Eendracht	17 dec. 1617	f. 234.455: — : 8:	Amsterdam
Walcherem	17 dec. 1617	f. 137.397:10:10:	Middelbourg
Enckhuijsen	17 dec. 1617	f. 140.782: 4: 1:	Enkhuizen
Eenhoorn	14 jan. 1618	f. 145.786:15: 3:	Amsterdam
Wapen van Zeeland	14 jan. 1618	f. 243.773:10: 3:	Middelbourg
Total value of shipments		f. 1.007.527: 7: 3:	

Sources: Ms. ARA. VOC. 1066. ff. 65 – 70v., 73 – 74v.

1610 Jacques Specx, chief clerk (*opperhoofd*) at Hirado, had to despatch merchandise destined for Siam by a Japanese merchant ship;[4] indeed, he had to return to Patani to replenish stores.[5]

Specx returned to Hirado the following year on the yacht *de Brack* which supplied the depot with cloth, lead, ivory, damask linen and raw silk.[6] He then had to apologise for the interruption of trade: Shogun Tokugawa Ieyasu had allowed the Dutch to exercise their lucrative activities on the basis of satisfying the annual requirements of the Japanese market; he also had to deal with the calumnies heaped on his country by its enemies which had come to the ears to Japan's strong man.

Dutch Incursions around Japan

Dutch vessels putting into Hirado became increasingly numerous after 1615 and the activities of the Hirado depot grew in proportion.[7] The balance sheet for 1614 and 1615 shows that the volume of exports in 1614 rose to 66,172 guilders; the following year exports grew to 194,780 guilders while imports reached about 57,000. However, this increase in business was not necessarily linked to a growth in transactions for the Japanese domestic market.

Analysing invoices from this period one finds among the cargoes despatched from Firando not only Japanese goods but also merchandise from outside Japan such as Chinese raw silk, Indian and Persian cotton goods, drugs, aromatics and spices. Furthermore, one finds among cargoes despatched from Japan both arms and ammunition and other items for the equipment of armies.

For example the three vessels that took part in the expedition of 1615, the junk *de Hoope* bound for Siam, the junk *de Fortuijne* and the ship *Enckhuijsen* bound for Bantam loaded as much Japanese silver and copper as arms, ammunition and other re-forwarded merchandise; the latter commodities are considered as exploitation on the part of the Dutch.

In the case of the ship *Vlissingen* which sailed from Hirado for the Moluccas on December 30th 1617, exports consisted of silver to the value of 266,982 guilders, construction wood, victuals, war materials produced in Japan as well as Chinese and Indian merchandise.

So Firando at this time functioned as a base and depot for the VOC in order to sustain naval operations against the Iberian navies and to maintain Dutch mastery of the Moluccan sea and fortify its central base of Bantam or Jakarta.

I should like to dwell here a bit on shipments to Holland at the end of the second decade of the seventeenth century. Dutch ships bound for Europe from the East Indies in 1617[8] are listed in Table 4.

With the exception of the *Oranjieboom* and the *Postaret*, Firando was mainly sending prize goods. At this period the VOC depots to which merchandise was allocated were known as Bantam, Jakarta (later Batavia), Patani, Firando and the Coromandel depots. Indian merchandise such as indigo, cotton goods and cloth were stored at Coromandel; Moluccan spices, pepper and other goods from regions near Java were stocked at Bantam or Jakarta, while goods from the Malay and Indo-Chinese peninsulas were for a while kept at Patani. As previously mentioned Firando was used for storing Japanese merchandise such as silver, copper, iron and camphor but also booty seized by the VOC from the Spanish and Portuguese and Chinese. The stocks were finally assembled at Bantam or Jakarta, the VOC's central bases in the East Indies from which the fleet would set forth for Europe.

The proportion of goods despatched from Firando in the cargoes of the returning fleet in 1617 were: 21.11 per cent of the total cargo of the *Eendracht*, 27.59 per cent of the *Walcheren*, 21.92 per cent of the *Walcheren*, 21.92 and 45.27 per cent of the *Wapen van Zeeland*.

Japanese goods such as silver, copper, iron, foodstuffs and munitions were almost all re-sold by the VOC in Asia to finance its military and commercial operations: only silk and silk goods came to Europe where they where acquired by the Dutch to the annoyance of their enemies.

The piratical extortion of the VOC came to a head in 1620 when the Anglo-Dutch mutual defence fleet was assembled at Hirado to oppose the Iberian naval force: this was the result of the defence treaty signed in 1619 by the British and Dutch East India companies.

Conclusion: Contradictions in Japanese Foreign Policy

The Shogun Tokugawa Ieyasu, who granted the Dutch a certain freedom to trade in his country, gave identical privileges to other foreigners provided that their presence was felt to be peaceful and friendly. He it was who put an end to the endemic civil wars that had been ravaging the country and it was he who in so doing re-established the authority of the central government. As far as his relations with foreigners were concerned, the Shogun operated a policy based on awareness of the pre-eminence of his territorial power: he permitted merchants to trade only on condition that they recognized his sovereignty over Japan and never opposed his decisions.

So the main plank of the Bakufu's diplomacy was to grant foreigners the right to trade and to protect them at the same time. This principle, elaborated during the first half of the seventeenth century, was subsequently considerably modified as the international situation in the region developed and the Shogunate began to act aggressively towards Christianity. Ieyasu's successor, Tokugawa Hidetada, continued with the main principles of his father's diplomacy; during his reign the Shogun's power was consolidated and control of foreign trade became more rigid.

Dutch and English acts of piracy were harshly criticized by the Portuguese and Chinese; the Bakufu objected to the methods of the former which it considered to be an attack on the integrity of the authority of Edo (the old name for Tokyo) by the fact that they cast anchor in its waters. As a result the Japanese government banned the Dutch and the English from exporting arms and ammunition and from employing Japanese as soldiers and sailors.

Because of the Shogunate's policy the VOC had to modify the methods hitherto employed. Above all after the 'Nuijts affair' the Batavian government opted for greater obedience to Japanese wishes and undertook a more peaceful business attitude in order to maximise profits from the Japanese market.

19

THE CARGO OF BROADCLOTH CARRIED IN THE EAST INDIA COMPANY'S EIGHTH VOYAGE

Anthony Farrington

The very idea of a substantial market for English woollen textiles in the climates of South, Southeast and East Asia with hindsight seems absurd. But we must not suppose that the Directors and servants of the East India Company were such poor merchants that they, too, did not quickly come to appreciate the difficulties of the endeavour. Unfortunately, the Company had little choice in the matter.

Early seventeenth century economic theory held that bilateral trade relations between countries should generate their own purchasing power and become self-financing. Left to itself it is probable that the Company, after the experience of its first few voyages, would have exported little other than precious metals; but it was subject to public and Parliamentary pressure to assist the national economy by creating overseas markets for English manufactures. The price paid for monopoly was the commercially irritating obligation to send out a certain proportion of its annual exports in goods as opposed to bullion or coin.

The second half of the seventeenth century saw particularly determined attacks on the Company's monopoly by the clothiers of Gloucestershire and the East Midlands, fronted by Parliamentary spokesmen. The monopoly survived at the cost of a legal obligation to home manufactures. The 1693 renewal of the Company's charter required an annual export of £150,000 worth of manufactured goods, and William III's re-grant of the charter in 1698 stipulated that 10% of annual exports must be in English goods.

It would certainly have been more profitable if the Company could have exported goods rather than precious metals. Sound commercial instincts must have gone against making cash payments in Asia if the commodities sought there could have been paid for with English goods yielding a second profit. But because of the structural imbalances in world trade in the seventeenth century the Company could not do so on any significant scale. Instead, reversing the old maxim, its survival required that the supply of English woollen textiles should create a demand.

The Company's Eighth Voyage of 1611 represents the early stages of commercial apprenticeship in Asia. Hopes for the sale of English manufactures were still relatively sanguine, although becoming tinged with caution at home and increasingly subject to the realism produced by accumulated experience overseas. What makes the voyage a fascinating case history of the broadcloth 'problem' is a unique survival which enables individual lengths of cloth to be traced from London to Japan.

The buying-in account of cloth purchased for the voyage[1] is followed by a complete cargo inventory of one of the ships plus the voyage accounts up to the formal establishment of the Japan factory on 3 December 1613.[2] The latter continue in an early nineteenth century abstract of the factory accounts from January 1614 to August 1615[3] and are then taken over by the Japan account book of John Osterwick 1 September 1615 – 31 January 1617.[4] Added to these there are more than 100 items of correspondence from, to or within Japan for the years 1613 – 1615 alone.[5]

Leaving aside precious metals, the company's exports to Asia at the period were, first of all, woollen textiles, overwhelmingly broadcloth; secondly, unwrought metals — iron, lead, tin, copper, quicksilver; and thirdly, miscellaneous luxury goods such as coral, ivory, swords, sporting guns and assorted *objects d'art*. The inventory of the ship *Clove* confirms the pattern. The total cargo value of £10,399 6s 1d was made up of £6,450 in silver coin and £1,591 for 100 broadcloths, with the remaining £2,358 6s 1d representing, in order of importance, 124 elephant tusks, 1951 bars of iron, 100 barrels of gunpowder, 70 pieces of kersey, 844 bars of lead, 80 fowling pieces, 18 cwt of tin, silver-gilt tableware, 10 cwt of oak galls and finally, miscellaneous items — wine, olive oil, spirits and clothing.[6] Thus broadcloth formed 40% of the ship's investment in goods and 15% of the total investment, while if the kerseys are added in the figures for woollen textiles become 47% and 18% respectively.

Broadcloth derived its name from its width 1.25 yards, as opposed to 'narrow' cloths like kersey, which were only 27 inches wide. The cloth length varied from 26 to 35 yards, with a few up to 38 yards, and there were great varieties of texture and weight,[7] with corresponding price differentials between coarse and fine qualities. The buying-in account for the voyage records the purchase of 216½ cloths. The descriptions attached to the entries reveal their origins in Gloucestershire, Suffolk and Warwickshire, and numerous individual clothiers are named.[8] It is also made clear that finishing to the Company's specifications was charged additionally and the text abounds with the technical terms of the English cloth industry — rowing, shearing, mantling, pressing, tacking, drying and dressing.

When he drew up his inventory of the *Clove*'s cargo Richard Cocks assigned a number to each cloth. The *Clove* carried 100, while the remaining 116½, carried on the other ships of the voyage, the *Hector* and *Thomas*, are detailed, again with their numbers, at the beginning of his voyage account. It is Cock's meticulousness which makes it possible to trace their fate, for the appropriate numbers were referred to in subsequent transactions. The predominant colours were red, black, green and blue, with a wide range of other shades from 'popinjay' to 'gallant colour',[9] and there was an enormous cost price variation over the 216½ cloths, from £9 to £23. For instance, the Venice reds, of 26 to 30 yards length, cost £13 10s and £14, but the finer stamett reds, of 33 and 34 yards length, were between £20 10s and £23. The cloths were packed at four to a bale and subsequently, from knowledge gained in the present voyage, they were first wrapped in thin sheets of lead with further sheets between the folds.

The three ships of the Eighth Voyage, the *Clove, Hector* and *Thomas*, left the Downs on 18 April 1611 under the command of General John Saris and chief merchant Richard Cocks.[10] Saris had previously served as a factor at Bantam between 1606 and 1609, where he had gathered information on commodities vendible in Japan, including 'broad-clothes of all sorts, viz. blackes, yellowes and reds' especially 'such as is low shorne'.[11] Cocks was a new employee, a member of the Clothworkers Company of London, possessing a background of trade and intelligence experience in the Basque country. The Company's instructions for the voyage[12] were to go to Surat in order to follow up the Sixth Voyage under Sir Henry Middleton who, the Company hoped, had established English trade at that port. If a sufficient lading could be obtained there all three ships were to return direct to England. If he could not reach Surat in 1611 Saris was ordered to fill in time by an experimental voyage to Mokha. Failing trade at Surat, the ships were to sail for Bantam. From there the *Hector* and *Thomas* were to be provided with cargoes for England and the *Clove* was to go on to Japan, where the Englishman William Adams was known to occupy a special position of friendship with the Shogun.

The course of the voyage followed the latter pattern, with an important side episode which mainly solved this particular broadcloth problem and provided Saris with Asian goods to exchange for Asian goods, at a handsome second profit.

The monsoon, as predicted, prevented direct sailing to Western India, and so Saris opened negotiations at Mokha in March 1612, only to learn that Sir Henry Middleton had been repulsed at Surat and was returning to the Red Sea to lie in wait for the annual Gujarati trading fleet. The combined fire-power of the ships of the Sixth and Eighth Voyages forced the Indian traders to a barter of cargoes in May and June 1612, two-thirds to Middleton and one-third to Saris.

The Eighth Voyage dumped on the helpless Indians no less than 148 broadcloths, which had cost £2,111 9s in England but which were now valued at £4,611 13s 4d, a margin of 118%. In return Saris took 49,686½ pieces of Indian textiles, valued by him a £5,346 16s, or 153% more than the cost price of the broadcloth. After deducting cloth given as presents at Mokha, this one-off manoeuvre reduced the Eighth Voyage's stock to 65½ out of the original total of 216½.

Saris then followed his alternative instructions. The *Hector* and *Thomas* left Bantam for England in December 1612 and January 1613. The *Clove* sailed for the Moluccas and Japan on 15 January 1613, reaching the port of Hirado off western Kyūshū on 12 June. When she quitted Hirado on 5 December 1613 the *Clove* left behind a new factory under the direction of Richard Cocks. The fascinating history of the factory's ten-year life cannot be explored here, but we can follow through the remaining broadcloth.

During the first weeks of negotiation at Hirado 7 whole and 3 half cloths were given as presents. An initial sale, on 30 August 1613, of 16.25 yards of sad blue for £32 10s against a cost price of £17 for the whole cloth of 29 yards seemed to augur well for future profit margins. Two cloths were used at the end of November to make clothing for the *Clove*'s crew, and when the ship left in December the opening stock of the factory was reckoned at 50 whole cloths and 6 remnants. But in the same month William Adams pointed to the dangers of competition from other Europeans importing broadcloth — 'such thinges as he [Saris] had brought was not veri vendibel . . . cloth at this present was very cheep becass both from Nova Spaynna, Manilia and out of Holland within this 4 years there caem very much, soum sold and verry much unsold'.[13] Cocks hoped that while 'as yet they are so addicted to silke that they doe not enter into consideration of the benefitt of wearinge cloth . . . tyme may alter their myndes',[14] and in his final orders to the new factory Saris urged 'make awaye your braudcloath . . . for the Fleming hath great store . . . and ours is verye evell condityoned'.[15]

When serious trading began in January 1614 Richard Wickman was sent up to Edo and Shizuoka with 15 cloths and William Eaton to Ōsaka and Kyōto with 8. Further consignments, respectively, of 9 and 3 plus a remnant were forwarded to them in the following July. Meanwhile another 8 cloths were carried to mainland Southeast Asia in March 1614 on a hired junk which was never heard of again, although it was later discovered that the chief English factor had been murdered in Annam.

Wickam and Eaton slowly disposed of their cloth, with much grumbling about prices and quality. Faced by Dutch superiority on both counts Eaton resolved 'to put awaye all that I have, although but for smale profit, rather then I will kepe them',[16] and some of the market forces and mechanisms were gradually revealed. It soon became clear that broadcloth was in demand for anything but clothing. The Japanese used it for saddle-coverings, linings for weapons and armour boxes, and occasionally for military surcoats (*jinbaori*), an extremely narrow market limited to the *samurai* and *daimyō* classes. If they were in town or warlike preparations were pending prospects might be hopeful. Wickham noted with envy Dutch sales to 'this nobillyty which are come upp [to Edo] about the castle building',[17] while at the same time Eaton complained that 'all the gentellmen that would bye cloth are there at Edo'.[18]

The English also had to cope with the vagaries of Japanese taste and the fluctuating fashion cachet attached to high-priced foreign imports. In general 'sad' colours were preferred, a reflection of Japanese *shibui* ('simple yet refined'), and it was realized that 'the nature & condition of these Japaners, especially of the better sort whoe are most comonly marchantes for our comodytyes, is to buy those comodytys that are most rare & at the time when they are most dearest'.[19] In addition, they had to come to terms with Japanese credit trading methods, allowing middlemen to hold cloth on a sale or return basis and giving them a small profit on any orders which they produced. The accounts for August 1615 record a hiccup in this system — the writing-off of 2.25 yards sold on credit to one Watanabe 'Croanasque' of Ōsaka, who had been 'slain in the wars'.

But when sales were made the profit was normally high. For instance, the Shogun bought 3 fine cloths for £166 6s 9d against a cost price of £48 15s, a gross margin of 240%, and another brought £42 against £19 cost. On the other hand, much of the cloth which had ended up in Japan and which was being marketed some five years after packing, with over two years in a ship's hold, was found to be 'vilely eaten all over the midest . . . with woorm holes cleane through'.[20] Packing and transport posed their own perennial problems, and partly because of its condition much of the cloth in Japan was disposed of as short lengths of one or two yards.

By the summer of 1615 the stock of broadcloth was reduced to about half a dozen plus a few odd pieces. Fortunately the second English ship to arrive, the *Hosiander* on 31 August 1615, did not bring any more. The next arrivals, the *Thomas* and *Advice* in June and July 1616 brought another 94½ cloths — a disaster, for by then the English were restricted to Hirado and Nagasaki and could no longer chase the market into the main cities of Japan. Apart from that given away in desperation as presents, most of the second consignment was still rotting in the warehouse when the English left Japan in 1623.

The Eighth Voyage was unusual in being able to unload so much broadcloth by an act of near-piracy, but its later commercial vicissitudes in Japan illustrate vividly the Company's continuing problem of having to satisfy pressures at home by carrying out this most difficult of commodities.

20

THE *EISCH BOEK* IN DUTCH-JAPANESE TRADE

Minoru Ōmori

*The necessity for the study of articles of exchange in the
history of Dutch-Japanese trade*

The trade and cultural exchange between the Netherlands and Japan in
the period from the seventeenth to the nineteenth century, are of
noteworthy concern within the study of the history of East-West
negotiations. There has been a trend to study this period by portraying
the characters involved, such as men like Engerbert Kämpfer, Carl
Peter Thunberg, Philipp Franz von Siebold and Izaac Titsing. Although
the literature concerning this trade and cultural exchange is comparatively well studied, we do not find any systematized reference to the
articles of exchange, themselves, particularly involving plants and
animals.

These reports, representing an emphasis on economic history, dealt
primarily with the movement of trading goods from place to place and
the current prices. The well-written book by K. Glamann entitled
Dutch-Asiatic Trade, 1620 – 1740 (1958 Copenhagen, 's Gravenhage)
can be given as an example. However, one must realize that even from
the view of economic history, not all of the items involved have been
investigated.

We know well that articles of trade have much to do with our culture,
how we live, and our mentality. Therefore, I have examined the *Eisch
Boek* for the articles involved in negotiations between Japan and the
Netherlands. Despite the many difficulties that presented themselves in
this research, I wish to report here on my findings.

Eisch Boek

The origin and format of the Eisch Boek

At the time of the Dutch Factory Head's travel mission to the
honourable Shogun's court in Edo, which began in the fourteenth year

of Keichō (1609), it was the policy of the Dutch East India Company to present many rare articles to the Shogun, called *rariteijten*. This was believed to lead to smooth and increased trading relations.

It is evident from the Dutch records of trade with Japan that it was not only to the Shogun that various rarities were presented, but also to 'Rōjū'[1] and 'Jisha-bugyō'[2] and others. And the numbers of articles readied for the Shogun and other high officials were usually more than enough, and the presents to be given were chosen from them after the mission arrived at Edo. The remnants were sold to the public. These presents and selling by the Dutch greatly aroused the interest of these limited few Japanese in items made abroad. There is no doubt that these Japanese then began to order the foreign products they had actually seen or imagined existed. It is likely that orders were placed orally at first. Then, it seems, the diverse articles ordered, along with the name of the persons placing the orders, gradually came to be recorded in the existing *Eisch Boeken*, or order books.

The *Eisch Boek* is a written document in which the ordered articles are found which were requested to the Dutch Factory by the Japanese in the period from the seventeenth to the nineteenth century. To the best of my knowledge, the *Eisch Boek* has only been treated in W. T. Kroese's 'De Eisch van Zijn Keizerlijk Majesteit' (The Demand of His Imperial Majesty),[3] and has been rarely studied heretofore. Within this *Eisch Boek*, the number of written names is not great, but they represent men of authority like the Shogun and 'Nagasaki Bugyō', governor of Nagasaki, political potentates or the people who had connections with Dutch-Japanese negotiations — 'Nagasakikaisho-shirabeyaku', commissioner of 'Nagasaki-Kaisho', interpreters and such. They were the people in a logical position to adopt forms of European civilization through the Dutch. Therefore the *Eisch Boek* reveals to us what sort of things the Japanese in those days desired. For this reason, the *Eisch Boek* has a great importance both in the history of trade and in the history of cultural exchange.

The *Eisch Boeken* are located in the Algemeen Rijks Archief (General State Archives) in The Hague. The *Eisch Boeken* are bound notebooks made of Japanese paper, and although they vary a bit in size, they are approximately 21 cm × 31 cm. The front covers are inscribed with such titles as 'Keizerlijk Eischen van 't jaar voor Aanstaande A≙1786' (Imperial Order for the Following Year, A.D. 1786) or 'De Eisch van Zijn Keijzerlijk Majesteit voor 't Aanstaande Jaar A≙1810' (The Order of His Imperial Majesty for the Following Year, A.D. 1810). Within, varieties of articles are listed in Dutch with brush and Indian ink. There are also signatures reading 'T Collegie' which had been written in brush and Indian ink, signifying that they were written by the Japanese interpreter colleagues for the Dutch language in

Nagasaki. In addition, either the red square seal of 'Cambang' trading place[4] (Cambang trading means private trading), or the red seal of reporter-interpreter[5] is stamped on them. The first *Eisch Boek* can be estimated to be from 1685, in which year 'Cambang' trade was given approval by the Shogunate, but this is a matter of conjecture. The *Eisch Boek* might possibly have had its start in 1685. In this year the Tokugawa government gave the permission for 'Cambang' trade. The oldest *Eisch Boek* which has the above-mentioned format is from 1785 for 1786. But judging from the contents, the ninth Shogun Tokugawa Ieshige's order sheet for horses, written in 1725, is an older order. Therefore, judging from both the format and the contents, it can be said at present, that the oldest of the *Eisch Boeken* is the one prepared in 1725 for 1726. Following this, those for the intermittent years 1765, 1785, 1809 and 1813, are found. It is evident, though, from the notes in the order books made in later years, that books for the intervening years were also made, and from 1817 on, the order books for each year are preserved.

The contents of Eisch Boeken—ordered articles and their requisitioners

When we look into the existing *Eisch Boeken*, we find the names of various textiles, animals, plants, daily wares (e.g., mirrors, spectacles, cruet stands, glassware, dishes, lamps), medical articles (medicines, bottles for medicine and drugs), stationery (e.g., knives, ink, papers), scientific apparatuses (e.g., timepieces, telescopes, microscopes, octants), munitions (e.g., pistols, gunpowder), books (dictionaries, encyclopedias, almanacs, literature in specialized fields), and special things such as drawing instruments and 'Duikers klok' (a diving bell). All of these articles have their ordered number of pieces enumerated in the books. Birds, timepieces, lamps, glassware are in some cases accompanied by sketches in colour, and textiles sometimes have sample pieces attached.

As to who ordered these articles is an interesting question. The titles of the persons who placed the orders which appear in the order book at the starting period of the *Eisch Boek* are 'Keijzerlijk Majesteit', namely the Shogun,[6] 'Gouverneur van Nagasaki',[7] 'Rente Meester,'[8] 'Commissaris der Geldkamer' or Commissioner of 'Nagasaki-Kaisho',[9] 'opperburgermeester' or upperburgomaster,[10] and 'het Collegie' or Japanese interpreter colleagues for the Dutch language.[11] But in those *Eischen Boeken* made later than 1820, 'Eerst Raad Heer',[12] 'Tweede Raad Heer'.[13] and 'Daimyō'[14] are seen as the purchasers. Moreover, people other than the Shogun and the Japanese interpreter colleagues for the Dutch language, have their personal names written down.

Below are given the main articles ordered, arranged under the designation of the person placing the order, taken from the order book entitled 'De Eisch van Zijn Keizerlijk Maijesteit voor 't Aanstaande Jaar A ≙ 1810' (The Order of His Imperial Majesty for the following year, A.D. 1810):

Shogun:* Plants: Seedlings of pepper tree and 8 other plants; seeds of saffron and other plants. *Animals: a brace of small camels, 5 brace of 'glattig',[15] 2 brace of musk cats. *Books: Batavian almanac, Dutch astronomical almanac, book written by E. Kaempfer (could be *De Beschrijving van Japan*). *Textiles: 'Armozijn', 'Taffecelas', 'Chitzen' and 'Hamans'. *Medical articles: herbs, gall nuts, indigo, saffron crocus. *Jewels: diamonds, lapis lazuli, crystal. *Scientific instruments: telescope. *Special articles: 'Duijkers Klok'[16] or diving bell.

Magaribuchi Kai no Kami,[17] governor of Nagasaki: *Textiles: 'Laken', 'Taffacelassen'. *Daily wares: small glass dish, glass bottles, glass lamp, liqueur glass. *Animals: a brace of small canaries, 5 brace of five kinds of small birds. *Scientific instruments: Telescope and table clock. *Special articles: iron stone.

Tsuchiya Ki-i no Kami,[18] governor of Nagasaki: *Textiles: 'Armozijn'. *Daily wares: picture drawn on a glass mirror, glass bowl with lid. *Animals: 3 kinds of parrots. *Scientific instruments: telescope. *Books: books about artillery and fireworks. *Maps: world map. *Medical articles: saffron, Venetian theriaca.

Takaki Sakuyemon, manager of trade account office[19]: *Animals: a brace of small birds from Batavia, a brace of small birds from Bengal.

Yakushiji Kyūzaemon, commissioner of Nagasaki Kaisho[20]: *Animals: 11 brace of small birds including five kinds; a brace of dogs.

Takaik Seiemon, commissioner of Nagasaki Kaisho: *Textiles: linen. *Daily wares: chair, chain for watch. *Animals: 5 brace of small birds. *Scientific instruments: pocketwatch.

Takashima Shirobei, upperburgomaster: *Textiles: 'Taffacelassen'. *Daily wares: square glass. *Animals: kinds of parrot, a bird with white head. *Books: book on various kinds of birds. *Scientific instruments: tool to polish glasses of telescope, small celestial globe and small terrestial globe.

Takashima Sakubei, upperburgomaster: *Daily wares: parquet. *Animals: red parrot. *Scientific instruments: two kinds of clock.

Fukuda Jūrōyemon, upperburgomaster: *Daily wares: a silver watch, pieces of flowered Dutch materials. *Animals: 3 brace of birds from Bengal.

Hisamatsu Zenbei, upperburgomaster: *Textiles: 'Taffacelassen', 'Chitz'. *Daily wares: square glass. *Animals: musk cat.

Gotō Sōtarō, upperburgomaster: *Textiles: 'Taffacelassen'. *Books: Pijbo Steenstra's astronomical table. *Scientific instruments: thermometer, barometer. *Medical articles: surgical instruments. *Maps: astronomical chart, world map.

Fukuda Shichijūrō, upperburgomaster: *Animals: two kinds of parrots.

Hisamatsu Kihei, upperburgomaster: *Textiles: 'Taffacelas'. *Daily wares: turnstile. *Animals: small dog. *Medical articles: lancet, scissors, catheter, knife, Venetian theriaca.

Japanese interpreter colleagues for the Dutch language. *Daily wares: glasses, mirror, glass bottle, chain for watch. *Foods: butter, liqueur, wine. *Jewels: amber. *Stationery: paper, pencil, quill pen and knife. *Scientific instruments: thermometer and telescope. *Books: herbal, Chomel's encyclopedia 9 volumes, La Lande's astronomy book, the book written by E. Kaempfer, new world atlas, geography book, English-Dutch and Dutch-English dictionaries, Heister's surgical book, newly-designed world map, book about Russia, Pijbo Steenstra's astronomy book with table, Pieter Marine's dictionary and Buy's dictionary. *Medical articles: theriaca, fresh-water lobster eye, turpentine oil and gum turpentine.

As to the several kinds of textiles mentioned above, they were described as follows:[21]

'Taffacelas', 'Taffacelassen': the material is cotton but sometimes with silk; plain fabric or striped.

'Chitzen',' Chiz', and 'Sitsen': light printed cotton. This cloth was in fashion in western Europe from the latter half of seventeenth century until the middle of the eighteenth century.

'Armozijn': the material is silk, thinly-made and limp.

'Hamans': cotton cloth.

'Laken', 'Laaken': woollen cloth.

There is indeed a great variety of items, including living organisms. In later years, the variety increased, and lands of origin represented by these products were, among others, Holland, India, Persia, Arabia and Indonesia.

Although considerable numbers of the articles were mere curiosities or precious objects of great value, many had a purely practical use. Examples of the later category, such as horses, medical articles, scientific instruments and books, contributed much to Japan's industrial, technical and academic fields in those days. This was the period after the middle of the Edo era, when there was an economic reconstruction under the Tokugawa Shogunate, combined with a promotion policy in production and great strides in the academic field. Thus, it can be substantiated from the order books, which items were in great demand at the time, and this can be correlated with the social circumstances of the period. From the fact that octants were in frequent demand, it can be inferred that for purposes of coastal defence, there was felt an urgent necessity for measuring the distance of foreign vessels at sea.

Circumstances under which the ordered articles were shipped to Japan: the case in 1825

Of the various items, including living organisms, that were mentioned in the previous section on the contents of one *Eisch Boek*, not all were always shipped to Japan in the following year as ordered. When the ordered articles were not delivered to Japan, the same orders were often repeated. When an article was ordered, specifications were given as to the material, dimensions, design and other details based on the experiences in the past. Such instructions presumably were quite troublesome to the Dutch. In examining one *Eisch Boek*, we can see that some of the ordered articles had been checked one by one as regards to their specifications, and in others, we can see traces of the ordered numbers having been revised, or the ordered articles, themselves, having been eliminated. From these facts it is clear that the merchandise was not always transported to Nagasaki as ordered.

Among some of the historical documents seen in Japan, there are several which tell us the circumstances under which the ordered articles written in the *Eisch Boek* were shipped, — as an example, 'Bunsei Hachinen Torinotoshi Oranda-sen Mukimuki-sama O-a-tsu-ra-e nar-abini Motolata Wakini Sashidashichō'[22] contrasted with 'Eisch van Zijn Kejzerlijk Majesteit voor 't Aanstaande A ≙ 1825/ 't Collegie'. In the latter, articles are recorded as ordered by the Shogun, in addition to 19 individuals and the Japanese interpreter colleagues for the Dutch language. The total number of different kinds of items adds up to 618. The largest order came from Takahashi Echizen no Kami, governor of Nagasaki, who ordered 95 kinds of items.[23] And the smallest order, which came to 1, was placed by Ōkubo Kaga no Kami,[24] councillor for state affairs. Generally, in all of the order books, the number of diversities ordered by the governor of Nagasaki was large.

In the former, the articles which were shipped for the people mentioned in the latter, are written out one by one, and the total number of all descriptions adds up to 274 kinds. The percentage of the number of articles shipped versus the number of articles received as ordered is approximately 44.3%. Although this is merely one example, it is presumable that the circumstances with ordered articles sent to Nagasaki in other years were much the same.

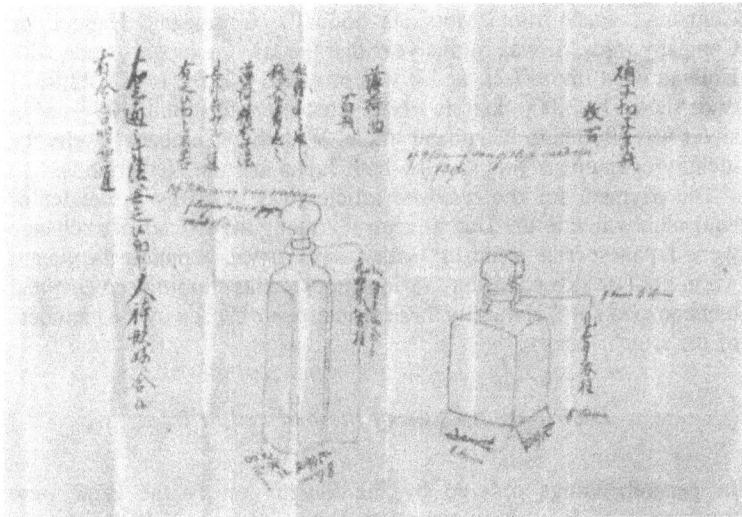

An example of an illustration in *Eisch Boek*, from *Eisch Boek* for 1827 (inv. no. 1419, het Algemeen Rijks Archief, Den Haag, Holland).

As for the articles ordered by the Shogun, the Dutch often treated them as articles of presentation or gifts. For the articles ordered by others, they were settled as 'Cambang Handel', that is as private trade. These facts are evident from the historical documents titled 'Cambang Reekening' or private reckoning. 'Cambang Handel' or private trading was called 'Wakini Shōbai' by the Japanese, and it is shown in the historical documents of both Japan and the Netherlands, that the transaction of ordered articles was recorded under private trading.

In 1685, 'Cambang Handel' was formally approved by the Tokugawa Shogunate as a private trade by the members of the Dutch East India Company, apart from 'Motokata Shōbai', 'Compagnie Handel' or Company trade. It was in this year that the law for Japan's trade with Holland went into effect, and it was provided that the total volume of trade should be 3,000 'kan' in silver. Apart from this limit, 400 'kan' in silver was allotted to 'Cambang' trade. With this 'Cambang' trade, the identity of interests was seen by both Japan and the Netherlands.

The payment for the received articles was made by a transfer of equivalent value to the Dutch factory. Among the articles of exchange were Japanese rice wine or 'sake', soya sauce, Japanese lacquered ware, gold or silver lacquer, various implements, folding screens, and bamboo crafts etc. Naturally these articles were chosen by the members of the Dutch factory.

Distribution route of the ordered articles

In general, things ordered by the Shogun or by the Rōjū were transported to Edo. It is natural that the articles which the Shogun ordered were treated with utmost care, and when they left Nagasaki they were brought across land or by sea, according to the circumstances. When the sea route was chosen, a ship named *Hiyoshi-maru* belonging to the Nagasaki governor's office, was used. In the case with the Rōjū, it can be imagined that the articles were given care proportionately, and sometimes after being received they were retransported to the province from which the Rōjū came. It can be generalized that articles ordered by cabinet members of the Shogunate were transported to the member's territorial domain.

In the Edo era, the only way to transport the goods overland was by horses or by bearers, and when by sea route, of course by vessels. The sea route was cheaper.

The sea route from Nagasaki to Edo was as follows:
  A. From Nagasaki to Kokura or Shimonoseki
  B. From Kokura or Shimonoseki to Ōsaka through the Inland Sea

C. From Shimonoseki to Edo through the Inland Sea and the
    Naruto Strait
D. From Ōsaka to Edo.
The overland route was as follows:
E. From Nagasaki to Kokura through Saga (the Nagasaki Road)
F. From Kokura to Shimonoseki (by ship)
G. From Shimonoseki to Ōsaka (the Sanyō Road)
H. From Ōsaka to Kyōto
I. From Kyōto to Edo (the Tōkaidō Road)

It is thus clear that the possibilities were either the sea route or the overland route, or a combination of one of the routes in A through D, with a part of the route indicated in E – I. The merchants in 1767 specified which articles should be conveyed overland, and which by boat,[25] thus, the transport route differed according to the kind of articles to be conveyed.

There were some items ordered by the Shogun that remained in Nagasaki, such as a diving bell. The diving bell was ordered by the Shogun in 1793 and was ultimately delivered to Nagasaki in 1834,[26] and was left there.

The articles ordered by the governor of Nagasaki, appointed in Nagasaki, commissioner of 'Nagasaki Kaisho', upperburgomaster of Nagasaki, and the Japanese interpreters for the Dutch language (all of whom were Nagasaki residents), were individually handed over to them. These purchasers in Nagasaki resold a part of their merchandise, to other regions of Japan. Shūhan Takashima[27] as an upperburgomaster, ordered many things, but resold such items as pocket watches, telescopes, guns, firestones, and saltpetre.[28] In 1848, a Japanese interpreter for the Dutch language, on his way to Edo from Nagasaki to deliver the articles for presentation from the Dutch Factory Head to the Shogun, sold some of his Dutch books in Ōsaka, and those that he could not sell there at a desirable price, were brough to Edo,[29] because in Edo the Dutch books would be sold at the private schools where Japanese studied Dutch. In 1654, Ōmetsuke[30] Masashige Inoue received the Vesalius' anatomy book which was ordered in 1650 from a Japanese interpreter for the Dutch language. This is one of the older examples. There is no doubt that such transactions occurred frequently.

By their nature, books are often retained for long periods of time, and the existing number of Dutch books imported in the Edo era was found to attain to about 6,000 volumes, according to an investigation begun in 1953. These books were brought to Nagasaki upon the order from the Japanese or at the discretion of the Dutch, in a 'Cambang' trade or private trade transaction, before they were conveyed to other parts of Japan. The existing Dutch books are found from Nagasaki and Kagoshima in the southern Kyūshū area to as far north as Hakodate in the Hokkaido area. From this it can be seen that imported articles, such as books, shipped to Nagasaki, were conveyed to many parts of Japan in contact with the transportation routes of the Edo era.

In conclusion, the ordered articles imported into Japan during the period from the seventeenth to the nineteenth century give a clear indication of the demands, and hence of the attitudes of the Japanese at the time.

21

THE FIRST TRADE ROUTES AND RELATIONS
BETWEEN JAPAN AND MEXICO

Arcadio Schwade

Introduction

The first Europeans to reach the shores of Japan around 1543 were
Portuguese sailors. The Portuguese, who for almost one century carried
out trade relations with Japan, usually sailed from Lisbon via Goa,
Malacca and Macao to Nagasaki. By using this maritime route they
took at least two years and four months for reaching Japan from
Portugal.[1] This was the longest route. The shortest one was that of the
Dutch, who were able to reach Japan within about ten months. The
Dutch Asian-bound fleets, after having passed the Cape of Good Hope,
used to steer eastward between 36° and 42° of southern latitude until
they reached the south-east trade winds where they set a northerly
course for the straits of Sunda. Their 'general rendevouz' in Southeast
Asia became the Javanese port of Jakarta, after it had been seized,
fortified and renamed Batavia by the Dutch on 30 May 1619.[2]

The route used by the Spaniards, from Sevilla to Mexico (New Spain)
and then from Acapulco over Manilla to Japan, was supposed to take
about fourteen months.[3] The maritime communication of the Spaniards
with Japan developed after Portugal and Spain had been united in a dual
monarchy under the rule of King Felipe II (1527 – 98; reigned 1556 –
98). Between 1584 and 1600 a good number of Spanish ships from
Manila bound for Macao or Mexico were blown off their course and
forced to take refuge in some Japanese port.[4]

First attempt at Japanese-Mexican trade relations

The Japanese ruler Tokugawa Ieyasu (1542 – 1616; reigned 1600 – 16)
from the beginning of his reign, showed great interest in obtaining
miners, shipbuilders and navigators from the Spaniards for opening
Japanese trade relations with Mexico.[5] During the past decades the
Japanese had, with the help of the Portuguese, developed their own
flourishing trade communication with the Philippine Islands and with

Southeast Asia.[6] A favourable opportunity for Ieyasu achieving his goal arose, when in September 1609 Don Rodrigo de Vivero y Velasco, during his voyage from the Philippines to Mexico, was shipwrecked in Iwawada, off the coast of Kazusa in the Kantō area. When the Japanese local officials discovered that the former Spanish interim-governor of the Philippines was among the shipwrecked, they made the necessary arrangements for Vivero to meet with Tokugawa Hidetada (1578 – 1631; reigned 1616 – 23) in Edo and with his father Ieyasu in Sumpu, the modern Shizuoka.

Vivero was a native of a noble Spanish family living in Mexico. During his youth he had spent some years at the Spanish court in the service of King Felipe II. Back in his native country he occupied such posts as Major Officer of Justice in Puebla and later that of Major of the Port of San Juán de Ulúa and, after the death of his father, he succeeded him in the post of the mining town of Taxco. Some time later he was sent to the new provinces of Durango and Chuhuahua (the old New Viscaya) with the purpose of exploring the recently discovered silver mines in the northern region of Mexico.

Since Vivero was familiar with the work and problems connected with the exploitation of silver mines, he was the ideal person with whom Tokugawa Ieyasu could discuss the possibilities of exploiting the Japanese silver mines using Western techniques. Two days after Vivero's first audience with Ieyasu, the minister of foreign affairs, Homda Kōsuke no suke Masazumi (1565 – 1673) told him that the ruler of Japan was going to offer his own ship, the second that Will Adams had made in Japan.[7]

While Vivero visited other parts of central and western Japan, the Franciscan missionary Luis Sotelo went from Miyako to the court of Sumpu to negotiate an agreement over a draft of treaty, which had been prepared by Vivero.[8] After Vivero's return to the court of Ieyasu, an Agreement and Peace Treaty was signed on 4 July 1610, containing the following clauses:

1. The ships from Mexico would be given a port, selected by the Spaniards, where the crew could build their homes.

2. The friars would be permitted to go to any part of Japan.

3. The ship from Luzón, on their route to Mexico, would be able to enter any Japanese port and continue the voyage at their discretion.

4. In case the Spanish ships needed repairs or it was necessary to build a new vessel, they would be provided with all the materials, as well as the workers, at a fair price.

5. The Spanish ambassador to Japan would be well received.

6. The Japanese ships that sailed to Mexico would be well received.

7. The merchandise brought to Japan for trade would be sold at low and fair prices and without coercion.[9]

This treaty was noteworthy because of the concessions made by Ieyasu to the Spaniards. The clause that most interested him was that which provided for the opening of trade with Mexico. Vivero's efforts to obtain from Ieyasu the expulsion of the Dutch from Japan ended in failure, because the Japanese ruler had already given the Dutch permission to stay in Japan.

Ieyasu, after having discussed the matter with Vivero, sent the Franciscan Fray Alonso Muñoz as his ambassador to Mexico and Spain. Muñoz took with him personal letters from Ieyasu and Hidetada to the King of Spain, in addition to copies of the treaty with Japan.[10]

Vivero, after outfitting the ship, using the financial aid of approximately four thousand ducats given to him by Ieyasu, renamed the ship *San Buenaventura*, and finally, on 1 August 1610 left Japan bound for Mexico, with Fray Alonso Muñoz and twenty-three Japanese merchants. Vivero's return voyage to Mexico had been, according to his report, 'the most prosperous and happy one ever made on the southern seas'. His ship arrived at the port of Matanchel on 27 October, 1610, and a few days later at Acapulco. The Japanese enjoyed the hospitality of the several cities they visited in Mexico.[11]

Plan of Sebastián Vizacíno's expedition for the discovery of the 'Rich Gold and Silver Islands'

The arrival of Don Rodrigo de Vivero coincided with the preparations in Mexico for sending an expedition to discover the 'Islands of Gold and Silver', a group of rich islands that were supposed to be about 150 miles off the eastern coast of Japan. The legend of the 'Rich Gold and Silver Islands' probably developed from a report of a cosmographer, named Andrés de Aguirre, who had accompanied Miguel López de Legazpi in 1564 on his expedition to the Philippine Islands. Aguirre, in a letter (probably of 1583 or 1584) to the Archbishop and Viceroy of Mexico, Pedro Moya de Contreras,[12] reports the discovery of very rich and densely populated islands, located east of Japan, between 35° and 40° northern latitude. Captain Pedro de Unamuno reports that he and his companions, after having taken off from a group of islands north of the Philippines, sailed in the direction of the islands called 'Rich in Gold' and 'Rich in Silver', but failed to reach them on the latitude indicated on a contemporary map. He therefore concluded that the said islands did not exist at all.[13] The names of the islands called 'Rica de Oro and Rica de Prata' appeared for the first time in Antonio de Morga's book, *Sucesos de las Islas Filipinas*, published in Mexico in 1609.[14]

No wonder that the above reports on the legendary 'Rich Gold and Silver Islands' once again impelled the Spanish authorities in Mexico and in Spain to order their search in the Pacific. As early as May 1607 the Viceroy of Mexico had recommended to the Spanish King that he send Sebastián Vizcaíno as general of the planned expedition. Vizcaíno had carried out several exploratory expeditions along the Mexican and Californian coast between the years 1596 and 1604 for finding safe ports for the Mexico-bound ships coming from the Philippine Islands. While on a visit to Spain in 1606, Vizcaíno was ordered to develop the harbour of Monterey in California. But this royal order was replaced by that of September 1608, commanding him to lead an expedition for the discovery of the 'Rich Gold and Silver Islands'.

The order of the Spanish King was not carried out immediately because of diverging opinions among Manila, Madrid and Mexico concerning the question, from where the planned expedition should depart. The Spanish Council of the Indies at first wanted to have it start from Acapulco under the responsibility of the Viceroy of Mexico. But later, influenced by the procurator of the Philippines, Hernando de los Rios Coronel, who was visiting Spain from the end of 1608 to 1609, the Council of the Indies decided on 20 March 1609 that Vizcaíno's expedition should take Manila as its departing point and that it should be supported by the Spanish Governor of the Philippines. The Council's decision was confirmed by the royal order of 13 May 1609. But because this royal order was strongly opposed by the Spanish Viceroy of Mexico (Oct. 1609), the Council of the Indies decided on 23 April 1610, to entrust the Spanish authorities in Mexico with the power to solve the question. As the procurator of the Philippines, on his return trip from Spain to Manila, had to pass over Mexico, all was arranged in such a way, that he could take part at the meeting of the Advisory Council to the Viceroy there, which took place towards the end of 1610, after Vivero's arrival from Japan with the group of 23 Japanese merchants.

Rios Coronel, in a letter from Mexico dated 31 December 1610, informed the Spanish King that Vizcaíno had to bring back to Japan a group of native merchants, and that he personally thought it better, that the expedition for the discovery of the 'Rich Gold and Silver Islands' should set off from Japan. Finally the Viceroy of Mexico, Luis de Velasco II, in a letter of 12 March 1611, informed the King of Spain that the ship bought from Japan was being equipped for bringing the Japanese merchants back to their homeland, from where Vizcaíno was to carry out the projected expedition. Thus the mission entrusted to Vizcaíno included the following duties: to visit the Japanese political authorities as ambassador of the Viceroy of Mexico; to return to Japan the 23 Japanese merchants who had come to Mexico with Vivero; to sound the eastern and southern coast of Japan with the permission of the Japanese authorities in order to find a safe trading port for the Spaniards; and to send out from Japan the expedition for the discovery of the 'Rich Gold and Silver Islands'.[15]

The first direct voyage from Mexico to Japan (1611)

The group of Japanese merchants under the guidance of Tanka Shōsuke left the capital of Mexico together with the members of Vizcaíno's mission to Japan on 7 March 1622. After having stayed for three days in Acapulco, they took off on 22 March in a ship named *San Francisco*, which had arrived from the Philippines during the winter and had not been sufficiently repaired and outfitted with provisions for the long voyage to Japan. After having sailed for eight days at the latitude of 12° the ship took a west-south-west direction. The travellers continued to enjoy favourable winds until, at the beginning of May, they reached the vicinity of the Ladrones Islands [Marianas], located at a latitude of about 15° and around 1,400 leagues distant from Acapulco.[16] So far Vizcaíno and his companions had sailed the same route which was used by the Spanish vessels annually, going from Mexico to the Philippines, as described by Antonio de Morga in his *Sucesos*:

In the ordinary way the ships sail and are despatched at the end of February, or at the latest by the twentieth of March. They sail westwards towards the Las Velas, or Ladrones Islands [Marianas], one of which, Guam, lies in thirteen degrees of latitude. Sometimes the ships run into calms, after leaving Acapulco, so they swing southwards from sixteen and a half degrees latitude (in which the port is situated) into ten or eleven degrees latitude in search of favourable winds. By this route they ride before continuous, fresh, fair winds and in good weather, without altering their sails for a distance of eighteen hundred leagues and without sighting any mainland or island. They leave the Barbudos [in the Carolines] and other islands on the southern side and then, gradually increasing their position to thirteen degrees latitude, continue until they sight the island of Guam and above it, lying in fourteen degrees, the island of Çarpana [Saipan]. This voyage to the Ladrones Islands generally lasts seventy days.[17]

According to Vizcaíno's report, a quarrel arose at the beginning of the voyage between the Japanese and the Spaniards about the use of the fireplace on the ship. Vizcaíno placated both parties by threatening with the death penalty anybody who would not obey his orders. The leader of the Japanese succeeded in controlling his group so well that he was later invited by Vizcaíno to have dinner with him.

Driven by favourable winds from south and south-east, the vessel
continued sailing in a northeasterly direction until 27 May when at
midnight it was struck by a hurricane that caused a serious leakage,
which the sailors managed to repair. But while the ship continued to
sail, it was struck by a second hurricane, more frighful than the first
one, on 1 June. After the storm was over, the vessel was driven by
strong winds from southwest in a northeasterly direction. Finally, when
on 6 June a strong wind began to blow from the south-east, the leaders
on board the ship decided to approach the next coast as soon as
possible. All members of the voyage were greatly relieved, when at
noon on 8 June they sighted land. On the following day, after having
reached a point above the latitude of 38°, the vessel was pushed by a
strong north-west wind along the coast until in the evening it reached
the entrance of a great bay. Then a sudden new change of wind
direction, threatened to drive the ship on to the shore.

Finally on the morning of 9 June eight Japanese boats approached the
Spanish vessel. Four Japanese came on board the ship and informed the
travellers that they had reached the coast of Fuginahama [Kuji-
nahama?], and that they were over forty leagues away from Uragawa,
and twenty-five leagues from the port of Unakami, the modern Chōshi.
With the help of one of the Japanese who boarded the ship, Vizcaíno
and his companions continued sailing along the coast of Japan and
passed before the harbour of Unakami around four o'clock in the
afternoon. But instead of entering it, they preferred to use the
favourable winds and weather for getting to the port of Uragawa as
soon as possible, which they entered safely on the evening of 10 June,
1611.[18]

Results of Vizcaíno's mission

Vizcaíno, after his arrival in Uragawa, wrote a letter to Ieyasu and
another to Hidetada presenting himself as an envoy of the King of Spain
and of the Viceroy of Mexico, and explaining the purpose of his
mission.[19] Some weeks later Vizcaíno was admitted to an audience with
Hidetada in Edo, and in September to an audience with Ieyasu in
Sumpu. The petitions presented by Vizcaíno to Ieyasu included the
following:

1. To take port soundings from Nagasaki to the northern province of
Akita for discovering those ports best suited for Spanish shipping.

2. To grant him the permission for the purchase of ships and
provisions necessary for this purpose at just prices.

3. To allow him the construction of a new ship to carry Japanese
goods to Mexico with the understanding that the ship would return in

the following year in order to keep up friendly commercial relations between both countries.

4. To obtain authorization for the Spanish ships to sell their goods in Japan free of duties, in the same way that the Japanese on the previous journey to Mexico had been permitted to do.

After Ieyasu had accepted all the above-mentioned requests, Vizcaíno demanded that the Japanese authorities expel the Dutch from their country, as a condition for maintaining good relations between Japan and Spain in the future.

Soon after receiving the red-sealed permissions for the port soundings, Vizcaíno and his party returned to Uraga. There they tried to sell their commercial goods and to effect some repairs on their ship. In October they travelled to Sendai, the capital city of the province of Ōshū, then governed by Date Masamune. This powerful daimyō received the Spaniards with great hospitality and offered them his ports for commercial trade with the Philippines and Mexico.[20]

Around mid-November Vizcaíno and his group began the survey of the eastern coast of Japan, while some time later his first mate, Lorenzo Vázquez, explored the southern coast of the principal island, Honshū, between Uraga and Ōsaka. The results of the exploration were recorded on a map, of which four copies were made. Ieyasu and Hidetada each received a copy. This study was finished in July 1612, and Vizcaíno requested permission to leave, saying that he would return to Mexico; but in reality he was going to search for the 'Rich Islands of Gold and Silver'.[21]

Vizcaíno left Uraga on 16 September 1612, and after   fruitless search, he returned to the same port on 7 November, his ship damaged by a storm. For about five months Vizcaíno made vain appeals to Ieyasu and Hidetada for getting aid. Finally the daimyō of Sendai offered Vizcaíno to finance the construction of a new ship for the return voyage, if he would supervise its construction. Date's plan, supported by Fr Sotelo, was to send a personal embassy to Felipe III of Spain and to the Pope with the intention of promoting direct trade between his fief and Mexico. Vizcaíno accepted the arrangement.

The ship was completed in October 1613 and sailed from Tsukinoura at the end of the same month with Vizcaíno and Date's embassy to Mexico and Europe, and with Hasekura Rikuemon and Luis Sotelo as envoys. Aboard the ship Vizcaíno felt himself to be no more than a powerless passenger, because the actual command of the ship was given to Fr Sotelo.[22]

The failure of Vizcaíno's mission in Japan was to a great extent the result of his own misgivings. His refusal to accept Japanese court etiquette and his pompous attitude antagonized the Japanese and later even the Franciscans. His repeated denunciations of the Dutch, and his request for their banishment as a condition *sine qua non* for the establishment of regular commercial relations between Japan and the Spanish empire were highly tactless. No more diplomatic was his hostility towards Will Adams, the most influential European at the court of the Tokugawa rulers. A group of miners brought by Vizcaíno from Mexico to Japan made such a poor impression that they were not accepted by the Japanese. What Rodrigo de Vivero by his prudent and tactful behaviour had done for the opening of friendly communication between Japan and Mexico, was ruined by Vizcaíno's ill-advised displays of stiffnecked pride. His subsequent complaints of supposed mistreatment he had received in Japan, and the news of the outbreak of the Christian persecution there, reaching the authorities in Mexico after Vizcaíno's return, further deteriorated the early relations between both countries to such a point, that a break resulted which lasted for over two centuries.[23]

22

THE AGE OF SUQUA, 1720 – 1759: THE EARLY
HONG MERCHANTS

W. E. Cheong

Although the ports of China were thrown open in 1684, European trade at Whampoa did not begin until 1699. Amoy, profiting from English voyages there in the 1670s and early 1680s, attracted nine vessels and Macao, one, during this period. However, determined efforts by the court and the accommodating attitude of local officials and merchants soon reversed the trend in Canton's favour.

Upon the establishment of the new Hoppo's (revenue commissioner's) Customs House in 1685, the 2% surcharge on measurage was dropped; in 1686, Whampoa upriver, was opened to foreign shipping and the maritime customs quota was reduced by 80% to just a little over 40,000 taels. In 1696, the rate of measurage on European ships was reduced to the rate for Asian bottoms. The reduction for the three classes from 3,500 taels to 1,400 taels, 3,000 taels to 1,100 taels and 2,500 taels to 600 taels respectively, entailed a loss of 30,285 taels in state revenue. The next year, Portuguese ships at Macao began to be assessed at the rate for Chinese ocean-going junks.

A period of intense rivalry between Amoy, Ningpo (Tinghai on Chusan Island) and Canton for the European business ensued for five years, with seven, twelve and eight ships, respectively, calling at the ports. By 1705, as a matter of choice, the English trade had concentrated at Canton. As early as 1689, a relocation from Amoy to Tinghai or Canton had been mooted, and from 1703, the English had concluded that Canton was preferable to Amoy and both to Tinghai; ships were therefore directed to Canton for 'it was a port of better usage, quicker dispatch and cheapest prices.'

Itinerants and Transients

As trade picked up at Whampoa, merchants from other ports converged on Canton, attracted by the increased traffic and encouraged by European supercargoes and other Chinese merchants. Some were from

Ningpo or even further beyond; the majority however, were practition-
ers in Amoy and most had family seats in Ch'üanchou. A number were
itinerant operators moving between the three ports and most were
transients at Canton.

Amoy Tinqua was in Canton as early as 1700 and so was Linqua, an
Amoy merchant of Ch'üanchou origin. Amoy Anqua traded at Canton,
Amoy and Ningpo between 1700 and 1704 whence he joined Linqua in
a duopoly which lasted until 1720. Kimco, a leading merchant in
Amoy, was persuaded by the supercargo of the *Loyale Cooke* to trade at
Canton in 1703; the end of the year saw him with his cargoes in Canton.
He was the later Cumshaw or Suqua. There was a 'Tartar merchant
newly arrived at Canton' in 1704 and a Chusan merchant peddling
Japanware in Canton through Linqua. Hunqua, Cawsanqua (Cudgin),
Chu Tonqua, Quiqua, Chinqua, Pinqua and Amoy Imqua (Empshaw)
were also all from Amoy. These merchants became principals in the
trade for the next two to four decades; some, like Suqua (1795) and
Tinqua (1770), continued well into the century.

The move south was, for a start, only a seasonal expedient to include
the European trade in the merchant's catchment of activities. Hence the
end of the trading season saw many returning to family seats in
Ch'üanchou or to more business in Amoy. As the heyday of the
Portuguese trade with Japan had attracted Fukienese merchants to
Macao, now the bilateral trade with Europe of the English and French
attracted their cupidity.

With the merchants came their house silk-weavers to cope with the
exacting European specifications. Chinese teas and silks came down
overland or by junks as supply by sea was still permitted at this time.
Some of the merchants' previous overseas business was now also
conducted out of Canton. These included trade with Japan, a strength of
Ningpo-Chusan merchants until the closure of the northern Super-
intendencies in 1522, shipments to Manila and Batavia, the traditional
specialities of Fukienese ports and trade with Cochin China and
Annam, a trade conducted mainly by Kwangtung merchants. The staple
for Batavia was tea, and for Manila and Japan, silk, nankeens and
luxury items. From Batavia, tin and sundries were the return cargoes;
from Manila, Spanish silver; from Japan, Japanware and copper and
from Cochin China, gold.

This was an extensive portfolio, and the early merchant could well be
described as a dabbler; in another sense however, he was a mercantile
thoroughbred, stranger to no branch of trade in the region which now
included the European business at Canton. The southward movement of
the merchants actually also described the southward drift of China's
maritime mercantile activities in this period. However, a reversion to
the traditional routes and specialists between 1715 and 1740, changed

the trading pattern and the mercantile commitments of the Canton merchants.

The duopoly of Linqua and Anqua lasted until Linqua's death in 1720; this started a renewal of the mercantile ranks. Suqua became the chief merchant until 1740 although Cudgin (1725 – 28) and Tinqua (1723 – 34) were briefly chiefs. Young Linqua, Anqua, Imqua, Youngqua and Boqwa left Canton or died in the next four years. By 1740, Hunqua, Chinqua, Quiqua, Tonqua, Cudgin and Pinqua had also disappeared; Cowlo and Chonqua, probably of the same vintage, had also gone.

Several new merchants who entered the trade in the 1720s also failed to survive their first decade. Such were Sinqua, Poor Robin Hunqua, Pinkey, Chocqua, Amoy Tiqua, Beau Khequa, Amoy Joss Hinqua, Shiqua, Young Khequa, Simon Manila, Phyllis Hunqua, Emmanuel Quinqua, Felix and Mandarin Quiqua. As their names suggest, some were clearly from Amoy and others from Manila.

Natural attrition — death, retirement or failure — had, it seemed, brought a cyclical renewal of the mercantile ranks. However, the mass exodus of merchants in these twenty years, suggests a generic affliction common to old and new merchants. Major changes in the character of the merchants and in the trade between 1715 and 1740, supports the postulation that a *décalage* had opened up between the expertise of the old type of merchant and the new conditions and trade to be conducted.

Withdrawal from Fukien

The initial phase of the itinerant merchant had passed although new arrivals from the north and abroad often disrupted trading practices and prompted the Co-hong of 1720 to single them out for restraint — an early sign of a settled merchant's proprietorial behaviour. However, many merchants were no more settled in their habits and activities than transients in Canton. Most of the leading merchants in Canton had a residence and warehouses in Amoy and commuted seasonally between Canton, Amoy and their hometown of Ch'üanchou. Thus several were reported returning in 1722 and in 1728, most of them left for Amoy during the off-season. The to-ing and fro-ing continued well into the 1730s, but came to a virtual end by about 1740.

Thus, throughout the 1720s, Suqua often left his partner, Tonqua, with his Canton business while he was in Amoy. Mandarin Quiqua's firms of the same name — Qouycong — in Canton and Amoy, kept him moving between the ports and his hometown in Ch'üanchou until he quitted Canton definitively in 1737. Hunqua and Cowlo had residences and warehouses at both ports. Old Quiqua, Cowlo's partner, had his second son, Tinqua, formerly in Canton, as the second ranked merchant in Amoy by 1734.

Cudgin left his Canton business to Leonqua in 1732 and retired to Ch'üanchou. In 1734, he was promoting the Canton-Amoy trade of his friend and relation, Monqua, an established merchant in Amoy. A former aide of Linqua and Anqua became an agent travelling between Canton, Amoy and Batavia in the 1720s. Beau Khequa retired to his hometown, Ch'üanchou, in 1734, after incurring the ire of Canton officials; his partner, Amoy Tiqua, inherited his Canton business, but the Beau retired in 1750 and became the chief merchant.

The seasonal migration and operations of Canton merchants in Amoy remained innocuous until discontentment with conditions in Canton raised the spectre of merchants and foreigners leaving Canton for Amoy or Ningpo permanently. A crisis of confidence had descended on the trade in the 1720s.

The demise of the duopoly in 1720 and the Co-hong in 1721, brought the mandarins back into the trade. Suqua for example was Viceroy Yang Lin's factotum. The lower military had also been particularly obstreperous. By 1723, the credit of most of the old merchants was ruined by debts to officials and Parsees. In 1724, Governor-Hoppo Nien Shih-yao sold the whole season's European trade to Boqua until Suqua made a counter-offer. The regime of Governor-Hoppo Yang Wen-ch'ien (1725 – 28) provoked outcries from merchants and the foreigners because of new duties and improved collection of charges; Suqua was dislodged as chief merchant and Yang's favourite, Cudgin, made chief until 1728 when he withdrew from the trade upon becoming a mandarin. Yang's suppression of official participation in the trade aroused the officials to launch an impeachment against him in 1727, but they were unsuccessful.

The official oppression and signs of a tightening of control prompted the merchants to contemplate seriously the abandonment of Canton. It thus turned into a crisis of identity for the merchants. On their return from Amoy in 1722, they invited the English to move their trade there as they had built residences and bought warehouses in preparation. The English were tempted but desisted, fearing that facilities, merchants and officials at Amoy might not meet their needs especially as the silk weavers had long before migrated to Canton.

Prompted further by the merchants and a favourable report from a country ship which had traded in Amoy, the English were ready to move in 1727, but inexplicably, the leaders, Suqua, Hunqua and Mandarin Quiqua were no longer interested. Hearing of the overtures made by the merchants to the English Viceroy K'ung Yü-hsün and Hoppo Yang in 1726 threatened Suqua and probably the others, with forfeiture of their property and trading rights in Canton if they moved away or colluded in re-opening the Amoy trade. This was an ultimatum for the Hong merchants to make a definitive commitment to Canton and trade there. Their rejection of the English offer thus virtually converted the transients into immigrants.

The conditions however, improved in Canton as the trade expanded with new European trade partners. The monopoly of the small élite, initiated by Yang in 1725, had become a vested interest to protect. The curb on the official trade begun under Yang had been extended to the Hoppo after Hoppo Tsu-ping-kuei was impeached in 1732 for that transgression. Thus the merchants re-emerged in full control of the European trade in Canton by the mid 1730s. The earlier defeat over relocation to Amoy inflicted by the Viceroy and Hoppo-Governor had now been assuaged by a triumph over official interlopers, who had encroached on their trade for more than thirty years.

The disgruntled English, misled by the continuing seasonal movement of merchants between ports and a report in 1734 that three senior Hongists had retreated to Chüanchou, dispatched two ships to Amoy (1734, 1735) and another to Ningpo (1736). But they all returned to what they now realized were superior conditions in Canton. The extortionate practices, in the northern ports, of merchants in collusion with officials, arbitrary levies and a six months delay in delivery were intolerable. Cudgin came to Amoy from Ch'üanchou and advised that English needs could not be met by Amoy producers whose goods were for a different market; at Ningpo, officials had to send to Soochow, which had eclipsed Ningpo in the northern trade, for merchants and cargoes.

In short, purveying for the English trade had become the speciality of Canton and its merchants. The strength went beyond facilities, port administration, duties and usages to the merchants, supply of goods to specification and delivery deadlines. The English disappointments in the north underlined the ascendancy of the Canton Hong merchants in national terms over the European trade in China, to match their local dislodgement of their main rivals in the trade, the officials. The traditional specialists in the European trade — the Fukienese merchants in Canton — thus took up where the Fukienese traders in Macao, a century before, had left the declining Portuguese commerce.

The end of the English interest, for the time being, in trade with Amoy and Ningpo, thus coincided with the loosening of ties between Fukienese emigrés in Canton and Amoy. By 1734, Hunqua alone of the Canton merchants still had a residence in Amoy. The death and retirement or failure of old merchants rid Canton of transients. Merchants with divided loyalty like Mandarin Quiqua, Cudgin and Beau Khequa, made a choice for Fukien, like many others who retired there.

The itinerant and transient had finally become an immigrant permanently settled in Canton; the residual transitoriness in attitude towards doing business in Canton gave way to a full commitment to the system and the expanded European trade. Officials had finally forced a choice on the merchants, and their ascendancy on the local as well as national level over the trade, had done the rest in making a specialist of the Hong merchant.

These changes on the domestic front were complementary to the contraction of the Hong merchant's interest in the Japanese, Manila and Batavian trade, a contraction which took place during this same period.

Contraction of Overseas Commitments

The trade with Japan was the first to decline. It reverted to the Ningpo-Chusan merchants whose traditional dominance had been, for more than a hundred and fifty years before 1684, usurped by the southerners. After 1684, Kwangtung-Fukien interest revived strongly but was soon overtaken by trade out of Yangtse ports. Whereas the share of the south was thirty junks against five in 1685 and thirty-six against twenty-six in 1688, it was only five against twenty-one in 1716.

Shogun Yoshimune's limitation of trade to thirty junks in 1716 and K'ang-hsi's ban on overseas trade from Ningpo between 1717 and 1722, set the trade on the path of decline throughout the rest of the century. A guild of eight merchants with a chief was established in Ningpo in 1728 for the trade, but by 1736, the port had been eclipsed by Soochou. The Hong merchant's interest in the trade had declined in tandem. Cowlo for example, who had a monopoly to supply Japanese copper to the state under guarantee from Old Quiqua's son in Amoy (Tinqua), was reported in 1728 to have defaulted for some years on the engagement.

The imperial prohibition (1717) of overseas trade lasted longer in Kwangtung (1723) and Fukien (1727). Trade with Annam and Portuguese shipping from Macao were excluded from the ban in 1718 upon petition by Viceroy Yang Lin of Liang Kwang. A three-year amnesty for Chinese abroad to return and prohibition of the landing of those settling overseas after 1717, was another caveat. Upon final repeal in 1727, junks from Kwangtung and Fukien were required to return only to Amoy or Whampoa. All these had important consequences on the Hong merchant's interest in the Manila and Batavia trades.

The junk trade from China to Manila revived rapidly between 1684 and 1715, but declined sharply during the prohibition; although it recovered afterwards, it never regained the peak of the 1701 – 1715 period:

1671 – 85	1686 – 1700	1701 – 15	1716 – 30	1731 – 45
78 (junks)	234	264	156	203

Junk trade was supplemented by occasional Portuguese or Armenian ships from Macao. The prohibition also brought the Spaniards back to the China coast. They were exempted from customs duties in Canton and the exemption was extended to Amoy in 1739. The privileged access to Fukienese ports which the Spaniards enjoyed since earliest days was formally reconfirmed by the Grand Council in 1748. There was a special relationship between Fukien and the Philippines, and the Manila trade had traditionally been a speciality of the Fukinese ports.

The share of the Hong merchants was probably partly conducted out of Amoy where they still had establishments well into the 1730s. In Canton, Suqua, Hunqua and Chonqua, of the old merchants, were known investors, some of their trade going through Macao and probably under Portuguese colours.

Investment for Manila from Canton, no doubt, increased significantly with the return of Chinese settlers in Manila to Canton. In fact the amnesty had brought 2,000 overseas settlers back to China by 1727. Merchants in Canton with Christian names were obviously returned from Manila and the firms they attached themselves to probably also had previous business with the Philippines. Manila was in the firm of Old Quiqua and Cowlo between 1729 and 1732; Manuel was an independent merchant. Emmanuel Quiqua and Felix became sometime partners of Young Hunqua who himself had only appeared in Canton in 1727. There were also Phyllis Hunqua and Simon and Tsetsyau (Suqua's successor as chief merchant in 1740) who appeared in Canton in 1734.

Mandarin Quiqua and his last manager in Canton (1736 – 37) Phuankhequa, were the most prominent of the repatriates. Mandarin Quiqua successfully re-established his Manila firm, Qouycong, in Amoy and Canton. With an assertiveness and single-minded devotion to profit, he made Qouycong the principal house in Amoy and became very rich in Canton; but he also became very tough. He was from Ch'üanchou and there he retired in 1737. Phuankhequa was also from the same hometown. During residence in Manila, he became fluent in Spanish and was converted to Christianity. On his return to Canton, he was apprenticed to Mandarin Quiqua and eventually became his manager when still only in his early twenties. His ties with Manila and linguistic skill enabled him to monopolize the trade of Spanish ships in

Canton and probably also invest for Manila. He stayed on to become
chief merchant between 1758 and 1788, when he died.

Amoy and Ch'üanchou no doubt also had their own returned
merchants from Manila, but Canton probably benefited from the
prolongation of the ban on sailings from Fukien until 1727. At any rate,
during the prohibition and afterwards, sampans owned or captained by
Chinese Christians were reported in Manila. However, the resumption
of direct trade by the Spaniards on the China coast, mopped up some of
the business that would have otherwise gone on junks.

After the ban was lifted, sailings from Amoy increased significantly,
and so did the Portuguese and Spanish carrying activity; Canton's share
in junk trade declined:

	Port/Sp/(China)	Junks (Canton)	Junks (Amoy)
1716 – 30	8	8	7
1731 – 45	12	6	68

(figures only of ships declaring their port of origin)

Thus after the prohibition, the traffic returned to the traditional
carriers — the Amoy merchants. No doubt, the retreat of Hong
merchants from Amoy in the early 1730s was a symptom as well as
contributory cause of their disengagement from the trade with Manila.

The trade with Batavia was also reduced to secondary importance in
the Canton merchant's portfolio by the mid-1730s; it also drifted back
into the control of the traditional carriers — the Fukienese merchants.
Batavia was an important vent for Chinese staples, teas especially, for
the European market before 1720. The English and French had only an
average of three ships in Canton per year in that period, and surplus
from the Canton operations were sent to Batavia and other ports 'at any
price', it was reported in 1716.

Linqua and Anqua were active in it before 1720; Anqua claimed, as
early as 1700, to have been in Batavia to drum up Dutch interest in the
Canton trade. Their goodwill was inherited by an aide who commuted
between Canton, Amoy and Batavia in the 1720s. Suqua and Hunqua
were also principals in the trade. No doubt, there were many others,
and as in the case of Manila, probably also returned settlers from
Batavia, but these are unverifiable.

The trade during the 1720s went on unlicensed junks from Canton,
Amoy, Ch'üanchou and Ningpo. The bulk of the Canton merchants'
consignments however, went on chartered Portuguese ships from
Macao. Hence when the ban was lifted on Ningpo in 1722, the
Portuguese ships were expected to be laid up when the law was repealed
in Kwangtung and Fukien. However, the heavy consignment in the

large Portuguese ships periodically occasioned higher prices and shortages in Canton during the decade.

In 1720, an English ship was unable to load teas in Canton because of shipments to Batavia and the provisioning of an earlier English ship and an Ostender. In 1721, three to four junks from Chusan with good teas competed with six to seven Portuguese ships from Macao laden with sweepings from the previous year's trade in Canton. In 1722, several unlicensed junks were reported again in Batavia. By 1723, the Canton Hongists had lost heavily for three consecutive years on teas for Batavia.

The repeal of the ban on Chinese overseas trade intensified rivalry and increased indebtedness. In consequence, in 1728, the Dutch seized up to 25,000 taels from junks off Banka to recover debts to them and Portuguese shipowners. Consignments of cheap teas continued however, causing a serious shortage and high prices in Canton that year.

In 1730, twenty junks from China and six Portuguese carriers from Macao brought 20,000 piculs of black teas to Batavia for Europe and a further 5,500 piculs for local consumption. A glut in both outlets inflicted heavy losses on Canton merchants arising from shipments in 1731; Suqua for example, lost 30,000 taels. More losses were incurred when prices in Canton fell from 18 taels to 13.5 taels per picul within a month.

The trade had been overdone. Bad teas, excessive shipment and the cost of the charter party exacerbated operational losses for more than a decade. The end was in sight. In 1734, eight Amoy junks entered Batavia but no junks or Portuguese ships from Canton or Macao. The expensive flag of convenience had thus been abandoned. It seemed also that the Fukienese, the traditional masters of the commerce, had recaptured what remained of the trade, as they had done with the Manila trade.

The prolonged malaise in the trade beginning from 1720, no doubt, originated from the direct supply of European markets by the European Companies. The extensive Ostender trade and the revival of the French operations at the beginning of the decade, were preludes to the return to the China coast by the Dutch in 1729 and the arrival of the Danes (1730) and Swedes (1732), the last two being direct successors of the Ostend Company.

The extensive commercial network of the Hong merchant thus contracted perceptibly between 1715 and 1740. Establishments and operations from Amoy and trade with Japan, Manila and Batavia had all virtually ended. In each case, the traffic had reverted to the traditional routes and the control of the traditional carriers. Only the trade with Cochin China remained unimpaired, having been spared prohibition in 1718. The gold it brought attracted the interest of the Europeans in the

1720s and 1730s, but although a continuing source of profit and activity, it declined in importance as the European trade itself became the major preocupation of the Hong merchant.

A distinctly more sedentary role remained for the Hong merchant in the European trade at Canton. This was specialization. Specialization was, at first, a strength fostered by success in depriving the northern ports of the European trade and by changing conditions and commercial traffic on the Chinese littoral. Only later did it deteriorate into parochial narrowness of expertise and experience, and inflexibility, as the next generic crisis in the 1770s – 1790s demonstrated.

The contraction of the Hongists' mercantile world, after all, was more physical and geographical than commercial. Asian goods came on the European ships and on junks required since 1727 to return either to Amoy or Whampoa. Although the Japan trade was lost and profit and activities in Batavia and Manila limited, the supply of Spanish America and Europe continued, not at Manila or Batavia, but in Canton itself where the Europeans now traded themselves.

However, it was here in Canton that the first sign of attenuated versatility became perceptible: the Hong merchant was now more a factotum than the dealer and consigner that earlier merchants had been. Ownership of vessels, extensive contacts with shipowners and shippers and activities abroad which had made the Hong merchant's name and movements in China household words among junkowners in Batavia and Manila, were roles and distinctions left behind in his transformation.

Merchants in the Administration

The mass extinction of merchants in the 1730s was thus something of a generic end of the old type of merchant. The new merchant was a specialist in the European trade at Canton, in all ways committed to the trade and system, and a permanent resident except for a family seat, usually in Ch'üanchou. But he was only a pale shadow of his versatile, ubiquitous and somewhat unsettled predecessor.

This was however, not a history of unremitting denudation of the merchant's talent and skills, for in the twenty years after 1740, administrative skills and delegated authority reconstructed the moribund mercantile thoroughbred into a merchant-bureaucrat. From 1736, permanent residence and commitment to the Canton trade and system was turned into positive participation in it, and eventually, into its defence.

In that year, Hoppo Cheng Wu-sai started to assign individual merchants to secure European ships, conferring a non-transferable monopoly of a ship's whole trade on the securing merchant. With it came responsibility for the ship's formalities while in port, duties and charges due on its trade and the conduct of its crew and officers. The compradors, linguists and functionaries attending to the ship and its victualling and trade, also came under the supervision of the security merchant. The managerial function, thus transferred, was legalized in 1745.

To the non-commercial duties was added power delegated in the 1740s by officials. Rivalry between the Hoppo and the territorial officials in the previous five decades had led to the virtual suspension of the separate post of Hoppo during the 1740s: incumbent Viceroys and Governors assumed its powers, if not title. But because of heavy responsibilities elsewhere, the actual administration was left to their Chungquans, who, in turn, delegated the routines to the securities. The accretion of administrative function and development power left the merchants to manage matters to their own advantage. By the same process, officials disengaged themselves from direct involvement in the trade, merchants and foreigners.

By 1750, the English were describing the merchants as 'our opponents who are now aiming at giving the law to the whole place'; they feared the Hongists would 'impose on us in matters of more consequence.' In fact, official and mercantile interests, in confrontation twenty-five years before, were now approaching convergence. The crisis in Anglo-Chinese relations during the 1750s provided the occasion to demonstrate and complete the bureaucratization of the Hong merchant.

The confrontation had been gathering momentum in the 1740s, with many long-established practices becoming regulations; these aggravated foreigners' discontent with the merchants' management of the port and trade. The formal recognition of the monopoly of the six leading merchants in 1755, was the last straw. The English dispatched two ships to Ningpo, hoping to find better conditions there, and presumably to threaten Canton with desertion.

The merchants who thirty years before had contemplated abandoning Canton for Amoy with the English, now adopted a totally different attitude. Despite severe indebtedness, partly attributable to official squeeze during the long tenure of Hoppo Li Yung-piao (1752 – 54, 1755 – 59), they rallied behind officials to oppose the resumption of trade in the rival northern port. At stake were the monopoly now secured and the managerial authority now vested in them — both absent in the 1720s and 1730s.

The Emperor was disinclined to close the northern ports and preferred to discourage the English at Ningpo. Trade on the Canton model seemed to be contemplated when a customs administration for the Ningpo-T'aichou circuit with a Hoppo from the *nei-wu-fu* and a schedule of duties identical to those at Canton, were ordered. This last was necessary as duties at Ningpo, as at Macao, had remained at rates for Chinese ocean-going ships, whereas duties for Europeans at Canton had increased with accretions since Min-Che and Liang Kwang duties were stardardised in 1735.

Fortunately for Canton interests, the Viceroy of Liang Kwang, Yang Ying-Chü, was charged with implementing both orders when the incumbent Viceroy of Min-Che, K'o-er-chi-san, died. Duties on staples — teas, silks and chinaware — were doubled, tripled and quadrupled, and the English were threatened with the ancient measurage abandoned in Canton in 1698, and Hong-yung. When these still failed to dislodge the English, Yang ordered their expulsion in December, 1757; an edict in Canton required all European ships to trade, henceforth, only at Canton. In 1759, the Emperor confirmed the *fait accompli*.

This crisis was the occasion for the Hong merchants to withdraw from yet another domestic theatre of activity. Strong links had been maintained with the Yangtse area for supplying the European trade in Canton. Runners were sent up-country on urgent commissions and during shortages, as Sweetia did in 1757 and 1759. His partner, Yongshaw, exchanged market reports with a brother Yongquan — the leading purveyor of the English at Ningpo at the head of a syndicate of four merchants. Other private arrangements probably also existed among the other Hongists.

Some thirty merchants and crew from Canton and Macao appeared in Ningpo with the English. Wang Sheng-i (Shingyquan) and his son, Lan-shui, were then active collaborators and they consigned to the English in Canton overland as late as 1759. In that year, the English dispatched Cainqua inland to report on the tea and silk country; other Europeans presumably had similar channels for market intelligence and trade.

The risk of the trade relocating to Ningpo was thus serious, but in the conflict between maintaining residual interests in the producing areas and defending the local monopoly of the merchants and the national monopoly of Canton, the latter again prevailed as it had against Amoy, in the 1720s. The defeat of the northern rival was followed by the prohibition of the direct trade between up-country suppliers and Europeans in Canton, and the investment of foreigners in the interior in 1759.

The price of the further protection of the Hong merchant's specialization was thus his exclusion from directly supplying his own needs from the interior. Only at second-hand, by joint operations with up-country suppliers or establishing a relative in the northern trade, could Canton merchants occasionally breach their mercantile prison wall. Legally, physically and functionally, the Hong merchant had become in 1759, a parochial specialist, as a sedentary middleman in the European trade at Canton.

Ironically, Yang Ying-chü was the son of Governor-Hoppo Yang Wen-ch'ien (1725 – 28) who in 1726 had prevented the flight of the merchants with the English trade to Amoy only by threatening Suqua and others with reprisals. Thirty years later, the son had the unstinting support of the merchants to foil the English desertion of Canton; the merchants even paid some 20,000 taels to have their case favourably heard in Peking.

Significantly, some of the principal merchants in the 1750s were the very delinquent ones of the 1720s or their successors: Suqua, Tinqua and the two apprentices, Chowqua and Phuankhequa, of the earlier errant Mandarin Quiqua. Others were men of the new generic type, recruited in the 1720s and 1730s — Beau Khequa (chief), Chai Hunqua (previously Young Hunqua) and his relative Chai Suequa, Teunqua, Chetqua (son of Suqua), Teinqua, Chinqua (not the original Chinqua), Fat Hunqua, Geequa, Sweetia and Footia.

Those thirty years had seen the Hong merchants inducted into the administration and assimilated into conformity. The transient whose commitment to Canton was so tenuous that he considered defection at the first sign of a system closing in on him, was now a permanent resident who participated in, managed and defended the system with a convert's fervour. Acting in concert with officials, the merchants' interests were now almost indistinguishable from official policy.

As if to underline his total assimilation, the substance of authority was now gilded with purchased titles, ranks and degrees. This also was a development of the Age of Suqua. The Kim*co* who arrived in 1704 from Amoy, became Cum*shaw* until his elevation from a petty trader into a fully-fledged merchant in 1716, styled Su*qua*. His rival, Cudgin, went further to become the first recorded case of a Hong merchant buying himself into official ranks and out of the lowly mercantile class in 1728; he promptly withdrew from active trade. Others followed, but without the need to observe the propriety of distance from material gain.

The pursuit of actual power and the purchase of the trappings of power thus came into the sights of the merchant's objectives alongside commercial profit. Success in trade ceased to be the sole measure of the merchant's attainments — blunted appetite for mercantile achievements and deflected aims being further indicators of generic change.

Conclusion

This paper is about generic change in the Hong merchants of Canton, but it was a change in which the contraction of their commercial activities in Fukien, Chekiang and overseas were important criteria. The paper is therefore also about the redrawing of the map of China's maritime commercial routes and trade, twice, in the period 1684 – 1759, initially on their southward course with the merchants to Canton, and then back to more traditional patterns in which the European commerce at Canton now had discrete place.

The Canton Hong merchant, in the end, was a separate breed in China's maritime trade history, but he was also a Fukienese. Hence, the reversion of the Japanese trade to the Yangtse ports apart, this is really also a history of the reassertion of Fukienese ascendancy, not only in the trades they traditionally dominated — with Manila and Batavia — but also in the new bilateral trade out of Canton with the Europeans.

23

CHINESE TRADE WITH BATAVIA IN
THE SEVENTEENTH AND EIGHTEENTH CENTURIES:
A PRELIMINARY REPORT

Leonard Blussé, Jan Oosterhoff and Ton Vermeulen

Introduction

Traditionally historians have devoted considerable attention to early
Chinese voyages and trade with overseas countries during the Sung and
Ming dynasties. Only recently has an increasing interest been shown
towards Chinese shipping during the Ch'ing dynasty. Doctoral theses
on the trade with the kingdom of Siam have been produced by Sarasin
Viraphol and Jennifer Cushman, studies by Iwao Seiichi and Uamawaki
Teijiro have thrown new light on Chinese trade with Tokugawa Japan,
Ng Chin-Keong has analysed the role of the Amoy traders in Chinese
coastal shipping, and George Souza in his recent thesis on Portuguese
trade from Macao has described the orientation of Portuguese trade
towards Indo-China and the Indonesian archipelago after Japan shut its
doors to the Iberians in 1640.[1] While Ng, Viraphol and Cushman
largely depended on Chinese sources, Iwao and Yamawaki combined
Dutch materials with Japanese sources. The same can be said of Souza,
who added much pertinent evidence from Dutch archives to the
Portuguese sources of the Macao archives. Unfortunately, only little
Chinese evidence remains of what was during the early eighteenth
century one of the most important Chinese trade links: the commerce
with the headquarters of the Dutch East India Company in Asia,
Batavia. In 1979, Leonard Blussé, one of the contributors to the present
article, mainly on the basis of Dutch source materials, provided a short
overview of Chinese trade with Batavia during the seventeenth and
eighteenth centuries. Deriving his information from printed sources
like the edicts and resolutions by Governor-General and Council, in
connection with Chinese trade and the so-called *Generale Missiven*, the
bi-annual letters that the Batavian government sent to the *Heren XVII* in
the Republic, he was able to show the changing policies of the Dutch
towards the Chinese trade and the way in which these policies effected
the decline of the junk trade at the end of the eighteenth century. The

scope of that survey, published in the special issue on the South China Sea of the French journal *Archipel*, however, did not permit further processing of the ample amount of quantitative data on Chinese shipping to Batavia which are kept in the *Algemeen Rijksarchief* in The Hague. Of recent years the contributors to this article have joined forces to collect quantitative data on the number of junks sailing to and from Batavia, the cargoes, the goods that were purchased, et cetera. These data have gradually been classified and put into a computer, and here we should like to present some preliminary results of our research, which will soon be published in book form. In order to put these figures into a conceptual framework, we shall very briefly review the development, or better said, the rise and fall of the junk grade during the V.O.C. period.

Shortly after the VOC had moved its headquarters in 1619 from Bantam to nearby Jakarta (which was rebaptised Batavia) great effort was made by the Dutch authorities to keep all Chinese shipping away from other Javanese coastal towns and to funnel all Chinese goods into Batavia. Initially this trade did not live up to the expectations and in the vicinity of Amoy a new trading post was set up on the island of Formosa. In between 1624 and 1661 (when the Dutch were expelled by the Chinese sea lord and Ming loyalist Cheng Ch'eng-king (Coxinga), Chinese goods were mainly brought by Chinese shipping to the Formosan trade-factory Zeelandia castle, and from there transported by Dutch ships sailing in different directions, to, for example, Siam, Japan, the Indonesian archipelago, India and Persia. Chinese trade to Batavia did not come to a complete halt in these years, but never amounted to more than four or five junks a year.

In 1661 the Chinese emperor issued an edict forbidding his subjects to participate in any coastal and maritime trade. Although this prohibition policy was not exercised with the same rigour everywhere the results were sharply felt in Batavia. Only after the conquest of Formosa in 1683 by the imperial forces, was the ban on overseas trade lifted. Not surprisingly a great increase in Chinese shipping to Batavia can be perceived from 1684 onwards. It is around this date that the Batavian authorities began to draw up shipping lists and started to make an inventory of the amount of goods purchased from and sold to the Chinese, Portuguese from Macao and other foreign merchants. These sources form the main evidence for our present research. Data concerning junk shipping before the 1680s have primarily been drawn from entries in the Diaries of Batavia Castle (*Dagregisters van Batavia*). These figures have already been collected by M. S. de Vienne in her unpublished doctoral thesis.[2]

The period between 1685 and 1730 may be characterized as the heyday of the junk trade. Contrary to the policies of the English East

India Company which established direct trade links with China around the turn of the century, the VOC preferred for the time being to be served by Chinese shipping. Problems with quality-control of Chinaware and tea that were ordered via Chinese *nachodas* who visited Batavia, forced the *Heren XVII* to new initiatives, and in 1727 a new direct trade link was established with Canton, much to the dislike of both the Chinese *nachodas* and the Governor-General in Batavia. The latter feared, not without reason, that this blow to the Chinese shipping would hit Batavia indirectly also, as it would inevitably result in a decrease in the traffic with China. In the years that followed adjustments were made in the sea routes of the Dutch China-bound vessels — they were eventually also permitted to call at Batavia — but the misgivings of the Indian government largely came true. A steady decrease of the junk trade set in. Many pronouncements made by Governor General and Council through the years point in this direction. All the same the quantitative data that we have collected now enable us to give a much more balanced view of what was actually happening.

Sources[3]

The VOC-archives in The Hague contain thousands of letters that the heads of the Asian factories had sent to their directors in the Netherlands, the Gentlemen XVII (*Heren XVII*). From the 1680s onwards these Letters and Papers Received (*Overgekomen Brieven en Papieren*) contains lists of foreign shipping and trade to and from the Asian headquarters of the VOC, Batavia.

The Chinese who called at Batavia were dealt with in separate shipping lists, while the Portuguese from Macao were recorded together with other European vessels. These lists note the date of arrival, the name of the captain or *(a)nachoda*, the name or type of vessel, the tonnage, the number of guns and the crew, the home-port and the date of departure to a specific harbour. In the Chinese lists are also mentioned the number of people on the junks that entered Batavia and left it again, officially at least.

On these ships Chinese and Portuguese carried a large variety of goods. These can be divided in two groups: those to be sold on the local Batavian market, and the merchandise that was meant to be bought by the merchants of the VOC. The former part consisted of small wares like combs, fans, all sorts of earthenware as well as tobacco, flour, aniseed etc. These goods were very important for the local economy. Already in 1647 when only two Chinese junks had arrived, the *Heren XVII* thought it detrimental of the citizens, 'because they (the Chinese) supply a lot of commodities and create a lot of trade . . .'[4]

The small wares for the local market were not recorded, but the other part of the cargo, bought by the Honourable Company officials, was recorded in the so-called *Samengetrokken Lijsten*, collected lists of the merchandise bought from and sold to the foreign merchants. On the left, the clerks registered the goods bought from foreigners, and on the debtor side the articles which were delivered out of the Company warehouses. Nearly all merchandise on these collected lists were Portuguese and Chinese. One or two shipments from Manila or India were also involved. European ships like the English, French, Danish, Swedish and Prussian called mainly at the Batavian roadstead for refreshments.

Shipping

From the 1680s onwards till 1793, some 400 Portuguese vessels from Macao and 1200 junks from China called at Batavia. Although more than 140 ships had as their home port Ning-po in the province of Chekiang, most of the Chinese trading vessels originated from Fukien and Kwantung harbours.

Half the total amount of Chinese ships departed from Amoy (Hsia-men) and about one-sixth or 200 from Canton (Kuang-chou), the main harbours in Fukien and Kwantung. Some Chinese junks also called at Batavia from places outside China; until the middle of the eighteenth century some 70 from Tonkin, and others which sailed from Japan or Siam.

The junks sailed south along the Chinese, Vietnamese and Cambodian coasts, across the Gulf of Siam to Bangka Strait in between the islands of Bangka and Sumatra, and finally onwards to Batavia, where they arrived at the roads near the Watercastle. In all, the voyage would take twenty to forty days. The seasonal passages depended upon the monsoon winds. The ships left China around the turn of the year when the North-east monsoon (October-March) was blowing and most of them went back in June and July, sailing down the South-west monsoon (March – October).

Ships of different types and sizes were used, but 85% of the Chinese *nachodas* commanded a junk of 150 – 200 tons. At the same time a smaller type of junk, the *wankang*, sailed across the South China Sea to Batavia. The Portuguese used mainly European-type vessels, like sloops (*chaloup*), ships and yachts, armed with 6 – 12 guns, while the Chinese lacked this weaponry. Not only were the vessels different, but also the flow of their shipment. The Chinese were masters of the trade route to Batavia and only some curtailments at the hands of their own authorities could increase the Portuguese share. Especially in the second and third decade of the eighteenth century the Macao shipowners profited from an imperial bull, which forbade overseas trade (1717 – 1727). A number of junks evaded this decree, but most Cantonese merchants hired cargo space on Portuguese ships to Batavia.[5] The number of their vessels decreased again from the 1730s onwards to a mere two or three a year.

The Chinese shipping was struck another severe blow in 1740, when the Chinese town population of Batavia was massacred. In the years that followed, the junks continued to call at the 'Queen of the East', but never regained their number of pre-1740, although a slight increase can be observed in the 1780s (Table 2).

But the Chinese massacre was not the only explanation for this decay. As time went by the *anachodas* were progressively troubled by the monopolistic tendencies of the VOC. Between 1710 and 1740 some twenty ships from the Middle Kingdom entered the Batavian harbour every year. Initially the junks constituted the only connection with China, but in 1728 the directors started to send Dutch ships to Canton in face of the keen competition from the English and Ostend companies. Between 1734 and 1756 these China-bound ships sailed from Batavia as a result of the fierce opposition evoked in Batavia to a direct European-China connection. Governor-General and Council feared for detrimental effects on the Chinese junk trade, that upheld the local economy. The Dutch ships destined for Canton were forbidden to load any goods that were carried by the junks. However in 1756 a direct trade between China and the Netherlands was established, and Batavia was a port of call only in order to load some merchandise on the way to Canton.[7] Consequently the Chinese and Portuguese traders lost the greater part of their trade to the VOC-shipping. The literature states that these developments marked the ultimate decline of the junk trade, but surprisingly the number of junks hardly decreased after 1706, and increased again slightly in the 1780s. The Chinese traders focused more on the local Batavian market, but the character of their trade with the Company changed. We shall consider the transformation in the business dealings between John Chinaman and Jan Compagnie.

Buying and Selling of the VOC

Purchases

During the seventeenth century the Dutch considered porcelain and silks as the most important Chinese merchandise. At the end of the century tea was more and more in demand in Europe, and the junks

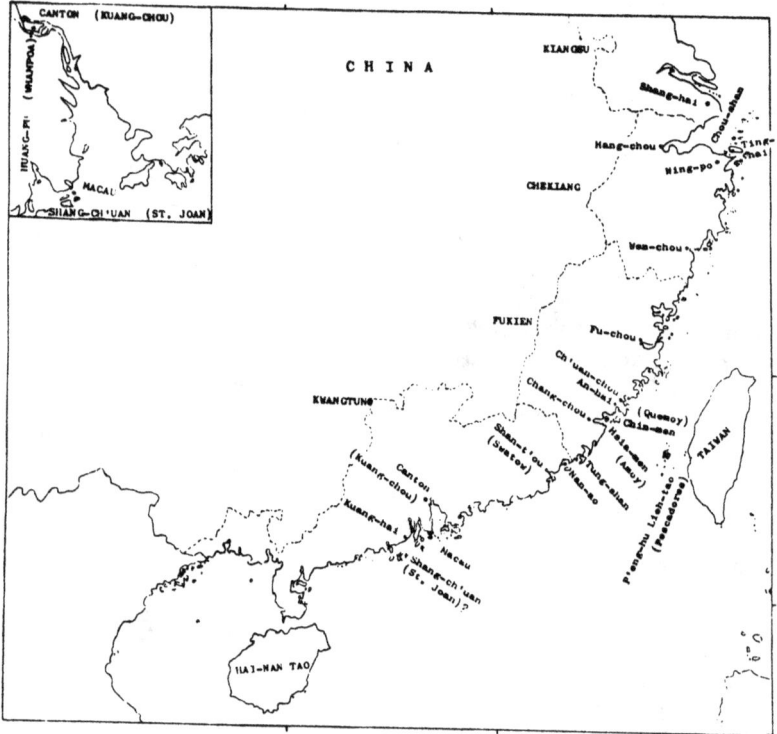

Fig. 1. Home ports in South-east China.

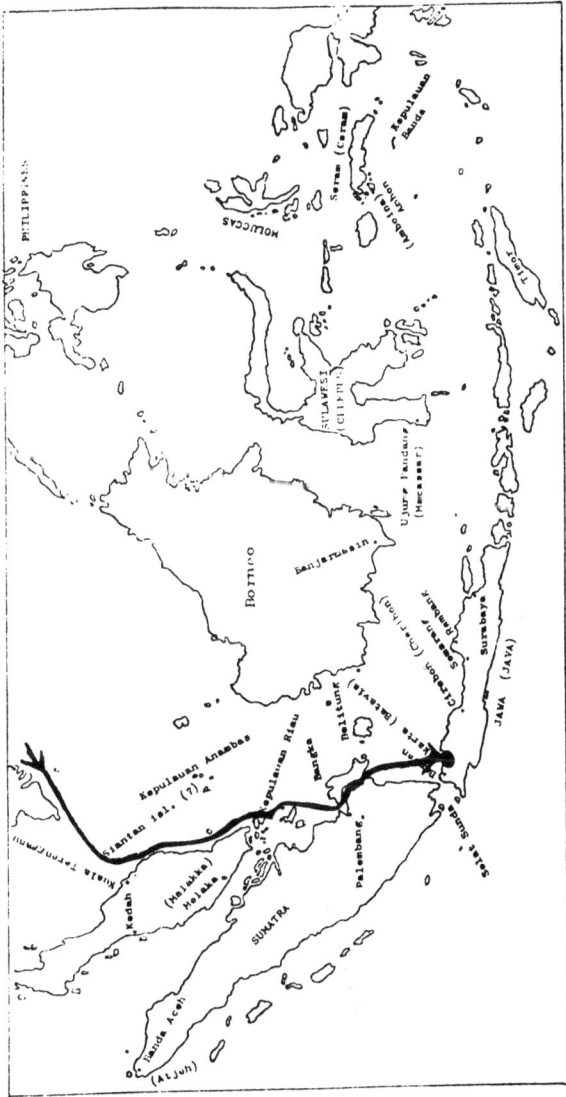

Fig. 2. Indonesian archipelago.

Table 1. *Types of vessels plying between China and Batavia*

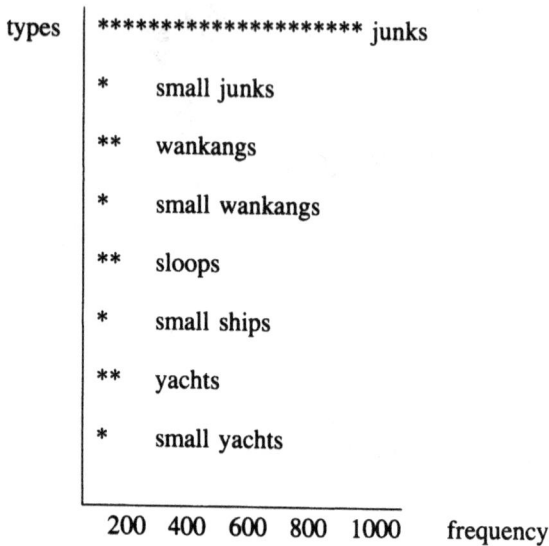

types	
******************** junks	
*	small junks
**	wankangs
*	small wankangs
**	sloops
*	small ships
**	yachts
*	small yachts

200 400 600 800 1000   frequency

Table 2. *Number of incoming ships (average per annum)*[6]

	Chinese	*Portuguese*	*Total*
1680 – 1690	9.7	1.8	11.5
1690 – 1700	11.5	1.6	13.1
1700 – 1710	11	2.9	13.9
1710 – 1720	13.6	5.9	19.5
1720 – 1730	16.4	9	25.4
1730 – 1740	17.7	4.8	22.5
1740 – 1750	10.9	4.1	15
1750 – 1760	9.1	1.8	10.9
1760 – 1770	7.4	2.4	9.8
1770 – 1780	5.1	3	8.1
1780 – 1790	9.3	3.9	13.2
1790 – 1793	9.5	3	12.5

freighted it in ever larger quantities to Batavia (Table 3). A peak was reached in 1738, when 15,229 piculs (of 125 Amsterdam pounds) were bought by the Company for 412,198 rix dollars. In contrast to the English in Canton most of the tea was of the black variety, especially Bohea from Fukien Province. After this period a sharp decline can be noticed, and in 1741 the last substantial quantity was sold by Portuguese and Chinese traders on the Batavian market.

Table 3. *Tea purchased by the VOC (average per annum)*

	quantity (piculs)	*value* (rix dollars)
1700 – 1710	400	?
1710 – 1720	745	46,215
1720 – 1730	3439	184,003
1730 – 1740	6048	149,023
1740 – 1750	810	16,347
1750 – 1760	0	0
1760 – 1770	0	0
1770 – 1780	3	116
1780 – 1790	4	147
1790 – 1793	0	0

This decline was the result of the VOC-policy to buy tea in Canton and transport it in her own ships. Besides, the Chinese and Portuguese tea shipped to Batavia was wrapped in bamboo-leaves, whereas the merchants in Canton packed tea in chests lined with lead. Several times these different packing methods were compared after 1730 and the balance of evidence was in favour of the lead-lined cases. The VOC at Batavia stopped buying tea, but it seems that the supply kept on going, because in 1743 private individuals were allowed to freight tea to Europe in the holds of VOC-ships, and the local Batavian market needed it too.

In the business dealing of the Dutch East India Company with the Chinese in Batavia, tea was replaced by various other products, which fluctuated considerably: cowries, pearl-shells, porcelain, radix China, camphor, ginger, turtle shells, bezoin, etc. However, metals topped the list, and the value of copper, zinc, pewter, tin and lead in the 1760s was twice that of tea in its heyday. At that time metals amounted to almost three million Amsterdam pounds (one pound = 0.49 kg) a year.

At first especially tin and lead were used by Chinese and Portuguese as ballast commodities for their trip to China, but this situation changed after 1740. Instead of buying, they sold increasing quantities to the Dutch authorities (Table 4). This is a surprising development as the export of copper and tin was strictly forbidden in China.

Table 4. Metals purchased by the VOC (average per annum)

	copper, zinc, pewter		tin, lead		total	
	quantity (piculs)	value (rix dollars)	quantity (piculs)	value (rix dollars)	quantity (piculs)	value (rix dollars)
1700 – 1710						
1710 – 1720						
1720 – 1730	209	2,929			209	2,929
1730 – 1740	126	2,269			126	2,269
1740 – 1750	99	2,629	3,621	59,103	3,720	61,732
1750 – 1760	619	16,648	9,681	153,994	10,300	170,642
1760 – 1770	562	13,623	22,773	356,663	23,336	370,286
1770 – 1780	610	14,380	16,762	250,143	17,372	264,523
1780 – 1790	628	17,082	21,456	321,166	22,084	338,248
1790 – 1793	344	8,959	9,224	138,357	9,568	147,316

The merchants from China carried a lot of other goods as well, but —
as mentioned above — they were of less importance or only had some
significance for a short period of time. Bullion, for instance, in the
1720s amounted to almost 30% of the total VOC-purchases, but
dropped the next decennium to a mere 2400 rix dollars a year (Table 5).

Table 5. *Precious metals purchased by the VOC (average per annum)*

	value (rix dollars)		value (rix dollars)
1700 – 1710		1750 – 1760	0
1710 – 1720	16,407	1760 – 1770	35,640
1720 – 1730	85,919	1770 – 1780	0
1730 – 1740	2,417	1780 – 1790	16,730
1740 – 1750	3,565	1790 – 1793	0

Sales

The money that the Chinese and Portuguese made from their sales was
used to buy a cargo for their trip home. Already before the coming of
the Dutch they purchased pepper in different ports of the archipelago,
but from the 1620s onwards they had to purchase it at Batavia, because
of the centralizing policy of the VOC. In the eighteenth century,
however, the importance of pepper declined because of the direct VOC-
trade with Canton and was surpassed in value by other (fine) spices
(Table 6).

Of the spices like cinnamon, cloves, nutmeg and mace, cinnamon
from Ceylon was the most important merchandise. Contrary to the
voluminous pepper trade, cinnamon was sold in relatively small
quantities. This luxury item was mostly freighted to Spanish Manila, a
port with which the VOC never had a direct trading link.

During the last forty years of the eighteenth century the amount of
cinnamon decreased whereas the decay of the spice trade with the
Chinese at Batavia on whole had begun two decennia earlier. Yet, a
curious recovery took place after 1780. The Fourth Anglo-Dutch war
(1780 – 1784) disrupted the European trade, and the company
warehouses were filled with spices. Portuguese and Chinese had ample
opportunity to buy large quantities for sale in China, because the VOC-
shipping to Canton was also momentarily brought to a halt.

Table 6. *Pepper and fine spices sold by the VOC (average per annum)*

| | pepper | | fine spices | (cinnamon) | | total value |
	quantity (piculs)	value (rix dollars)	value (piculs)	bales (piculs)	value (rix dollars)	(rix dollars)
1700 – 1710	15,421	107,871	45,945	462	35,546	153,816
1710 – 1720	11,675	116,128	49,408	919	73,523	165,536
1720 – 1730	11,515	115,149	77,034	735	59,080	192,183
1730 – 1740	8,135	73,164	87,686	941	75,298	160,850
1740 – 1750	4,662	55,917	52,402	521	41,998	108,319
1750 – 1760	1,049	14,529	103,251	669	90,534	117,780
1760 – 1770	878	14,293	35,225	139	29,337	49,518
1770 – 1780	544	9,076	23,197	67	14,530	32,273
1780 – 1790	2,669	43,839	68,753	145	31,166	112,592
1790 – 1793	0	0	0	0	0	0

Table 7. *Tin sold by the VOC (average per annum)*

	quantity (piculs)	value (rix dollars)
1700 – 1710	–	–
1710 – 1720	–	–
1720 – 1730	2,907	44,843
1730 – 1740	2,683	46,115
1740 – 1750	1,792	31,994
1750 – 1760	1,154	24,263
1760 – 1770	2,580	48,569
1770 – 1780	971	17,476
1780 – 1790	5,379	100,793
1790 – 1793	350	8,750

This upsurge during the Anglo-Dutch war can also be observed by the VOC-sales of tin, which were augmented five-fold (Table 7). But the purchases of tin far exceeded these sales.

From 1757 onwards, the sale of another product exceeded that of all others sold to the Chinese and Portuguese, viz. opium or as the Dutch called it *amphioen*. During the 1720s and 1730s the VOC had endured a lot of trouble in combating the smuggling of opium by Company servants to whom it constituted a short cut to the amassing of private fortunes. In 1745 the opium trade was laid in the hands of the Opium Society. By provision, the VOC delivered a minimum of 1200 chests a year at 450 rix dollars a piece.[8]

Table 8. *Opium sold by the VOC (average per annum)*

	number of chests	value (rix dollars)
1757 – 1760	1,133	510,000
1760 – 1770	721	337,740
1770 – 1780	581	293,431
1780 – 1790	842	575,692
1790 – 1793	582	442,199

An embargo was laid on opium by the Chinese emperor, and to prevent any difficulties the VOC forbade its personnel in 1756 to take it along in the China-bound ships. The *anachodas* took this opportunity to buy opium and smuggle it into Amoy, Canton and other harbours. In 1757 and 1758 the Company sold 1200 chests at the invoice value. But later on the price increased (Table 9). Opium became the most important product, which the VOC sold at Batavia. In value its share grew from 46% in the 1760s to 67% between 1780 and 1790.

The total sales of the VOC reflected this increase at the end of the 1750s and stayed at a high level (Table 9). Due to opium and the Anglo-Dutch war, in the period 1780 – 1790 the Company sold goods at a value of over 850,000 rix dollars a year. On the other side, the purchases also reflect a major increase. Why then did contemporaries complain about the decline of the junk trade in the second half of the eighteenth century?

Decline of the Junk Trade

Most complaints about the decline of the junk trade were uttered during the 1770s and indeed the trade decreased in that period. That the number of ships remained stable for long and even increased a bit afterwards, may be explained by the important role they played as passenger carriers to and from China. The local Batavian market could not fall into complete decay, because the number of Chinese inhabitants kept on growing. No steep decline can be observed in the VOC-sales either, apart from 1790 – 93, when the value per ship fell considerably.

The only possible answer to the question is that the Chinese and Portuguese may have had less to sell to the VOC. During the second half of the eighteenth century, the value of goods purchased by the VOC from foreigners increased, but this was very largely accounted for by tin. In all probability the Chinese and Portuguese *anachodas* were not the major transporters involved in this trade. Apart from Malacca, tin was found on the island of Bangka and the VOC had acquired an unstable monopoly on its trade. The sultan of Pelembang, ruler of the island, had signed treaties from 1662 onwards in which was stated that tin was to be delivered to the VOC.[9] If we subtract the tin from the total Company purchases, a meagre trade remains in comparison with 1720 – 40 (Table 9).

In this respect one can say that the junk trade declined, but on the other hand the number of junks stabilized, the VOC-purchases per ship did not decrease and, because of opium, the VOC sales grew to a high level in the second half of the eighteenth century. Further research may prove these preliminary conclusions to be premature.[10]

Table 9. *VOC-trade with foreign merchants (average per annum): value in rix dollars*

Period	VOC-purchases		VOC-sales	per ship (Ch+Port)		
1690 – 1700	191,197		322,949			
1700 – 1710	100,781		229,570	7,250		16,516
1710 – 1720	87,220		269,926	4,473		13,842
1720 – 1730	302,727		344,481	11,918		13,562
1730 – 1740	165,990		354,883	7,377		15,773
1740 – 1750	171,679	(112,576)	250,063	11,445	(7,505)	16,671
1750 – 1760	270,943	(116,949)	506,996	24,857	(10,729)	46,513
1760 – 1770	454,933	(98,270)	739,383	46,422	(10,028)	75,447
1770 – 1780	338,228	(88,085)	490,458	41,757	(10,875)	60,550
1780 – 1790	622,943	(301,777)	859,069	47,193	(22,862)	65,081
1790 – 1793	299,875	(161,518)	489,999	23,990	(12,921)	39,200

Between brackets = tin excluded.

24

DOMESTIC SEA-BORNE TRADE ALONG THE CHINA COAST AT THE BEGINNING OF THE EIGHTEENTH CENTURY

Bodo Wiethoff

An Introduction to Documents

A number of fairly detailed reports on private Chinese trade carried out overseas along the China coast at the beginning of the eighteenth century between ports south of the river Yangzi and Tianjin are conveniently accessible to students of Asian Trade Routes. With one exception these reports all date from the Yongzheng-era (1723 – 1735/ 36). The total number of reports at present available is thirteen, as itemized below.

Sources

Until 1976 only three such reports were available. They were contained in three documents found in the archives of the Qing-dynasty after its downfall and published in the series *Collection of Documents* (*Wenxian congbian*) which was edited by the Office of Documents (*Wexian guan*) of the National Palace Museum Beiping (*Guoli Beiping gugong bowuyuan*) between 1930 and 1937 which in turn were photo-graphically reproduced in two volumes by the Defence Publishers (*Guofang chubanshe*), Taibei, in 1964.[1] The documents were listed under the heading 'Historical materials on customs and excise from the Yongzheng-court of Qing' (*Qing Yongzheng-chao guanshui shiliao*), vol. 1, 332 – 7.

Since all entries in the *Collection of Documents* were type-transcripts and thus only representations of the original documents, there was no way here to affirm their authenticity. Furthermore, there was no way of knowing whether these documents, and thereby the reports, were representative of a whole series of similar communications, or whether they were the only ones of their kind that ever existed or survived.

Since 1976 ten more reports have become available to the student with no direct access to the remnants of the Qing archives. The reports are contained in eight documents which were reproduced photographically between 1976 and 1980 by the National Palace Museum, Committee for Edition Documents from the Palace (*Guoli gugong bowuyuan, Gugong wenxian bianji weiyuanhui*) in the multi-volume series *Secret memorials of the K'ang-hsi period: Ch'ing documents at National Palace Museum* [Original title in English] (*Gongzhong-dang Kangxi-chao zouzhe*) and *Secret palace memorials of the Yung-cheng period: Ch'ing documents at National Palace Museum* [Original title in English] (*Gongzhong-dang Yongzheng-chao zouzhe*). The documents here are listed chronologically.[2]

Although there are some minor discrepancies as regards the documents published in both series, the latter reproductions not only corroborate the reliability of the *Collection of Documents* but also testify to the serial format of the reports contained therein.

Reports

These are available as shown in Table 1. The reports were written by officials of middle rank, i.e. Intendant of Tianjin, Head of Customs, Intendant of Salt.

The memorials (documents) were written by officials of high rank, i.e. Governor-General and Governor.

The first figure s.v. source refers to the volume of the respective new series.

Formats

The available documents are characterized by a high degree of conformity; this applies to the routine of the documentary process as well as to the reporting procedure.

Documentary process:

— The official (officials) in charge of customs report the arrival of the ships in question to the Governor-General of Zhili at the latest after the end of the north-going season.

— The Governor-General memorializes the report (reports) to the Emperor with reference to the ruling that all the sea-borne arrivals have to be reported, regardless of whether they originate within the Qing domain or outside, at the latest before the end of the year in question.

— The Emperor comments on the memorial.

Table 1. *Availability of reports*

No. of report	author	No. of documents	author	date	source
1	Zhu Gang	1	Zhao Hongxie	KX 56, 9, 1	7, 116 – 118
2	Lu Yunshi Duan Ruhui	2	Li Weijun	YZ 1, 8, 11	1, 603
3	Lu Yunshi Duan Ruhui	2	Li Weijun	YZ 1, 8, 11	1, 603
4	Lu Yunshi Duan Ruhui	2	Li Weijun	YZ 1, 8, 11	1, 603
5	Gao Kuang	3	Li Wei jun	YZ 2, 9, 1	3, 104 – 105
6	Gao Kuang	4	Cai Ting	YZ 3, 9, 1	5, 64 – 65
7	Gao Kuang	5	Cai Ting	YZ 3, 9, 7	5, 99 – 100
8	Gao Kung	6	Cai Ting	YZ 3, 10, 3	5, 243
9	Pu Wenzhuo	7	Li Fu	YZ 4, 9, 22	6, 632
10	Jiang Shu	8	Tang Zhiyu	YZ 7, 7, 27	13, 753
11	Jiang Shu	9	Tang Zhiyu	YZ 7, 8, 9	14, 156 – 157
12	Cheg Wenhua Peng Jiabing	10	Liu Yuyi	YZ 9, 12, 15	19, 251 – 258
13	Peng Jiabing	11	Li Wei	YZ 10, 11, 7	20, 759 – 761

Reporting procedure:
— Period or beginning of period covered in the report (arrival at or report to customs).
— Number of arrivals covered in the report.
— Type of ships arrived.
— Province, Prefecture, District of origin of ships arrived.
— Code and number of registration of ships arrived.
— Name of supercargo (var: Name of shipmaster)
— Number of sailors.
— Itemized and quantified cargo of ships arrived. (var: Cargo itemized only) (var: Cargo of all ships arrived summarized).

Examples

In order to demonstrate the routine, scope and contents of the reports under consideration two examples are presented here in tabulated form, as shown at Tables 2 and 3.

Perspectives

Due to their highly identical format, the documents under consideration can be used, without adducing external, associative evidence, to generalize concerning the:
— control and administration of domestic sea-borne trade along the China coast at the beginning of the eighteenth century at the point of destination Tianjin,
— identification and classification of the means of transport.

Due to their itemized and quantified contents the reports contained in the documents can be used, by applying various numerical evaluations, to generalize concerning the:
— volume and development of this kind of traffic within the time and locality under consideration,
— composition and distribution of this trade with regard to its origin,
— size of the ship's companies and participation of the supercargoes,
— composition, volume, and development of cargoes per ship, per year (season), and per period under consideration.

Since similar reports on this kind of trade from other destinations are not available, no general statement can be made on the:
— network and timing of domestic sea-borne trade along the China coast in general,
— nature and development of the return-trade from Tianjin,

Table 2.

	Report 7	*Report 8*
date of arrival	YZ 3,8,8 (14.09.1725)	YZ 3,9,10 (15.10.1725)
number of ships	1	1
type of ships	Min	Min
origin of ships	Fujian, Quanzhou, Tong'an	Fujian, Fuzhou, Jinjiang (error for: Quanzhou, Jinjiang or Fuzhou, Minxian)
code and number	Tong 1178	Zhou (?) 18 (Zhou is not standard for Jinjiang nor Minxian)

Table 3.

name of supercargo	Li Yuanmei		Lian Dejie	
number of sailors	22		18	
cargo (in order of listing)	white sugar	602 sacks	dried bamboo-shoots	478 baskets
	brown sugar	543 sacks	maochang-paper (fibre long-paper?)	134 quires
	sugar candy	33 barrels		
	orange cake	31 barrels	black prunes	29 baskets
	shark's fins	3 sacks	tea leaves	31 baskets
			white sugar	42 sacks
	fragrant mushrooms (*lentinus edodes*)	1 basket	ganglian-paper (carry joint-paper?)	
	tea leaves	486 baskets		1,875 baskets
	star-aniseed (*illicium verum*)	12 sacks	gulian-paper (old joint-paper?)	
	crystallized fruit	26 barrels		2,433 baskets
	sapan-wood	2,888 pounds	lianqi-paper (joint seven-paper?)	11 quire
	zhu-paper (bamboo-paper [unspecified])	5 baskets	zhishi (medicinal herbs: unripe fruits of *citrus aurantium, citrus medica, poncirus trifoliata*)	5 bags
	planks of pine-wood	1 set		
	sweet-potato flour	4 bags	zucao-paper (grass [wrapping]-paper)	400 quires
	coarse bowls	11,670 pieces	Fujian lotus-seed	2 bags

— economics of the trade per unit (partial cargo, full cargo, ship, fleet).

To cull the reports for corroborative evidence in support of historiographic projections or erudite associations with regard to life in Qing times in general and interregional trade in particular is rejected here as unacceptable.

A preliminary numerical analysis of the contents of the reports has been published under the title 'Wirtschaftsnachrichten aus Tianjin vom Beginn des 18. Jahrhunderts' in *Bochumer Jahrbuch zur Ostasienforschung* (1986), 82 – 140.

NOTES

Notes to Chapter 3

1 See e.g. Heltzer, *Rural Community*; idem, *Goods, Prices*; idem, *International Organization*; Liverani, 'Royauté syrienne'; idem, 'Communautés'; Astour, 'Great powers'; Linder, 'Thalassocracy'.

2 See Polanyi, 'Comparative treatment'; idem, 'Traders and trade'; Dalton, 'Polanyi's analysis;' Humphreys, 'The work of Karl Polanyi'; Veenhof, *Old Assyrian Trade*, pp. 345 – 57; Adams, 'Anthropological perspectives'; Powell, 'Götter, Könige'; Gledhill and Larsen, 'Polyanyi paradigm', esp. pp. 197 – 200.

3 Cf. Edzard, 'Problèmes de la royauté'; Larsen, 'The city and its king'; Grégoire, 'Noms de fonction'; Brin, 'Title'; Imparati, 'Signori'; Kitchen, 'King list'; and for the seals: Nougayrol, *PRU* III, pp. xxxvi – xliii; Schaeffer, *Ugaritica* III, pp. 66 – 83.

4 See Heltzer, *Rural Community*, pp. 75 – 9, 92 – 101; Boyer, 'L'ancien droit oriental'; Klengel, 'Sībūtum; Mcdonald, 'Assembly'; Pardee, 'YPH'; Loewenstamm, 'Yāpeʻḫ'; Gelb, 'Sîbût'.

5 See Heltzer, *Internal Organization*, pp. 141 – 52; Millard, 'Assyrians and Arameans'; Greenfield and Shaffer, 'Tell Fekherye'.

6 See Heltzer, *Goods, Prices*, pp. 139 – 42; idem, *Internal Organization*, pp. 152 – 4; Liverani, 'Due documenti'; Astour, 'Merchant class'; Veenhof, *Old Assyrian trade*, pp. 309 – 10; Mazar, 'Philistines', pp. 3 – 5, Gledhill and Larsen, 'Polanyi paradigm', esp. pp. 208 – 13.

7 See Nougayrol, *PRU* III, pp. 45 – 126 (dossiers); Heltzer, *Internal Organization*, pp. 158 – 59 n.87; idem, *Goods, Prices*, pp. 121 – 47 (tamkar); Rainey, 'Business agents'; Liverani, 'Dotazione'; Macdonald, 'Guilds'; Zaccagnini, 'Merchant at Nuzi', pp. 172 – 3 nn. 11 – 12; Gledhill and Larsen, 'Polanyi paradigm', esp. pp. 205 – 6.

8 See Dornemann, 'Excavations'; Margueron, 'Nouvelles perspectives'.

9 See Astour, 'Maʻḫadu'; Stieglitz, 'Ugaritic Mḫd'; Gledhill and Larsen, 'Polanyi paradigm, esp. pp. 206 – 8.

10 See Heltzer, *Goods, Prices* pp. 17 – 120; Stieglitz, 'Commodity prices'; cf. Pardee, 'Ugaritic', pp. 270 – 2.

11 See Sasson, 'Maritime involvement'; Linder, *Maritime Texts*; idem, 'Thalassocracy'; Heltzer, *Internal Organization*, pp. 188 – 91 (Excursus I); Xella, 'Ausrüstung'; Lipiński, 'Ugaritic letter'; Fensham, 'Shipwreck'; Ziskind, 'Sea loans'; Pardee, 'Bottomry loan'; Schaeffer, *Ugaritica* VII, pp. 371 – 81 ('Remarques sur les ancres en pierre d'Ugarit').

12 See Nougayrol, *PRU* III, pp. 101 – 8 (Sinaranu); Heltzer, *Internal Organization*, pp. 161 – 3; Astour, 'Ugarit and the Aegean'.

13 See Astour, 'Etrangers'; Yaron, 'Foreign merchants'; Heltzer, *Goods, Prices*, pp. 137 – 8; Rainey, 'Canaanite'; idem, 'Canaanites again'.
14 See Sasson, 'Maritime involvement', esp. pp. 130 n. 21, 138 n. 61; Young, *Phoenician Expansion*; Mazar, 'Philistines'; Larsen, 'Tradition of empire', esp. pp. 100 – 1; Frankenstein, 'Phoenicians', esp. p. 286; Polanyi, 'Comparative treatment', esp. pp. 347 – 8; Humphreys, 'The Work of Karl Polanyi', esp. pp. 191 – 6.
15 See Dollinger, *Hansa*, pp. 411 – 13: Doc. 26 = Hansisches Urkundenbuch 9, 584: Privy Council, dated 1469.

Notes to Chapter 4

1 The ancient bias toward the big institutions affects modern reconstructions. For instance, A. L. Oppenheim, 'Essay on Overland Trade in the First Millennium B.C.', *Journal of Cuneiform Studies* 21 (1967): 236 – 54, assumes that all caravan trade coming into Babylonia had to pass through Babylon for royal inspection, even when the text mentions a shipment arriving at Uruk.
2 For years, some scholars thought that in the 2nd Millennium the Mesopotamians did not eat fish, since there was little or no mention of them in tablets. This notion was held despite the fact that archaeologists routinely excavated quantities of fish bones from houses occupied during the era of supposed taboo. The simplest answer for the lack of records of fish is that for some reason the big institutions just got out of the fish business and the government seems not to have even taxed it. More recently, it has been proposed that the average Mesopotamian could not afford to eat meat, even though bones of sheep, goat, cow, pig, tortoise, bird, gazelle and other animals are plentiful in even small, insignificant houses exposed by excavation.
3 Perhaps as early as the 3rd Millennium B.C., the trees in Assyria had been greatly reduced by human activity.
4 Although Babylonia lies between the Euphrates and the Tigris, it was essentially the product of the Euphrates. The Tigris, for most of its length in the alluvium, cuts very deeply so only in the far south could its waters be used for irrigation. However, the Tigris was responsible for a great part of the marshes and these afforded Babylonia an especially rich resource area that Assyria lacked. But most central governments could not effectively control the marshes, especially those on the east fed directly by the Tigris. I suspect that in most periods, the eastern marshes were essentially independent of all control and the inhabitants would have been more willing to trade with Elam and the upriver Tigris states than with Babylonia.
5 See A. L. Oppenheim, 'The Seafaring Merchants of Ur', *Journal of the American Oriental Society* 74 (1954): 6 – 17 for a discussion of the Babylonians' Gulf trade in the nineteenth century B.C. Oppenheim sees a royal monopoly. I would propose that parts of the trade were government sponsored, while some ventures could be privately backed in whole or in

part, since royal records do not account for all the kinds of items found archaeologically.

6 J. A. Brinkman, 'Foreign Relations of Babylonia from 1600 to 625 B.C.: the Documentary Evidence', *American Journal of Archaeology*, 76 (1972): 275.

7 Ibid., p. 278.

8 J. A. Brinkman, 'Babylonia c. 1000 – 748 B.C.', *Cambridge Ancient History* (2nd ed.) III/1 (Cambridge, 1982): 300.

9 Ibid. pp. 301 – 4.

10 Ibid. p. 304. J. A. Brinkman, 'Notes on Arameans and Chaldeans in southern Babylonia', *Orientalia* 46 (1977): 304 – 25 details the basic differences between Arameans and Chaldeans. The Arameans rarely occupied cities of their own, were composed of as many as 40 small tribes, and took no part in Babylonian political life. The Chaldeans occupied cities of their own, were composed of five large tribes, were much more assimilated into Babylonian life and politics, sometimes took Babylonian names, engaged in date cultivation and took part in trade. Brinkman has argued that the evidence will not allow the notion that Chaldeans were a subgroup of Arameans, but the structure of those large corporate kin groups and the economic basis for their solidarity needs to be investigated more thoroughly. (Brinkman is in process of doing so.) One would expect some Arameans, having been settled in Mesopotamia for several centuries, to have evolved a variety of social and economic structures, especially if there was a strong economic base such as long-range trade to consolidate wealth and power in the hands of one or two powerful lineages. In recent Iraqi history, the formation of the Muntafiq confederation of southern Iraq would seem to offer a parallel. If the Chaldeans were new to Mesopotamia in the ninth century, their organization and economic foundations must be sought in some other area. Perhaps, like the great Arab tribe the Shammar of recent times, the Chaldeans arrived in Mesopotamia with a stratified, ranked society already formed on the fringes of the settled area on the basis of trading activities, herding and raiding.

11 J. A. Brinkman, 'Babylonia under the Assyrian Empire 745 – 627 B.C.' in M. T. Larsen, ed., *Power and Propaganda* (Copenhagen, 1979), p. 236.

12 Israel Eph'al, *The Ancient Arabs: Nomads on the Borders of the Fertile Crescent, 9th – 5th Centuries, B.C.* (Leiden, 1982), p. 162.

13 The Wadi Sirhan area includes the Dumah oasis. Since it is known from Assyrian and Babylonian sources that the Wadi Sirhan (Dumah) region was occupied in the early 1st Millennium, it is apparent that the Arabs of that time either left little or nothing for a surface reconnaissance to find or the sherds are not being correctly identified. In the Eastern Province I found that the 'Hellenistic' label covered Achaemenid sherds and probably earlier ones as well. More recent survey work in Arabia may very well have filled the gap.

14 Richard S. Bulliet, *The Camel and the Wheel* (Cambridge, Mass., 1975) has a wealth of evidence on the use of the camel and summarizes its advantages over horses, donkeys, and wheeled transport in the Near East. His

bibliography allows full study of the use of the camel from a variety of viewpoints.

15 Ibid., pp. 57ff. gives a good discussion of archaeological, philological and technological evidence on the date of domestication. The possibility of the domestication of the bactrian camel well before the dromedary is also discussed there. Since the dromedary (one-humped) is the variety best adapted to Arabia's hotter climate, the prior domestication of the bactrian may not have influenced events in the Arabian Peninsula, even though it must have had a profound impact on Iran, Afghanistan and Central Asia.

16 J. A. Brinkman, 'Notes on Arameans and Chaldeans', p. 277.

17 Paula Wapnish, 'Camel Caravans and Camel Pastoralists at Tell Jemmeh', *The Journal of the Ancient Near Eastern Society of Columbia University* 13 (1981): 101 – 121, reports from this Palestinian site only a few camel bones in 2nd Millennium contexts (1400 B.C. being the earliest level with camel), while many were found in levels dated from 700 – 200 B.C.

18 D. E. McCown and R. C. Haines, *Nippur I.* Oriental Institute Publication 78 (Chicago, 1967), p. 93 lists two camel figurines in Kassite context and ten others in later levels. M. Gibson, Judith A. Franke, *et al.*, Excavations at Nippur, Twelfth Season. Oriental Institute Communication 23 (Chicago 1978), Fig. 48:7, shows a figurine found in a building datable to about 1250 B.C.

19 Eph'al, *The Ancient Arabs*, p. 21.

20 Ibid., pp. 93ff.

21 Ibid., p. 106, n. 360 lists booty or tribute taken by four Assyrian kings.

22 Bulliet, *The Camel and the Wheel*, pp. 57 – 86 argues that the spread of the domestic camel was related to the incense trade. There are significant mentions of incense in the economic documents of the early Neo-Babylonian period. The Assyrian references to kings of Sheba bring into focus the biblical account of the visit of a queen of Sheba to King Solomon, arguably a real event of the tenth century, reflecting the long-range contacts already established by camel caravan at that time.

23 Ephal, *The Ancient Arabs*, pp. 179ff. has presented a convincing reconstruction of Nabonidus's strategy as it related to the economy.

Notes to Chapter 6

The author would like to express his sincere gratitude to the owners of the private papers used: the late Mrs Guglielmina Marcopoli, Viceconsul of Italy, the late Dr A. Poche, Consul of Belgium (both Aleppo) and Marchese G. de Ghantuz Cubbe, Rome, in addition to Mr Alfred Girardi, Consul General of Denmark and Mr Georges Antaki, Consul of Italy (both Aleppo) who have facilitated my work in every possible way. I have catalogued the *Marcopoli Papers* prior to 1874, in my article quoted in note 19, pp. 151 – 2.

1 *Encylopaedia of Islam*, articles Ḥadjdj and 'Īd al-Aḍḥā.

2 Paul Masson, *Histoire du commerce français dans le Levant au XVIIe siècle*, Paris 1896, pp. 377 – 8; Niels Steensgaard, *Carracks, Caravans and Companies: The structural crisis in the European-Asian trade in the early 17th century*, Copenhagen-Odense 1973, p. 37.

3 [Helmuth von Moltke], *Briefe über Zustände und Begebenheiten in der Türkei aus den Jahren 1835 bis 1839*, Berlin-Posen-Bromberg 1841, p. 290 (letter of 20 July 1838).

4 Information kindly given to me by the late Consul Paolo Marcopoli in December 1975.

5 *Marcopoli Papers* (deposited in the Italian consulate, Aleppo). Fratelli Castelli e Compagnia: Copia Lettere no. 3, p. 139 (1826 15/3, to Ceccardi, Genova).

6 *Marcopoli Papers*. Fratelli Castelli e Compagnia: Copia-Lettere 1824-25, pp. 26 and 43 (1824 3/12 and 11/12, to Marino Mattei, Cyprus).

7 Ibid., pp. 290-1 (two letters of 1825 7/7 to G. Oliva and to F. Persico, both at Genova).

8 *Marcopoli Papers*. Copie-lettres Nicola Marcopoli no. 7, p. 57 (1863 14/11, to Giovanni Marcopoli, Mossul).

9 M. P. Charlesworth, *Trade Routes and Commerce of the Roman Empire*, 2nd ed. London 1926, reprint Chicago 1974, p. 39; Robert Boulanger ed., *Moyen Orient* (Les Guides Bleus). Paris 1965, p. 236.

10 Public Records Office, London (PRO) FO. 618/4, e.g. 1837 25/12.

11 Ibid., 1839 29/12.

12 *Archivio di Stato Trieste* (AST). I.R. Governo del Litorale (Küstenländisches Gubernium). Atti Generali classe 8/6 (Affari consolari) busta 1341 (1834 – 38 fasc. 13) Gub. 28967/5392 ex 1835: Küstenländisches Gubernium to Hofkammer, Vienna.

13 PRO. FO. 618/4, *passim*. Of my 12 examples, three are from 1838, six from 1839, and one from each of the years 1837, 1840, 1841.

14 *Poche Papers* (Belgian Consulate, Aleppo). Brief Copie 1821 – 1823 Ignaz Zahn, letters of 1822 13/2, 24 – 26/4, 16/5, 21 – 22/5.

15 Information from the late Consul Paolo Marcopoli.

16 Summarized in the document quoted supra note 12.

17 *Archives de la Chambre de commerce, Marseille*, série L-IX no. 774 (Fonds Roux Frères, B. Rostand & Cie, Aleppo, to P. H. Roux, Marseilles, 1815 18/8); Oeuvres complètes de Volney, Paris 1838, pp. 254 – 5.

18 Volney, op. cit., pp. 243 and 246

19 Ibid., p. 251; Thomas Riis, 'Affaires et vie quotidienne à Alep (1820 – 1870): la maison Giustiniani e Nipoti, puis Vincenzo Marcopoli & Cie. Les sources orientales. — Un bilan provisoire', *Bulletin d'Etudes Orientales* XXXIV, 1984, p. 143 with note 2.

20 Volney, op. cit., p. 250.

21 Ibid., p. 246.

22 *Archives de la Chambre de commerce, Marseille*, liasse 'Liban — Syrie', fasc. Alep an XIII — 1867: copie d'une lettre du Ministère des Affaires Étrangères au préfet des Bouches du Rhône, 1820 18/5.

23 Fr. Charles-Roux, *Les échelles de Syrie et de Palestine au XVIIIᵉ siècle*, Paris 1928, p. 121.

24 *Poche Papers.* Brief Copie 1821 – 1823, Ignaz Zahn to A. Svoboda, Baghdad 1822 18/8.
25 Charles-Roux, op. cit., pp. 141-8. By 1833 Beirut was considered the port with most foreign trade in all Syria (AST. I.R. Governo per il Litorale. Atti generali 8/6 busta 1341 fasc. 13, Gub. 482/94 ex 1836).
26 Consequently costs were almost the same on either route, see *Cubbe Papers (Rome).* Copia Lettere d'Europa 1831 – 1843: Cubbe, Aleppo, to D. & J. Marini, Marseilles, 1835 21/5.
27 Volney, op. cit., pp. 240 – 1 and 244; Charles-Roux, op. cit., p. 122. In 1833, two trading firms of Trieste sent an envoy to Syria. He found that Latakia was becoming the port of Aleppo to the disadvantage of Alexandretta, because of the latter's unhealthy climate, (same document as the one quoted in note 25). *Marcopoli Papers.* Fratelli Castelli e Compagnia: Copia Lettere no. 3, p. 256 (1826 25/7, to Capt. Vzo Samlich, p.t. Alexandretta).
28 PRO. SP. 105/343 (Richard Wood to Werry, 1837 3/1).
29 *Cubbe Papers.* Copia Lettere per la Costa di Soria — Messieurs B[no] — Cie, Marseille, 1843 – 1846: Cubbe, Aleppo, to Capt. E. Dasso, 1845 3/7.
30 Ibid. Cubbe, Aleppo, to Capt. Casso, 1845 18/8.
31 Ronald E. Coons, 'Steamships, Statesmen, and Bureaucrats. Austrian Policy towards the Steam Navigation Company of the Austrian Lloyd 1836 – 1848', *Veröffentlichungen des Instituts für Europäische Geschichte Mainz LXXIV*, Abteilung Universalgeschichte, Wiesbaden 1975, pp. 131 and 184 – 5. Cf. also the French consul's letter to the Ministère des affaires étrangères according to which the opening of a French steamship line to Syria would be profitable to the postal communications with Aleppo (Archives du Ministère des affaires étrangères, Paris, CC Alep vol. 29, fol. 304 r. – v., Aleppo to Aff. Etr. 1836 12/10). The French line's concentration on passenger and mail transport was not profitable (Haus-, Hof- und Staatsarchiv, Vienna (HHStA.), Administrative Registratur F 38 Karton 8, fasc. 1848 – 55, fol. 142 r. – v., report from the consul general in Alexandria 1848 23/10).
32 *Archives of the DDSG, Vienna*: Bilanz. Sitzungs-Protokoll der General-versammlung 1829 – 42, Generalversammlung 1840 10/2, pp. 14 – 5.
33 The relatives of the Austrian consul general opened a rival postal service, see *Marcopoli Papers.* Giustiniani e Nipoti: Copia Lettere no. 2, pp. 203, 211, 221, 243 (1839 28/6, 13/7, 23/7, 13/8 to Hays, Alexandretta) and 207 – 8 (1839 29/6 to Autran, p.t. Alexandretta).
34 Ibid., p. 243 (1839 14/8 to Hays, Alexandretta, referring to an express letter dated 29 July from DDSG's agent in Baghdad).
35 Ibid., pp. 260 (1839 11/8 to Rostand, Beirut) and 271 – 2 (1839 20/9 to Autran, Constantinople). Marcopoli moved his mail service to Beirut as a consequence.
36 Ibid., pp. 518 (1840 9/11 to J. Rostand, Beirut), 523 – 4 (1840 20/11 to A. Autran, Constantinople), 545 – 6 (1840 31/12 to J. Rostand, Marseilles).
37 An article on the agreement between the two steamship companies is in preparation (Thomas Riis, Der Vertrag zwischen dem Österreichischen

Lloyd und der Ersten Donau Dampfschiffahrtsgesellschaft vom 13. Jänner 1834: Wirtschaft oder grosse Politik?).

38 *Bulletin des lois de la République Française* no. 411, loi no. 3057 du 8. juillet 1851, offprint in Archives Nationales, Paris sous-série F[12] no. 6767, pp. 18, 23 and 29.

39 HHStA. Administrative Registratur F 38 Karton 9, fasc. 1852/53 fol. 35 – 36 v. (1853 2/2 with annexe) and fol. 89 r. (timetable from 1 March 1853).

40 The distances are given (in *lieues marines* of three nautical miles) in the report to the general assembly of shareholders by the administrative council of the Messageries 1873 29/5, p. 18. The printed report is to be found — with other papers concerning the Messageries — in Archives Nationales, Paris, sous-série F[12], liasse 6767.

41 PRO. FO. 78/1452 fol. 59 r. – 60 r., report by F. Sankey, Alexandretta, 1859 10/1.

42 *Cubbe Papers.* Copia Lettere di Levante 1831 – 37 (1839): Cubbe, Aleppo to Capt. A. Pioggio, 1834 11/3 and 17/3. These instructions were confirmed a week later (ibid., idem to idem, 1834 24/3).

43 Ibid., 1834 9/5, Cubbe to Pioggio in Beirut.

44 Ibid., 1834 7/6. In his letter of 24 March Cubbe had informed the captain that the caravan bound for Aleppo from Baghdad accompanied the one bound for Damascus.

45 In his letter of 12 February 1844 to Captain E. Dasso at Latakia Cubbe complimented him for having bought silk instead of sesame the price of which at Leghorn was not known (*Cubbe Papers.* Copia Lettere per la Costa di Soria — Messieurs B[no] Rostand & Cie, Marseille, 1843 – 46).

46 Cf. PRO. FO. 78/1452 fol. 156 r. (return of shipping at Alexandretta 1858 no. 4).

47 *Marcopoli Papers.* Agence d'Alep des Messageries: Copie-lettres 1861 – 73, N. Marcopoli to J. Talon, directeur des services maritimes des Messageries, Marseilles, no. 1340 Sécrétariat, 1862 24/12.

48 Ibid., N. Marcopoli to direction des Messageries, Marseilles, 1864 6/1.

49 Jacques Thobie, Intérêts et impérialisme français dans l'empire ottoman (1895 – 1914), Paris 1977, p. 164.

Notes to Chapter 7

Prices in the Darxat Province at the beginning of this century: 'The informants talked about *tugriks*. This Mongolian money did not exist at that time so they probably meant roubles, or Chinese money. Therefore, I translate the term as "money" ' (Badamxatan, p. 31). These amounts were paid by the Russian Merchants:

1 sheepskin	1 money
1 sheep	5 money
1 wolf	3 – 4 blocks Russian tea
1 sable	20 – 24 money
1 horn of deer	270 – 432 blocks tea

1 *jin* wool = circa 0.6 kg   0.5 money
1 *púú* fish = circa 16 kg   7 – 8 money
1 Dolgix, B.O., *Rodovoj i plemennoj sostav narodov Sibiri v XVII. v.* Moscow 1960 (Trudy IEMM. nov. ser. LV), p. 389.
2 E.g. Carruthers, D., *Unknown Mongolia, I.* London 1924, p. 220.
3 Pêrlêê, X., *Mongol and ulsyn êrt, dundad úeijn xot suuriny tovčoon.* Ulan Bator 1961, p. 140, Majdar, D., *Arxitektura i gradostroitel'stvo Mongolii.* Moscow 1970, pp. 216, 228, 230 – 231. Kyzlasov, L.P., *Srednevekovye goroda Tuvy:* SA No. 3. 1953, pp. 66 – 75.
4 Rašid-ad-Din, *Sbornik letopisej T. I. kn. 1.* Moscow — Leningrad 1952, p. 151.
5 Sanždorž, M., *Xalxad xjatadyn mòngò xúúlêgč zudaldaa nêvtêrč xòlžsòn n' (XVIII. zunn).* Ulan Bator 1963 (Studia historica III/5), pp. 10 – 16.
6 Šinkarev, L.J., *Szibéria.* Budapest 1977, pp. 66 – 7.
7 Cimitdoržiev, S.B., *Vzaimootnošenija Mongolii i Rossii XVII-XVIII. vv.* Moscow 1978, pp. 21 – 2, 41 – 3, 45, 91.
8 *Istorija Tuvy I.* Moscow 1964, p. 233.
9 Sanždorž, p. 46.
10 Šinkarev, pp. 444 – 51.
11 Čimitdoržiev, pp. 36, 44, 46 – 8.
12 Sandag, S., *Mongolyn uls tòrijn gadaad xarilcaa. 1. 1850 – 1919.* Ulan Bator 1971, p. 37. About the trade through Kyaxta cf. Gmelin, J.G., *Reise durch Sibirien von dem Jahr 1733 bis 1743 I – IV* Göttingen 1751 – 1752. (Sammlung neuer und merkwurdiger Reisen zu Wasser und zu Lande.) I, pp. 451 – 5, III. pp. 38 – 51.
13 Sanždorž, pp. 36 – 7, 40, 47.
14 Čimitdoržiev, pp. 102 – 3, 99 – 100.
15 Badamxatan, S., *Xòvsgòlijn darxad jastan.* Ulan Bator 1965 (Studia Ethnographica III, 1), p. 75, p. 26.
16 Čimitdoržiev, p. 107.
17 Sanždorž, pp. 50, 52.
18 Čimitdoržiev, pp. 105, 106.
19 Sandag, pp. 72 – 3.
20 Šinkarev, pp. 92, 121, 63.
21 Sandag, p. 86.
22 Badamxatan, p. 32.
23 Dolbežev, V.A., *Darxatskij okrug.* St. Petersburg 1911. (Trudy SKOURGO, T. XII, vyp. 1 – 2), pp. 101 – 2.
24 Sandag, pp. 55 – 6, 166, 135, 173 – 80.
25 Dolbežev, p. 104.
26 Sandag, p. 149.
27 Olsen, Ø., *Et primitivt folk.* Kristiania 1915, pp. 151 – 6.
28 Carruthers, I., pp. 109, 113 – 14.
29 Haslund-Christensen, H., *Jabonah.* Stockholm 1947, pp. 220 – 34.
30 Badamxatan, pp. 38 – 9.

Notes to Chapter 8

1 Olufsen, p. 146
2 From Schultz, p. 58.
3 Olufsen, p. 103.
4 Schultz, p. 261.
5 Adamec, p. 66.
6 Wood, pp. 198f, 243, 252.
7 Olufsen, pp. 123, 145.
8 Shor, p. 685.
9 Wood, pp. 199, 243f.
10 Olufsen, p. 171.
11 Wood, p. 251.
12 Wood, p. 251.
12 Grötzbach, p. 252.
13 Kussmaul, p. 26.
14 Ibid., p. 68; Snoy, pp. 122, 124ff; Huwyler, p. 9.
15 Grötzbach, pp. 61f.
16 Shor, p. 674.
17 Ibid., p. 677.
18 Singer, p. 159.

Notes to Chapter 9

1 After the military-Putsch of 1978 the Khirgiz fled to Pakistan. They are living in Turkey today.
2 Grancy, Roger S. de and R. Kostka, *Grosser Pamir* Graz 1978.
3 See also Raunig, W. 'Pamir und Wakhan — ein kaum Bekannter Kreuzweg der Kulturen in Zentralasien', *Schriften-Reihe des Zentralinstituts für fränkische Landeskunde und Allgemeine Regionalforschung an der Universität Erlangen-Nürnberg*, Vol. 21 Erlangen-Nürnberg 1982, pp. 125 – 34; 'Spuren alter Besiedlung auf den Talterrassen des östlichen Wakhan (Nordostafghanistan)', in Snoy, P. (ed.), *Ethnologie und Geschichte: Festschrift für Karl Jettmar, Beiträge zur Südasienforschung*, Bd 86 Wiesbaden 1983, pp. 496 – 805; 'Problems of Settlement of the Eastern Wakhan Valley and the Discoveries Made There in 1975', *Journal of Central Asia*, Vol. VII No. 2, Islamabad Dec. 1984, pp. 15 – 19.
4 See Patzelt, G. and Grancy, R. S. de, 'Die Ortschaft Ptukh im östlichen Wakhan' and Kuschel, W., 'Unbewohnte und Verfallene Gebäude im Talbecken von Sarhad', both in *Grosser Pamir*, 1978, pp. 215 – 47 and 249 – 61. See also Grancy, R. S. de, 'Siedlungsbild und Hausformen der Ortschaft Wark im Wakhan', in: Gratzl, K. (ed.) *Hindukush, Österreichische Forschungsexpedition in den Wakhan 1970*, Graz 1972, pp. 61 – 76; *Siedlung und Gehöft der Wakhi in Nordost-Afghanistan*. Diss. Graz 1980.

5 Stein, M. A. 'A Chinese Expedition Across the Pamirs and Hindukush, A.D. 747', *The Geographical Journal*, Feb. 1922, pp. 110 ff., and Hennig, R., *Terrae Incognitae*, Vol. 2, Leiden 1950, pp. 116 – 26.

Notes to Chapter 10

1 I. Wallerstein, 'Rise and future demise of the Capitalist World-Economy', in *The Capitalist World-Economy*, Cambridge, 1979, p. 26. Cf. arguments of F. Perlin in *Review IV*, 2, 1980 and K. N. Chaudhuri, ibid., V, 2, 1981.

2 This is an opinion of N. Steensgaard, 'The Indian Ocean network and the emerging World Economy c.1550 – c.1750', Report for the 16th ICHS, Stuttgart, 1985. Cf. his 'Asian Trade 15th – 18th Centuries. Continuity and Discontinuities', in *XVe Congres International des Sciences Historiques*, Rapports, II, Bucharest, 1980.

3 The further arguments are mainly based on my two Polish books, *The Factory and Fortress: The Pepper Trade over Indian Ocean and Portuguese Expansion in the 16th Century*, Warsaw, 1970 and *Kerala: From Equilibrium towards Backwardness*, Warsaw, 1976.

4 Cf. J. Kieniewicz, *Pepper Gardens and Market in Precolonial Malabar*, *Moyen Orient et Océan Indien*, 3, Paris 1986, p. 1 – 36. There is only scant and enigmatic information about production of pepper in D. Barbosa, *O Livro*, Lisboa, 1867, pp. 341 – 5 and T. Pires, *The Suma Oriental*, London, 1944, p. 362, G. da Orta, *Coloquios dos simples e drogas da India*, Lisboa, 1891, vol. II, pp. 241 – 3 is not better. Cf. *Cartes de Affonso de Albuquerque seguidas de documentos que as elucidam*, vol. II, Lisboa, 1903, pp. 258, 398; vol. VII, Lisboa, 1935, pp. 175, 176. The first detailed account of this of F. da Costa /about 1615/, Relatorio sobre o trato da pimenta, *Documentação Ultramarina Portuguesa*, vol. III, Lisboa, 1963, pp. 350-2. This is the reason why relatively little attention has been paid to this subject in V. M. Godinho, *L'économie de l'empire portugais aux XVe et XVIe siècles*, Paris 1969, pp. 578 – 80 and K. S. Mathew, *Portuguese Trade with India in the Sixteenth century*, New Delhi, 1983, p. 123. Cf. J. Kieniewicz, *Factory and Fortress . . . op. cit.*, pp. 83 – 95.

5 J. Kieniewicz, *Kerala . . . op. cit.*, pp. 60 – 1, reports and memoirs of Leyden, Brown, Tyler, Ewer, Senton and others. Cf. *Malabar Special Commission, 1881 – 1882. Malabar Land Tenures*, Madras, 1882, vol. II, pp. 211, 399 and W. Logan, *Malabar Manual*, Madras, 1887, vol. II, app. I, tab. 10.

6 W. H. Horsley, 'Memoir of Travancore, Historical and Statistical', in *Selections from the Records of Travancore*, vol. I, Trebandrum, 1860, p. 21.

7 *Cartas . . . op. cit.*, vol. I, Lisboa, 1884, p. 44; vol. III, p. 398; T. Pires, op. cit., p. 357; V. M. Godinho, op. cit., p. 374.

8 J. Kieniewicz, *Kerala . . . op. cit.*, pp. 154 – 61.

9 *Cartas . . . op. cit.*, vol. III, pp. 381, 394. About Syrian Christians cf. *Die Zeitgenössischen Quellen zur Geschichte Portugiesisch-Asiens und seines Nachbarländerzur Zeit des Hl. Franz Xaver*, ed. G. Schurhammer,

Leipzig, 1932, No. 99, 121; L. da Costa, in *Documentação Ultramarina Portuguesa*, vol. III, pp. 378, 379. British Museum, Mss Add. 28461, f.57v.

10 D. Barbosa, op. cit., p. 332; *Cartas* . . . op. cit., vol. I, 329; vol. III, p. 394. V. M. Godinho, op. cit., p. 632 is of a different opinion. Cf. also P. B. Alaev, *Yujnaia India*, Moscow, 1964, p. 293 and A. Disney, *Twilight of the Pepper Empire: Portuguese Trade in Southwest India in the Early Seventeenth Century*, Cambridge Mass., 1978, p. 34. The interesting information about advances in F. Buchanan, *A Journey from Madras Through the Countries of Mysore, Canara amd Malabar*, vol. II, London, 1807, p. 532 and India Office Records, Bombay Commercial Proceedings, 414/65, p. 374.

11 S. Botelho, 'O tombo do Estado da India' in *Subsidios para a história da India Portuguesa*, Lisboa, 1868, pp. 25, 26; *Colecção de São Lourenço*, vol. 1, Lisboa, 1973, pp. 133, 146 /M. A. de Sousa 24 XII 1537/. Cf. *Documentação Ultramarina Portuguesa*, vol. III, pp. 310, 312, 33.

12 *Cartas* . . . op. cit., vol. III, p. 258.

13 There are many descriptions in F. Pyrard de Laval, *Voyage*, vol. I, Paris, 1615, pp. 429 – 39; P. de S. Bartolomeo, *Viaggio alle Indie Orientali* . . ., Roma, 1796, passim; Buchanan, op. cit. and B. S. Ward, 'Memoir of the Travancore Survey', British Museum, Add Mss 14379, pp. 10, 90. About local roads see B. Ziegenbalg, *Ausführliche Beschreibung der Malabari-sche Heidentums*, Leipzig, 1926, p. 211 and opinions in India Office Records, Mackenzie Collection, Gen. 45, p. 145; Home series, Misc. 456B, p. 599.

14 D. Barbosa, op. cit., p. 302; G. da Orta, op. cit., p. 241; *Livro que trata das cousas da India e do Japão*, ed. A. de Almeida Calado, *Boletim da Biblioteca da Universidade de Coimbra*, 24, 1960, pp. 46, 47; F. da Costa, op. cit., pp. 315, 351. Cf. P. van Dam, *Beschryvinge van de Oostindische Compagnie*, s-Gravenhage, 1928 – 1943, vol. II, 2, pp. 291, 292; H. A. van Rheede, *Officieel afschrift van het corspronkelijk gedenkschift geschreven in 1677 A.D.*; Selections from the records of the Madras Government, Dutch Records No 14, Madras, 1911, p. 31; S. Van Gollenesse, 'Memorandum on the Administration of the Malabar Coast /1743/' in *Dutch in Malabar*, ed. A. Galletti, Madras, 1911, p. 57; P. da S. Bartolomeo, op. cit., p. 77; F. Buchanan, op. cit., p. 531.

15 P. da S. Bartolomeo, op. cit., pp. 79 – 81.

16 *Cartas* . . ., op. cit., vol. VII, p. 175; *Die Zeitgenössischen Quellen* . . . op. cit., no. 157. Cf. K. S. Mathew, op. cit., p. 208.

17 D. Gonçalves, *Historia do Malavar*, Münster, 1955, p. 47.

18 *Cartas*, op. cit., vol. VII, p. 174; F. da Costa, op. cit., p. 315.

19 F. Buchanan, op. cit., p. 537.

20 Josephus Indus, in S. Grynaeus, *Novus orbis regionum ac insularum*, Basileae , 1555, p. 207; *Lettera di Giovanni da Empoli a Leonardo suo padre* . . ., Archivio Storico Italiano, III, Firenze, 1846, p. 87; *Cartas*, op. cit., vol. VII, p. 173; J. de Barros, *Da Asia*, IV,1,12; F. Sassetti, *Lettere edite e inedite*, Firenze, 1855, p. 433; *Die Zeitgenössischen Quellen* . . . op. cit., no. 1703; F. da Costa, op. cit., p. 350.

21 D. Gonçalves, op. cit., p. 47.
22 Cf. F. Pyrard de Laval, op. cit., vol. I, p. 470.
23 J. Kieniewicz, 'The Stationary System in Kerala', *Hemispheres*, No. 1, Warsaw, 1985, pp. 7 – 40.
24 Cf. M. N. Pearson's and A. Das Gupta's research concerning Gujarat.
25 J. Kieniewicz, 'Contact and Transformation: The European Precolonial Expansion in the Indian Ocean World-System in the 16th-17th centuries', *Itinerario* VIII, 1984, 2, pp. 45 – 58. More in my paper prepared for the ICIOS II, Perth, 1984, 'Overwhelming and Exchange: Forms of Contact in the Portuguese Expansion in the Indian Ocean World-System during the Sixteenth Century.'
26 J. Kieniewicz, 'L'Asie et l'Europe pendant les XVIème – XIXème siècles. Formation de l'état arrieré et confrontation des systemes des valeurs', in *L'Histoire à Nice. Actes de colloque franco-polonais d'histoire*, vol. III, Nice, 1983, pp. 220 – 5.
27 The difference and the complementarity of the littoral and the interior seems to be crucial in the recently opened discussion: A. Disney, 'The Portuguese Empire in India c. 1550 – 1650. Some suggestions for a less seaborne, more landbound approach to its socio-economic history', in *Indo-Portuguese History. Sources and Problems'* ed. J. Correia-Afonso, Oxford 1981, p. 153 (a paper read at the Ist ISIPH, Goa 1978); J.C. Heesterman, 'Littoral et intérieur de l'Inde', *Itinerario*, IV, 1980, 1, pp. 87 – 92; M.N. Pearson, 'Littoral Society: The Case for the Coast', *The Great Circle*, VII, 1, 1985, pp. 1 – 8. Cf. also N. Steensgaard's opinions in a closing lecture at the IIIrd ISIPH (Goa 1983) and comments of G. Winius in *Itinerario*, VII, 1983, 1, p. 7.

Notes to Chapter 11

1 This paper is a shortened and slightly changed version of chapter 2 of my thesis *De Verenigde Oostindische Compagnie in Gujarat en Hindustan, 1620 – 1660*, Krips Repro, Meppel. Only a few references are added here.
2 *Generale Missiven, II*, p. 33, 18 – 12 – 1639.
3 VOC 867, p. 387, A. van Diemen and Council to P. Croock, Batavia, 11 – 6 – 1643.
4 *Generale Missiven, IV*, pp. 166, 167, 13 – 12 – 1677.
5 N. Steensgaard, *The Asian trade revolution of the seventeenth century*, *passim*.
6 VOC 1236, p. 331, L. Winnincx and Council to J. Maetsuycker and Coucil, Surat, 11 – 4 – 1661.
7 Bibliothèque Nationale, F.Fr. 14614, G. Rogues, La Manier de Negocier, p. 295.
8 F. S. Gaastra, De VOC in Azië tot 1680, in, E. van den Boogaart a.o., *Overzee, Nederlandse Koloniale geschiedenis 1590 – 1975*, Haarlem, 1982, pp. 58, 59.
9 VOC 1209, f.485r., Remonstrantie G. Pelgrom to J. Maetsuycker, 24 – 5 – 1655.

10 A. Das Gupta, *Indian merchants and the decline of Surat, c.1700 – 1750*, p. 15.

Notes to Chapter 12

1 A survey of the country trade *in folio* is given by Holden Furber in the brilliant chapter: Country Trade and European Empire, in his *Rival Empires of Trade in the Orient 1660 – 1800* (1976), cf. also the references to this article.

2 The Tranquebar shipping statistics are preserved in two series. The one is a register of sea passes issued from 3 June 1793 to 31 December 1805, with a gap from 1 April 1799 to 17 May 1802 (Ostindiske journalsager 1797:328, 1802:63; 1805:178 and 1806:410, with a parallel list of sea passes 3 June 1793 – 31 December 1797 from the papers of the Commission to Investigate into the Misuse of Danish Sea Passes, all in Kommercekollegiets Arkiv, Rigsarkivet, Copenhagen). The other is a register of ships' arrivals at Tranquebar from 1 August 1796 to 31 December 1806, with a gap from 1 August 1796 to 31 May 1797 and during the British occupation from 12 May 1801 to 17 August 1802 (Ostindiske journalsager 1797:328, 1798:278, 1802:22, 93 & 153, 1803:208 and 1805:201, cf. above). The statistics of arrivals from 1 August 1804 to 31 December 1806 are among the sequestered papers of the ship Fædres Minde (High Court of Admiralty, Prize Papers 32:1030. Public Record Office, London).

3 The impression is among other sources based upon the regularly written reports of the governor of Tranquebar to the Kommercekollegium, and the valuable annual Reports on External Commerce with their abundant statistics for Calcutta 1795 – , Madras 1802 – and Bombay 1801, in the India Office Library, London.

4 Governor of Tranquebar 8 February 1797 to the Kommercekollegium (Ostindiske journalsager 1797:328), cf. also Frantz von Lichtenstein 5 February 1794 to the Minister of Finance (Schimmelmannske papirer vedk. Tranquebar etc. Kommercekollegiets Arkiv, Rigsarkivet, Copenhagen).

5 Governor of Tranquebar 7 February 1796 to the Kommercekollegium (Commission to Investigate etc., cf. note 2).

6 Governor of Tranquebar 12 February 1801 to the Kommercekollegium (Ostindiske journalsager 1802:128).

7 For an example of combined country trade and Europe trade, see my Dutch Batavia trade via Copenhagen 1795 – 1807. A Study of Colonial Trade and Neutrality. *Scandinavian Economic History Review* 21, 1973.

8 The annual Reports on the External Commerce of Madras and Bombay and especially of Calcutta contain extremely detailed information about the various branches of country trade under Danish colours and about the realities behind the neutral camouflage.

9 Valuable statistics on shipping to and from Isle de France are published by Auguste Tousaint in *La Route des Iles. Contribution à l'histoire maritime des Mascaregnes* (1967).

10 See, *inter alia* Bengal Foreign Consultations 10 January 1805 (India Office Library, London), and the sequestered papers of the ship Graf Bernstorff (High Court of Admiralty. Prize Papers 32:656. Public Record Office, London).

11 Besides the reports referred to in note 3, attention should be drawn to the volume *Papers Respecting Illicit Trade*, published by The English East India Company in London 1799.

12 Lord Fitzgerald 7 May 1799 to Secretary of State, marked 'Secret and Confidential' (Foreign Office. Denmark, 22:34. Public Record Office, London).

13 Governor-General of Bengal 30 January 1800 to Henry Dundas, marked 'private' (Copy in Foreign Office. Denmark. 22:37. Public Record Office, London).

14 A good example of such trade in ships is given in the Report on the External Commerce of Bengal 1804 – 1805, dated 10 June 1806 (India Office Library, London).

15 Material dealing with English agents in Tranquebar is found in Madras Secret Proceedings 6 January 1801 and 22 May & 4 September 1804, and in Madras Secret Letters Received 18 April & 13 August 1799 and 18 March 1801 (India Office Library, London). Cf. also Governor-General of Bengal 6 February 1799 to Secretary of State (Foreign Office. Denmark. 22:34. Public Record Office, London).

16 Cf. the ruling of the judge in the case of the Danish ship Fædrelandet, formerly the British ship Priscilla (Court Minute Book. Prize. High Court of Admiralty. 28:43. Public Record Office, London).

17 See pp. 171 – 177 in my *India Trade under the Danish Flag 1772 – 1808: European Entreprise and Anglo-Indian Remittance and Trade* (1969).

18 Secret Letters Received from Bengal 9 April & 31 October 1801 and 1 January 1803 (India Office Library, London). In *Trade and Finance in the Bengal Presidency 1793 – 1833* (1956), Amales Tripathi has very convincingly demonstrated the Governor-General's financial dependence upon the Calcutta agency houses.

Notes to Chapter 14

1 Raschke, p. 605.
2 van Leur, p. 90.
3 ibid., pp. 158 – 82.
4 Coedes 1928.
5 Malleret 1960, 1962.
6 Preserved in Chinese histories and encyclopaedias, Pelliot.
7 Wheeler, pp. 206f.
8 Raschke, p. 653.
9 Landes.
10 Walker and Santoso.
11 Bronson, pp. 28 – 30 and Fig. 7.
12 Aung Thaw.

13 Crib.
14 Beck
15 Rajpitak 1979, 1983, Rajpitak and Seeley.
16 Glover 1980.
17 Glover 1983; *et. al.* 1984.
18 Natapintu, Bennett.
19 Pliny, Natural History, XX, 76 – 9, page 1962; X, 225 – 7.
20 Bellwood, pp. 276f.
21 Glover *et. al.* 1984
22 Beck, pp. 387f. and Pl. LXXI.
23 Dikshit, p. 14 and Pl. IV.
24 Gupta, K.P., personal communication, June 1983.
25 Unpublished, but one is on display in the site museum.
26 Fox, Colour Pl. 1A.
27 Bellwood, pp. 275f and Fig. 10.
28 Aung Thaw, Fig. 76.
29 Zuo Ming.
30 e.g. Jamal Hasan 1982, p. 133.
31 Glover 1983.
32 Marshall, Vol. III, Pl. 496.
33 Rajpitak and Seeley.
34 Rajpitak and Seeley, pp. 27 – 30.
35 Batchellor.
36 Sørensen, Fig. 22.
37 Rajpitak 1983, pp. 131 – 519.
38 Lal, p. 89 and Pl. XLVI B; I.A.R. 1956 – 7: Pl. XLIV B and Nath, A., personal communication, 11/9/85.
39 Cat. No. 1867: 4.27.1.

Notes to Chapter 15

1 Van Leur, p. 3.
2 ibid., p. 55.
3 ibid., p. 55.
4 ibid., p. 56.
5 ibid., p. 64
6 ibid., p. 71.
7 ibid., p. 47.
8 Meilink-Roelofsz, p. 8.
9 Steensgaard, p. 11.
10 Meilink-Roelfosz, p. 11.
11 Polanyi 1944.
12 Wallerstein, pp. 347 – 51.
13 Mai.
14 Evers 1988, pp. 206 – 7.
15 Pigeaud, p. 503.
16 Siegel, p. 22.

17 Census 1891, XV, p. 15.
18 Thurston, pp. 250, 253.
19 Census 1961, Village Survey Monographs No. 14:9.
20 Weerasooria, p. 155.
21 Adas 1974b, p. 396.
22 Evers 1964, p. 75.
23 John Capper 1877, cited by Weerasooria, p. 15.
24 Singapore Guide and Street Directory, Ministry of Culture, 1972, p. 21.
25 Sandhu, p. 118.
26 Andrus, p. 66.
27 Adas 1974a, p. 66.
28 Report of the Burma Provincial Banking Enquiry Committee, 1929 – 30, Vol. 1, p. 204, Adas 1947b, p. 391.
29 p. 677.
30 Evers and Pavadarayan.

Notes to Chapter 16

1 The author would like to thank both the Social Science Research Council and the Carlsberg Foundation, for providing the necessary financial support and encouragement to permit the realization of this project, 'The Textile Production in Vietnam 1880 to 1980', notably for facilitating extensive and numerous visits to France for archive research. I would also like to thank Dr. Carl-Axel Nilsson and Dr. Ole Hyldtoft, from the Institute of Economic History, University of Copenhagen, respectively, for their valuable suggestions and comments. Special thanks go to Tove Nørlund and Angela Zassenhaus who read this article and helped to improve its general readability.

2 A rather cursory and marginal contemporary study was made by chief of statistics in Indo-China, F. Leurence: *La balance commerciale de l'Indochine de 1913 à 1922* (BEI 1924). This short study mainly deals with the methodological problems involved in estimating the trade balance, suggesting in fact some advanced methods of calculation. However, this is not an analysis of the actual development. In the 1930s some major studies dealing with the Indo-Chinese economy and trade relations appeared, i.e. Paul Bernard: *Le problème économique de l'Indochine française*, Paris 1934 and Charles Robequain: *L'Évolution économique de l'Indochine Francaise*, Paris 1939. Both of these studies, however, consider trade relations only as a minor aspect of a broader economic analysis. Paul Remy has written the only book specifically dealing with Franco-Indo-Chinese trade relations: *Le problème des relations commerciales entre l'Indochine et la France*, Nancy 1938. The chapters treating the tariff policies of the metropolitan France are particularly useful. But those chapters dealing with trade development suffer from the methodological weakness of employing measures solely expressed in current prices and of considering only the development of total accumulated trade volume. Measuring trade development solely in terms of current prices obviously leads to overestimating its

importance during the 1920s, when inflation of the franc was high, and consequently tends to underestimate the actual trade development at the turn of the century.

Recently the French historian Jacques Marseille has published his Ph.D. thesis entitled, *Empire colonial et capitalism française*, Paris 1984, whose analysis of French colonialism goes a long way towards revising certain generally held assumptions about its economic nature.

3 By applying fixed prices to specific commodities every year, a basis for the addition of the various other categories can be devised. The fixed price is based on the year 1914. The total price of each category is divided by the tonnage in 1914 in order to determine a unit price. This unit price is then multiplied by the tonnage for each successive year. The prices for 1914 seem a reasonable point of departure, since they are not yet inflated by the onset of World War I.

4 The 19 export commodities are: 1. raw silk 2. silk cloth 3. ginned cotton 4. raw cotton 5. rubber 6. anthracite 7. cement 8. zink 9. buffaloes 10. pigs 11. dried fish 12. corn 13. pepper 14. cinnamon 15. copra 16. white rice 17. cargo rice 18. broken rice 19. paddy.

5 The 31 import commodities are: 1. jute sacks 2. unbleached cotton fabrics 3. bleached cotton fabrics 4. coloured cotton fabrics 5. pure and mixed silk cloth 6. silk cloth and light silk commodities from China 7. ginned cotton 8. unbleached cotton thread 9. unbleached twisted cotton thread 10. porcelain 11. wheat flour 12. refined sugar 13. table wine 14. fruits and vegetables 15. refined petrol 16. galvanized iron 17. iron bars. 18. iron and steel wire 19. steel bars 20. locomotives 21. tools 22. rails 23. iron goods 24. nails 25. sprigs 26. screws 27. peanuts 28 Chinese tea 29. Chinese noodles 30. Chinese paper 31. joss sticks.

6 The main trading partners of Indo-China outside France and the empire. Percentage of the total value.

Imports to Indo-China

	1913	1920	1929
Hong Kong	28%	34%	16%
China	8	7	6
Singapore	9	11	3
Japan	2	1	2
USA	2	4	5
England	2	6	2
Dutch Indies	–	–	7
other countries	6	10	8
(France)	(43)	(26)	(49)

Exports from Indo-China

	1913	*1920*	*1929*
Hong Kong	33%	36%	32%
China	7	3	7
Singapore	12	16	10
Japan	6	2	7
USA	1	6	1
England	2	–	3
Dutch Indies	–	–	10
other countries	15	26	8
(France)	(26)	(13)	(24)

Sources: Annuaire statistique 1913 – 22, 1923 – 29

7 There is no disagreement as to the dominant position held by the Chinese merchants of Indo-China in the processing of rice and the control of its internal trade. As for the export trade of rice, the role of the Chinese merchants is handled much more superficially in the literature, but it is usually assumed that here also Chinese merchants play a major role. Yves Henry in *L'Économie agricole de l'Indochine* (Hanoi 1932), contends that 'Les Chinois jouent dans les transactions du paddy et du riz un role prépondérant. Si pour l'exportation ils travaillent concurrentement avec les firmes européenes, ils détiennent entierement le commerce intérieur . . .' (p. 344). Paul Bernard in *Le problème économique Indochinois*, maintains that, 'Ces artérioles sont communes aux deux systemes de circulation: elles amenent jusqu'aux points les plus reculés des campagnes les produits d'importation, principalement Chinois, mais en revanche elles drainent tout le paddy que reste entre les mains des ta-diens et des petits proprietaires, et le livrent d'abord au marchand ramasseur de paddy qui le dirige vers le marchand de demigros du chef-lieu, et, enfin, grace à l'organisation de transport, connexe de tout commerce de riz en gros, vers les magasins des gros exportateurs de Cholon ou aboutit la circulation des paddy destinés a l'export, ce qui ferme le cycle de commerce chinois.' (p. 30). Charles Robequain, describing the role of the Chinese merchants in the rice trade, insists that, 'La coeur de cette organisation est à Cholon, ou les gros acheteurs, les usiniers, les exportateurs agissent en liaison étroite, dans un enchevetrement d'intérets tres difficile a démeler. Le Chinois préside encore au commerce d'autres denrées exportées par l'Indochine, comme le poisson et les pays . . .' (p. 47).

Notes to Chapter 17

1 Chen, p. 117.
2 Wang Gungwu.
3 Ji.
4 Shi Ji = SJ 116:2297 – 98, Watson, p. 296.

5 SJ 116:2293 – 94, Watson, pp. 291 – 93.
6 SJ 123, Watson, pp. 264 – 89.
7 Cf. Hervouet, Chapter 2.
8 SJ 123:3166, Watson, p. 270.
9 SJ 123:3170 – 71, Watson, p. 275.
10 SJ 116:2996, Watson, p. 294.
11 SJ 123:3171, Watson, pp. 275f.
12 SJ 116:2997, Watson, p. 295.
13 SJ 123:3166, Watson, pp. 269f.
14 Cammann, p. 6.
15 For a discussion, see Chen, pp. 118f.
16 Pirazolli-t'Serstevens, pp. 84f.
17 SJ 116:2996, Watson, p. 294.
18 SJ 123:3166, Watson, p. 270.
19 SJ 129:3261, Watson, p. 485.
20 Hou Han Shu (=HHS) 86:2849.
21 Huayangguo Zhi (=HYGZ) 4:60.
22 HYGZ 4:60.
23 Yun, p. 95.
24 Aung-Thwin, unpublished paper.
25 SJ 123:3171, Watson, p. 276.
26 Kennedy, p. 25.
27 Lattimore, p. 175.
28 HHS 2:121.
29 ibid.
30 Wang, p. 86.
31 SJ 113:2969, Watson, p. 240.
32 Yunnan Qingtongqi, pp. 16ff.
33 Wang, pp. 46 – 53.
34 SJ 129:3261 – 62, Watson, p. 485.
35 Yunnan Qingtongqi, pp. 3ff.

Notes to Chapter 18

Acknowledgement: This paper was translated from the French by Richard Bailey, London.
1 Iwao, Seiichi, 'Kinsei Nisshibōeki ni kansuru sūryōteki kōsatsu' in *Shigaku zasshi* LXII – 11, 1952.
2 Okamoto, Yoshitomo, 'Jūroku-shichi-seiki Nihon kankei Kōbunsho' in *Nippo Kōtsū dai 2 suū*. pp. 174 – 87.
3 Memoria de las mercaderias que lleva la nao de Portugueses de la China al Japón. (Archivo de Indias, Sevilla), Collim-Pastels. III. pp. 219 – 220.
4 Copie missive van Jacques Specx aen Lambert Jacobsz. Heijn in Siam, dd. Comptoir Firando, 3 Nov. 1610. Ms. ARA. 1054.
5 Van Dijk, L.C.D. *Iets over onze vroegste betrekkingen met Japan.* Amsterdam 1858, p.34.

6 Adams, William 'Letter to My unknowne Friends and Countri-men', *Hakluytus Posthumus or Purchas His Pilgrimes*. Glasgow 1905. Vol. II. p. 338.

7 Copie Staet is 't Corte van 't Comptoir tot Firando in Japan sorterende onder Jacques Specx, [Firando, 3 Maijo 1616.]. Ms. ARA. VOC. 1061. ff.88 – 89v.

8 J. R. Bruijn, F. S. Gaastra, I. Schöffer (eds.) *Dutch-Asiatic Shipping in the 17th and 18th Centuries*. Vol. III (R.G.P. 167). Den Haag, 1679, pp. 20 – 21.

Notes to Chapter 19

1 India Office Records: *H/39 ff.2 – 7* Account of cloth purchased 15 Sep. 1610 – 21 Mar. 1611 for the Eighth Voyage.

2 IOR: *L/MAR/C/6* Cargo inventory of the *Clove* 4 Apr. 1611, by Richard Cocks, with his voyage accounts (Ledger A) 20 May 1612 – 3 Dec. 1613.

3 IOR: *G/12/9* A collection of materials on Japan made by East India Company Library clerk Peter Pratt in 1822, which includes some abstracts of 'Ledger B' Jan. Jan. 1614 – Aug. 1615. The original accounts have been lost, probably during weeding of the Company's archives in the 1860s. Pratt's collection has been published as *History of Japan . . . by Peter Pratt 1822*, ed. M. B. Paske-Smith (Kobe, 1931).

4 British Library Dept. of Mss: *Cotton Vesp.F.XVII*. I was directed towards this previously unknown source by the late Professor Ralph Davis, F.B.A. The accounts form the second half of a manuscript which begins with a totally unrelated 'Diary of Public Events 1509 – 21' and the catalogue of the Cotton collection merely gives 'Merchant's Accounts 1615 – 17'. Osterwick arrived on the second ship to reach Japan, the *Hosiander* on 31 August 1615, and he remained there as book-keeper.

5 Mainly in IOR:*E/3/1 – 2* 'Original Correspondence' series, and *G/12/15* Letter Book of Richard Wickham.

6 This category was made up of 100 shirts and 325 pairs of shoes!

7 The average weight was about 90 lbs.

8 For example '9 longe Gloster whittes, Jacke Smythe's'; '4 fine Suffolke blewes, Fowler's'; '3 longe whittes, Stradforde's'; Richard Waters, Edward Lightfoot, John Gregory, Edward Hall, George Howe.

9 The complete breakdown was: azure 2; blue 16, sad blue 4; black 29; cinnamon 10; gallant colour 5; green 5, French green 1, sad green 2, grass green 2, sea green 14; lemon 2; murrey in grain 2, peach murrey 2; plunkett 2; popinjay 4; pink 2; primrose 7; Venice red 64, stamett 17; silver 2; sad tawny 1; violet in grain 12; yellow 2, deer colour 2; flame colour 2; hair colour 2; straw colour 1; willow colour 1.

10 The major part of the log of the *Clove* [IOR: *L/MAR/A/XIV*] has been published as *The voyage of Captain John Saris to Japan 1613*, ed. E. M. Satow, Hakluyt Soc., 2nd ser. vol. 5 (London, 1900). Logs of the other ships have not survived, but there is a general account in *Purchas his Pilgrimes* vol. 1 bk.4, pp. 334 – 413 (London, 1625).

11 *Purchas*, op. cit. pp. 394 – 5.
12 IOR: *B/2 ff.140 – 48* Commission to John Saris 4 Apr. 1611.
13 IOR: *E/3/1 no. 122* William Adams at Hirado to the East India Company in London, 1 Dec. 1613.
14 IOR: *E/3/1 no. 121* Richard Cocks at Hirado to the East India Company in London, 30 Nov. 1613.
15 IOR: *E/3/1 no.125* John Saris' commission to Richard Cocks, Hirado, 5 Dec. 1613.
16 IOR: *E/3/2 no. 140* William Eaton at Ōsaka to Richard Wickham at Edo, 20 Apr. 1614.
17 IOR: *G/12/15 pp. 1 – 2* Richard Wickham at Edo to Richard Cocks at Hirado, 26 Apr. 1614.
18 IOR: *E/3/2 no. 144* William Eaton at Ōsaka to Richard Wickham at Edo, 12 May 1614.
19 IOR: *G/12/15 pp. 5 – 6* Richard Wickham at Edo to Richard Cocks at Hirado, 25 May 1614.
20 IOR: *G/12/15 pp.3 – 4* Richard Wickham at Edo to Richard Cocks at Hirado, 22 May 1614.

Notes to Chapter 20

In the Japanese-Dutch trade, we had two kinds of trade method. One is 'Compagnie Handel', company trade or Motokata Shōbai' and the other 'Cambang Handel', private trade or 'Wakini Shōbai'. Motokata Shōbai is the official trade between Japan and the Netherlands. It began in 1609, in which year a Dutch factory was first established at Hirado and after the movement of the factory to Deshima in Nagasaki in 1641, this continued. Wakini Shōbai is the private trade between the Japanese and the members of the Dutch East India Company. This trade was called 'Cambang Handel' by Dutch people. The meaning of the word 'Cambang' is not clear. 'Wakini' means 'non-official goods'.

1 Rōjū, namely councillors of state, of which there were usually four or five, were in normal times the highest officials in the Shogunate. They were selected from among feudal daimyō with a revenue of 25,000 koku or more. The Rōjū performed their duties in turn, each one taking responsibility for a month at a time. These were actually the central authorities of state affairs.
2 Jisha-Bugyō. An office charged with the supervision of temples and shrines throughout the country and the handling of affairs pertaining to their maintenance. The office had existed earlier in the Kamakura and Muromachi Shogunates, but in the Edo Shogunate it was made the highest of the three bugyō, the jisha-bugyō, kanjō-bugyō and machi-bugyō, and placed directly under the direction of the Shogun.
3 Dr. W. T. Kroese 'De Eisch van Zijn Keizerlijk Majesteit', *Overdruk uit Textielhistorische Bijdragen*, no. 14, 1973.
4 Wakini Kanjoba. Accounting office for private trade.
5 Nenbanyakushi. Two interpreters chosen in order annually from the Japanese interpreters for the Dutch language. They were called 'Rapporteur

Tolk' or reporter-interpreter by the Dutch in the Dutch factory in Deshima, and worked as managers for the entire group of interpreters, and acted as the liaison personnel between the Dutch and Japanese.

6 Shogun. Literally 'the general commanding an army'. The term applied to the administrative rulers, as distinguished from the sovereigns, of Japan. Also known as 'Taikun'.

7 Nagasaki Bugyō. Bugyō is a word of frequent occurrence in the title of Tokugawa officials who were governors of towns, or were in charge of certain branches of the administration. In this case, the word, Bugyō, has the former meaning.

8 We have two opinions about 'Rente Meester': Shihai Kanjō. Lower officer of the finance ministry of Shogunate government, who handled the practical business of finance, such as tax collecting and the managing of the Shogunate finances; Nagasaki Daikan. Lower governor of Nagasaki. Daikan means literally 'Representative official', and is applied to the governors of the Shogun's domain and territories ruled by the Tokugawa government.

9 Commissioner of 'Nagasaki Kaisho', Nagasaki Kaisho Shirabeyaku. Nagasaki Kaisho Shirabeyaku is the chief officer of Nagasaki Kaisho. Nagasski Kaisho was the office for trade, founded at Nagasaki by the Tokugawa Shogunate in 1697, which managed Japanese-Dutch and Japanese-Chinese trade.

10 Upperburgomaster, Nagasaki Machitoshiyori. Head of native officials in Nagasaki. They assisted the governor of Nagasaki, taking part in trade and management of town-government.

11 Oranda Tsūji. Japanese interpreters for the Dutch language. They were custom house officials as well.

12 See note 1.

13 Wakatoshiyori. Assistant councillor for state affairs.

14 Daimyō. During the Edo era, the term 'daimyō' was commonly used to designate military leaders who were recognized by the Shogun as possessors of domains with a revenue of ten thousand koku or more of rice and who had large numbers of retainers in their service. They were also referred to as 'hanshu', 'domain lords', or 'shokō', 'feudal lords'.

15 A bird sometimes spelled 'grattig', with white colour on head and breast and black colour from back to tail. This bird is a native of Indonesia.

16 Diving bell or small diving room shaped like a bell.

17 Period of office 1806 – 1812.

18 Period of office 1809 – 1810.

19 Shihai Kanjo. See note 8.

20 Nagasaki Kaisho Shirabeyaku. See note 9.

21 Description of cloth from Dr. W. T. Kroese 'De Eisch van Zijn Keizerlijk Majesteit', *Overdruk uit Textielhistorische Bijdragen*. nr. 14, 1973.

22 Bunsei Hachinen Torinotoshi Oranda-sen Mukimuki-sama O-a-tsu-ra-e narabini Motokata Wakini Sashidashichō. An order book for official trade and private trade in the eighth year of Bunsei (1825). This document belongs to the Nagasaki prefecture library.

23 Takahashi Echizen no Kami Shigekata (period of office 1822 – 1826).

24 Ōkubo Kaga no Kami Tadazane (Period of office 1818 – 1837).

25 Meian Chōhōki, Vol. 6. (Nagasakikenshi Shiryōhen Vol. 4, p. 553).

26 Cf. J. Mac Lean: 'The Enrichment of the Royal Cabinet of Rarities at 's Gravenhage with Japanese Ethonological Specimens from 1815 to 1848'. *Japanese Studies in History of Science*, no. 14, 1975.

27 Shūhan Takashima (1798 – 1866). Gunnery expert of the late Edo period and one of the originators of European style military art in Japan.

28 According to the existing documents, Takashima sold such articles to shimazu han in Satsuma province, nabeshima han in Saga prov., hosokawa han in Higo prov., Noriyoshi Murakami who was his pupil in Mikawa prov. and Tarozaemon Egawa who was also his pupil in Izu province. In other years he also sold some articles.

29 According to the Genki kusaka's letter to his parents dated on 17 January 1848.

30 Ōmetsuke. Major overseers, were officials responsible for supervision of the activities and personnel of the Shogunate. Because they were also in charge with supervision of the diamyō, they are often called daimyō metsuke. There were four or five persons appointed to the office. Ōmetsuke Ino-u-e Chikugono Kami Masashige (1585 – 1661), became Ōmetsuke in 1632 and governor of Christianity policy later. He ordered many kinds of articles which he received.

Notes to Chapter 21

1 Schütte, *Valignanos Missionsgrundsätze für Japan*, I/1, pp. 123 – 32.

2 Schwade, *The Sea Routes*, p. 129.

3 Schütte, op. cit., pp. 131 – 3; Morga, *Sucesos*, pp. 319 – 23.

4 Schwade, ibidem, p. 126; Boxer, *The Christian Century*, pp. 155 – 71.

5 Murakami, *Zōtei ikoku*, pp. 238 – 40.

6 Boxer, op. cit., pp. 260 – 6.

7 Monbeig, *Rodrigo de Vivero*, pp. 5 – 10; Vivero, *Relación*, pp. 53 – 66; Schwade, *The First Diplomatic Relations*, pp. 101 – 2.

8 Vivero, *Relación*, pp. 66 – 72; Pastells, *Historia*, VI, pp.XLVII – LVII; Schwade, ibidem, pp. 102 – 3.

9 Murakami, *Don Rodrigo*, pp. 140 – 2; DNS, XII, pt. 7, pp. 222 – 5; Schwade, ibidem, pp. 103 – 4.

10 For the text of the letters see Murakami, *Ikoku ōfuku*, pp. 93 – 5; Pastells, *Historia*, VI, pp. LII – LIII.

11 Pastells, *Historia*, VI, pp. LIV – LVIII; Murakami, *Don Rodrigo*, pp. 111 – 25; DNS, XII, pt. 7, pp. 241 – 3.

12 Reigned as Viceroy of Mexico from 1584 to 1585.

13 Nachod, Ein unentdecktes Goldland; in: MOAG, VII (1900), pp. 320 – 6; Knauth, *Controntación transpacífica*, p. 197.

14 See p. 321 in the ed. of J.S. Cummins of 1971; Nachod, ibidem, p. 327.

15 Nachod, ibidem, pp. 331 – 41.

16 Vizcaíno, *Relación*, in *Documentos inéditos*, VIII, pp. 102 – 5; DNS, XII, pt. 8, pp. 746 – 8.
17 Morga, *Sucesos*, pp. 319 – 20.
18 Vizcaíno, ibidem, in: *Documentos inéditos*, VIII, pp. 105 – 13; DNS, XII, pt. 8, pp. 748 – 55; Nachod, op. cit., pp. 342 – 3.
19 The Spanish text of the letters is included in Vizcaíno's report: *Documentos inéditos*, VIII, pp. 114 – 6; DNS, XII, pt. 8, pp. 756 – 8.
20 Vizcaíno, ibidem, *Documentos inéditos*, VIII, pp. 117 – 58; DNS, XII, pt. 8, pp. 758 – 85; Schwade, Sebastián Vizcaíno in Japan, pp. 205 – 8.
21 Vizcaíno, ibidem, in: *Documentos inéditos*, VIII, pp. 159 – 85; DNS, XII, pt. 8, pp. 787 – 819; Schwade, ibidem, pp. 208 – 10.
22 Vizcaíno, ibidem, in: *Documentos inéditos*, VIII, pp. 185 – 98; DNS, XII, pt. 9, pp. 964 – 79, pt. 12, pp. 14 – 21; Schwade, ibidem, pp. 210 – 11.
23 Vicaíno, ibidem, in: DNS, XII, pt. 8, p. 814; pt. 12, pp. 111 – 12; pp. 124 – 7; Nachod, ibidem, pp. 370 – 2; Schütte, Vivero and Vizcaíro in Japan, pp. 88 – 99; Schwade, The First Diplomatic Relations, pp. 106 – 109.

Notes to Chapter 23

1 Cushman, J. W., *Fields from the sea: Chinese junk trade with Siam during the late eighteenth and early nineteenth century*, Ph.D. diss. Cornell 1975; Iwao Seiichi, 'Kinsei nitchū boeki ni kansuru shuryoteki Kosatsu', *Shigaku zasshi* 62 – 11; Ng Chin-keong, 'Trade and society: the Amoy metwork on the China coast 1683 – 1735', unpublished thesis, Canberra 1980; Souza, G.B., *Portuguese Trade and Society in China and the South China sea 1630 – 1754*, Ph.D. Diss. Cambridge 1981; Viraphol, S., *Tribute and Profit: Sino-Siamese trade 1652 – 1853*. Cambridge Mass. 1977; Yamawaki Teijiro, *Kinsei Nichi-chu Boeki-shi no kenkyu*. Tokyo 35.
2 Blussé, L., 'Chinese trade to Batavia during the days of the VOC', *Archipel* 18 (1979) 195 – 213; Vienne, M.S. de., 'Les Chinois dans l'archipel Insulindien au XVIIe siècle d'après les Dagh Register de Batavia', Thèse doctorat de IIIe cycle Paris 1979.
3 For a description of the Algemeen Rijksarchief (ARA) in The Hague: *Itinerario* 1980 – 2. Special issue on the ARA.
4 ARA, VOC 317, Letters of the Gentlemen XVII to GG and Council 1644-1647, 4 – 10 – 1647. 'Alsoo deselve veel commoditeijten aenbrengen en neringe maecken . . .'.
5 Souza, *Portuguese trade*, 277 – 9.
6 This and other tables have been based mainly on archive materials and partly on data given by Souza, *Portuguese trade*, 396 – 404.
7 Jörg, C. J. A., *Porcelain and the Dutch China trade*. The Hague 1982, pp. 15 – 45; Hullu, J.de., 'Over den Chinaschen handel der OIC in de eerste dertig jaar van de 18de eeuw', *Bijdragen van het Koninklijk Instituut voor Tall-, Land- en Volkenkunde* (BKI) 73 (1917), pp. 32 – 151; ibidem, 'De instelling van de commissie voor den handel der OIC op China in 1756', *BKI* 79 (1923), pp. 523 – 45.

8 Furber, H., *Rival empires of trade in the Orient 1600 – 1800* (Minneapolis 1976) 257 – 9, 279 – 80, 292; Chijs, J. A. van der., *Nederlandsch-Indisch plakaatboek 1602 – 1811*, 17 volumes (Batavia and The Hague 1885 – 1900) vol. V, 1743 – 1750, 296 – 306, 708 – 10; ibidem vol. VI 1750-1754, 502 – 10.
9 Kamp, A.F. *De standvastige tinnen soldaat. De N.V. Billiton Maatschappij 1860 – 1960*. The Hague 1960, pp. 19 – 21.
10 See Leonard Blussé, 'The VOC and the Junk Trade to Batavia: a Problem in Administrative Control', in Leonard Blussé, *Strange Company: Chinese Settlers, Mestizo Women and the Dutch in VOC Batavia*, Verhandelingen KITLV), 1986 Dordtrecht-Holland, pp. 97 – 155. The data of the junk trade to and from Batavia are interactively accessible via the text version of Chronos Historical Data Archive System, Leiden University; see P. K. Doorm (ed.), *Netherlands Historical Data archive II*, Swidoc/Steinmetzarchief, Herengracht 410 – 12, 1017 BX Amsterdam, 1990.

Notes to Chapter 24

1 Ch'iu K.M. 'Chinese Historical Documents of the Ch'ing Dynasty, 1644 – 1911' *Pacific Historical Review* 1, 1932, pp. 324 – 36. Peake C.H. 'Documents Available for Research on the Modern History of China', *American Historical Review* 38, 1932, pp. 61 – 70; Köster H. 'The Palace Museum of Peiping'. *Monumenta Serica*, 2, 1936 – 37, pp. 181, 187; Fairbank J. K./Teng S. Y. *Ch'ing Administration*, Three studies. Cambridge, Mass., 1960, pp. 69, 72; Wilkinson E., *The History of Imperial China: A Research Guide*, Cambridge, Mass., Harvard 1974, p. 8.
2 Ho Y. P./Liu K. C. 'The Importance of the Archival Palace Memorials of the Ch'ing Dynasty; The Secret Palace Memorials of the Kuang-hsü Period, 1875 – 1908'. *Ch'ing-shih wen-t'i* 3, 1, 1974, p. 81; Bartelett B.S. 'Ch'ing Palace Memorials in the Archives of the National Palace Museum', in: *National Palace Museum Bulletin* 13, 6, 1979, p. 1.
   Since the completion of the Yongzheng-series, the editors have begun to publish the memorials from the Qianlong era. These documents have not been checked for the present survey.
   In addition to the 400,000 documents stored in the National Palace Museum, Taipei, there are some 8 to 9 million documents in the 'Number One Historical Archive' (Diyi lishi dang'anguan) Beijing. Publication of a selection thereof and/or a list of holdings is in the process of preparation.
   Cheng P. K., 'A Visit to the Ming-Ch'ing Archive in Peking', *Ch'ing-shih wen-t'i* 4, 1, 1979, pp. 94-100; Kühn P.A., 'News from the First Historical Archives, Beijing' *Ch'ing-shih wen-t'i* 5, 2, 1984, p. 137.

REFERENCES

References to Chapter 2

The present account is based on the following works:

Attman, A. *The Bullion Flow between Europe and the East, 1000 – 1750* (Acta Regiæ Societatis Scientiarum et Litterarum Gothoburgensis: Humaniora 20). Göteborg 1981.

—— *Dutch Enterprise in the World Bullion Trade, 1550 – 1800* (Acta Regiæ Societatis Scientiarum et Litterarum Gothoburgensis: Humaniora 23). Göteborg 1983.

References to Chapter 3

Adams, R. 'Anthropological perspectives on ancient trade', *Current Anthropology* 15, 1974, pp. 239 – 58.

Astour, M. 'Les étrangers à Ugarit et la statut juridique des Habiru', *Revue d'assyriologie et d'archéologie orientale* 53, 1959, pp. 70 – 6.

—— 'Ma'ḥadu, the harbour of Ugarit', *Journal of the Economic and Social History of the Orient* 13, 1970, pp. 113 – 27.

—— 'The Merchant class of Ugarit', in D. Edzard (ed.), *Gesellschaftsklassen im alten Zweistromland und in den angrenzenden Gebieten* (RAI XVIII), Munich 1972, pp. 11 – 26.

—— 'Ugarit and the Aegean: a brief summary of archaeological and epigraphic evidence', in H. Hoffner (ed.), *Orient and Occident: essays presented to Cyrus H. Gordon* (AOAT 22), Neukirchen-Vluyn 1973, pp. 17 – 27.

—— 'Ugarit and the Great Powers', in G. Young (ed.), *Ugarit in Retrospect: fifty years of Ugarit and Ugaritic*. Winona Lake, Indiana 1981, pp. 3 – 29.

Boyer, G. 'La place des textes d'Ugarit dans l'histoire de l'ancien droit oriental', in J. Nougayrol (ed.), *Le Palais Royal d'Ugarit* III. Paris 1955, pp. 283 – 308.

Brin, G. 'The Title ben (ha)melekh and its parallels', *Annali dell' Instituto Orientale di Napoli* 19, 1969, pp. 433 – 65.

Cutler, B. and Macdonald, J. 'The unique Ugaritic text UT 113 and the question of "guilds" ', *Ugarit-Forschungen* 9, 1977, pp. 13 – 30.

Dalton, G. 'Karl Polanyi's analysis of long-distance trade and his wider paradigm', in J. Sabloff and C. Lamberg-Karlovsky (eds.), *Ancient Civilization and Trade*. Albuquerque 1975, pp. 63 – 132.

Dollinger, P. *The German Hansa*. London 1970.

Dornemann, R. 'The Excavations at Ras Shamra and their place in the current archaeological picture of ancient Syria', in G. Young (ed.), *Ugarit in*

Retrospect: fifty years of Ugarit and Ugaritic. Winona Lake, Indiana 1981, pp. 59 – 69.

Edzard, D. 'Problèmes de la royauté dans la période présargonique', in P. Garelli (ed.), *Le Palais et la Royauté* (RAI XIX). Paris 1974, pp. 141 – 49.

Fensham, F. 'Shipwreck in Ugarit and ancient Near Eastern law codes', *Oriens Antiquus* 6, 1967, pp. 221 – 4.

Frankenstein, S. 'The Phoenicians in the Far West: a function of Neo-Assyrian imperialism', in M. Larsen (ed.), *Power and Propaganda: a symposium on ancient empires*. Copenhagen 1979, pp. 263 – 94

Gelb, I. 'Šîbût Kušurrā'im, "witnesses of the indemnity" ', *Journal of Near Eastern Studies* 43, 1984, pp. 263 – 76.

Gledhill, J. and Larsen, M. 'The Polanyi paradigm and a dynamic analysis of archaic states', in C. Renfrew, M. Rowlands and B. Segraves (eds.), *Theory and Explanation in Archaeology*. New York 1982, pp. 197 – 229.

Greenfield, J. and Shaffer, A. 'Notes on the Akkadian-Aramaic bilingual statue from Tell Fekherye', *Iraq* 45, 1983, pp.109 – 16.

Grégoire, J. 'Remarques sur quelques noms de fonction et sur l'organisation administrative dans les archives d'Ebla', in L. Cagni (ed.) *La Lingqu di Ebla*. Naples 1981, pp. 379 – 99.

Heltzer, M. *The Rural Community in Ancient Ugarit*, Wiesbaden 1976.

—— *Goods, Prices and the Organization of Trade in Ugarit*, Wiesbaden 1978.

—— *The Internal Organization of the Kingdom of Ugarit*, Wiesbaden 1982.

Humphreys, S. 'History, economics, and anthropology: the work of Karl Polanyi', *History and Theory* 8, 1969, pp. 165 – 212.

Imparati, F. ' "Signori" e "figli del re" ', *Orientalia* 44, 1975, pp.80 – 95.

Kitchen, K. 'The king list of Ugarit', *Ugarit-Forschungen* 9, 1977, pp. 131 – 42.

Klengel, H. 'Zu den šîbūtum in altbabylonischer Zeit', *Orientalia* 29, 1960, pp.357 – 75.

Larsen, M. T. 'The City and its king', in P. Garelli (ed.), *Le Palais et la Royauté* (RAI XIX) Paris 1974, pp. 285 – 300.

—— 'The Tradition of empire in Mesopotamia', in M. T. Larsen (ed.), *Power and Propaganda: a symposium on ancient empires*, Copenhagen 1979, pp. 75 – 103.

Linder, E. *The Maritime texts of Ugarit: a study in late Bronze Age Shipping*. Brandeis University, 1970.

—— 'Ugarit: a Canaanite thalassocracy', in G. Young (ed.), *Ugarit in retrospect: fifty years of Ugarit and Ugaritic*, Winona Lake, Indiana 1981, pp.31 – 42.

Lipiński, E. 'An Ugaritic letter to Amenophis III concerning trade with Alašiya', *Iraq* 39, 1977, pp. 213 – 17.

Liverani, M. 'Due documenti ugaritici con garanzia di presenza', in C. Schaeffer, *Ugaritica* VI, Paris 1969, pp. 375 – 8.

—— 'La royauté syrienne de l'age de bronze récent', in P. Garelli (ed.), *Le Palais et la Royauté* (RAI XIX), Paris 1974, pp. 329 – 56.

—— 'Communautés de village et palais royal dans la Syrie du IIème millénaire', *Journal of the Economic and Social History of the Orient* 18, 1975, pp. 146 – 64

—— 'La dotazione dei mercanti di Ugarit', *Ugarit-Forschungen* 11, 1979, pp. 495 – 503.

Loewenstamm, S. 'Yāpeᵉḥ, Yāpiᵃḥ', *Comparative Studies in Biblical and Ancient Oriental Literatures* (AOAT 204) Neukirchen-Vluyn 1980, pp. 137 – 45.

Macdonald, J. 'An assembly at Ugarit?', *Ugarit-Forschungen* 11, 1979, pp. 515 – 26.

Margueron, J. 'Ras Shamra: nouvelles perspectives des fouilles', in G. Young (ed.), *Ugarit in Retrospect: fifty years of Ugarit and Ugaritic*. Winona Lake, Indiana 1981, pp. 71 – 8.

Mazar, B. 'The Philistines and the rise of Israel and Tyre', *Proceedings of the Israel Academy of Sciences and Humanities* I, 1967, pp.1 – 22.

Millard, A. 'Assyrians and Arameans', *Iraq* 45, 1983, pp. 101 – 8.

Nougayrol, J. *Le Palais Royal d'Ugarit* III. Paris 1955.

Pardee, D. 'The Ugaritic text 2106.10 – 18: a bottomry loan?', *Journal of the American Oriental Society* 95, 1975, pp. 612 – 19.

—— 'YPH "witness" in Hebrew and Ugaritic', *Vetus Testamentum* 28, 1978, pp. 204 – 13.

—— 'Ugaritic', *Archiv für Orientforschung* 28, 1981/82, pp.259 – 72.

Polanyi, K. 'On the comparative treatment of economic institutions in Antiquity', in C. Kraeling and R. Adams (eds.), *City Invincible*. Chacago 1960, pp. 329 – 50.

—— 'Traders and trade', in J. Sabloff and C. Lamberg-Karlovsky (eds.), *Ancient Civilizations and Trade*. Albuquerque 1975, pp. 133 – 54.

Powell, M. 'Götter, Könige und "Kapitalisten" im Mesopotamien des 3. Jahrtausends V.U.Z.', *Oikumene* 2, 1978, pp. 127 – 44.

Rainey, A. 'Business agents at Ugarit', *Israel Exploration Journal* 13, 1963, pp. 313 – 21

—— 'A Canaanite at Ugarit', *Israel Exploration Journal* 13, 1963, pp. 43 – 45.

—— 'Ugarit and the Canaanites again', *Israel Exploration Journal* 14, 1964, p. 101.

Sasson, J., 'Canaanite maritime involvement in the second millennium B.C.', *Journal of the American Oriental Society* 86, 1966, pp. 126 – 38.

Schaeffer, C. *Ugaritica* III. Paris 1956.

—— *Ugaritica* VII. Paris 1978.

Stieglitz, R. 'Ugaritic Mḫd — the harbor of Yabne-Yam?', *Journal of the American Oriental Society* 94, 1974, pp. 137 – 8.

—— 'Commodity prices at Ugarit', *Journal of the American Oriental Society* 99, 1979, pp. 15 – 23.

Veenhof, K. *Aspects of Old Assyrian Trade and its Terminology*. Leiden 1972.

Xella, P. 'Die Ausrüstung eines kanaanäischen Schiffes (KTU 4.689)', *Die Welt des Orients* 13, 1982, pp. 31 – 5.

Yaron, R. 'Foreign merchants at Ugarit', *Israel Law Review* 4, 1969, pp. 70 – 9.

Young, G. *The Historical Background of Phoenician Expansion into the Mediterranean in the early first Millennium B.C.*, Brandeis University 1969.

Zaccagnini, C. 'The merchant at Nuzi', *Iraq* 39, 1977, pp. 171 – 89.

Ziskind, J. 'Sea loans at Ugarit', *Journal of the American Oriental Society* 94, 1974, pp. 134 – 7.

References to Chapter 4

Brinkman, J. A. 'Babylonia c. 1000 – 748 B.C.', *Cambridge Ancient History* (2nd ed.) III/1. Cambridge: Cambridge University Press, 1982.

—— 'Babylonia under the Assyrian Empire 745 – 627' in M. T. Larsen (ed.), *Power and Propaganda*, Copenhagen: Akademisk Forlag, 1982, pp. 223 – 250.

—— 'Foreign Relations of Babylonia from 1600 to 125 B.C.: the Documentary Evidence', *American Journal of Archaeology* 76: (1972): 271 – 81.

—— 'Notes on Arameans and Chaldeans in Southern Babylonia', *Orientalia* 46 (1977): 304 – 325.

Bulliett, R. S. *The Camel and the Wheel.* Cambridge, Mass.: Harvard, 1975.

Eph'al I. *The Ancient Arabs: Nomads on the Borders of the Fertile Crescent, 9th – 5th Centuries, B.C.* Leiden: Brill, 1982.

McCown, D. E. and R. C. Haines, *Nippur I.* Oriental Institute Publication 78. Chicago: University of Chicago, 1967.

Oppenheim, A. L. 'Essay on Overland Trade in the First Millennium B.C.', *Journal of Cuneiform Studies* 21 (1967): 236 – 54.

—— 'The Seafaring Merchants of Ur', *Journal of the American Oriental Society* 74 (1954): 6 – 17.

Wapnish, Paula. 'Camel Caravans and Camel Pastoralists At Tell Jemmeh', *Journal of the Ancient Near Eastern Society of Columbia University* 13 (1981): 101 – 21.

References to Chapter 7

Badamxatan, S., *Xövsgölijn darxad jastan.* Ulan Bator 1965 (Studia Ethnographica III, 1.)

Carruthers, D., *Unknown Mongolia,* I. London 1924.

Čimitdoržiev, S.B., *Vzaimootnošenija Mongolii i Rossii, XVII – XVIII.* Moscow 1978.

Dobležev, V.A., *Darxatskij okrug* Trudy SKOURGO, T. XII, vyp. 1 – 2, St Petersburg 1911.

Dolgix, B.O., *Rodovoj i plemennoj sostav narodov Sibiri,* v XVII. Moscow 1960. (Trudy IEMM. nov. ser. LV).

Gmelin, J.G., *Reise durch Sibirien von dem Jahr 1733 bis 1743,* I – IV. Göttingen 1751 – 1752. (Sammlung neuer und merkwürdiger Reisen zu Wasser und zu Lande.)

Haslund-Christensen, H., *Jabonah.* Stockholm 1947. *Istorija Tuvy I.* Moscow 1964.

Istorija Tuvy I. Moscow 1964.

Kyzlasov, L.P., *Srednevekovye goroda Tuvy:* SA No. 3. 1953.
Majdar, D., *Arxitektura i gradostroitel'stvo Mongolii.* Moscow 1970.
Olsen, Ø., *Et primitivt folk.* Kristiania 1915.
Pêrlêê, X., *Mongol ard ulsyn êrt,* dundad üeijn xot suuriny tovčoon. Ulan Bator 1961.
Rasid-ad-Din, *Sbornik letopisej,* T. I. kn. 1. Moscow-Leningrad 1952.
Sandag, Š. *Mongolyn uls tórijn gadaad xarilcaa.* 1. 1850 – 1919. Ulan Bator 1971.
Sanždorž, M., *Xalxad xjatadyn mòngò xüülêgê xudaldaa nêvtêrč xòlžsòn n',* (XVIII. zuun). Ulan Bator 1963. (Studia historica III/5.)
Šinkarev, L.J., *Szibéria.* Budapest 1977.

References to Chapter 8

Adamec, Ludwig E. (ed.) *Badakhshân Province and Northeastern Afghanistan.* Graz 1972.
Grötzbach, Erwin. 'Kulturgeographischer Wandel in NO-Afghanistan seit dem 19.Jh', *Afghan. Studien,* Bd.4.Meisenheim 1972.
Huwyler, Edwin. Die Wirtschaft im Munğantal. Univ. Basel 1975. (MS — not published)
Kussmaul, Friedrich. 'Badaxšan und seine Tağiken', *Tribus* No. 14, 1965.
Olufsen, Olaf. *Through the unknown Pamirs, Vakhan and Garan.* London 1904. (Repr. New York 1969).
Raunig, Walter. 'Zu den materiellen Lebensgrundlagen der Bewohner des Wakhân', in *Grosser Pamir.* Graz 1978.
——'Einige Bemerkungen zu Verkehr und Handelstendenzen in der afghanischen Provinz Badakhshân'. *Wirtschaftskräfte und Wirtschaftswege* IV: Übersee und allgem. Wirtschaftsgeschichte. Bamberg 1978.
——'Pamir und Wakhân — ein kaum bekannter Kreuzweg der Kulturen in Zentralasien', *Schriftenreihe des Zentralinstituts für fränkische Landeskunde und allgemeine Regionalforschung an der Univ. Erlangen-Nürnberg* Bd. 21, 1982.
Schultz, Arved v. 'Bericht über den bisherigen Verlauf meiner Pamirexpedition 1911/12', *Petermanns Mitteilungen* 58.Jg. Juli-Heft 1912.
Shor, Jean and Franc. 'We Took the Highroad in Afghanistan', *The National Geographic Magazine* Vol. XCVIII, no. 5, Nov. 1950.
Singer, André. 'Problems of Pastoralism in the Afghan Pamirs', *Asian Affairs* (J.R.S.A.A.), 63, 2, 1976.
Snoy, Peter. 'Nuristan und Muğan'. *Tribus* No. 14, 1965.
Wood, John. *A Personal Narrative of a Journey to the Source of the River Oxus by the Route of the Indus, Kabul, and Badakshân* . . . London 1841, 2nd. ed. 1847.

References to Chapter 12

Das Gupta, Ashin. The Letter Books of Francis Jourdan. *Bengal Past and Present*, 75. 1956

Das Gupta, Ashin. *Malabar in Asian Trade 1740 – 1800*. Cambridge 1967.

Dermigny, Louis. *Cargaisons indiennes. Solier & Cie 1781 – 1793*. I – II. Paris 1959 – 60.

—— *La Chine et l'Occident. Le commerce à Canton au 18e siècle. 1719 – 1833*. I – II Paris 1964.

Feldbæk, Ole. *India Trade under the Danish Flag 1772 – 1808. European Enterprise and Anglo-Indian Remittance and Trade*. Scandinavian Institute of Asian studies. Monograph Series No 2. Copenhagen 1969.

—— 'Dutch Batavia Trade via Copenhagen 1795 – 1807. A Study of Colonial Trade and Neutrality'. *Scandinavian Economic History Review, 21*. 1973.

—— 'Danish East India Trade 1772 – 1807. Statistics and Structure'. *Scandinavian Economic History Review, 26*. 1978.

Feldbæk, Ole, & Justesen, Ole. *Kolonierne i Asien og Afrika*. Copenhagen 1980.

Furber, Holden. *John Company at Work. A Study of European Expansion in India in the Late Eighteenth Century*. Cambridge Mass. 1951.

—— *Bombay Presidency in the Mid-Eighteenth Century*. London 1965.

—— *Rival Empires of Trade in the Orient 1600 – 1800*. In Boyd G. Shafer (ed.): *Europe and the World in the Age of Expansion*, II. Oxford 1976.

Mandal, B.L. *India's Trade Relations with Malaya and Indonesia (1793 – 1833)*. Allahabad 1984.

Marshall, Peter. *East Indian Fortunes*. London 1976.

Mookerjii, R..K. *A History of Indian Shipping*. Calcutta 1957.

Nightingale, Pamela. *Trade and Empire in Western India, 1784 – 1806*. London 1970.

Parkinson, Cyril Northcote. *Trade in the Eastern Seas 1793 – 1813*. Cambridge 1937.

—— *War in the Eastern Seas, 1793 – 1815*. London 1954.

Rasch, Aage. Dansk handel på Isle de France. *Erhvervshistorisk Aarbog, 5*. Aarhus 1953.

Sen, S.P. *The French in India 1763 – 1816: First Establishment and Struggle*. Calcutta 1958.

Toussaint, Auguste. *History of the Indian Ocean*. London 1966.

—— *La route des Iles. Contribution à l'histoire maritime des Mascaregnes*. Paris 1967.

Tripathi, Amales. *Trade and Finance in the Bengal Presidency 1793 – 1833*. Calcutta 1956.

References to Chapter 13

The most important Danish unpublished source material is in the archives left from the chartered companies, now held in the Danish National Archives. It is inventoried in:

J. O. Bro-Jørgensen & Aage Rasch, · *Asiatiske, vestindiske og guineiske handelskompagnier* (Rigsarkivet, Copenhagen 1969).
Other archive groups in the Danish National Archives contain essential information, e.g. that of the Board of Commerce on sea passes. In addition, foreign archives hold papers of interest; see survey in the book mentioned below by Feldbæk (1969).
Critical surveys of the literature on Danish chartered companies and tropical colonies are found in:

Erik Gøbel, 'Danske oversøiske handelskompagnier i 17. og 18. århundrede. En forskningsoversigt'. *Fortid og Nutid* vol. XXVIII, 1980, pp. 535 – 569.
Remaining literature written by Danish historians includes the following works:

Ole Feldbæk, *India Trade under the Danish Flag 1772 – 1808. European Enterprise and Anglo-Indian Remittance and Trade*. Copenhagen 1969.
—— 'Danish East India Trade 1772 – 1807. Statistics and Structure', *Scandinavian Economic History Review* vol. XXVI, 1978, pp. 128 – 144.

Ole Feldbæk & Ole Justesen, *Kolonierne i Asien og Afrika*. Copenhagen 1980.

Kristof Glamann, 'The Danish East India Company', in Michael Mollat, ed., *Sociétés et compagnies de commerce dans l'Océan Indien*. Paris 1970, pp. 471 – 479.

Erik Gøbel, 'The Danish Asiatic Company's Voyages to China 1732 – 1833', *Scandinavian Economic History Review* vol. XXVII, 1979, pp. 22 – 46.

Aage Rasch, 'Dansk handel på Isle de France, in *Erhvervshistorisk Årbog* vol. V, 1953. pp. 7 – 27.

Tim Velschow, 'Voyages of the Danish Asiatic Company to India and China 1772 – 1792', *Scandinavian Economic History Review* vol. XX, 1972, pp. 133 – 152.

Vore Gamle Tropenkolonier vol. V – VII, ed. by Johannes Brøndsted. Copenhagen 1967.
One of the most important non-Danish publications dealing with country trade, with mention of the role of Denmark, and with further references to the international literature is:

Holden Furber, *Rival Empires of Trade in the Orient 1600 – 1800*. London 1976.

References to Chapter 14

Aung Thaw, U. *Report on the Excavations at Beikthano*. Archaeological Survey, Ministry of Culture, Rangoon 1968.

Batchellor, B. C. Post 'Hoabinhian' coastal settlement indicated by finds in stanniferous Langat River alluvium near Dangkil, Selangor, Peninsular Malaya. *Federation Museums Journal* (n.s.) 1978, 22.

Beck, H. C. Etched carnelian beads. *Antiquaries Journal* XIII, 1933, pp. 384 – 98.

Bellwood, P. Archaeological Research in Minahasa and the Talaud Islands, Northeastern Indonesia. *Asian Perspectives* XIX (2), 1978, pp. 240 – 88.

Bennett, A. *Metallurgical Analyses of Iron Artifacts from Ban Don Ta Phet, Thailand.* B.Sc. Report, Institute of Archaeology, University of London, 1982.

Bronson, B. Excavations at Chansen, Thailand, 1968 & 1969: a preliminary report. *Asian Perspectives* XV, 1973 (for 1972), pp. 15 – 46.

Chin You-di. *Ban Don Ta Phet: preliminary excavation report, 1975 – 76.* (In Thai) Bangkok: National Museum, 1976.

Christie, A.H. Lin-i, Fu-nan, Java. pp. 281 – 7 in *Early South-East Asia.* R. B. Smith & W. Watson (eds.) Oxford University Press, 1979.

Coedes, G. The excavations at P'ong Tuk and their importance for the ancient history of Siam. *Journal of the Siam Society* XXI, 1928, pp. 195 – 209.

Coedes, G. *The Indianized States of Southeast Asia.* ed. W. F. Vella, translated by S. B. Cowing. Canberra 1968.

Crib, J. The date of the symbolic coins of Burma and Thailand. *Seaby Coin and Medal Bulletin* 75, 1981, pp. 224 – 6.

Dikshit, M. G. *Etched Beads in India.* Deccan College Monograph Series 4. Poona, 1949.

Fox, R. B. *The Tabon Caves.* Monograph 1 of the National Museum, Manila 1970.

Glover, I. C. Ban Don Ta Phet and its relevance to problems in the pre- and protohistory of Thailand. *Bulletin of the Indo-Pacific Prehistory Association* 2, 1980, pp. 16 – 30.

—— Excavations at Ban Don Ta Phet, Kanchanaburi Province, Thailand, 1980 – 81. *South-East Asian Studies Newsletter* 10: 1 – 3, 1983.

—— Archaeological survey in West-Central Thailand; a second report on the 1982 – 83 field season. *Asian Perspectives* XXVI(1): 109, 1987.

—— Pisit Charoenwongsa, Alvey, B. A. R., and Narawat M. Kamnounket. The cemetery of Ban Don Ta Phet: results from the 1980 – 81 excavation season. *South Asian Archaeology 1981* 1984, pp. 319 – 30.

IAR. Excavation at Jaugada, District Ganjam. *Indian Archaeology — a review* 1956 – 57, pp. 30f.

Jamal Hassan. The distribution and types of beads in the Gangeatic Valley. *Puratattva* 11 (1979 – 80) 1980, pp. 131 – 40.

Lal, B. B. Sisulpalgarh 1948: an early historic fort in Eastern India. *Ancient India* 5, 1949, pp. 62 – 105.

Lamb, A. Some observations on stone and glass beads in early South-East Asia. *Journal of the Malay Branch of the Royal Asiatic Society* 38, 1965, pp. 87 – 124.

Landes, C. Piece d'epoque romaine trouvee a U-Thong, Thailande. *Journal of Silpakorn* 26(1), 1982, pp. 113 – 5.

Leur, J. C. van. *Indonesian Trade and Society*. Selected Studies on Indonesia 1. (2nd ed., English translation from the Dutch.) The Hague, 1967.

Mackay, E. Decorated carnelian beads. *Man*, September 1933, pp. 143 – 6.

Malleret, L. *L'Archeologie du Delta du Mekong II. La Civilization materielle d'Oceo*. P.E.F.E.O. Vol. 43, Paris 1960.

—— *L'Archeologie du Delta du Mekong III. La culture du Founan*. P.E.F.E.O. Vol. 43, 1962. Paris.

Marshall, J. *Taxila: an illustrated account of the archaeological excavations*. Cambridge 1951.

Mourer, R. Un cas de changement technologique dans la fonte du cuivre a Phsar Dek (Camboge): aspects techiques, economiques, et sociaux, in *The Diffusion of Material Culture*. H. H. E. Loofs-Wissowa (ed). Asian & Pacific Archaeology Series 9, S.S.R.I., Honolulu 1980, pp. 333 – 50.

Natapintu, S. *Prehistoric iron implements from Ban Don Ta Phet*. B.A. Report, Faculty of Archaeology, Silpakorn University 1976. (In Thai).

Pelliot, P. Le Fou-nan. *Bulletin d'Ecole Française d'Extreme Orient* 3, pp. 248 – 303.

Pliny. *Natural History*, Book XXXVII. ed. R. E. Eicholz, Loeb Classical Library Vol. 8. London 1962.

Possehl, G. Cambay beadmaking. *Expedition* 23(4), 1981, pp. 39 – 47.

Rajpitak, W. *The Development of Copper Alloy Metallurgy in Thailand in the pre-Buddhist period, with special reference to high-tin bronze*. Ph.D. thesis, Institute of Archaeology, London, 1983.

—— *The Technology of copper-alloy artifacts from Ban Don Ta Phet, Thailand*. B.Sc. Report, Institute of Archaeology, London 1979.

Rajpitak, W. & Seeley, N. The bronze bowls from Ban Don Ta Phet: an enigma of prehistoric metallurgy. *World Archaeology* 11(1), 1979, pp. 26 – 31.

Raschke, M.G. New Studies in Roman Commerce with the East. pp. 605 – 1361 in *Aufstieg und Niedergang der Romischen Welt* II.9. Berlin, New York, 1978.

Sorensen. P. Prehistoric iron implements from Thailand. *Asian Perspectives* 16(2), 1973, pp. 134 – 73.

Strabo. *The Geography*, Jones, H. L. (ed.), Loeb Classical Library, London, 1930.

Walker, M. & Santoso, S. Romano-Indian rouletted pottery in Indonesia. *Asian Perspectives* XX(2) for 1977, 1980, pp. 228 – 35.

Wheatley, P. *Nagara and Commandery: origins of the Southeast Asian Urban Traditions*. Department of Geography Research Papers 207 – 8, University of Chicago, 1983.

Wheeler, R. E. M. *Rome Beyond the Imperial Frontiers*. Harmondsworth, 1954.

Williams, L. *A New Approach to the Study of Bead-making Workshop Practices, with special reference to Carnelian and Agate Beads from Ban Don Ta Phet, Thailand*. B.A. Report, Institute of Archaeology, London, 1984.

Wolters, O. W. *Early Indonesian Commerce: a study of the origins of Srivijaya*. Ithaca 1967.

Zuo Ming. Etched carnelian beads found in China. *Kaogu* 1974 (6), pp. 382 – 5.

References to Chapter 15

Adas, M. *The Burma Delta*. Madison: University of Wisconsin Press, 1974a.
—— 'Immigrant Asians and the Economic Impact of European Imperialism: The Role of the South Indian Chettiars in British Burma', *Journal of Asian Studies* 33, 3:365 – 401, 1974b.
Andrus, J. R. *Burmese Economic Life*. Stanford, CA.: Stanford University Press, 1947.
Evers, H.-D. *Kulturwandel in Ceylon*. Baden-Baden: Nomos, 1964.
—— 'Chettiar Moneylenders in Southeast Asia' in D. Lombard et J. Aubin (eds.), *Marchands et hommes d'affaires asiatiques*, Paris: Editions de l'EHESS, pp. 199 – 219, 1988.
Evers, H.-D. and J. Pavadarayan, 'Religious Fervour and Economic Success: The Chettiars of Singapore', in: Kernial Singh Sandhu (ed.), *Indians in Southeast Asia*, Singapore, forthcoming.
Geertz, C. *Peddlars and Princes*. Chicago: University of Chicago Press, 1963.
Horridge, A. *The Prahu, Traditional Sailing Boat of Indonesia*. Kuala Lumpur: Oxford University Press, 1981.
Mai, U. 'Small-town Markets and the Urban Economy in Kabupaten Minahasa (North Sulawesi, Indonesia)', Working Paper No. 36, Sociology of Development Research Centre, University of Bielefeld, 1983.
Meilink-Roelofsz, *Asian Trade and European Influence in the Indonesian Archipelago between 1500 and about 1630*. The Hague: Martinus Nijhoff, 1962.
Pigeaud, T. G. T. *Java in the Fourteenth Century*. Vol. IV, The Hague: Martinus Nijhoff, 1962.
Polanyi, K. *The Great Transformation*. New York: Holt, 1944.
Polanyi, K. *Trade and Market in the Early Empires: Economies in History and Theory*. Glencoe, IL.: Free Press, 1957.
Sandhu, K. *Indians in Malaya*. Cambridge: Cambridge University Press, 1969.
Siegel, J. T. *The Rope of God*. Berkeley: University of California Press, 1969.
Steensgaard, N. *The Asian Trade Revolution of the Seventeenth Century: The East India Companies and the Decline of the Caravan Trade*, Chicago: University of Chicago Press, 1974.
Thurston, E., *Castes and Tribes of Southern India*. Madras: Government Press, 1909.
Van Leur, J. C., *Indonesian Trade and Society. Essays in Asian Social and Economic History*. The Hague: van Hoeve, 1955.
Wallerstein, I., *The Modern World-System I. Capitalist Agriculture and the Origins of the European World-Economy in the Sixteenth Century*. New York/London: Academic Press, 1974.
Weerasooria, W. S., *The Nattukottai Chettiar Merchant Bankers in Ceylon*, Dehiwala: Tisara Prakasakayo, 1973.

Wertheim, W. F., 'The Trading Minorities in Southeast Asia', in: Hans-Dieter Evers (ed.): *Sociology of Southeast Asia*. Kuala Lumpur: Oxford University Press, pp. 104 – 120, 1980.

References to Chapter 16

Administration des douanes et regies. *Indochine Française. Rapports sur les statistiques des douanes*. Saigon, yearly 1885 – 95.

Annuaire statistique de l'Indochine. Premier volume. Recueil de statistique-relatives aux années 1913 a 1912. Imprimerie d'extreme-orient. Hanoi 1927.

Annuaire statistique de l'Indochine. 2ème volume. 1923 – 29. Imprimerie d'extreme orient. Hanoi 1930.

Bernard, P. *Le problème économique Indochinois*. Nouvelles Editions Latines. Paris 1934.

Bulletin Économique de l'Indochine. Imprimerie d'extreme orient. First published in 1897. (BEI)

Henry, Yves. *Économie agricole de l'Indochine*. Gouvernement generale de l'Indochine. Hanoi 1932.

Leurence, F. *Étude statistique dur le développement économique le l'Indochine de 1899 à 1923*. Extrait de BEI no 171, nouvelle série, 1925.

Leurence, F. *La balance commerciale de l'Indochine de 1913 a 1922*. BEI 1924.

Marseille, J. *Empire colonial et capitalism français. Historie d'une divorce*. Paris 1984.

Remy, P. *Le problème des relations commerciales entre l'Indochine et la France*. Nancy 1938.

Robequain, Ch. *L'Évolution économique de l'Indochine Française*. Paris 1939.

References to Chapter 17

Aung-Thwin, Michael. 'Burma before Pagan: the Status of Archaeology today'. Unpublished paper 1984, 25 pp. text with maps and plates.

Cammann, Schuyler Van R. 'Archaeological Evidence for Chinese Contacts with India during the Han Dynasty', *Sinologica*, Vol. V, No. 1, 1956, pp. 1 – 19.

Chen Qian. 'Preliminary Research on the Ancient Passage to India from Sichuan via Yunnan and Burma', *Social Sciences in China*, Vol. II, no. 2, 1981, pp. 113 – 48.

Hervouet, Yves. *Un poète de cour sous les Han: Sseu-ma Siang-jou*, Paris 1964.

Hou Han Shu. Zhonghua-ed. Beijing 1965.

Huayangguo Zhi. Sibu Beiyao-ed. Repr. Taibei 1976.

Ji Xianlin. *Zhong-Yin Wenhua Guamxi Shi Lunwen Ji*, Beijing 1982.

Kennedy, Jean. 'From Stage to Development in Prehistoric Thailand: an

Exploration of the Origins of Growth, Exchange and Variability in Southeast Asia', in Hutterer, Karl (ed.), *Economic and Social Interaction in Southeast Asia: Perspectives from Prehistory, History and Ethnography*, Ann Arbor 1977, pp. 23 – 38.

Lattimore, Owen. *Inner Asian Frontiers of China*, New York 1940.

Pelliot, Paul. 'Deux itinéraires de Chine en Inde à la fin de VIIIe siècle', *BEFEO* t. IV, Nos. 1 – 2 (1904), pp. 131 – 413.

Pirazolli-t'Serstevens, Michelle. *La Civilisation du royaume de Dian a l'époque Han*, Paris 1974.

Shi Ji. Zhonghua-ed. Beijing 1962.

Wang Gungwu. 'The Nanhai Trade: a Study of the Early History of Chinese Trade in the South Sea', *JMBRAS*, Vol. 31, Pt. 2 (1958), pp. 1 – 135.

Wang Zhongshu. *Han Civilization*, New Haven 1982.

Watson, Burton (trans). *Records of the Grand Historian*, Vol. II, New York 1961.

Yunnan Qingtonggi. Beijing 1981.

Yun Qin, 'Dong Han Yongchang Junzhicheng Zhi Weizhi', *Sixiang Zhanxian* (Kunming), No. 2, 1981, p. 95.

Yü Ying-shih. *Trade and Expansion in Han China*, Berkeley 1967.

References to Chapter 20

(with the exception of books and articles mentioned in the text)

Arima, S. *Takashima Shūhan*, Yoshikawa-Kō Kōbunkan. Tōkyō, 1958.

Dagregisters Gehouden bij De Opperhoofden van het Nederlandsche Factorij in Japan, vol. 1, Tōkyō Univ., 1974.

Ikeda, T. Nihon Kenzai Ransho Mokuroku, *Nisshin Igaku*, vol. 43, no. 7 – vol. 50, no. 12.

Iwao, S. (ed.) *Biographical Dictionary of Japanese History*, Tokyo, 1978.

—— *Kinsei no Yōgaku to Kaigai Kōshō*, Gannandō, Tōkyō, 1979.

Mac Lean, J. 'The Introduction of Books and Scientific Instruments into Japan, 1712 – 1854'. *Japanese Study of History of Science*, no. 13, 1974.

Ogata, T. (ed.) *Edo-Bakufu Kyūzo Ransho Sōgō Mokuroku, List of Dutch Books Collected by Tokugawa Shogunate*, The Japan-Netherlands Institute. Tōkyō, 1980.

Ōmori, M. 'Edo-Jidai ni Okeru Oranda karano Yunyū Buppin Mokuroku, A List of Some of the Items Imported from the Netherlands during Edo Era', *Bulletin of the Faculty of Liberal Arts of Hōsei Univ*. no. 24, 1976.

—— 'Edo-Jidai ni Okeru Oranda-sen niyoru Yunyū Buppin Mokuroku (2), A List of some of the Items Imported by Dutch Ships to Japan during Edo Era'. *Bulletin of the Faculty of Liberal Arts of Hōsei Univ*. no. 28 Tōkyō, 1977.

Toyoda, T. and others (ed.) *Tokushi Sōran*, Jinbutsuōrai-sha, Tōkyō, 1966.

Umetani, N.: *Ogata Kōan to Tekijukusei*, Shibunkaku, Ōsaka, 1984.

Yamawaki, T. 'Oranda-sen Stat Tiel Gō no Tsumini', *Nagasakidansō*, no. 49.

References to Chapter 21

Boxer, C. R., *The Christian Century in Japan, 1549–1650*, Berkeley/Los Angeles/London 1967.

DNS: *Dai Nihon Shiryō* [Japanese Historical Documents] vol. XII, pt. 7, Tōkyō Teikoku Daigaku, 1904; pt. 8, Tōkyō, 1906; pt. 9, Tōkyō, 1906; pt. 12 Tōkyō 1909.

Knauth, L., *Confrontación transpacúfica. El Japón y el Muevo Mundo Hispánico, 1542-1639*. México, Universidad Nacional Autónoma de México, 1972.

Kuno, Y.S., *Japanese Expansion on the Asiatic Continent*, vol. II, New York, 1967.

Monbeig, J., *Rodrigo de Vibero, 1564–1636. Du Japon et du bon gouvernement de l'Espagne et des Indes*. Paris, École Pratique des Hautes Études, 1972.

Murakami, N., *Bisukaino kingintō tanken hōkoku* [Report of Vizcaíno's quest for the 'Gold and Silver Islands']. Tōkyō, Yūsandō, 1970.

—— *Don Rodrigo Nihon kembunroku* [Don Rodrigo's memoirs of Japan]. Tōkyō, Yūsandō, 1970.

—— *Ikoku ōfuku shokanshū* [Collection of letters exchanged with foreign countries]. Tōkyō, Yūsandō, 1970.

—— *Zōtei ikoku nikki-sho* [Extracts from diaries on foreign affairs]. Tōkyō, Yūsandō, 1970.

Morga, A. de, *Sucesos de las Islas Filipinas*. Transl. and ed. by J.S. Cummins, Hakluyt Society, Cambridge Univ. Press, 1971.

Nachod, O., 'Über ein unentdecktes Goldland'. In: *Mitteilungen der Deutschen Gesellschaft für Natur- und Völkerkunde Ostasiens*: MOAG [: abbrev. for Mitteilungen der Ostasien Gesellschaft], Vol. VII, Tōkyō, 1900, pp. 311–451.

Nutall, Z., 'The Earliest Historical Relations between Mexico and Japan'. In: *American Archaeology and Ethnography*, vol. 4, no. 1, Berkeley, 1916.

Pastells, P., *Historia General de Filipinas*, see Torres Lanzas.

Schütte, J.F., *Valignanos Missionsgrundsätze für Japan*. Vol. I: Von der Ernennung zum Visitator bis zum ersten Abschied von Japan (1573 – 1582). Pt. 1: Das Problem (1573 – 1580). Roma, Edizioni di Storia e Letteratura, 1951.

—— 'Don Rodrigo de Vivero de Velasco and Sebastián Vizcaíno in Japan'. In: *30th. International Congress of Human Sciences in Asia and North Africa* [30 ICHSANA], Seminars: Asia and Colonial Latin America, ed. by Ernesto de la Torre, México, El Colegio de México, 1981, pp. 77–99.

Schwade, A.: 'The Sea routes between Japan and the East Asian Countries during the Sixteenth and Seventeenth Centuries'. In: *Actes du XXIXe Congrès International des Orientalistes*, Japón, vol. 2, ed. by Harmut Rotermund, Paris, L'Asiathèque, 1976, pp. 124 – 32.

—— 'The First Diplomatic Relations between Japan and Mexico (1609 – 1616)'. In: *30 ICHSANA*, Seminars: Asia and Colonial Latin America, ed. by Ernesto de la Torre, México, 1981, pp. 100 – 9.

Schwade, A., 'Sebastián Vizcaíno in Japan'. In: *30 ICHSANA*, Proceedings 1: Japan and Korea, vol. 1 ed. by Graciela de la Lama, México, El Colegio de México, 1982, pp. 205 – 12.

Torres Lanzas, P., *Catálogo de los documentos existentes en el Archivo de Indias de Sevilla* [preceded by a '*Historia General de Filipinas*' by Pablo Pastells, vol. VI, Barcelona, 1931].

Vivero, Rodrigo de, 'Relación y notícias de el reino de Japón, con otros avisos y proyectos para el buen govierno do la monarchia española'. In: Monbeig, *Rodrigo de Vivero*, pp. 47 – 131.

Vizcaíno, S., 'Relación del viaje hecho para el descubrimiento de las Islas llamadas 'ricas de oro y plata', situadas en el Japón'. In: *Colección de documentos inéditos, relativos al descubrimiento, conquista y organización de las antiguas posesiones españolas de América y Oceanía, sacados de los Archivos del Reino, y muy especialmente del de Indias*. vol. VIII, Madrid, 1867; in: *DNS*, vol. XII, part 8, pt. 9 and pt. 12.

References to Chapter 23

Sources

Algemeen Rijksarchief The Hague:
VOC archives 317. Letters of the Gentlemen XVII to GG and Council 1644 – 1647.
1342 – 3971. Received letters and papers 1680 – 1794.
Archives of the Comité Oost-Indische Handel en Bezittingen 55. Received letters and papers 1795.

Literature

Blussé, L. 'Chinese trade to Batavia during the days of the VOC', *Archipel* 18. Paris 1979, pp. 195 – 213.

Chijs, J. A. van der. *Nederlandsch – Indisch plakaatboek 1602 – 1811*, 17 volumes. Batavia and The Hague 1885 – 1900.

Cushman, J. W. *Fields from the Sea: Chinese junk trade with Siam during the late eighteenth and early nineteenth century*, Ph.D. diss. Cornell 1975.

Furber, H. *Rival empires of trade in the Orient 1600 – 1800: Europe and the world in the age of expansion*, volume II. Minneapolis 1976.

Hullu, J. de. 'Over den Chinaschen handel der OIC in de eerste dertig jaar van de 18de eeuw', *Bijdragen van het Koninklijk Instituut voor Taal-, Land- en Volkenkunde (BKI)* 73, The Hague 1917, pp. 32 – 151.

—— 'De instelling van de commissie voor den handel der OIC op China in 1756', *BKI* 79. The Hague 1923, pp. 523 – 45.

Iwao Seiichi, 'Kinsei Nitchū boeki ni kansuru shuryoteki Kosatsu', *Shigaku zasshi* 62 – 11.

Jackson, J. C. 'Mining in 18th Century Bangka: the pre-European exploitation of a tin island'. *Pacific Viewpoint* 10, 1969, pp. 28 – 54.

Kamp, A. F. *De standvastige tinnen soldaat. De N.V. Billiton Maatschappij 1860 – 1960* The Hague and Nijmegen 1960.

Ng Chin – keong, 'Trade and society: The Amoy network on the China coast 1683 – 1735', unpublished thesis, Canberra 1980.

Souza, G. B. 'Portuguese trade and society in China and the south-China Sea 1630 – 1754', Ph.D.diss. Cambridge 1981.

Vienne, M.S. de, 'Les Chinois dans l'Archipel Insulindien au XVIIe siecle d'apres les Dagh Register de Batavia', unpublished These de doctorat de IIIe cycle, Paris 1979.

Viraphol, S. *Tribute and profit: Sino-Siamese trade 1652 – 1853*. Cambridge, Mass. 1977.

Yamawaki Teijiro, *Kinsei Nichi-chu Boeki-shi no kenkyu*. Tokyo 35.

For Product Safety Concerns and Information please contact our EU
representative GPSR@taylorandfrancis.com
Taylor & Francis Verlag GmbH, Kaufingerstraße 24, 80331 München, Germany